G000070745

"STAND TO"

A Diary of the Trenches
1915 – 1918

By
CAPTAIN F. C. HITCHCOCK,
M.C., F.R.HIST.S.

Late 2nd Battalion The Leinster Regiment

With a Preface by
MAJOR-GENERAL SIR JOHN CAPPER,
K.C.B., K.C.V.O., C.B.

Illustrated with Photographs and Maps

PUBLISHED BY
THE NAVAL & MILITARY PRESS

PREFACE

"*STAND TO*" is a narrative of the day-by-day life of a
Subaltern on the Western Front in the Great War.

Captain Hitchcock gives no highly coloured account of
his and others' emotions under the stress of war, but states the
bare facts of the conditions under which the Infantry lived—
and died—conditions which can hardly be realised by those who
have not experienced them.

And this life—what was it ?

Days mostly spent in stinking muddy trenches, infested with
huge rats, the only shelter a damp and comfortless dug-out
which too often gave but inadequate cover.

Both officers and men were constantly wet through and half
frozen, exposed day and night to sniping and bombardment
by every kind of shell and gas, whilst always liable to sudden
attack.

Day and night at work improving their defences and frequently
seeing their labour wasted by the destruction caused by enemy
shells.

It is easy to realise what a terrible strain such a life imposed
on all.

" Rest "—so called—though much of it was spent in carrying
heavy stores up long and twisting communications, and digging
support and reserve defences, too often meant but a return to
ruinous and draughty buildings which were absolutely devoid of
any sort of comfort.

Yet through it all the men showed a wonderful spirit and a
great patience.

The 2nd Leinsters, one of those very fine South Irish regiments,
was indeed a battalion to which any man might be proud to have
belonged.

The men were stout fighters, good marchers, and splendid
workers, their trenches were always kept as well as circumstances
permitted, and, as I saw myself, when blown in by artillery-fire,
the men set to work at once, without orders, on rebuilding them.

They were wonderfully cheerful and always ready with some
quaint answer to a question, or a witty remark on some unusual
incident.

PREFACE

Though apt to be rather reckless in attack—in raids (for two of which the detailed orders are given in the Appendices) they showed individually the strict obedience and restraint by which alone a raid can be brought to a successful conclusion.

I cannot close without paying my special tribute to that young and very gallant officer Lieut.-Colonel Murphy, a thorough soldier, an excellent C.O., and possessor of a very lovable personality.

And I must also mention the noble Padres of the Battalion, men fearless in the service of their God, who constantly risked their lives in order to give the last comforts of their Faith to men dying in the front-line trenches or on the battlefield.

The 2nd Leinsters are—alas—no more in being. It was a sad day when they left the Division, a sadder still when they were disbanded.

Let us hope that in happier times the Regiment may rise again to take its place in the loyal defence of the British Empire and all that the Empire stands for.

Mapor

Major General
late G.O.C. 24th Division

BRANDEAN,
November 30th, 1936.

THE DISBANDED IRISH REGIMENTS

THE 31st July, 1937, will mark the fifteenth anniversary of the disbandment of the five Southern Irish regiments, which were mustered out of the Army List in consequence of the reorganisation of the Constitution of Ireland and the establishment of the Irish Free State.

While they served, the Royal Irish Regiment, the Connaught Rangers, the Prince of Wales's Leinster Regiment (Royal Canadians), the Royal Munster Fusiliers and the Royal Dublin Fusiliers embodied and perpetuated the noblest traditions of the British Army.

The 18th Royal Irish, who were raised by Charles II in Ireland from independent companies of pikemen and musketeers, could boast a record of 238 years' unbroken service to the Crown at the time of their dissolution. In their initial continental campaign they gave full proof of their fighting qualities in storming the fortress of Namur under the personal supervision of William III, and won the admiration of the whole army. For their gallantry they were granted the privilege of bearing the King's escutcheon, "The Lion of Nassau," on their colours, with the motto "*Virtutis Namurcensis Prœmium*" (the Reward for Valour at Namur), which incidentally is the first instance of a battle honour having been granted to a British regiment.

Here also it received the Royal prerogative for its distinctive title, Royal Regiment of Ireland, and last, but not least, the Harp and Crown as a distinguishing emblem for their head-dress, which they forthwith proceeded to carry most conspicuously throughout Marlborough's victories. Two hundred years later the Royal Irish were destined to be drawn up in modern battle array—rifle-pits—at almost the identical spot where they had fought one of their earliest engagements, and to bear the full brunt of von Kluck's hordes at Mons, and to join battle with them as vigorously as their forebears had crossed bayonets with the white-clad columns of Monarchical France at Malplaquet.

CONNAUGHT RANGERS

The Connaught Rangers were embodied in Connaught during the throes of the French Revolution, and from the cradle they were nourished on gunpowder. Designated with the fascinating nomenclature, Connaught Rangers, and officered entirely by the gentry of the West of Ireland, they were launched into the fighting arena, Flanders. Here they came under the orders of the luckless Duke of York—during that inglorious campaign against the revolutionary forces.

After the disastrous expedition to Buenos Ayres, the 88th, nothing daunted by reverse, were dispatched to the Peninsula, where they got full opportunity for displaying true Celtic impetuosity and fighting phlegm, gaining a reputation second to none at Fuentes d'Onor, Ciudad Rodrigo, and Badajoz for their conspicuous, if not reckless, gallantry, and also the marked approval of the Iron Duke.

It was in this campaign where the regiment was given their nickname of The Devil's Own by General Picton. For their services in that year of desperate fighting, 1914, the Rangers reaped more battle honours than any other regiment.

THE LEINSTERS

The Leinsters had a decidedly eventful career, and were justly proud of their unique origin, as they were the only British regiment which represented two Colonies in their constitution ; for the 1st Battalion, the Royal Canadians, was raised in Canada from Canadian Irishmen, whilst the 2nd Battalion came from the East India Company's service, the old 3rd Bombay Europeans, which was largely composed of Irishmen, and had rendered such yeoman service throughout the Central India campaign, particularly in the capture of Jhansi, where Bugler Whirlpool, *alias* Conker, of Dundalk, gained the regiment its first Victoria Cross.

Both battalions were appropriately domiciled to Ireland officially under the Cardwell system in 1881. Niagara was the Leinsters' first action, though their first casualty list, amounting to 200 men, had been incurred years previously by shipwreck off the coast of Newfoundland. The sword and scarlet sash worn by Sergt.-Major Patrick Dempsey, and the drum-sticks which actually beat the assault on Niagara were preserved in the mess of the 100th down to the last days of its existence.

In its first European Campaign the Leinsters were awarded four Victoria Crosses. The 2nd Battalion appeared in a Special Divisional order in February, 1918, when their Divisional Commander placed on record his " great appreciation of this fine Battalion. The 2nd Leinster Regiment has always maintained a high standard of discipline and a magnificent fighting spirit."

THE " DIRTY SHIRTS "

Two of the regiments, in the Munsters and the Dublins, were of Indian origin. The Munsters were raised officially almost on the eve of Plassey, in which battle they received their baptism of fire, but they could claim lineal descent from a handful of armed men who were despatched from England to protect British interests, i.e. the factories of the John Company, established at Madras, Calcutta, and Bombay, by Charles II. Their finest battle honour was embodied in their nickname, " The Dirty Shirts," and they earned this quaint soubriquet at the Battle of Bhurtopoore in the year 1805.

Having discarded their scarlet tunics in order to be less encumbered, they had entered " the ring " to return dirty and gory, but elated with victory, to an appreciative General who addressed them as " Dirty Shirts," and from this remote period the nickname was cherished with pride down to disbandment.

The 2nd Munsters were with the " Old Contemptibles " at Mons, and fought a brilliant rear-guard action at Etreux, where they man-handled teamless guns out of action in the face of a regiment of Uhlans, which they badly mauled. In the official history of the war a complete chapter is devoted to recording the heroic feats of the Battalion during the retreat.

The 1st Dublins were the oldest of the John Company units, tracing their pedigree back to the reign of King Charles I, and the 2nd Battalion claimed direct descent from the original British force despatched to garrison the Island of Bombay—the first of our possessions in India, which was part of Catherine of Braganza's dowry on marrying the Merry Monarch.

THE DUBLINS IN INDIA

The Dublins jealously treasured battle honours of their own shared by no other regiment, gained in the conquest of the great Mogul Empire. They paved the way for the conquest of India, fighting under leaders of the calibre of Stringer Lawrence and Robert Clive.

Clive was their first recorded Colonel, and Plassey their first battle honour. To have these traditions were sufficient in themselves to ensure perpetual gallant service down through the centuries. One hundred and sixty years later this celebrated regiment was called on to co-operate with their compatriots, the 1st Munsters, in one of the severest tests of discipline and self-sacrifice in the annals of warfare—the seemingly impossible task of landing on the shores of hostile Gallipoli from exposed rowing boats in the teeth of a tornado of artillery and machine-gun fire rained on them from the commanding Turkish defences. How gallantly they acquitted themselves with the 29th Division, " The Incomparables," in spite of overwhelming casualties has been well and deeply carved into the annals of military history.

It was in order to commemorate the gallantry displayed by the Irish regiments in South Africa that the Irish Guards were raised in April, 1900, and the 2nd Dublins had a fair share for the responsibility for the well-known order of the same date :

" Her Majesty the Queen is pleased to order that in future upon St. Patrick's Day all ranks in her Irish regimènts shall wear, as a distinction, a sprig of shamrock in their head-dress to commemorate the gallantry of her Irish soldiers during the recent battles in South Africa.—Wolseley."

REUNION DINNERS

The disbanded regiments still keep up their annual dinners and old comrades' reunions, when the spirit of Irish camaraderie pervades throughout these ceremonies, as it did in the days of yore. These are some all too brief hours in which to talk of the days spent " with the old battalion at Bareilly," or " up at Wipers "—some incident laughingly described, which rekindles with vividness the glories of the old regiment and the life that made it live. But the phantom battalions have marched into history as resolutely as they strode into action under Marlborough, Clive, and Wellington, as courageously as they advanced at Colenso, Gallipoli, and Guillemont, on through the devastating barrages and the low-lying mists which enshrouded the shell-churned morasses of sinister Passchendaele, and on into oblivion.

From the scorching plains of India, the sun-baked banks of the Nile, and the forlorn Silesian terrain, the battalions heard the " dismiss " sounded. One of the regiments, returned from its last and gallant fight in Malabar, was carrying out its last ceremonial under the eyes of its Colonel-in-Chief, the heir to the throne, when the bombshell burst. Amidst the historic associations of Fort St. George, Madras, they swung past, colours flying, to the lilting strains of the regimental quickstep, " Come back to Erin." Well, they came back—but for disbandment.

THE COLOURS

The Colours of the line battalions were surrendered to King George V for safe keeping, and they now provide another tone of stately splendour to the glories of St. George's Hall, Windsor.

" We are here to-day in circumstances which cannot fail to strike a note of sadness in our hearts. No regiment parts with its Colours without feelings of sorrow. A knight in days gone by bore on his shield his coat-of-arms, token of valour and worth ; only to death did he surrender them. Your Colours are the record of valorous deeds in war and of the glorious traditions thereby created. You are called upon to part with them to-day for reasons beyond your control and resistance. By you and your predecessors these Colours have been reverenced and guarded as a sacred trust—which trust you now confide in me.

" As your King I am proud to accept this trust, but I fully realise with what grief you relinquish these dearly prized emblems ; and I pledge my word that within these ancient and historic walls your Colours will be treasured, honoured, and protected as hallowed memorials of the glorious deeds of brave and loyal regiments."

So spoke His late Majesty, deeply moved, on this impressive and final parade in the history of the gallant Irish regiments, which had played such a conspicuous rôle in the building of his Empire.

18th Royal Irish, Rangers from Connaught, Leinsters, Munster Fusiliers, and Dublin Fusiliers, you are now but a memory, but your gallant exploits will be handed down to posterity as the proudest records of the Irish race.

Reproduced by permission of the " Irish Times," for which paper the author wrote the above memoriam.

"STAND TO"

1915

16th May. Sunday.

ORDERS for the Front! I had been stationed at
Victoria Barracks, Cork, attached to the 3rd Battalion
Leinster Regiment, which was commanded by Lieut.-
Colonel A. Canning.[1] The Adjutant, Captain C. C. Harman,[2]
gave me instructions to proceed to Queenstown forthwith,
and report to the C.O. of the 4th Battalion Royal Irish
Regiment, as I was to conduct a draft of 200 N.C.O.s and men
of this regiment overseas. Several other fellows serving with the
3rd Battalion got active service orders at the same time. In
view of the casualties sustained by our 1st Battalion in the gas
attack at Ypres we had daily been anticipating orders for the
Front, in fact we had a farewell dinner-party at the Imperial
Hotel earlier in the week, consisting of George Read, Duncan,
Bailey, Ray Stirling, Jimmy Barry, Hartland-Rowe, Levis,
McCormick, Charles Renshaw, le Poer Trench, Fitz-Gerald (who
had lost an eye on the Aisne when attached to the 2nd Battalion
the Connaught Rangers), and " Wally " Morrogh,[3] who was the
first officer wounded with our 2nd Battalion in France.

With my valise rolled and reduced to 35 lb. weight in accordance with B.E.F. regulations, and encased in webbing equipment,
and complete with Smith & Wesson revolver, I set off in the
rain for Glenmire Station on Donovan's side-car with his well-
known grey between the shafts.

In spite of the fact that it was still pouring with rain when I
arrived at Queenstown, and that the whole platform was stacked
with coffins for the victims of the *Lusitania*, my morale was
excellent at the prospect of getting out to the Front. I stayed
the night in the Royal Irish mess, a house by the sea, where I

[1] Was awarded C.M.G. at Gallipoli later in the year.
[2] Later Lieut.-Colonel, D.S.O. and bar, Commanding 1st Battalion Royal
Sussex Regiment.
[3] Now Brevet Lieut.-Colonel, D.S.O., M.C., 5th Battalion Royal Tank Corps.

was treated in a most hospitable manner by the " Eighteenth " ; Brian-Bellew and Harris could not have done more for me.

17th May.

I reported to the C.O., Lieut.-Colonel de Montmorency.

A general air of depression hung over the town, owing to the torpedoing of the *Lusitania* by the Boche submarine ; hourly boats were bringing back bodies into harbour from the scene of the disaster. There were some half-dozen life-boats bearing the name of the ill-fated ship hauled up on the boat-slip beside the Yacht Club, where I was made an honorary member.

18th May.

The draft was paraded and inspected at 11 a.m., and I marched it off to the station. The strength was exactly 200 N.C.O.s and men, some of whom had already been out and been wounded in the Retreat from Mons and at Ypres. They were all in excellent fettle, and had small flags and pennants stuck in the muzzles of their rifles. We were played down from barracks by the regimental band to the tune of " Farewell Isobel," a song which at the time had ousted " The Girl I Left Behind Me." The band stopped suddenly and we realised that we were passing the boat-house of the Yacht Club, which was being used as a mortuary for the bodies of the victims of the *Lusitania* awaiting identification by their relatives. All ranks, from the Colonel downwards, came to the station to see the draft off, and we entrained and steamed out of the station to " Auld Lang Syne."

At Cork I was joined by Captain B. C. Riall, who also was under orders for the Front with a large draft of the Leinsters. The men behaved well on the journey up to the North Wall, considering that at Mallow, Thurles, Ballybrophy, Portarlington and most of the other stations along the line, relatives and friends came to say good-bye, and as parting gifts handed bottles of whisky and porter into the compartments for " me darlint Jimmy (or Michael) whose goin' to the WAAR."

Eight boxes of S.A.A. caused me some trouble, and they, with their escort, were nearly shunted back to Cork at Thurles. Eventually they turned up, attached to another train at Dublin. Food was issued by the buffet at the military siding. I gave my sword and Sam Browne to my father, who came to see me off, as a parting gift, and embarked my draft.

In the gathering darkness we weighed anchor in a decidedly choppy sea. The Irish Channel was rough, and the boat, which was a cattle and cargo-boat, pitched a great deal. There were some half-dozen officers in the boat belonging to Irish regiments.

19th May.

Arrived at Holyhead at 4 a.m., where we got breakfast and entrained for Southampton, which we reached at noon. Here we detrained, and marched into the embarkation shed where we piled arms, took off equipment, and awaited further orders. All ranks were C.B., and we spent the time watching horses belonging to the Canadian Army being slung on board a large transport. Later we were joined by a draft belonging to the 20th Hussars, and embarked at dusk. As we mounted the gangway, every officer and man was handed Lord Kitchener's message to troops proceeding on Active Service :

(This paper is to be considered by each soldier as confidential, and to be kept in his Active Service Pay Book.)

You are ordered abroad as a soldier of the King to help our French comrades against the invasion of a common Enemy. You have to perform a task which will need your courage, your energy, your patience. Remember that the honour of the British Army depends on your individual conduct. It will be your duty not only to set an example of discipline and perfect steadiness under fire but also to maintain the most friendly relations with those whom you are helping in this struggle. The operations in which you are engaged will, for the most part, take place in a friendly country, and you can do your own country no better service than in showing yourself in France and Belgium in the true character of a British soldier.

Be invariably courteous, considerate and kind. Never do anything likely to injure or destroy property, and always look upon looting as a disgraceful act. You are sure to meet with a welcome and to be trusted ; your conduct must justify that welcome and that trust. Your duty cannot be done unless your health is sound. So keep constantly on your guard against any excesses. In this new experience you may find temptations both in wine and women. You must entirely resist both temptations, and, while treating all women with perfect courtesy, you should avoid any intimacy.

Do your duty bravely.
Fear God.
Honour the King.
KITCHENER,
Field-Marshal.

Life-belts were issued out, we inspected our drafts in them, and reported " All Correct " to Bertie Riall, who was O.C. ship. We sailed at 8 p.m., and we were accompanied by a destroyer.

All lights were extinguished on board and smoking was forbidden on the decks.

20th May.

Had a smooth crossing, and slept passing Le Havre. We sailed up the Seine to Rouen, where we disembarked. It was a lovely morning, and I will not forget my first impressions of the smiling country-side of La Belle France. The French peasants, who were working in the fields attired in their picturesque blue smocks, came over to the river banks to cheer, and some yelled " Good-bye."

A Faugh-a-Ballagh[1] subaltern, who, like myself, was going out for the first time, asked another officer, who had already been blooded in France, why they yelled " *Good-bye*," and not " *Au revoir*." The answer he got was—" These Froggies know a thing or two about this war ! ! "

At 11 a.m. we disembarked, and marched off to the Base Camp, receiving quite an ovation from the inhabitants as we went through Rouen, in spite of the fact that the War had been going on for nine months.

I handed over my draft to the O.C. 4th Divisional Base, as it was earmarked to reinforce the 2nd Royal Irish Regiment, and then I was instructed to report to the O.C. 6th Divisional Base. Here I found to my delight that I was posted to the 2nd Leinster Regiment, the battalion I was particularly anxious to join, and learned that movement orders for the front would follow later.

21st May.

With a subaltern of the 2nd Durham Light Infantry marched a party of 400 men down to the Docks for fatigue duty at 7 a.m. We had breakfast in the town, and took the party, which had been employed unloading flour and forage, back to camp. Two Leinsters in Captain Prendergast and 2nd Lieut. Gamble arrived.

22nd May.

Usual camp routine, inspections, and musketry parades. I got a servant called McCafferty from the 2nd Battalion draft. Had orders to stand to for the front line, but these were cancelled. Went into Rouen with some other fellows for dinner, and by an odd coincidence met Bertie Biddulph of the Queen's Bays (2nd Dragoon Guards), son of the Master of the King's County Foxhounds, whose Kennels were at Kinnitty, Birr, where my father was Rector.

[1] Royal Irish Fusiliers ; a soubriquet from Peninsula War days, meaning " Clear the Way " in Gallic.

23rd May. Sunday.

Detailed to march a party to an open-air service. Afterwards I had to censor a number of the men's letters.

There were some fifteen officers in our Base camp, which was ideally situated overlooking the town; one of them belonged to the 1st Royal Dragoons,[1] a regiment which had had the Kaiser as Colonel-in-Chief. Prior to the War this officer had sported several German decorations. He used to get chaffed about losing his medal ribbons which he had to remove on the declaration of war.

We invariably dined in Rouen—a delightful old town. It was full of our troops, and was also the Base for the Indian Expeditionary Force; one would catch sight of stately-looking Sikhs riding in and out of the traffic with a very colourful and typically French background of boulevards. Sitting out under the awning of a café opposite the quayside one evening, a sudden commotion upset several tables and sent glasses crashing to the ground. Some boatloads of Boche prisoners who had been working down the river were passing. This was too good a sight for the excitable Froggies to miss ! !

24th May.

Left the Base with Prendergast and Gamble, for the Front. I had enjoyed my sojourn in Rouen, where the "Entente Cordiale" pervaded everybody and everything.

The majority of troops in the train belonged to the Highland Regiments of the 9th Scottish Division. Trucks marked

40 HOMMES
8 CHEVAUX

were allotted to the men. Our train left Rouen at 5.30 p.m.

ARMENTIÈRES

25th May.

Arrived at our destination, Bailleul, at midday, after some eighteen hours in the train, which passed through Abbéville, Boulogne, Calais, St. Omer, and Hazebrouck. At Bailleul we

---

[1] In the Officers' Mess of the Royal Dragoons now stationed at Shorncliffe, hangs a portrait of the ex-Kaiser. It was banished from the Mess during the War and for the immediate post-War years, but it has now been restored being a matter of historical interest.

Pre-War, the German Emperor sent a laurel wreath annually to decorate their regimental guidon in commemoration of the capture of the Colour surmounted with the Eagle belonging to the 105th French Regiment at Waterloo by Captain Clarke of The Royals.

heard the guns firing during an attack at La Bassée. Here the
2nd Battalion officers' mess cart was awaiting us, and we drove
off to Armentières. At the regimental transport lines, we were
met by Padre Moloney, Lieut. W. S. Caulfeild, the transport
officer, and 2nd Lieut. R. L. Piper, Indian Army, attached to the
2nd Battalion. After tea, the Padre volunteered to take me up to
Battalion Headquarters, and as it was getting dark, we could
walk up the road without using the trench. The Commanding
Officer, Major Bullen-Smith, shook hands with me and welcomed
me to his battalion. This kindly greeting made me feel instantly
at home with the Regiment. He ordered me to report to Lieut.
N. G. Young, O.C. A Company in the front line, and a runner
was called to guide me up to his Company Headquarters.

Entering a shallow communication trench which ran parallel
with a small stream called the " Little Nullah," we got into the
firing line within ten minutes.

It was now quite dark, but every now and then Véry lights
were sent up by both sides, and I was able to discern the course of
the German trenches. When I arrived the Company was " Standing to." This is one of the trench warfare routines carried out
every morning and evening.

I duly reported to Young, who was going round the line. He
was a fine-looking fellow, who had won the first Military Cross
awarded to the Battalion for bravery on the Aisne in September.
He had been at school—St. Columba's College, Dublin, with my
brother. The other officers in A Company were Tim Laville,
Barnett, and Will, who had played Rugger for Scotland as wing
three-quarter.

I did my first tour of duty from 4 a.m. to 6 a.m. with Company
Sergeant-Major Kerrigan, who was wearing the ribbon of the
D.C.M. as well as his two South African ribbons. He gave me
a lot of information about trench warfare and the routine in the
line.

Our trenches appeared to be very formidable ; they were duck-
boarded, and the parapets and paradoses were completely
revetted with sand-bags. The parapets were 6 feet high, and the
wooden fire steps being 1½ feet in height, gave a fire position of
4½ feet. Owing to the low-lying nature of the terrain the trenches
were breast-works.

I was given command of No. 3 Platoon, strength about 40.
Sergt. O'Connor was my platoon sergeant, and Sergt. Keating
was the supernumerary sergeant in the platoon. Both were old
campaigners, having seen service in the South African War.

An advanced post called Water Wheel Farm came into my
platoon frontage. It had been reduced to a few crumbling walls

from shell-fire and trench mortars, but it still boasted a deep cellar, which harboured the men belonging to the post when off duty. Here they slept and cooked their food. The post had an evil reputation, as it was continually subjected to trench-mortar strafes.

In company with the C.S.M., I visited the listening posts, which consisted of an N.C.O. and two men, lying prone some 50 yards in advance of the front line. Their rôle was to warn the Company in case of a night attack, and to wipe out hostile patrols.

The Battalion was over 1000 strong in trenches, and we had a new army battalion of Highlanders belonging to the 9th Division attached to us for instruction.

At 6 a.m. I turned into my dug-out, which was full of straw, and slept soundly until " Stand to."

At " Stand to " the Roll was called, and day sentries posted.

Roll of the 2nd Battalion officers at Armentières on the 25th May, 1915 :

Headquarters.

Major G. M. Bullen-Smith.
Lieut. A. D. Murphy, Adjutant.
Lieut. J. V. Macartney, M.C., Machine-Gun Officer.
Lieut. W. S. Caulfeild, Transport Officer.
Lieut. and Quartermaster H. O. Squire.
Rev. Father J. P. Moloney.

A Company.

Lieut. G. N. G. Young, M.C.
Lieut. S. E. B. Laville
2nd Lieut. D. O. Barnett
2nd Lieut. J. G. Will.

B Company.

Lieut. L. D. Daly.
2nd Lieut. J. H. Monaghan.
2nd Lieut. T. Hickman.
2nd Lieut. J. K. Ducat.
2nd Lieut. H. Pearman.

C Company.

Capt. E. W. C. Munro, Royal Irish
Rifles (attached).
Lieut. N. Algeo.
2nd Lieut. J. F. Marsland.
2nd Lieut. R. L. Piper (unattached list, Indian Army).

D Company.

Lieut. E. H. M. de Stacpoole.
Lieut. J. J. O'Brien.
2nd Lieut. G. Murray.
2nd Lieut. T. H. Poole.

Regimental Sergt.-Major C. H. Smith, D.C.M.

The Battalion was holding l'Epinette sector of the Armentières front, so called from the village of that name, through which the front line ran. L'Epinette had been in German hands up to the 12th March, on which date it and the adjacent farm were captured in an attack made by the 17th Brigade.

The 6th Division was composed of the following regiments.
The G.O.C.[1] was Major-General W. N. Congreve, V.C., M.V.O.;
who had on this date taken over command of the Division from
Major-General J. L. Keir.

16th Brigade.

1st Battalion The Buffs	3rd Foot
1st Battalion Leicester Regiment . . .	17th Foot
1st Battalion King's Shropshire Light Infantry .	53rd Foot
2nd Battalion York and Lancaster Regiment .	84th Foot

17th Brigade.

1st Battalion Royal Fusiliers	7th Foot
1st Battalion North Staffordshire Regiment . .	64th Foot
2nd Battalion The Leinster Regiment (R.C.) .	109th Foot
3rd Battalion Rifle Brigade	

18th Brigade.

1st Battalion West Yorkshire Regiment . .	14th Foot
1st Battalion East Yorkshire Regiment . .	15th Foot
2nd Battalion Sherwood Foresters . . .	95th Foot
2nd Battalion Durham Light Infantry . . .	106th Foot

R.F. Artillery 2nd Brigade. Batteries 21, 42, 53.   R.G.A.
    ,,   24th   ,,   ,, 110, 111, 112. Heavy
                                        Battery.
    ,,   38th   ,,   ,, 24, 34, 72. No. 24.
    ,,   12th   ,,   Howitzer 43, 86, 87.
Royal Engineers. 12th and 38th Field Companies. 6th Signal
                                          Company.
C Squadron 19th Hussars and 6th Cyclist Company.
R.A.M.C. 16th, 17th and 18th Field Ambulances.

To each Brigade was attached a Territorial Battalion.
The 16th Brigade . . 1/5th Battalion Loyal North Lan-
                                       cashire Regiment
The 17th ,,   . . 1/2nd Battalion London Regiment
The 18th ,, . . . Queen's Westminster Rifles

While at Armentières the 19th Brigade, consisting of the
    2nd Battalion Royal Welch Fusiliers
    1st Battalion The Cameronians
    2nd Battalion The Argyll and Sutherland Highlanders
    with the 5th Territorial Battalion Scottish Rifles (attached),
formed part of the 6th Division.

[1] Major-General Congreve won his Victoria Cross at Colenso when endeavouring to save the guns with Lord Roberts' son, who was mortally wounded and posthumously awarded the V.C. General Congreve's eldest son also won the V.C. later in the War, and was killed on the Somme in 1916. This was another case of a father and son winning this coveted decoration.

26th May.

My platoon paraded in the trench for rifle inspection. They were a fine body of men ; the majority hailed from Tipperary, King's and Queen's Counties, and Westmeath, and were time-serving soldiers. The German lines were only about 150 yards away, and one could see their parapets beyond dense masses of barbed wire and *chevaux de frise.*

The C.O. and Adjutant came round to inspect the front line. With the exception of occasional sniping and trench-mortar activity in the evening, everything was very quiet.

We had a good mess in Company Headquarters, and we got country beer from a brasserie in Armentières. Hudson, who had been Colonel Craske's servant, functioned as mess cook.

27th May.

Shelled by " whiz-bangs " or " Little Willies " in the morning. In the evening we were strafed by trench mortars, and some landed close to Company Headquarters. I could see the trench mortars coming through the air. They weighed about 60 lb., and made a colossal explosion on striking the ground. The craters they formed were about the same size as a 5·9.

We got news of a successful French attack at Carency and Souchez. Met Marsland of C Company.

The Company was relieved at 9 p.m. by D Company. Brought my platoon back to the support line. Got shelled throughout the night. I was very cold, as I had neither greatcoat nor blanket.

28th May.

Had breakfast in the Support Company H.Q., which was farther back beside the Little Nullah. Here I met Macartney, the Battalion Machine-Gun Officer, with whom I became great friends afterwards.

He kept us all laughing at breakfast with some amusing yarns. He wore a monocle, and, like Young, the ribbon of the Military Cross.

Explored our support line, which ran under the Armentières-Lille railway. The Huns shelled Chapelle d'Armentières with 5.9 shells, or " coal-boxes " as the men called them. I was trans-ferred to C Company. Piper, who had been an Under-Officer of H Company at Sandhurst, came along to guide me over to C Company H.Q. Captain Munro, attached from the Royal Irish Rifles was O.C. Company. I took over command of No. 9 Platoon.

My Platoon-Sergeant, by name Ginn, was a Cockney, the only one in the Battalion. His people owned a flower shop near Victoria Station. He was a fine soldier, and the youngest sergeant

in the Battalion, having just four years' service on the outbreak
of war. (He was killed at Hooge on the 15th March, 1916.)

Roll of No. 9 Platoon on the 29th May, 1915 :

Platoon Sergeant 9560 Sergt. S. Ginn.

No. I Section.

Sergt. Bennett.
10269 L/Corpl. Geard.
Pte. Corrigan.
  ,, Coghlan.
  ,, McClean.
3038 Pte. Brown.
Piper Farrell.
Pte. Cox.
  ,, Walsh.
  ,, Shea.
  ,, Duffy.
  ,, Bowes.
  ,, Keenan.

No. II Section.

L/Corpl. Bates.
Pte. Brady.
  ,, Dolan.
  ,, Duffy.
  ,, Farrell.
  ,, McKenna.
  ,, Kavenagh.
  ,, Scott.
  ,, Hugh.

No. III Section.

2881 L/Corpl. O'Neill.
Pte. Flood.
  ,, Hogan.
3467 Pte. Daly.
Pte. Mara.
  ,, Richards.
3604 Pte. Daly.
Pte. Donovan.
  ,, Clarke.
8212 Pte. Brown.
Pte. Murray
8243 Pte. Jackson.

No. IV Section.

Corpl. Mahon.
Pte. Bracken.
  ,, Digan.
  ,, McMahon.
  ,, Nolan.
  ,, O'Halleron.
  ,, Kelly.
  ,, Sheernan.
  ,, Eldridge.
  ,, Burgess.
  ,, Smith.
  ,, Bland.
  ,, McCafferty.

Strength, 48.

My platoon was on the left flank of the Battalion, in touch with
the 1st Royal Fusiliers. For the first time I watched an air duel
between one of our planes and a Boche Taube over the lines.

I was most tremendously struck with the men and their
physique. Daily the platoons paraded for rifle inspection, with
the exception of the men on sentry-go. Even in trenches the men
turned out scrupulously clean, and were always shaved before
10 a.m. There was a splendid *esprit de corps* throughout the
Battalion.

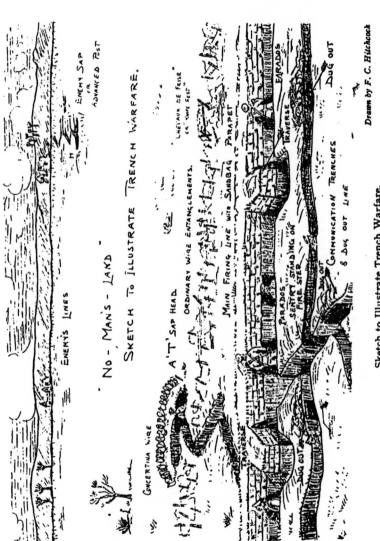

Sketch to Illustrate Trench Warfare.

No. 3235 Pte. Foran was killed by a trench mortar near the l'Epinette corner. He was the first man I saw killed in the War, his body was hoisted up behind the parados and covered with a ground sheet to wait until darkness, when the stretcher-bearers would bring him back for burial. Strong rumours afloat that the 6th Division were moving up to the Ypres area and that the 27th Division, to which our 1st Battalion belonged, would relieve us.

Marsland brought me down to see his sector on the right flank of the Company, and afterwards I had a tot of rum with him in his dug-out. He had fought throughout the South African campaign. Just before the War he won the individual bayonet-fighting championship open to both Services, at Olympia. In December, he had been promoted in the field for bravery, having gone out with the Battalion as Regimental-Sergeant-Major.

While I was with him, the Germans suddenly opened rapid fire, we went into the fire bays, and found the men standing on the parapets firing rapid back !

Marsland ordered them back into the trench, and started firing up star shells, as it was quite dark. I dashed off as hard as I could to get back to my platoon. The bullets were ricochetting off the walls of two old ruined houses, through which the line went, as I passed. This was the first burst of rifle fire " in anger " I had heard.

It turned out that the reason for this outburst was that the Huns had located a wiring party of the Royal Fusiliers in No-Man's-Land, thinking that we were forming up for a night attack they had " got the wind up " (the B.E.F. expression for fear), and had opened fire. We had no casualties, but the Fusiliers had a few men hit.

29th May.

The Company stood-to at about 4 a.m. The men were practised in gas-respirator drill. This consisted of putting a piece of gun-cotton between the teeth and tying a piece of crape round the mouth. This gear had proved fairly successful in a last gas attack at Ypres. Each man had, in addition, a bottle of hypo solution, with which he was to keep his mask moistened in a pukka gas attack.

The enemy had one of their sausage-shaped balloons up some way behind their lines. It was attached to a railway truck, and when shelled it retired hastily out of range.

Had a sniping duel with a German who signalled inners, outers, and magpies, with a white flag. The troops opposite belong to a Saxon regiment.

We put up some old biscuit tins behind " Barrier " house, and had revolver practice. At dusk one of our G.S. wagons came up the road to the Company dump, just behind the front line, with barbed wire, stakes, and duck-boards.

The official *communiqué*, which we got daily, stated that the 29th Division had made a most successful advance on the Gallipoli Peninsula. The field company conduct sheets were handed over to me for custody and keeping up-to-date. This is always one of the duties meted out to the junior subaltern in a Company on active service. The C.O. came round the line with our Brigade-Commander, Brig.-General G. M. Harper, D.S.O.

30th May.

"Stand to" at about 4 a.m. Munro discovered two men in the line belonging to our 1st Battalion, which had arrived in Armentières the night before. They both had brothers in the 2nd Battalion, and had come up to see them. Munro strafed them for being absent from their battalion, and later strafed Piper and myself for having taken off our boots at night.

We inspected the rifles and "iron rations." These latter consist of a small packet of tea and sugar in a sealed tin, a small bag of very small biscuits ironically called "elephants," and a tin of bully beef. These rations had to be kept and shown on inspections. They were for use in case of emergency, and then only with the C.O.'s permission.

During the morning we received orders for our relief by the 1st Battalion North Staffordshire Regiment, and that we would proceed to billets in the Asylum, Armentières. Relief orders also stated that the 6th Division would move immediately up to the Ypres sector. Ypres had the name of being a death-trap throughout the Army, whereas Armentières was considered "cushy," and had been ever since the line had been established in October.

The 2nd Battalion took a prominent part in this advance with the 3rd Corps. The casualties of the Battalion had been particularly heavy. Captains W. G. Montgomerie and H. T. Maffett and Lieutenants Gaitskell, Lecky, and Cormac-Walshe being killed, and Captains Whitton, G. Orpen-Palmer (O.P. 2), and 2nd Lieut. Budgen wounded, while Lieutenants Hamilton, O'Connor, and Barton were captured. The strength of the Battalion was reduced to 500, the majority of the casualties occurring in the capture of a small hamlet called Premesques, south-east of Armentières.

It was here that Macartney was awarded the Military Cross and Sergt. Bennett, the Battalion Machine-Gun Sergeant, the D.C.M. Other D.C.M.s awarded were to Sergt.-Major Smith and Pte. Regan. Bennett and Regan were also decorated with the

Russian Order of St. George, but they never received the actual medal owing to the downfall of Imperial Russia.

Relieved at 10 p.m. After I had handed over my line to the incoming subaltern of the 1st North Staffords, we proceeded to the Company rendezvous about a mile away.

Here we were joined by the other platoons (Piper's No. 1, Algeo's No. 11, and Marsland's No. 12), and marched down the cobbled road to the strains of the bagpipes played by Sergt. Moran and Pte. Farrell. It was dark when we got to our billets in the Asylum, but C.Q.M.S. Wall was waiting for us with lamps, and guided the platoons to their various rooms. Our servants had left the trenches in advance, and had made down our valises in padded cells ! ! We sat up into the early hours of the morning in the Company Mess. So far I had thoroughly enjoyed my time at the Front. I was being well broken in, the weather had been excellent and I liked the spirit of camaraderie in the trenches. But Armentières was not Ypres, and this fact I had yet to discover ! ! Turning in at night, one could see the Véry lights going up every now and then from the trenches. The Asylum was only 2 miles as the crow flies from the front line.

31st May.

" Jung "[1] Murray of the 1st Battalion came to see us.

Platoon inspections, respirator drills, and general cleaning up of equipment and kit. The men were very comfortable. I was orderly officer, but without sword or Sam Browne belt. George Murray of D Company made hot punch, and we sat up into the night chatting.

1st June.

Munro drilled the Company in the field behind the Asylum. The men handled their arms well. The majority wore peculiar caps with flaps for the ears, which could be turned down in the cold weather.

The Asylum was a large building surrounded by a high wall, with a small chapel in the centre of the compound, and a large bed of rhododendrons. There was a story current in the Battalion that a newly joined subaltern had once taken refuge under these bushes when the Germans bombarded the Asylum in March. This strafe incidentally cost the Battalion many casualties as it commenced in the early hours of the morning when all, bar the

---

[1] His actual nickname was " jungalee wallah." He thought more about fighting than his personal appearance. He was a real slayer of Huns, and later Turks, and wound up the War with a D.S.O. and an M.C. and Lord Kitchener's niece as his wife. Now Commanding 4th Battalion Royal Tank Corps.

Quarter Guard at the gates, were asleep. Went into Armentières with Marsland in the evening. There was much "scrapping" down at La Bassée and the sky at night was lit up by the shell flashes.

2nd June.

We got movement orders for the Ypres salient at 10 a.m. and started packing up. The Battalion paraded at 5.50 p.m., and marched off for Bailleul. Although it was a longish march for men who had been cooped up in trenches for months on end, yet none fell out. Munro got badly kicked on the shin by his company charger, which cow-kicked as he was about to mount and he had to go off to a dressing-station. Command of the Company devolved on Algeo. We reached our destination at 9.30 p.m. Piper and I were billeted over an estaminet, Algeo and Marsland in a house which we used as the Company mess. The men got distributed in various large barns, and soon settled down with their blankets in quantities of straw.

3rd June.

Lieut.-Colonel W. T. M. Reeve, who had had his arm shot off in November, rejoined and took over command of the Battalion from Lieut.-Colonel Bullen-Smith, who had only just been gazetted to the temporary rank. Colonel Reeve suddenly and unexpectedly appeared on parade, and B-S hastily departed to cut off his two stars from his cuffs. We were all exceedingly sorry for him. All officers attended a lecture on gas attacks in the town hall. Up to this period in the War Bailleul had not been shelled, but had been occasionally strafed by air raids. The R.F.C. had a large aerodrome outside the town. No naked lights were allowed at night. Bailleul was quite a fair-sized place, and we enjoyed our sojourn there.

4th June.

Battalion paraded and marched off from Bailleul at 5.30 a.m. with the 17th Brigade. Order of march was North Staffords, Royal Fusiliers, the Leinsters, and R. B's. It was a sweltering hot day, and we felt the heat greatly, being heavily equipped. The dust was bad throughout the long column, and the uneven cobbled roads made the march more tiring. Carried Pte. Farrell's rifle to enable him to play the bagpipes. Our route was Locre, Reninghelst, Vlamertinghe, and then proceeded to the woods north-west of Vlamertinghe.

Reached our destination at 1.30 p.m. The cookers came up with the transport, the men got their dinners, and we started

putting up bivouacs. At night we made large fires, and sat round
them chatting for some time.

The men had a wonderful knack of settling down ; within a
short time after arrival they had erected top-hole " bivies " as
they called them, with their ground-sheets, and were busy
brewing their tea.

YPRES

5th June.

The Company put out a bush fire in the morning. There were
detachments of French cavalry throughout our area. At 9 p.m.
we struck camp and moved off for the front line. We struck
the Ypres road at Vlamertinghe and marched to the cross-roads
at H.12.A. (a reference point on the artillery squared map, sheet
28). Here we branched off to the left, with intervals of 200 yards
between companies, for No. 4 Bridge, which brought us across the
Yser Canal north-west of Ypres, thus giving the town a wide berth.

Ypres was being strafed as we marched around it, and the sky
was all lit up from the flashes of the numerous shells. As we
marched on towards the higher ground near La Brique, we easily
located the front line in its salient formation, from the star-shells
which seemed to go up all round. And so the 2nd Battalion had
arrived at Ypres. Going on across country, we passed some of
our batteries which were in action, with their night-lights ahead
of them. At La Brique we got into a support line some 700 yards
away from this ruined village and took over from the 1st Battalion
Royal Irish Fusiliers, 10th Brigade, 4th Division. It was 12 p.m.
when the relief was complete. Double sentries were posted, and
orders given that no fires were to be lit in daytime, and that gas
masks were to be kept ready, as the wind was blowing from a
dangerous quarter, north-east, i.e. towards our line.

Besides the 120 rounds of S.A.A. carried in the web equipment,
every man carried two bandoliers of 50 rounds each, slung across
him. It was a pitch-dark night, but our front-line trenches on
the ridge in front were clearly defined by the continual spout of
the yellow-green star-shells. I found my exact position on the
map by the aid of these Véry lights, which silhouetted the
jagged ruins of the farmhouses in the vicinity.

Throughout the night the guns boomed, and the sky was continually lit up by the shells going over the lines. The Battalion
had some men killed and wounded getting into trenches. Turning
into a small dug-out or " funk-hole," I slept until " Stand to " at
3.30 a.m.

6th June.

The trenches had been well made and revetted, but the parapets were much lower than those at Armentières. No. 10 Platoon was on my right, and A Company was on my left flank across the La Brique–Langemarck road. The Battalion was in support to the Royal Fusiliers. Our support line ran from a point 300 yards west of Irish Farm, and across to some 200 yards south-west of English Farm, and back towards St. Jean. Company Headquarters was situated on top of the ridge where this village stood, which gave us a good view of the surrounding country, flat, barren wastes studded here and there with derelict farm-houses. There was practically no timber of any kind, with the exception of the usual few willow trees, which grow at random all over Flanders. Most of the land was in meadow, now bleached by the gas. It was a depressing sight ; behind us was the deserted and battered village of St. Jean, and off in the distance we could see the tower and pinnacle of the Church and Cloth Hall of Ypres. Everywhere there was the sickly smell of the gas which had been used on the Canadians in the 2nd Battle of Ypres. The Company was employed making a support line around the wood north of English Farm all night, and we got shelled. We knocked off work at 4 a.m. and returned to our trench. Here 2nd Lieut. J. Bourke joined the Company.

7th June.

Very hot weather. D Company on our right was shelled in the evening. Capt. de Stacpoole was severely wounded,[1] and some men killed. I saw de Stacpoole lying in his dug-out with his back peppered with shrapnel. D Company being on top of the St. Jean Ridge, his men had been walking about in the open, and had been spotted by the Huns. Every morning and evening we stood to with our respirators on.

There were French Turcos on our left ; they were a great nuisance as they kept up a rapid fire all night. The enemy retaliated on us, catching our working and wiring parties. These Turcos were quaint-looking troops in their short blue tunics and picturesque baggy red trousers. In the day-time numbers of them used to leave their trenches and go back at large to loot in Ypres.

Enemy aeroplanes undoubtedly had the upper hand at this period in the Salient, and flew over our lines every night. Our anti-aircraft guns (12-pounders R.H.A.) did not seem to worry them. Got my platoon making dug-outs, as the only cover they

---

[1] Now Lieut.-Colonel E. H. M. de Stacpoole, M.C., Commanding 1st Battalion The Royal Scots.

had were " funk-holes " cut out of the trenches, or sheets of corrugated iron spread across the parapets, with sand-bags on top to keep them from blowing away ! We got doors and rafters from Irish Farm. Daly climbed up on the roof and started taking down a window shutter which looked due north, towards the Hun lines. He was spotted instantly, and we were shelled heavily for an hour with " Black Marias " and " Jack Johnsons."

Moved my platoon farther along the trench, as they were getting direct hits on my parapet near the road.

After the smoke and debris of one shell had cleared away, Daly emerged from the farm gate with the shutter on his shoulder ! Our artillery, the 42nd and 112th Batteries, retaliated on the Hun lines at Canadian, Hampshire and Shell Trap Farms.[1] There was a terrible shortage of shells, at this period each gun was rationed to three shells per day. When Algeo rang up the gunners for retaliation, the answer he invariably got was : " Sorry, but we have expended our allowance, and if we fire any more shells off to-day, we will be left with none to repulse attacks with to-morrow ! " Company still on fatigue digging the communication trench near English Farm. As we had dug right through a swamp, the trench welled water, and we had to bale it out. Commencing our work at 8 p.m., we rarely finished until after 3 a.m. The smell from dead bodies lying round was ghastly, and in digging the trench we often had to dig up a corpse. Shells came over at intervals, but we had no casualties.

8th June.

We watched the effect of the Hun artillery on the tower of Ypres Cathedral, and on the three remaining pinnacles of the Cloth Hall. They got direct hits on two of the pinnacles, and then stopped, leaving the other obviously as a ranging mark for further strafing.

The Boche gunners strafed Ypres systematically every night ; and as the roads from Ypres radiated like spokes of a wheel, they knew that our transports had to pass going through from westward to eastward of the city.

I was sitting in a fire-bay one morning and overhead two old " toughs " discussing the situation and the shells which were incessantly whining over our heads towards Ypres. " Faith, Mick, Armentières was cushy compared to this spot. The shells down there were only connecting files, but here, begad, there's battalions of 'em—and in column of route, too ! "

---

[1] Later in the War this farm was renamed Mouse Trap Farm, as the name Shell Trap, it was considered, might have a demoralising effect on troops taking over that sector.

One particular shell, the 12-inch, made a " wr wr " sound in
the air.   This the men nicknamed " The Roscrea Mail."   We
were all greatly astonished at first by the colossal shell-fire and
the continual bombardment of Ypres.

Scrounging round, the men discovered a field of potatoes near
Irish Farm.   Naturally, this was a great attraction, especially to
Irish troops.   At all hours of the day the men used to get out
behind the trench and dig for national fodder.   In time, this drew

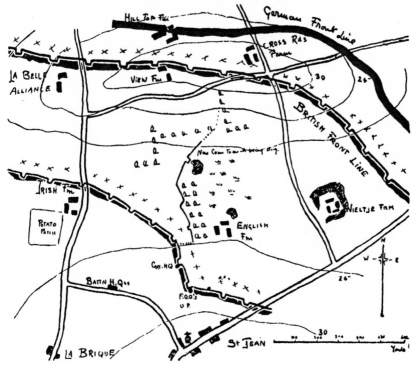

Sketch of the La Brique–St. Jean area N.E. of Ypres, June, 1915.

shell-fire on our line near the farm, and we got crumped with
8-inch shells or 5·9s.

Accordingly, orders were issued that men must not get out of
the trench in daylight.   However, two men of A Company went
out this evening to get their " buckshee " ration, as they called
it, and as ill-luck would have it, one solitary crump landed beside
them, killing one, No. 4734 Pte. Halligan, and missing his companion completely.   The C.O. of the Royal Fusiliers, Colonel
Fowler-Butler, happened to be passing at the time, and sent for
me, and told me that some Leinsters had been blown up behind

the farm. I got our stretcher-bearers and hurried off to the potato patch, where we found the terribly mangled body of Halligan lying on the brink of a smoking shell crater. Both his legs and one arm had been blown off. He was, of course, killed instantaneously, while his companion was absolutely unscathed, except for concussion and slight bleeding from the ears !

Just before the shell landed, one man had been seen holding a biscuit tin for his pal to put the potatoes into. It came out afterwards that Halligan had got permission to get " the spuds," but his companion had not. Such indeed was the irony of circumstance.

9th June.

Returned from fatigue at 3 a.m. We were all pretty jaded and disgruntled with this task. Every night on the same work, hacking through corpses and filling sand-bags ! The ground was a swamp, and churned up by shell-fire which prevented drainage. Nothing broke the monotony of this working party ; the same smell of gas, and sickening smell of decomposing human flesh hung round the locality. Every now and then shrapnel would burst over us to break the stillness of the night. Otherwise the only sounds were the sighing poplars and the everlasting croaking of the frogs. In the morning we built up the line which had been blown in near Irish Farm, and made large traverses to stop side bursts and, as usual, we dug up some bodies and had to re-bury them. At dark, we often cut the standing meadows in No-Man's-Land in order to get a better field of fire, in case the front line had to withdraw to our support line. On these grass-cutting expeditions we often came across the bodies of dead Canadians, which we buried. Received orders to move my platoon to the right flank of the Company, and got to my new position in the evening. I had a dug-out hard by to D Company's old headquarters where de Stacpoole had got knocked out. The weather broke, and rain descended in torrents.

10th June.

My platoon was in D Company's old line just north-east of St. Jean, our trench swinging round the high ground. We had to be careful not to show movement in this area on account of shell-fire and the bad state of the trench. Will, and five men of A Company were wounded.[1] Will was a good fellow, and a fine sportsman. He had been awarded his " Rugger " cap for Scotland in season 1913-14.

[1] He was later seconded to the R.F.C. and was killed flying on the 25th March, 1917, with the 29th Squadron.

I went out at 8.30 p.m. with the digging party, which consisted
of the whole Company, less one platoon, which was always left
behind to hold the line.

11th June.

Just as we got back from the working party at 2.30 a.m. it
started to rain heavily, and we got soaked through. I thanked
my lucky stars that I had made my batman, McCafferty, roof my
dug-out with a sheet of corrugated iron the day before. Algeo
came up to my dug-out as his had been flooded out, and he was
drenched. It rained a deluge for hours ; the men's dug-outs
caved in one by one, and their rations and packs were carried
away down the slope. This torrential rain created a young river
in the trench.

The rain stopped at 8 a.m. and the line, or what was left of
it, was in a terrible state. We spent the morning draining the
trench by digging big sump pits. In one place I had the parapet
pulled down, and let the water off down the slope towards English
Farm. The sun came out, and it remained fine all day. Captain
R. A. H. Orpen-Palmer took over command of D Company from
O'Brien, who had been temporarily commanding it since de
Stacpoole was hit. He got a rough reception on his arrival, as
the Huns strafed his company throughout the night, and blew in
his trench in many places.

Working party as usual at night ; discovered the new line
which we had just finished, completely flooded.

12th June.

Fine weather. Shelled all evening with " Little Willies " or
" whiz-bangs." The gunners forward observation post was blown
in. Monks, the gunner subaltern, had attempted to camouflage
his post, but his futurist screen had too many colours in it, and
did not resemble a hedge in the least. The Boche spotted it, and
accordingly strafed his position all day.

I met Orpen-Palmer for the first time when he came down to
see us. On account of the heat, like everyone else he was in
shirt-sleeves. He was always known as O.-P.1, his younger
brother, O.-P.2, had been seriously wounded in October. Got
orders from Battalion Headquarters to count the shells which
fell along the Company front. Algeo detailed his servant, Keegan,
to do this, and gave him a note-book. While we were having tea,
Keegan kept yelling out : " One shell, sir, on No. 9 Platoon,
four shells on No. 11 Platoon, direct hit on th' ould farm, one
gone off to blow up the Colonel, a Black Maria on me father's

section." (Keegan's father, a veteran of several wars, was actually serving in the Company.)

We noticed that more and more shells were coming our way, and after one large crump had landed slap behind our dug-out, I got up and looked over the parados, to find Keegan in his shirt-sleeves, note-book in hand, standing out in the open just behind Company Headquarters! He had been there the whole time, counting the shells and drawing fire on us! It was a marvel he hadn't been killed. Algeo was laughing so much that he couldn't curse him for being such a B.F.! C.S.M. O'Bryan was wounded, and Sergt. Morgan took over the duties of C.S.M.

13th June.

Got back with the working-party at 3 a.m. We had been digging a new firing-line behind the Wieltjze trenches. Found that some of my parapets had fallen in, and they had to be built up again. Company shelled in the evening; some men were wounded badly by a "Little Willie," which came right through the parapet, bursting in the trench. More digging at night.

14th June.

Shelled all morning and evening. We had working parties during the day employed in pumping the water out of my trench. However, as usual, the trench pumps would not function, and in the end we baled the water out with buckets. The enemy spotted us working, and sent over salvos of shrapnel which caught some of my platoon. 3129 Pte. Bland was killed, Pte. Smith and my servant McCafferty were wounded. Bland was the first man who had been killed since I took over command of No. 9 Platoon.

8243 Pte. Jackson became my new batman, and I was lucky to get him. A rum issue came up for the Company.

15th June.

Got orders to bring my platoon down to La Brique for the night, as the 4th Division were going to attack early next morning and the C.O. did not consider my trench would withstand a bombardment, as the Huns were bound to retaliate on our support lines. At dusk left the line for La Brique, where we got into some dug-outs round the hedges of a small field in front of one of our batteries. When the men had removed their packs, we paraded for fatigue, which consisted of carrying duckboards up to Company Headquarters. The fatigue finished, we returned to La Brique. I spent the night on a stone floor in the Battalion stores at La Brique.

16th June.

Having spent a most uncomfortable night, I got up at 3.30 a.m. when our bombardment started. It was not quite light, a mist enveloped the place, but in spite of this, I had an excellent view of our batteries in action, as two of them were less than 100 yards away. This was the first time I had seen batteries firing in a real pukka bombardment. The shells made a mighty roar as they went crashing off towards the enemy lines. Then the Germans started counter-battery work, and the woods, where our guns were placed, were subjected to a very severe shelling.

The morning sky was lit up by the numerous shells going backwards and forwards, and crossing each other in the air. An enemy crump landed close to one of our guns and silenced it. I afterwards heard that the complete crew had all been knocked out. The bombardment lasted until 5 a.m. The attack was successful, but after a few hours the enemy counter-attacked, and retook most of the ground gained. Our casualties were heavy, as the enemy wire entanglements had not been properly cut, and our men were held up in the open, and mowed down by machine-guns. It was not our gunners' fault, as they had done their work as well as could be expected, with the limited number of shells at their disposal. The 4th Division captured 50 prisoners.

Marched my platoon back to the trenches at 8 a.m., and got orders to go back to La Brique at night, and remain there until further notice. On fatigue all night, carrying foot-boards and stakes to the support line.

17th June.

My platoon worked on their dug-outs, and made them more splinter proof. Macartney, the Padre, and I went down in the evening to see Ypres. The city was deserted and desolate. The atmosphere was heavy with the smell of decaying bodies, for the first shells had surprised the inhabitants, and had caught many in their beds. A number of the houses had been knocked down by direct hits, and others had one of the walls blown down, showing the furniture of the stories above, like scenery in a theatre.

Few houses had been left unscathed. The square in front of the Cloth Hall was in a dreadful state, strewn all over with parts of British G.S. waggons, bones of dead horses, broken rifles, and web equipment. The streets throughout Ypres were pitted with shell craters, beside the Cloth Hall there was a crater of a 16-inch shell. I measured it, and found it was fifty-two paces around, 30 feet deep and 48 feet across from lip to lip.

We returned to La Brique, and I took a carrying party up to the support line near St. Jean.

18th June.

Marsland and I took up our platoons down to Ypres, and took down a number of the hall doors off the houses for dug-out roofs, and brought them back to La Brique in hand-carts. I got some dozen bottles of wine which I looted from a cellar. At dark, I brought the " hall doors " up to the line, and as the knockers had been left on most of them, at every halt the men amused themselves by knocking a tattoo! We dumped our loads in the support trenches, and returned early to our dug-out line.

19th June.

More carrying parties to Ypres. Took more hall doors down from houses in a street called Rue de Lille.

20th June. Sunday.

At 5 a.m. Sergt. Bennett woke me up, saying that one of our aeroplanes was landing near us on fire. I got out of the dug-out in time to see it crashing near our reserve trenches north-east of La Brique. It had been scrapping with an enemy Taube, which it sent down over the lines near Poelchapelle. Under heavy fire from hostile anti-aircraft guns our pilot turned towards our lines to continue his reconnaissance, when his petrol tank was hit. His machine then burst into flames, and he started to descend. The observer was seen getting out on to the wings to escape from the flames. When the plane crashed, both fell clear and we picked them up, badly burnt. The rounds in their revolvers had all gone off. The plane was now burning fiercely and the unexpended ammunition was going off. We salved the machine-gun and the " skull and cross-bones " which was in front of the body. The pilot was one of our " aces," and had got this honour for having downed many enemy machines. The men carried the pilot and observer off to the dressing-station, where our M.O. attended to them. They were both terribly burnt. The Huns, seeing the plane landing, and expecting we would go out to help the occupants, sent over shrapnel, but we all managed to get away in time. Six months afterward the pilot died from his injuries.

During the morning we salved all the serviceable portions of the plane and equipment which lay round it, field-glasses, revolvers, etc., all under shrapnel fire from the Huns who had got the exact range from the flames. More carrying fatigues from Ypres to the support line.

21st June.

Platoons still employed in Ypres all morning. An official photographer took a photograph of Marsland and myself, with some of the men, in front of the Cloth Hall, beside a derelict waggon.

Two R.F.C. officers came up to see about the crashed aeroplane, and took photographs of the wreckage. At night I brought up Bourke's platoon and my own to build dug-outs in the front line for A Company, 1st Royal Fusiliers (Captain Alexander's company). There we made dug-outs in a sort of rest-line behind the fire bays. One could see the Germans, who were out on grass-cutting expeditions in No-Man's-Land, quite easily when the star-shells went up ; and as the Fusiliers also had grass-cutting parties out, they let the enemy carry on in peace. Some of the Boches were singing, we supposed to create a peaceful atmosphere until they finished their job.

There were about 200 yards between the lines at this point— Cross Roads Farm. Finished our task at midnight.

22nd June.

More fatigues in Ypres. The town was being badly strafed all morning, so we did not remain longer than necessary. In the evening the 3rd and 4th Divisions carried out an attack at Hooge. All our artillery moved up nearer La Brique, and the howitzers took up positions along the canal bank.

23rd June.

At 4 a.m. the enemy put 96 crumps (5·9's) into a field just behind us. Evidently they thought they had located a battery. No damage was done. Worked in Ypres as usual. Rained throughout the day, and we got shelled spasmodically.

24th June.

Went across to watch the 42nd Battery in action. It was splendidly concealed behind a hedge, and all the guns were cleverly camouflaged. Kavanagh, of my platoon, was wounded by a premature burst of shrapnel from one of our guns. At night, my platoon was employed carrying stakes and barbed wire to B Company, beyond English Farm. There was a considerable amount of sniping, but I had no men hit.

25th June.

Rain all morning. Marsland and I went down to see the 42nd Battery. We heard that poor old Monks had been blown up some eight days past when observing from a new " O.P." at English

Farm. He had been badly mauled ; one of his arms was found some 25 yards away, with a wrist watch strapped on it, and still going ! News of the awards of the C.M.G. to the C.O. and the D.S.O. to Major Bullen-Smith, and to Marsland and Padre Maloney the M.C. We all got very wet as there was no roof to the Battalion stores where we lived. At 8 p.m. I was relieved by a platoon of the 1st East Yorkshire Regiment, and marched off to Ypres, where I was joined by the Company.

The N.C.O. in charge of our guides got tight, and we had to wait some time in the rain before our billets were found. We took over billets from the 2nd Durhams. Ypres was full of wine. Some of our company servants got drunk, and were returned to duty. We discovered that the cellar in our billet contained two hundred bottles of good red wine.

26th June.

We were in top-hole billets, near the Water Tower on the Poperinghe road. Piper, Marsland, and Algeo lived on the top floor, Bourke and I slept on mattresses on the ground floor. After lunch, Algeo, Piper, and I went to reconnoitre a position where we were to dig a new trench at night. We walked up the Menin Road to "Hell Fire Corner," where we met a sapper officer, who showed us the way. We were seen by the Huns, who sent over some shrapnel. This was the first time I had been on the Menin Road—an unhealthy route indeed. It was badly pitted with shell-holes, and the poplar trees which grew along it were badly scarred from shell-fire. We found the place after difficulty, and returned to our billets to guide the Company up.

At 8 p.m. we paraded and marched off with picks and shovels. I had 9 and 12 Platoons, Piper and Algeo 10 and 11. A sapper officer led me astray, mistaking us for a party belonging to the 1st Leicester Regiment. He brought me to Birr Cross Roads, before I discovered he was conducting me to the wrong place. As it was dark, I could not recognise the country. On the way, we were heavily shelled by shrapnel, which rattled on the shovels. A few men were hit—Daly and Mara. We narrowly missed being wiped out, as we had only just left the Cross Roads at Hell Fire Corner when some dozen crumps landed on top of it. I marched back just in time to meet the rest of the Company turning off towards the White Château. We started work on a communication trench,[1] which the sappers had taped out. As we were under shell-fire all the time, the men dug in like blazes, and soon made

[1] Communication trenches were dug wide enough to enable a stretcher to be carried through.

good cover. We had only two casualties in the Company, but D Company were very unlucky, a shell landing slap into one of their platoons, wounding J. J. O'Brien, and knocking out 15 men, of whom 5 were killed. The enemy, as usual, had been searching for our transports, which they heard rumbling along the roads.

27th June.

Carroll and Keegan unearthed some civilian clothes, and dressed up in the afternoon, which greatly amused the men. Their get-up was splendid, and they took us all in at first. Keegan came in to wait at dinner, complete in tail-coat and white shirt. He looked frightfully comical.

28th June.

I took my platoon off for a bathe in the Yser Canal, and took 9 and 12 Platoons out working at night to the same place, near Hell Fire Corner. Passing the Devil's Elbow, I was stopped by military police, who said that I should wait as the road was being heavily shelled. My orders were to report to an R.E. officer at 8.30 p.m., so on I went. As the road was all torn up by fresh shell-craters, I got the platoons into file, and doubled along until we had passed the dressing-station, which was on fire, and being heavily shelled. There were some Red Cross ambulances outside, and nurses and R.A.M.C. orderlies were evacuating the wounded on stretchers, as the shells plunked all round them. Got to our rendezvous, having given Hell Fire Corner a wide berth. We were only just into our trench when the enemy started a real strafe on the Menin Road. All the shells went well over us. Orpen-Palmer brought up D Company. At 3 a.m. we had finished the trench completely, and duck-boarded and revetted it, and returned to our billets. The guns had stopped for a time, and Ypres seemed as silent as the grave, as it always did when there was a lull in the shell-fire.

29th June.

C and D Companies left billets at the Water Tower for rest in the Vlamertinghe Woods. We were glad to leave Ypres. Shell-fire in the front line is expected, and one is prepared for it, but shell-fire in billets is most unpleasant. We were usually shelled at night when we were all asleep. One would be wakened by yells and screams for stretcher-bearers, and go out, to find a billet had fallen in on top of some men. D Company were very unlucky, for besides losing numbers of men on the working parties at night, they lost many in billets from shell-fire. There is rarely any cover in a town from shell-fire. There were cellars in Ypres, but to take refuge in them meant running the risk of having the house collapse on top of one. It is always advisable to leave a town which is being badly shelled, but what can be done when surprised in the middle of the night ?   " C'est la guerre," as the Flemish peasants used to say when they went back to Ypres to salve some of the household gods, only to find their old home completely demolished. Turning their horses' heads once more towards Vlamertinghe, they would drive away repeating : " C'est la guerre ! C'est la guerre ! "

Got to Vlamertinghe, where we had baths, and moved on to " A " camp north-west of this small town. The camp consisted of huts in the midst of a wood. The trees were in foliage, and everything seemed very peaceful after the noise in the salient.

30th June.

Parades, arm drill, musketry and bayonet exercises. In the evening, with Bourke, I took the Company for a march towards Poperinghe and back.

1st July.

Brought Nos. 9 and 12 Platoons for a march towards Elverdinghe. The Padre came round to see us on his black Uhlan horse. Its previous owner had actually surrendered to him at Le Cateau, when he was Chaplain to a Cavalry Brigade. It stood about 17 hands high, and had U.9 branded on the near side of its neck. It was known as the submarine. The C.O. came round to inspect our lines. He remarked that his arm gave him hell, and he could not sleep at night. Weather excellent.

2nd July.

Usual inspections of rifles, respirators, and iron rations. Marsland went on leave. Caulfeild, who had just been promoted Captain, took over the Company from Algeo. He brought with him as charger a splendid brown mare called Matilda which won the 6th Divisional Jumping Competition at Armentières with de Stacpoole.

3rd July.

Battalion left the woods for the line at Potijze. We again made a detour of Ypres as it was being shelled. The route was via Vlamertinghe, No. 4 bridge at Noordhofwyk Cross Roads south of La Brique, and along the Brigade road to Potijze. We were shelled rather badly on the way up with gas shells, and were all practically blinded ! Coughing and choking, and with our eyes smarting and streaming, we took over the support line from the 1st K.S.L.I., the 2nd York and Lancs having taken over our billets in the Vlamertinghe Woods. The trench relief was complete at 2 a.m. Dug-outs were plentiful.

4th July.

The new line was a great improvement on the trenches at La Brique. A and B Companies were in the front line astride the Ypres–Zonnebeke road. Our line in support ran south of this road from the Potijze Woods. The enemy had launched a gas attack here within the last week unsuccessfully. The stench of it hung round the dug-outs and the standing crops had a bleached, withered look. Company Headquarters was situated just south-east of the village in front of a belt of poplars, and Battalion Headquarters was situated slap in the wood at Potijze. We did not envy Battalion Headquarters their site, it threatened to become exceedingly " unhealthy."

5th July.

Spent the morning pulling down rafters from the houses in Potijze for dug-out roofs. The 14th Division lost part of a trench near Railway Wood. The 1st North Staffordshire retook it, but with casualties. Brought Sergt. Ginn and my four section commanders up to the front line to reconnoitre the sector, which we had to support.

6th July.

The 4th Division carried out an attack which did not materialise into any great success. They advanced, taking 200 yards of enemy trenches and a bag of 80 prisoners.

Working from 9 p.m. to 1 a.m. carrying R.E. material up to A Company from the Battalion dump in Potijze. We had just got clear of the village when the enemy started strafing. Potijze had had its share of shell-fire up to this time in the War. It was only a mere hamlet on a cross-roads, most of the houses were roofless, the jagged beams and rafters projected into the void, and fragments of cottage furniture and cooking utensils were strewn across the road. Here and there were twisted rifles and torn bits of khaki uniform. One house had a large pile of un-opened bully beef tins. From this heap the company replenished the deficiencies of iron rations, which they all said had been " destroyed entirely in the flood at La Brique."

Healy annexed a Belgian's dog, a nice little black and white mongrel, which he called Whisky. It gave the men some amusement and some " wag " made a gas mask for it. Young came down to see me ; he took exception to the position of my dug-out, and asked me to build another as he was relieving me. I returned with Young to the front line to look at his bomb store. The communication trench, which was called Bond Street, was a long one, and it took 20 minutes steady walking to get to the firing-line from our Company Headquarters. It was in this sector that the cavalry put up such a good show, dismounted in the Second Battle of Ypres. Cavalry bandoliers and sabres lay scattered all about the place, and two R.F.A. derelict limbers with hundreds of empty shell-cases were in the Potijze Wood. We made gas alarms of these shell cases, hanging them in the trench with an entrenching tool handle. To pass the time we practised sword drill with an abandoned sabre belonging to the Household Cavalry.

7th July.

Young and I were very nearly knocked out by a whiz-bang on our way down to Company Headquarters. The weather changed, and it turned cold. Young wore a Tommy's great-coat, as his own had been blown up by the Huns at Premerques in October. Young was very fed up with the War, and he told me that his nerves were beginning to feel the racket.

8th July.

We got badly crumped all day. The Germans were searching for our battery positions, which were close to our support line. The Gunner F.O.O. had his " O.P." in the top of an old willow tree behind Company Headquarters. We admired him for the way he stuck up in his position directing the guns through his megaphone with shrapnel bursting all round. Marsland returned from leave ; he had been presented with his Military Cross at Buckingham Palace by the King. He brought back a bottle of " John Jameson " in his pack from Tipperary. It disappeared with rapidity.

Working on our parapets all night ; the enemy sent some colossal shells into Ypres, "More Roscrea mails," as the men called them ironically. They certainly did sound like trains going through the air.

9th July.

Early a.m. my platoon was carrying rafters from an old farm hard by Potijze for dug-out roofs.

The official communiqué which was distributed daily to Companies in type-written form and which was alluded to as " Comic Cuts," stated that the conquest of German South-West Africa was now complete, by General Botha's forces.

Relieved A Company at midnight. Before going up I took my platoon to the Company dump in Potijze for S.A.A., sand-bags, and barbed wire. We narrowly missed being blown up ; just as we had moved off, over came some " 8-inches," and blew up the dump and the cross-roads. Some men of the 3rd R.B.s were hit, and the back of their water-cart was blown in. The horses bolted and went careering off towards Ypres without a driver ! We relieved A Company. My platoon found all listening posts, and I relieved Piper's covering party. A draft arrived from Cork, from which three, an N.C.O., Corporal Maher, and two men, were allotted to my platoon. The trenches were very fine indeed, with comfortable dug-outs, the advanced line being barely 150 yards from the enemy.

The enemy attacked on our right near Bellewaarde Farm. They got into some trenches held by the 14th Division, but were immediately ejected by a successful counter-attack. Weather excellent.

10th to 11th July.

The C.O. came round the line, making a tour of inspection. He was not in very good form, and was obviously suffering from the loss of his arm.

On night duty, and I visited all the listening posts. Earlier in the day I had been over to see D Company on the left, also down to A Company with my servant to see about barbed-wire from the Battalion dump. Valentine Williams, the war correspondent, visited the Battalion in the front line ; he was a friend of Louis Daly's. As it was a dark night, men were employed strengthening the parapets and deepening the new communication trenches called Duke and Jermyn Streets. Neville Young wounded in the shoulder by shrapnel.

12th July.

Improved our dug-outs. Learnt that the XIX Bavarians were opposite to us. Watched a German sentry through a periscope for a long time. Piper established a lot of sniping posts along the Battalion front. He was made O.C. snipers, and we called him " Lord of the Hate Squad." He was issued with some capital telescopic rifles by Brigade Headquarters. Heavy shell-fire all day at Railway Wood and at Hooge. Pte. Reilly was shot at night when out with a covering party. Marsland and Morrissey carried him in.

13th July.

At 5 a.m. the enemy started shelling the advanced post of D Company, which surrounded some old ruins called Stink Post.

I watched them sending over trench mortars for some time. They then burst salvoes of shrapnel and "whiz-bangs" over the position. The place was covered in smoke and red brick-dust from the already demolished houses in the vicinity, which completely obliterated the post from view. After a furious bombardment, in which the garrison were all either killed or wounded, the enemy rushed the post and bayoneted the few who happened to be badly wounded. Captain Orpen-Palmer organized a counter-attack, and drove the Germans out in less than ten minutes "scrapping."

There was no support from our covering battery, as the telephone wires had been cut in the bombardment. Our casualties were 7 men killed, and 2 officers and 27 men wounded. The killed were Ptes. Burke, Guinnan, Hyland, Murphy, Tuite, Watson and Smith. O.-P. was hit in the face, but remained at duty.

At 9 a.m. we were watching one of our aeroplanes reconnoitring the enemy lines (from 4000 feet up). It was being shelled by larger anti-aircraft shells than usual. The third shell got a direct hit, and it suddenly crumpled up, and came crashing down behind the enemy lines. It made a dreadful roaring noise, and we saw one man fall out. It crashed just out of view from our trenches as the Huns were on the high ground, but we saw the flames shoot up when it struck earth. The enemy cheered like blazes. A demoralizing sight. Reilly died from his wounds. The Germans attacked the 47th Division (Territorial), but got repulsed. The canal bank was gassed all day by gas shells. The Salient commenced getting very lively from this date onwards.

14th July.

At 5 a.m. one of our planes flew very low over the Hun lines. It was shelled a good deal, but carried on with its flight, and after some time flew back towards Ypres. At 7 a.m. four Boche planes flew over our lines towards Ypres.

Russians reported to be retreating "like a manœuvre"!

Supplied D Company with a covering party at night.

15th July.

The Huns strafed the tower of Ypres Cathedral all morning. Our artillery observation post found! Our Press used to amuse us immensely with its accounts of the Huns' "frightfulness" in bombarding churches. Both sides invariably used church towers as artillery observation posts.

Located a sniper in a tree, and gave Sergt. Bennett his position. A burst of the Vickers soon settled him, as he dropped like a stone. A new Boche Taube came over our lines; it had very large Maltese crosses on its wings. We opened fire on it, as it was flying quite low, but our fire did not seem to affect it in the least. It turned out to be plated with steel underneath. It continued to fly low over our lines every evening throughout this tour, and it was alluded to as "Iron-Arsed Fritz."

Severely shelled all evening. Sergt. Bennett had given away his machine-gun position by opening fire on the Boche plane.

The 3rd Rifle Brigade, who were on our right, had some men hit. The G.O.C., Major-General Congreve, V.C., came round the line and condemned a number of dug-outs as not being shell-proof. I brought out the covering party, which had to lie out in No-Man's-Land between Crump Farm and Stink Post all night. D Company very nearly opened fire on us, and would have, but for O.-P. recognising me in time. Captain Grant Saunders and Lieut. A. D. O'Morchoe of the 3rd Battalion joined.

16th July.
Terence Hickman[1] wounded, and Gamble invalided down the line. A tranquil day, but for an occasional "Little Willie."

17th July.
The weather broke and it rained throughout the day. Our advanced position became flooded. In some places the duck-boards were floating.

18th July.
Good weather again. Marsland, Piper, and I went up to see "Stink Post" in the evening. It was quite a job getting out to the end of the sap as the communication trench was frightfully low, and we had to crawl along as the enemy snipers were particularly hostile.

This C.T. ran through some old ruined houses, under which were the graves of the late owners, killed in the second battle. Horses' hoofs, too, stuck out at odd intervals from the parapets. The sickly smell of decaying flesh hung all about the place. No wonder it had been called "Stink Post," but it was marked on the maps as Odour Houses. We found the garrison sitting down, their rifles across their knees, and gazing into periscopes which were stuck up along the parados. There were no sniping plates of any description, and our snipers had to "chance their arm" and fire over the parapets. Whilst we were in the post, two of the Battalion snipers, 5970 Pte. Flanaghan, and 3784 Pte. Ward, were shot clean through the head. The former lived for just twenty minutes, and the latter for about the same time. Every

---

[1] Killed 27/6/16.

second bullets were snapping viciously against the ruined walls behind us. The men of this post were relieved every nine hours, and the Battalion snipers put in so many hours per day in the position. They were all keen men, both Flanaghan and Ward had been there on their own all day. The former had accounted for at least ten Huns during this tour. Through periscopes I saw the enemy working behind their trench, and I spotted a Hun in the trench wearing the famous *pickelhaube*. Evidently they were preparing for relief. At night the artillery on both sides were actively engaged in counter-battery work. The Potijze Wood came in for a lot of strafing.

19th July.

Macartney returned from leave. He also, like Marsland, had attended an investiture at Buckingham Palace, and had received his M.C. from the King.

The enemy had three captive balloons up observing our lines. At 7 p.m. when at dinner, we were all suddenly thrown on the ground by a colossal vibration. Getting up, we rushed out of the dug-out, to see, as it seemed, the whole of Hooge in the air !

A mine had been sprung by the 3rd Division, right under the German lines. The whole area has become quite dark, and we could still see the debris and earth falling from the sky from the explosion. The mine had made a deafening roar. Simultaneously, all our batteries opened. We then saw our troops getting out of their trenches and attacking in extended order. They disappeared into a great cloud of smoke, which was lit up now and then by the bursting of shrapnel shells. The Huns resented this bit of frightfulness on our part, and retaliated on all our front lines and back areas, " crumping " Railway and Potijze Woods considerably.

We next saw our supports going up through Railway Wood in artillery formation towards the Bellewaarde Ridge. The objective for the attack was the enemy line which ran along the crest of this ridge from Bellewaarde Farm to Hooge inclusive. Then the rattle of musketry and staccato of machine-guns firing could be heard above the bursting of the shells. Within a short time the hiatus seemed to die down at Hooge, the 3rd Division had captured their objectives. This was a most successful attack and brilliantly carried out. In the fighting the 2nd Battalion Royal Irish Rifles[1] greatly distinguished themselves.

The mine made a record crater right beneath the enemy front line, which included a strongly held redoubt. One hundred and forty-five dead Germans were counted, and many more were killed

---

[1] Now Royal Ulster Rifles.

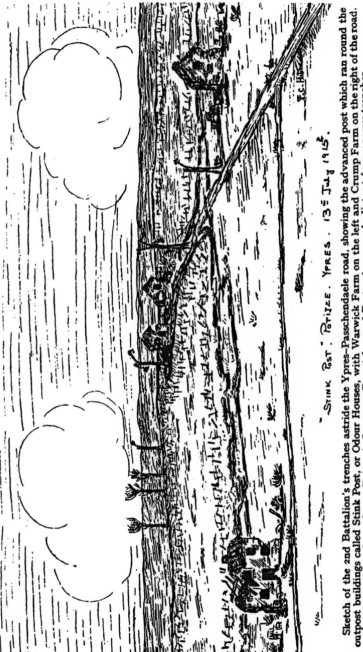

'STINK POST'. POTIJZE. YPRES. 13th July 1915.

Sketch of the 2nd Battalion's trenches astride the Ypres–Passchendaele road, showing the advanced post which ran round the outpost buildings called Stink Post, or Odour Houses, with Warwick Farm on the left and Crump Farm on the right of the road. Position held by Capt. Orpen-Palmer's Company D. Advanced Post only 20 yards distant from enemy trenches.

by the 1st Gordon Highlanders as they were endeavouring to extri-
cate themselves from the debris of shattered woodwork and earth.
Throughout the attack we were severely shelled. Every minute
one of our well-revetted parapets went sky-high. However, our
traverses being very formidable, afforded us great cover. Although
we were bombarded for six hours, and our trenches were blown in
in many places, yet the company had only one casualty I The
Machine-Gun Section lost some men ; one gunner who was up in
Stink Post had his head blown off. The 3rd Rifle Brigade had
some knocked out, and I met Padre Talbot going up to administer
the last rites of the Church to the mortally wounded. We were to
have been relieved at 9 p.m., but the unit which was relieving us
got held up on the far side of the Potijze Wood by the bombardment. The reason that this wood got shelled so heavily was that
one of our planes sent a wireless message in German saying that
the British were concentrating in it. This clever ruse had the
desired effect of easing the shelling on our front line.

Throughout the attack enemy aeroplanes were actively engaged
in dropping lights over our trenches to give their artillery the
exact range. Close on 2 a.m. we were relieved by Territorials, the
Honourable Artillery Company. They were a fine unit ; most of
their rank and file were public-school men.

By this time the shell-fire and musketry had died down at
Hooge, and we knew then that the 3rd Division had successfully
consolidated their gains. Platoons rendezvoused at Potijze at
2.30 a.m. and we marched off for the huts in the Vlamertinghe
Woods.

Ypres was very silent, and the crumbling ruins stood out very
forbiddingly in the early dawn, as we marched by the Cloth Hall
and Cathedral. The tramp of the two hundred pairs of ammunition boots on the uneven *pavé* re-echoed through the streets.
Suddenly Pte. Farrell broke into " Brian Boru " on his pipes,
and we all, who had felt the strain of the intense bombardment for
the past seven hours, cheered like blazes. It was not until we
had just got to Vlamertinghe that Farrell got " winded." Caulfeild lent me his horse for a part of the march.

20th July.

Got up at 11 a.m. The C.O.[1] went away on leave, and Major
Bullen-Smith again took over command of the Battalion.

Went into Poperinghe with Tim Laville and the doctor. We
got back to the woods in a staff car, which we stopped I

---

[1] Colonel Reeve was not medically fit enough to command a battalion in the
line, but he volunteered to take out a Garrison Battalion to Gallipoli and died
from the effects of his old wound on leaving the Peninsula.

21st July.

Drilled all morning, and we had a sing-song in the evening.

22nd July.

Drilled as usual. Brought the Company down to the Division baths in Poperinghe. On the way back we stopped at the Quartermaster's stores, and the men were issued out with clothing and boots. The transport lines and Quartermaster's stores were on the Elverdinghe road, and to get back to camp we cut across country. Rained hard all day.

23rd to 24th July.

Got issued with a new gas mask, a bag made from Army flannel to put over the head. It had talc eye-pieces and a rubber breathing

The first defensive measure against gas. A black gauze rag tied round the face, with a piece of gun-cotton soaked with a hypo solution, held between the teeth. Issued to troops in May, 1915, after 2nd Battle of Ypres.

The first respirator, well made out of old Army shirts. Called the P.H. helmet. Guarded both eyes and lungs. Came into use throughout Army in July, 1915. Breathing tube for mouth, and talc eye-piece. A very good improvement.

tube for the mouth ; the ends of the respirator had to be tucked under the jacket collar. They were all drenched with a solution of hypo, and were very sticky, messy gadgets.

We then marched the men off to watch a gas demonstration, a section of the Belgian defence trenches were covered over, and turned into a gas chamber. The officers put on their new masks and went into it. The gas was pumped out of a large cylinder. The gas was "hostile" looking stuff, and was of a greenish yellowy vapour. When we came out of the chamber our buttons were blackened and our watches had stopped, mine jibbed for ever afterwards, so I had to scrap it.

Had a sing-song in one of the huts after dinner. I believe Barnett was responsible for the following parody of the song: "I want to go back to the Farm." The words were:

> I want to go back, I want to go back,
>   I want to go back to the Hun
>   With his seventeen-inch gun
>   And his shell which weighs a ton.
> And his trench mortar, the one that oughter
>   Wake me up at 4 a.m.
> For I love old Wipers when it's full of snipers
> So I want to go back, I want to go back,
>   I want to go and chance my arm
> That's why I want to be, away back at Pot-ij-ze,
>   Down by Crump Farm.

Another song, which we sung to the tune of " We've been Married just one Year," ran:

> " We've been fighting just one year,
>   And we've got the wind up
>   We've got the wind up,
> We've got the bleeding awful wind up.
>
> For we expect a strafing,
>   The Hun is on his way,
> It's rumoured that he's got Warsaw,
>   And hopes to get Calais."
>   etc.

25th July.

Bourke and I took the Company up to the Vlamertinghe Château, Divisional Headquarters. Here we put up barbed-wire entanglements in front of a new reserve trench. Farrell played the pipes at night when we were at dinner. We dined by Company Messes all very close together under the trees. The men cheered when he played " Brian Boru." We then gave him a large whisky, " with not so much of the water, sir."

26th July.

At 5 am. I paraded the Company and marched off to the Vlamertinghe Château to carry on with the wiring. I was joined by D Company under Laville and Hickman. Met a subaltern of the 5th Dragoon Guards, who brought us along to their lines for a drink. Cavalry were having a good time at this stage in the War. The officers were under canvas, the men in top-hole bivouacs, and their horses were picketed under the trees. The 5th D.G.s belonged to the 1st Cavalry Brigade, the other two regiments of

which were the The Bays and the 11th Hussars. This Brigade
had been through the retreat and had put up an excellent show
against overwhelming odds at Nery with the famous L Battery
R.H.A. on 1st September. Piper went on leave to the " U.K.,"
as the British Isles were alluded to in official correspondence in
France.

27th July.

Orders for the front line. At 5 p.m. the Battalion paraded and
we marched off. Major Bullen-Smith being once more in command, rode ahead of the Battalion on his grey charger. We were
rather short of officers, and O'Morchoe had been invalided down
the line.

Marched through Ypres, as it was not being shelled, but with
200 yards interval between companies. Got on to a Brigade track
leaving the city and cut across to St. Jean, where we got into a
communication trench. By 10.30 p.m. we had taken over a line
on the left of Wieltje from Major Pratt's Company of the 2nd
Battalion York and Lancaster Regiment. Marching along the
Poperinghe–Ypres road we invariably had a halt in Vlamertinghe,
this evening we fell out just opposite the cemetery inside the
the gates of which I saw the grave of Capt. Francis Grenfell,
V.C., of the 9th Lancers, who had been killed during the 2nd
Battle out Hooge way. Ever afterwards when marching through
Vlamertinghe, I always glanced at the grave of this very gallant
soldier.

28th July.

Trenches excellent, well revetted and duck-boarded. Weather
good. Shelled all morning. Piper's platoon had 9 casualties from
a thirteenth shell. The C.O. and Adjutant made a tour of inspection.

FLAMMENWERFER

Our line was very straight, and we knew it well from La Brigue
days. Daly had a difficult job taking over his sector, as the
Company Commander from whom he relieved had a very bad
stammer ! His C.S.M. did interpreter !

29th July.

Bourke left on being seconded to the Machine-Gun School at
St. Omer. Our line was 350 yards away from the enemy. In the

middle of No-Man's-Land were the remains of a Canadian ammunition column which had got blown up in May. Marsland, Sergt. T. Flaherty and O'Leary were on patrol all night. They found the bodies of three men of the 2nd Royal Dublin Fusiliers, and collected their identity discs and pay books, and sent them in to Battalion Headquarters. Digging a communication trench round the Company Mess, and I was on duty all night. As usual, the Company servants went to meet the ration limbers. Keegan came back to Algeo with the handle only of a rum jar, and said " a lump of shell had broke the jar, and bad luck to it, but it has spilt all the beer ! " Keegan looked after Algeo in great style. If Algeo was short of anything, Keegan used to go scrounging round the other officers' kits to make up the deficiency !

30th July.

More fighting at Hooge. At 5 a.m. the Huns tried another form of frightfulness, *Flammenwerfer*, on the front-line troops astride the Menin Road. The troops, 8th and 9th Service Battalions of the R.B.s and 60th Rifles, who belonged to the 14th Division, were driven out of their trenches, and the positions gained by the 3rd Division on the 19th July were lost. The 14th Division carried out a counter-attack which did not meet with any success and incurred heavy casualties. Our 16th Brigade were pulled out of their rest billets to hold the new line. Daly's Company had a perfect view of the fighting from their positions round Wieltje, which was on the high ground. They stated that the " Liquid Fire " attack looked most demoralising.

Marsland and I went up to see B Company in the evening. We got a perfect view of our old line at Potijze and the Hooge sector from the 2nd Durham's trenches on Daly's right. There was a strafe going on at Hooge. C.Q.M.S. Wall brought us tragic news when he came up with the rations at night. Neville Young had died of his wounds at Boulogne. We were all very upset, and surprised, as he had only got a small piece of shrapnel in the shoulder on the 12th, but gangrene had set in. He had gone off to the dressing-station, saying, " Jammy one." Heavy artillery fire throughout the night at Hooge. We could see S O S rockets shooting up in the sky in thousands. 2nd Lieut. R. L. Stirling joined. He had been attached to the 2nd Royal Munster Fusiliers.

31st July.

Good weather. We were shelled all evening by large crumps. Corpl. Maher of my platoon narrowly missed being blown up by a direct hit on the parapet of fire bay he was in. His rifle was turned into a piece of twisted iron. More shell-fire at Hooge. Enemy aircraft very active all day.

We were supplied with full particulars regarding the "liquid fire" attack. It appeared that the enemy's method of launching this attack was with a number of men carrying on their backs a tank similar to a potato-spraying device with a hose. From this jet issued forth a flame of liquid which was estimated could shoot some 30 to 50 yards.

The defenders of this sector had lost few men from actual burns, but the demoralising element was very great. We were instructed to aim at those who carried the flame-spraying device, who made a good target.

It was reported that a Hun who had his cargo of frightfulness hit by a bullet blew up with a colossal burst. Counter measures against an attack were with rapid fire and machine-gun fire. As the flames shot forward they created a smoke-screen, so we realised that we would have to fire into "the brown."

1st August.

Marsland, Algeo, and I sat up on the parados of our trench near Company Headquarters to observe the Hun lines. We were spotted by a sniper, who fired, and very narrowly missed me, the bullet going right through my cap as I was looking through my field-glasses. It was a close shave, as the bullet left two holes in my cap and grazed the centre plume of my cap badge—the Prince of Wales' plumes being the Leinsters' badge.

A "Little Willie" blew up A Company's Mess. The destruction of the Mess was a standing joke in the Battalion for some time. Prendergast had discovered a very fine mahogany table in a house in St. Jean, and under the cover of darkness he sent a fatigue party for this table, but when it was brought up to the trench it was found to be too large to go through the dug-out entrance. "Prendy" had the dug-out pulled down, put the table on the old floor, and built a new dug-out around it. This was the largest I ever saw and, as it was dark, the men did not notice that it showed well up above the parapet, "just like a young house," as C.S.M. Kerrigan said !

At dawn the enemy immediately spotted it, and started shelling. They got a direct hit, which landed on the table, blowing up the whole place. When I saw it, Barnett, who had just returned from leave with lots of fodder, was on his knees rescuing some tins of sardines from the debris.

I missed being buried by a traverse which collapsed in a section of my trench. Went down to Battalion Headquarters which were situated in "Garden Villa," near St. Jean, for orders for a wiring

party. I met the C.O., who chatted to me. B Company got hell
all morning in Wieltje from trench mortars, aerial torpedoes, and
shrapnel. Their front line was badly smashed about. At night
I was in charge of a wiring party for D Company. The task was
difficult, as it was dark and the ground being pitted with shell-
holes, we fell about all over the place. To prevent the enemy
hearing us hammering, the wooden mallets were muffled with
sand-bags. Throughout the night there was heavy shell-fire at
Hooge. Rumours of the 6th Division doing an attack there to
retake the mine crater and lost trenches.

2nd August.

All morning our batteries shelled the Huns, and there was no
retaliation. B Company again were heavily shelled. Grant
Saunders was wounded ; also C.S.M. Boyer, and Hogan of my
platoon, who was employed as a Battalion sniper in the Wieltje
village. B Company were having a bad tour, but we, C, were
absolutely in clover regards a peaceful time.

Behind us were all the old ruins which we knew so well when at
La Brique—Wieltje and English Farms. Our line round Wieltje
village happened to be on a commanding position, so no wonder
the Huns strafed it.

From our observation posts there we could get splendid views
of the enemy back areas. Shell Trap Farm was behind the Hun
lines. Fierce fighting had gone on around this farm during the
Second Battle. The 2nd Royal Irish Regiment and 2nd Royal
Dublin Fusiliers had particularly distinguished themselves in the
defence of it. The Royal Irish were driven out of it by the gas,
but retook it immediately against large numbers of the enemy.
They had no supports whatever, and the Germans had at least
fifty men to every one of ours !

3rd August.

McClean of my platoon went away, time-expired. I was sorry,
as he was a fine old soldier, who had served in the South African
War. Macartney came round to say that " Comic Cuts " (the
official communiqué) stated that the Turks and British were
having a swimming match at Gallipoli across the Dardanelles !
Topic of conversation all day, an attack at Hooge by the 6th
Division to regain the lost ground.

4th August.

Orders issued for relief. Not unexpected, although we had been
given to understand we were in this sector for a long tour. Hooge
seemed a certainty. The Regiment which was to relieve us got

held up by shell-fire. L/Corpl. Jenkins brought our relieving Company up across country. At 1.45 a.m. we had handed over our sector to the 1st Battalion Wiltshire Regiment of the 7th Brigade, 3rd Division. We got out behind the trenches and cut across to the St. Jean road. It was a fine moonlight night, and only a few solitary shells were whining over our heads towards

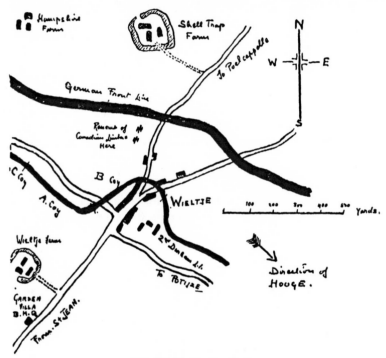

The Wieltje Sector, Ypres.

Ypres. We marched past the crumbling ruins of the St. Jean Church and its torn-up graveyard.

This graveyard had been badly shelled. All the crosses and tomb-stones had been smashed, and dead bodies and coffins were lying exposed on the brink of large craters. I fell out my platoon at the Menin Gate, the rendezvous, to wait for the Company.

We marched through Ypres, which was being spasmodically shelled. A few crumps landed uncomfortably close as we marched over the Cross Roads beside the Water Tower. Rain fell just after we had got clear of the town and the Poperinghe road seemed longer and uglier than ever as we marched along its uneven *pavé*. We got drenched, and when it stopped, a thick mist hung all round, which obliterated the countless poplars which belted the road ahead of us. We were tired and depressed. Even Sergt. Kells, who always had something to say, was silent.

5th August.

Reached our hutments in the Vlamertinghe Wood at 5 a.m. At 9 a.m., having had a short sleep, I started off on duty to the Louvie Château. West of Poperinghe I managed to lorry jump most successfully to my destination ; reported to the 6th Corps Headquarters, and managed to get a lift back in a motor ambulance. 17th Brigade under orders for Hooge. The woods, where we were, got shelled.

6th August.

16th and 18th Brigades ordered up to Hooge, and we, the 17th Brigade, ordered to consolidate. Orders cancelled, as the attack at Hooge was postponed.

7th August.

Short parades in the morning, and at 12.30 p.m. we carried out a trench assault before the C.O. The men carried picks and shovels on their backs, stuck through the cross-straps of their equipment.

8th August.

Major Gerald Boyd,[1] late 2nd Leinsters, G.S.O. 6th Division, came to see us. He won the D.C.M. and D.S.O. in South Africa, having been promoted on the field. I believe he was the only officer in the South African War to be wearing both these decorations. Paid out the Company in very dirty 5-franc notes, and signed my name scores of times in indelible pencil in their Army Books 64.

9th August.

At 4 a.m. the 17th Brigade "stood to." Zero hour for the attack at Hooge was timed at six o'clock. Our 16th Brigade were to attack with the 18th Brigade in support. We were the reserves.

The rôle for the Brigades in the attack was decided by the toss of a coin between the respective Brigadiers, and we lost. Throughout the early hours of this fine summer morning, we could hear the bombardment going on, and now and then some 15-inch naval guns, which were situated in our area, gave tongue.

At 9 a.m. we heard that the attack was successful, and that

---

[1] Afterwards became Major-General Sir Gerald Boyd and Colonel of the Regiment. Died in 1933 when Military Secretary at War Office.

all the objectives had been gained, and that the 2nd York and Lancs and the K.S.L.I. had linked up on the far side of the mine crater. Ten prisoners only reported captured.

At 4 p.m. we got orders to parade in battle order. We stacked our packs by companies, and marched off to some huts south-east of Vlamertinghe. Here we stayed for the night. The whole sky was lit up with the perpetual gun-fire east of Ypres. Further news of gains at Hooge stated we had captured 285 prisoners, of whom 75 were wounded. On our march to these huts, our bombers kept slipping on the cobbles under the heavy boxes of bombs which they were carrying.

BRITISH AND GERMAN BOMBS.

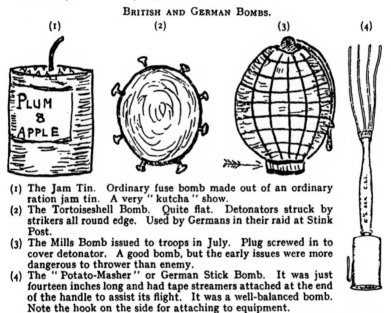

(1) The Jam Tin. Ordinary fuse bomb made out of an ordinary ration jam tin. A very " kutcha " show.
(2) The Tortoiseshell Bomb. Quite flat. Detonators struck by strikers all round edge. Used by Germans in their raid at Stink Post.
(3) The Mills Bomb issued to troops in July. Plug screwed in to cover detonator. A good bomb, but the early issues were more dangerous to thrower than enemy.
(4) The " Potato-Masher " or German Stick Bomb. It was just fourteen inches long and had tape streamers attached at the end of the handle to assist its flight. It was a well-balanced bomb. Note the hook on the side for attaching to equipment.

Morrissey lent me his stretcher to sleep on during the night. The fact that it was covered in blood-stains did not prevent it being comfortable.

10th August.

Germans attempted a counter-attack, but were driven back. All the gains were held with the exception of A.3, a trench running towards Bellewaarde Farm, which had to be vacated owing to enfilade fire. At 6.30 we got orders to move up to Hooge to work under the Sappers, Barnett and two platoons of A Company being attached to us. Marched off by platoons at 200 paces interval, and at the Water Tower we drew picks and shovels from one of our G.S. waggons. A few shells fell as we marched on through Ypres. When crossing the square we passed companies of the 2nd York and Lancs returning from Hooge to rest. Quite a number of them had German helmets stuck on the end of their rifles as souvenirs. They yelled out " Good luck, Micks." We were the only Irish regiment in the 6th Division. It was quite dark when we got to Birr Cross Roads. Shrapnel burst over us when crossing the railway line at Hell Fire Corner, without inflicting any casualties.

Hell Fire Corner was a station or " halt " on the Ypres–Menin road, the railway lines crossing it in the Roulers direction. It was also an important cross-roads, which led off to Potijze and Zillebeke, and the enemy was, therefore, perpetually shelling this junction. A few houses, and a small chapel, had once stood close by, but only a few heaps of red bricks remained, and a Crucifix, or Calvary, as the peasants called it, which stood up intact amidst the debris of brick and timber. We made a fine job of a communication trench, which ran parallel with the Menin Road, and a support line called H.12, near the culvert. Throughout our task we were heavily shelled. At 2 a.m. we formed up and marched back to Ypres, where we billeted in dug-outs on the ramparts beside the Menin Gate.

HOOGE

11th August.

These dug-outs had been cut out of the ramparts. C and B Companies were on the right side of the Menin Gate leaving the City, and A and D Companies were on the left. We got the Company into quite a small area as the dug-outs were built tier upon tier up from the road which ran from the Menin to Lille Gates. Steps had been made out of filled sand-bags up to the parapet of the ramparts.

We made a company mess out of an old ruined house. I reported on duty to Brigade Headquarters further down the ramparts, where I met Brig.-General Harper who stopped and talked to me. The C.O. had a " pow-wow " with all the officers in the Battalion. He told us that we were ordered to consolidate the new position at Hooge. He said we would have to dig in and wire all night, and that we must be prepared for a counter-attack. His final orders were : " Go and tell your platoons what they are up against, and what to expect." The ramparts were shelled all afternoon, the enemy was searching for a battery which was hard by the moat beyond the duckboard track. We watched their howitzer shells falling in to the moat, and hitting the walls of the ramparts below us. At 7 p.m. we marched off for Hooge in battle

order, each man carried sand-bags, and a pick or shovel. Algeo
was in charge of the Company, as Caulfeild had gone up in
advance to take over the front line. Marsland was attached to
Battalion Headquarters as Bombing Officer. We got to the front
line at Hooge after a rough journey under shell-fire, over dead
men and round countless shell-holes. At 11 p.m. we had taken
over the Hooge sector and the mine crater from the 1st Battalion
The Buffs—16th Brigade. The order of the Battalion in the
line was C and D Companies front line, with A and B in support
and reserve. We had hardly taken over the line, when the Huns
attacked our left flank, which was exposed. However, Algeo had
posted the Company Bombers there, and with a handful of men
armed with jam-tin bombs, succeeded in beating them back.
By the light of the moon and the glow from the green-white star-
shells one could make out the course of the trenches of both sides,
and could just distinguish the serpentine course of the German
lines running along the near side of the Bellewaarde or Château
Wood, only 50 yards away. The leafless trees stood out in their
shattered forms, and behind them was the lake reflecting the
moonlight.

The two front line companies were distributed in the following
order, from the right flank. C Company Bombers, Nos. 9, 10, and
11 Platoons holding from the barricade on the banks of the small
stream called Bellewaardebee to D Company, linked up with us
at the head of the communication trench, and extended to the
Menin Road inclusive. The mine crater came into D's sector,
their trench running round the near lips, but they held the far
side with an advanced post. We had No. 12 Platoon in support
at H.12, and D Company also had a platoon in support.

D Company connected with the 1st Royal Fusiliers, who held
the line running through the Zouave Wood. My left flank was in
the air, a barricade only separating us from the Germans. We
actually shared our front line with the enemy! How this strange
fact came about was as follows: The continuation of our front
line running up the Bellewaarde ridge which had been captured
by the 16th Brigade on the 9th had to be abandoned the same
evening, as the trench was untenable owing to the enfilade fire
which caused terrible havoc to the troops holding it. This
enfilade fire came from the German positions on the high ground,
on the extreme left flank at Bellewaarde Farm.

The 16th Brigade, therefore, evacuated this enfiladed section
and erected a strong, sand-bagged barrier in the trench with a
good field of fire. After about twelve hours, the Huns cautiously
worked their way along their old front line, from Bellewaarde
Farm, and found that our troops had withdrawn. After the

bombing attack had been successfully repulsed Algeo and his bombers flattened out the old German parapets, and filled in the trench in front of the barricade, so that the Huns could not approach this post under cover. Within 15 yards of our barricade, the enemy switched off their old front line into their old support line. Throughout the night, the enemy were very offensive with bombs and snipers. We did not retaliate, as we were too busily employed reversing the parapets, making fire-steps and deepening the trench everywhere, as we were antici-pating a bombardment and a counter-attack on the morrow. Sergt. Bennett and his Machine-Gun Section worked splendidly, and built two fine battle positions for their guns. All the men worked like Trojans on top of the parapets in their shirt sleeves.

The place reeked with the smell of decomposed bodies. They lay about in hundreds, on top of the parapets, in our trenches, in No-Man's-Land, and behind the parados. The British dead mostly belong to the 2nd York and Lancs, and the 2nd D.L.I. The dug-outs were full of dead Germans, those that were not, two only, were strengthened for occupation. While we were working bullets spat viciously all round, and we had several casualties.

12th August.

Dawn broke at 4 a.m. and within half an hour I had two casualties. Pte. Bowes was killed by an explosive bullet in the head, and Pte. Duffey was wounded by an enfilade bullet from the Bellewaarde Farm. We buried Bowes in a disused trench behind our line. One could now make out the country all round perfectly, and what an appalling sight it was. Everywhere lay the dead. The ridge in our rear was covered with dead men who had been wiped out in the final assault of the German position ; their faces were blackened and swollen from the three days' exposure to the August sun, and quite unrecognisable. Some of the bodies were badly dismembered ; here and there a huddled up heap of khaki on the brink of a shell-crater told of a direct hit. Haversacks, tangled heaps of webbing equipment, splintered rifles, and broken stretchers, lay scattered about. The ground was pitted with shell-holes of all sizes. A few solitary stakes and strands of barbed wire was all that was left of the dense mass of German entanglements by our artillery. Several khaki figures were hanging on these few strands in hideous attitudes. In front of us, in No-Man's-Land, lay a line of our dead, and ahead of them on the German parapet lay a D.L.I. officer. They had advanced too far, and had got caught by a withering machine-gun fire from the Bellewaarde Wood. There was not a blade of

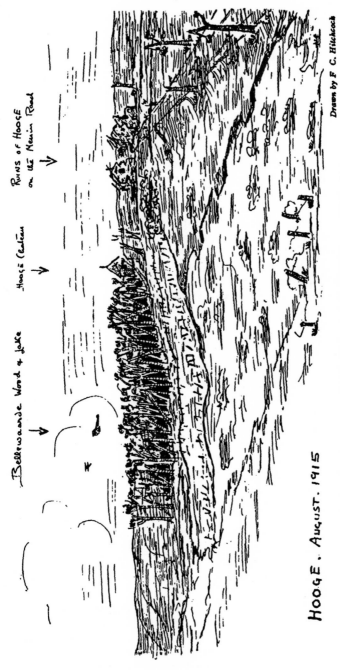

Bellewaarde Wood & Lake

Hooge Chateau

Ruins of Hooge on the Menin Road

Drawn by F. C. Hitchcock.

HOOGE. AUGUST. 1915

Sketch showing trenches held by the 2nd Leinster Regt. at Hooge, Ypres.

grass to be seen in No-Man's-Land or on the ridge, the ground had been completely churned up by the shells, and any of the few patches of grass which had escaped had been burnt up by the liquid fire. Some 50 yards away, around the edge of the Belle-waarde Wood, ran the sand-bagged parapet of the German line on its serpentine course towards the shattered remains of Hooge.

The wood itself had suffered severely from the shell-fire. Most of the trees were badly splintered, and some had been torn up by the roots. There was little foliage to be seen on any of the trees. All that was left of the once bushy topped trees which lined the Menin Road were shattered stumps, and the telegraph poles stood drunkenly at all angles. Although numbers of the Durhams and the York and Lancs lay about in the open, yet our trench was full of German dead belonging to the Würtembergers.

They lay in the dug-outs, where they had gone to seek refuge from our guns, in fours and in fives. Some had been killed by concussion, others had had their dug-outs blown in on top of them, and had suffocated. Our gunners had done their work admirably, and the strong cover made with railway lines and sleepers and with trunks of trees had collapsed under the fierce onslaught of our shells. The faces of the enemy dead, who had thus been caught or pinned down by the remnants and shattered timber of their death-traps, wore agonised expressions.

Here and there, where portions of the trench had been obliterated by the shells, legs and arms in the German field-grey uniform stuck out between piles of sand-bags. Thousands of rounds of fired and unexpended cartridges lay about the parapets, and grounded into the bottom of the trench. German Mausers, equipment, helmets, and their peculiar skin-covered packs lay everywhere. The ground was littered with portions of the enemy uniforms saturated in blood. Serving in the Ypres salient one was not unaccustomed to seeing men blown to pieces and, there-fore, I expected to see bad sights on a battle-field, but I had never anticipated such a dreadful and desolate sight as the Hooge presented, and I never saw anything like it again during my service at the front. The reason that Hooge was such a particu-larly bloody battle-field was due to the fact that it covered such a small area in the most easterly portion of the salient, and was not spread out over miles of open country like those battle-fields on the Somme in 1916. Hooge had been continually under shell-fire since the First Battle of Ypres in October, and the ridge which we had dug into had been captured and recaptured five times since April.

At 5 a.m. some shells fell all along our line. Then all was silent and we realised the meaning of those dozen shells which traversed our line from left to right, ranging shots for a pukka bombardment. Within fifteen minutes of the burst of the last shot, a steady bombardment started all along our line.

The enemy gunners carried out their work in a most systematic manner. They fired by a grouping system of five shells to a limited area, under 12 yards. Then they burst shrapnel over this area. This plan for shelling our position was undoubtedly successful, as three out of the five shells hit our trench, obliterating it, blowing in the parapet on top of the occupants, or exposing them to a deadly hail from shrapnel shells. Our casualties were beginning to mount up. A direct hit with a 5·9 knocked out six men of the Machine-Gun Section, Burlace, Cleary, and Scully being killed. As there was no communication trench, the walking wounded " chanced their arms " going back over the ridge which was being raked by shrapnel fire, but the badly wounded had to lie in the bottom of the trench and wait until the cover of darkness to be carried back by the stretcher bearers. Some of these stretcher cases were, unfortunately, hit for a second time and killed.

At 12.30 p.m. the shelling eased, and we got ready for a counter-attack. The order : " Pass along the word, fix bayonets," went along the line. We all, except the wounded who looked wistfully up at us, armed to the teeth, looked forward to Germans getting out of their trenches, but they did not. Although there were no wire entanglements of any description in front of us, as the single stretch of concertina wire had been cut by the first shells, yet we would have given hell to the Huns had they attacked. They obviously calculated on us retiring from our seemingly hopeless position, but we did not budge an inch. During the lull, the men dragged the wounded under better cover, dug out more funk-holes, and took the opportunity to " drum up their char." Shell-fire, the smell of powder, and the continual dust made us all very thirsty, and never did I relish a drink of tea more than that dixie-full which L/Corpl. Leonard and Pte. Coghlan shared with me. The dixie was chipped all round the edges and was blackened by smoke !

At 3 p.m. exactly, the enemy started a second bombardment of our line. All along our trench they put down a terrific barrage of shells of every description. High explosives and crumps exploded on our parapets, leaving burning and smoking craters, and torn flesh, and above, screeching and whining shrapnel burst over us. We were shelled from all sides by guns of every calibre. We could not have been in a worse position, and it seemed that every enemy gun around the Salient was turned on to our 400 yards of trench on the left of the Menin Road. Shells from the

Bellewaarde direction enfiladed us, and blew in our few traverses ; shells from the Hill 60 direction ploughed great rifts in our parados, and broke down our only protection from back-bursts, and now and then some horrible fragments of mortality were blown back from the ridge with lyddite wreaths.

The whole place had become quite dark from the shells and the clouds of earth which went spouting up to the sky. We could barely see twenty yards ahead throughout this terrible tornado of fire. Our casualties increased at such a rapid rate that we were all greatly alarmed, our trench had ceased to exist as such and the enemy shrapnel caused dreadful havoc amongst the practically exposed company. L/Corpl. Leonard, Privates Keenan, McKenna, Digan, and Shea of my platoon had been hit, and Algeo got a direct hit on his platoon, killing 6032 Pte. Fay, and 3642 Pte. Lysaght, and wounding Privates Healy and Rattigan badly, and four of his N.C.O.s. If this went on much longer, the Boches would walk into our position without any opposition, as we would all be casualties. The shells came down with tantalizing regularity, which was nerve-racking.

The blackened bodies of our dead, and the badly wounded, lay about at the bottom of the trench, and it was impossible to move without treading on them. Every few minutes the call for the stretcher bearers would be heard. Then along came Morrissey with his first-aid bag, closely followed by Reid. "Steady, me lad," they'd say to a man who had lost his leg, but could still feel the toes of the lost limb tingling, " 'tis a grand cushy one you've got. Sure you're grand entirely, and when darkness sets in we'll carry you off to the dressing station, and then ye'll get your ticket for Blighty." How they stuck it, those company stretcher bearers, Morrissey, Reid, Dooley, and Neary. White men all ! Sometimes a direct hit on the parapet would bury the occupants.

A most demoralising effect is that of being smothered in sand-bags. Twice I emerged out of a heap of demolished sand-bags to find men hit on either side of me. It was extraordinary how one got to know and understand the men under shell-fire. " 'Tis different now beyont in Killyon, sir," said a man in my ear. " Ye gods, yes ! " I replied. The man had seen me many times pre-war, as Killyon was only three miles from my home.

It was exasperating, sitting there getting crumped to blazes, while our own guns kept silent. Nothing puts more life into weary troops under a fierce bombardment than the sound of their own shells screaming over them, but ours were obviously saving their ammunition to repel a counter-attack.

Suddenly and unexpectedly our guns from away back at Ypres started firing. The enemy must have been massing for a counter-attack. " Swish, swish, swish, bang, bang, bang," over went our shells, crashing on the enemy parapets. They went so low over us that we imagined they were hitting our own parapets. Shells of all calibres burst over the Boches' lines. The noise of them split our ears, and we all felt quite dazed by the brain-racking concussions. This retaliation was perfect, and cheered us immensely. Our howitzers raised great columns of earth and debris from the enemy trenches into the sky. The trees of the Bellewaarde Wood were being blown into the air and across the enemy parapets. Shells fell into the Château lake, and sent the water spouting up like fountains.

A battery of French ·75's lent to the Division was also in action. Their discharges were so rapid that they sounded as if they came from some supernatural machine-gun, their trajectory being low, it seemed that these wonderful ·75's passed close over our heads. The German lines on our left and in front were covered in a cloud of green lyddite fumes. What pleased us more than anything was that the Huns were showing unmistakable signs of " wind up " ; behind this curtain of smoke and fire we saw their S O S rockets shooting up all along his front to Hooge ! Evidently they expected us to attack. We, who had lost 65 men out of 120 (strength of the three platoons in front line) within the last seven hours !

We were still being shelled and having casualties. I went up to the bend where Company Headquarters was situated. They had just got a direct hit and the stretcher bearers were on their knees bandaging some lifeless-looking forms. Another yell rang out for stretcher bearers from close to a smoking crater, and off Dooley ran to give first aid along the top of the trench into the blackness, and disappeared from view. Healy and Rattigan who had been hit earlier in the day, lay alongside each other in the bottom of the trench. Algeo was standing beside Sergt. Bennett, who was sucking at an old clay pipe. Both wore an expression of defiance on their determined-looking faces. Rattigan was in a semi-conscious state, and blackened from head to foot with powder. Healy was in frightful pain ; he had been badly hit in the stomach, and kept calling for water. " Mister Algeo, for the love of God give me a drink." " Stay quiet now, Healy, and you'll be all right soon." But he would not stay quiet. He then spotted me, and asked me for my water-bottle, but I could not give it to him. Reid came along and rinsed his mouth with water. " Can't ye keep quiet now, for a few minutes. Shure 'tis meself that will be bringing you along to the dressing station." But Healy would not stay quiet. " Holy Mary, Mother of God ! " Bang, crash ! A shrapnel shell burst right over us, and Healy lay

quiet for all time. He had been hit for the second time. " 'Tis
as well, sir," said Morrissey. " He hadn't a hope ; a piece of
shell as big as your fist in his stomach ! "

As suddenly as the bombardment had opened at 3 p.m. it
ceased at 5.30 p.m. We all stood to, and Sergt. Bennett mounted
the tripod of his Vickers on a hastily built emplacement. But
the Germans did not leave their lines. It appeared that they
counted on us evacuating the position owing to the intense
shell-fire.

Right along the Company front, the men and the slightly
wounded stood to arms for some time in case an enemy attack
should materialise. The bombardment was over ; everything
was very calm except for the rumbling of artillery engaged in
counter-battery work. One of our aeroplanes flew up from
Ypres and across the lines towards Menin, to observe and direct
fire for our gunners. Having posted night sentries, we attended
to the wounded and buried the dead. We were all thirsty, and
our water-bottles were empty, but not hungry, although we had
had no food whatsoever since we had left Ypres the night before.
The sickening stench of the charred human flesh had driven away
all pangs of hunger. The men of the Company were very bitter
to think they had been shelled all day by an invisible foe, and had
lost some of their best pals, without a chance of retaliation.
Nothing would have pleased C and D Companies more than an
order for attack on the 132nd Würtembergers.

At " Stand To " an issue of rum, which had been sent up under
cover of darkness, was dished out, and was thoroughly appreciated. Sergt. Shields, Piper's platoon sergeant, who was somewhat ancient and had felt the strain of the day more than younger
men, took a double ration, and started firing up at the stars and
shouting out about the Battle of Colenso !

With the exception of sniping everything was calm until 9.30
p.m., when the Boches launched a fierce bombing attack on our
left flank, which was still in the air. They surrounded our small
post and hurled bombs into it. I opened rapid fire on my left
front to help Algeo, and prevented the Huns from coming further
up on the outside of the trench. Algeo and his half-dozen bombers
did wonders. With cigarettes in their mouths for lighting the
fuses of their jam-tin bombs, they drove back over thirty Huns
armed with Krupp's latest pattern bomb. Some of this gallant
little band were wounded by bomb splinters, but they refused to
leave Algeo.

Sergt. Flaherty got a bullet through the ear, but remained at
duty with his " souvenir shot " as he called it. 8212 Brown got
a bullet through the neck. With the exception of the sentries we

started deepening the trench and building up the parapets.
Nothing will resist shell-fire better than a really deep line. At
2 a.m. my platoon was relieved by No. 12 Platoon, and we went
back to the support line at H.12. I went to sleep on the wooden
fire step, but woke to find that I was lying underneath it. We
had been shelled, and the men pushed me under it for safety. I
had slept solidly for six hours, and would have gone on sleeping
but for heavy rain which awakened me. I discovered that L/Corpl.
O'Neill had been badly wounded in the stomach whilst I slept.

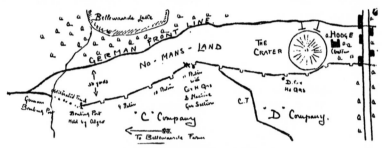

2nd Leinsters' trenches at Hooge.

13th August.

I was sharing some tea with Jackson when I got a chit ordering
me to relieve Caulfeild and Piper, as Algeo had been badly
wounded with three men of the Machine-Gun Section. Being
daylight, I ran up the shallow communication trench, which lay
parallel to the Menin Road, and which was being heavily strafed
with large crumps.

I met the wounded, with Algeo, at the head of the communication trench, being carried away. Algeo was laughing, and said
he had a jammy one. He was on Morrissey's back, as the stretchers
were wanted for the machine-gunners who were more severely
hit than he was. Algeo had his boots and puttees hanging round
his neck, as his legs and feet were swathed in bandages. His
wounds were far from being " jammy " ones, but it was typical
of him to make light of them. I arrived in the front line with a
full jar of rum, which I issued out with a large spoon. Ward, who
knew me well pre-War days, told me that " 'twas the grandest
medicine he'd ever taken."

The Company had been digging during the night and had
deepened the trenches by 2 feet. As we were still being badly
enfiladed from the high ground at Bellewaarde Farm, I had a
large traverse built near the bombing post. Padre Moloney came
up to visit the men. While he was with me, L/Corpl. Doonan
was badly hit in the neck, at the bombing post on my flank, but

the Padre, who was a very big man, insisted in going to see him, which he had to do on his hands and knees owing to the shallowness of the trench.

The Boches seemed to have suffered equally from the bombardment, and through a periscope I watched some Huns in their shirt sleeves mending up their parapets. I heard that O'Neill had died of his wounds. Jim Marsland came round the line and visited the bombing post. I went along to see Orpen-Palmer, and found him asleep in a fire bay, with two days' growth on his face. Shaving was out of the question. Later, he woke up, and he, Macartney, and I sat chatting in an old dug-out for some time. D Company's advanced post at the crater captured two men of the 132nd Würtembergers, and they were brought round to Company Headquarters to be interrogated by Macartney, who spoke German fluently.

Judging from the following extracts from a diary found on the field, the enemy had been having a pretty ghastly time at Hooge.

A SOLDIER'S DIARY—132ND REGIMENT

FRIEDERICH KRESSIS of the 6th Company, 132nd Regiment, was present at the capture of HOOGE CHÂTEAU on May 25th, and was slightly wounded at HOOGE on June 16th. After 10 days' rest and a visit to HILL 60, the Battalion returned to HOOGE hurriedly on August 1st after the flame jet attack. On July 19th he was buried by a shell and the shock evidently upset his nerves.

1st August, 1915.

Shrapnel flying like flies. A heavy bombardment of HOOGE. 2nd Battn. 132nd Regt. sent up to reinforce 126th, which has already lost half its men.

2nd August.

Joined 6th Company to-day. We lie 28 minutes distance behind the front in support trenches standing by. Building cover against shrapnel.

4th August.

Heavy artillery fire the whole night. The English are concentrating 50,000 Indians on our front to attack HOOGE and HILL 60. Just let them come, we shall stand firm. At 3.0 marched off to the Front. Watch beginning again.

5.0 marched off to the Witches' Cauldron, HOOGE. A terrible night again. H.E. and shrapnel without number. Oh, thrice cursed HOOGE ! In one hour 11 killed and 23 wounded and the fire unceasing. It is enough to drive one mad, and we have to spend three days and three nights here. It is worse than an earthquake, and anyone who has not experienced it can have no idea of what it is like. The English fired a mine, a hole 15 metres deep and 50 to 60 broad, and this " cauldron " has to be occupied at night. At present it isn't too badly shelled. At every shot the dug-outs sway to and fro like a weather-cock. This life we have to stick for months. One needs nerves of steel and iron. Now I must crawl into our hole as trunks and branches of trees fly in our trench like spray.

6th August.

To-night moved to the crater again half running and half crawling. At seven a sudden burst of fire from the whole of the artillery. From about 11.0 yesterday evening we lie out in the sap on our stomachs whilst the artillery fires as if possessed. This morning at 4.0 we fall back. We find the 126th have no communications with the rear as the communication trenches have been completely blown in. The smoke and thirst are enough to drive one mad. Our cooker does not come up. The 126th give us bread and coffee from the little they have. If only it would stop ! We get direct hits one after another and lie in a sort of dead-end cut off from all communication. If only it were night ! What a feeling to be thinking every second when shall I get it ! . . . has just fallen, the third man in our platoon. Since 8.0 the fire has been unceasing ; the earth shakes and we with it. Will God ever bring us out of this fire ? I have said the Lord's Prayer and am resigned.

THE END

One was badly wounded in the arm, and said he was afraid that we would shoot him. He said that on the 1st August his Regiment, the 132nd Würtembergers, had been sent up to reinforce the 3rd Battalion of the 126th, as the latter had lost half their men in our bombardment. He complained bitterly of the accuracy of our shrapnel and the French 75's. The F.O.O.[1] for the Gunners was a very good fellow, belonging to the Territorials. He and I went along D Company's line to see the crater. What a sight we saw ! At least two hundred German corpses in every imaginable

---

[1] Forward observation officer, R.F.A.

shape and form ; the place was one mass of torn and charred flesh !

The enemy had worked like ants in this vast mine crater since the 30th July, when they took it from the 14th Division. It resembled an ampitheatre, with its tiers of bomb-proof shelters scooped out of the crumbling sides of the chasm, and shored up with tree trunks.

But all shelters and dug-outs had collapsed under our terrific barrage on the 9th August. The 3rd Rifle Brigade were filling it in with chloride of lime. The little Cockneys were revelling in their task, searching the corpses for souvenirs, and then rolling them into the vast depths of the crater. The Château of Hooge and its stables had practically disappeared, only a few crumbling walls and heaps of red bricks remained. At 1.30 p.m. Caulfeild relieved me, and I left him sitting in an old German dug-out (which already had had two direct hits, and had not stirred), with a telephone orderly and C.S.M. Morgan. General Congreve[1] came up to inspect the front line and got held up by shell-fire.

I went back to H.12 where I got some food, bully beef and tea. At night I relieved Piper at the bombing post : later, I got orders to meet the 2nd London Regiment, Territorials, attached to our Brigade, and guide them up the Menin Road from Birr Cross Roads for fatigues. On my way down with Jackson we passed Marsland, Sergt. Flaherty and Pte. O'Leary going up with bombs.

The Germans were again attacking on our left flank, Piper having rung up Battalion Headquarters for more bombs. This was the last time I saw Jim alive. He was gaily going up the line for a " show " of any kind.

Met the Adjutant at Birr Cross Roads.[2] He also was waiting for the Londons, who had got held up by shell-fire. They turned up later, and I allotted them their task of digging a communication trench. Returning with my orderly to the front line, we lost our bearings, and nearly ran into the enemy trenches. Beating a hasty retreat to our front line, I tripped over a strand of barbed wire, and landed into a shell-hole full of dead men. Returned later to reserve line, Jackson carried my trophies, a *pickelhaube*, a rifle and a saw bayonet. We heard that Jim Marsland was seriously wounded, and had been taken to the 17th Field Ambulance, and was not expected to recover.

---

[1] We heard that the G.O.C. had brought up his youngest son as far as Ypres that day, who was in Boy Scout kit. An original way of spending his school holidays, we considered.

[2] This homely sounding name was given by our 1st Battalion during the 2nd Battle of Ypres. There was also a Leinster Farm hard by which will be seen marked on the maps.

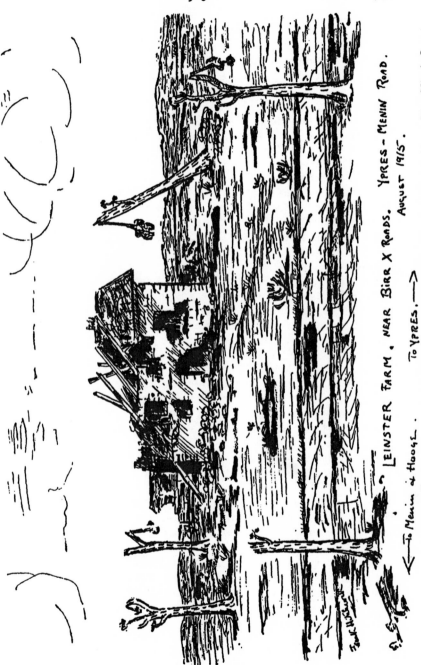

LEINSTER FARM, NEAR BIRR X ROADS. YPRES - MENIN ROAD.
AUGUST 1915.

← To Menin & Hooge.   To Ypres. →

F. HUTTON.

Leinster Farm, Ypres, so named by our 1st Battalion, and Birr Cross Roads, after the Regimental Depot, Birr, King's County.

14th August.

Got my first wash since " the twelfth," but I could not get the lice out of my clothes. I got these vermin from the dirty German dug-outs in the front line. Corpl. Hill gave me a cross made out of a Belgian copper bullet to hang on to my identity disc cord, and wear it as a charm. He said I would not be killed while I was wearing it, and added it was " hard to kill a bad thing ! " I have it to this day. The C.O. and Adjutant came round our reserve line, A and B Companies were holding the front line. The C.O. showed me where he wanted an advanced battle headquarters made. I started a fatigue party on it ; we were spotted, and got crumped badly.

Laville and Monaghan were wounded, and the two Gunner F.O.O.s were killed when relieving each other at B Company Headquarters (one of them was the Territorial[1] who had observed for me in the front line).

15th August.

Marsland died of wounds. I rather expected it, as the Colonel told me that he was very bad the night before. The doctor said that he was unconscious to the end. Sergt. Flaherty, who was with him on patrol, said that they were lying out in No-Man's-Land, and that he had withdrawn the pin from the Mills bomb ; that he was then hit by a bullet in the head and had released the bomb, which exploded, blowing off his hand. To the end, Marsland raved about a boxing match which he had been refereeing a few nights previously in billets. The C.O. came up and told Caulfeild that C and D Companies were to go back to the front line for two more days ! He said that Piper should strengthen the barricade, and put out barbed wire ; also that the positions had to be made as strong as possible, with traverses and flying traverses to stop the enfilade fire. He detailed me to bury all the dead at night.

At 5.30 B Company got heavily shelled for over 1½ hours. The shrapnel-fire was terrific, and their line was completely enveloped in a dense mass of smoke from the bursting shells.

We stood to in case of an attack, but the shell-fire did not materialise into anything. Daly's casualties were 7 killed and 21 wounded. These numbers included most of his N.C.O.s.

When it was dark I set off with two platoons to bury the dead. It was a most unpleasant duty, as they were all men of the Durhams and York and Lancasters, who had been killed on the 9th in the charge. There were many other bodies lying out in this shell-churned area, and the ghastly stench of mangled corpses

[1] Lieut. R. C. Woodhouse.

gripped us all by the throat as we carried out our task. It was very sad, but headless and armless got exactly the same treatment. We searched all for their identity discs, and their Army Books 64, and any other personal belongings for their next-of-kin. We salved their webbing equipment and rifles, and buried them in threes and fours in large graves. We buried some fourteen and returned to the reserve line, where we all got a rum issue. Barnett got a bullet through the stomach when he was guiding a working party of the 1st North Staffords along the Menin Road. Poole and Pearman were wounded and Louis Daly[1] slightly, but he remained at duty, being the only officer left in B Company. Ducat, who was transport officer, returned to duty to assist him. C and D Companies took over the front line again at 9 p.m.

16th August.

Barnett died of his wounds. The Doctor told us that he stuck his wound splendidly, and that men who were only hit in the arms and legs were groaning all round him in the dressing-station. Barnett had a presentiment that he would get killed, and told us so when we got orders for Hooge. I relieved " Cherrie " Piper and Caulfeild at 9 a.m. in the fire trench. The Brig.-General came round to inspect the line with the C.O. The Brigadier said the Battalion had done splendidly, and that the place was thoroughly consolidated ; he, however, objected to a German's leg which was protruding out of parapet, and I was told to have it buried forthwith by the C.O. I called Finnegan, and told him to remove the offending limb. As it would have meant pulling down the whole parapet to bury it, he took up a shovel and slashed at it with the sharp edge of the tool. After some hard bangs, he managed to sever the limb. I had turned away and was standing in the next fire bay, when I overheard Finnegan remarking to another man : " And what the bloody hell will I hang me equipment on now ? "

Three men of the Machine-Gun Section were wounded. We found a private of the York and Lancasters wounded and in a dying condition in a dug-out near the culvert, he appeared to have been there for days without any help. I had No. 11 Platoon carrying up bombs all night to the front line.

17th August.

On duty all morning in the advanced trench. The C.O. brought the C.O. of the North Staffords, Lieut.-Colonel de Falbe, up to look round the line. He gave me orders about burying some dead. In a hollow he had discovered three unburied. This was a sad

---

[1] Now Lieut.-Colonel, Commanding K.O.Y.L.I.

sight, as the trio consisted of a patient lying on a stretcher and the two stretcher bearers lying across him, with the slings of the stretcher still across their shoulders. All had been knocked out by the same shell.

We were only shelled in the support trench and at Railway Wood. At 10 p.m. we were relieved by the 1st North Staffords, and I handed over my line with its flank in the air joyfully ! After relief we did not return to billets, but found carrying parties for R.E. material to the Hooge crater. So back again we toiled along the Menin Road in Indian file, with duckboards, stakes, planks, and sand-bags. To make matters worse, it was raining hard and very dark. It was a tedious job ; fallen trees had to be negotiated and numerous shell-holes full of water had to be avoided. The enemy was sending up star-shells, and we had to halt until the flare fell and had burnt itself out. To have been seen by the enemy would have been fatal, as we were on the exposed Menin Road, right away from cover of any description. We finished our work at 1.30 a.m. and moved off for Ypres in the dark, and in heavy rain. The Battalion had had few casualties that day, but the bomb-store belonging to the left sector at H.12 was blown sky-high by a direct hit. Corpl. Leavy, Bombing N.C.O. of A Company, had a narrow escape.

We had no guide to meet us in Ypres, and we wandered about near the Lille Gate. Sergt. Sullivan, the Provost Sergeant, heard me cursing, and came to my assistance, and showed me our billeting area.

18th August.

We got up at about 11 a.m. for breakfast. We were in dug-outs which were built tier upon tier round a re-entrant into the ramparts beside the Lille Gate. Caulfeild, " Cherrie," and I shared a large dug-out, with beds taken out of the abandoned houses in the vicinity. B Company had their mess dug-out just opposite. Our mess was a kind of summer-house on the top of the ramparts ! We lazed about in the sun all day, and watched one of our 4.2 batteries getting crumped. At night " Cherrie " and I brought the Company up to Hooge, to work for the North Staffords. I dug a new line in front of H.12 near the culvert. The North Staffords got bombed all night. A high explosive burst beside Corpl. Sweeny and myself, knocking us down and covering us with earth. After midnight we had finished our task, and marched back along the Menin railway lines to the Lille Gate. It was very dark, and the men, utterly fatigued, kept stumbling and falling on the sleepers.

19th August.

Got up at 11 a.m. and had the usual breakfast; strong tea, bacon, and tinned tomatoes! Shelled at intervals throughout the day.

Had a long walk all round the ramparts. There was no doubt that Ypres[1] had been a beautiful city before the Boches started shelling it. Some of the houses had gabled fronts of timber; it was surrounded on three sides by high ramparts, which looked very grim and forbidding from the canal bank, and above all rose the battered remnants of the Cloth Hall and the tower of St. Martin's Cathedral. Only one of the old Gothic pinnacles remained of the famous tower of the Cloth Hall. Below lay the broad moat into which shells were plunging every few minutes. Except for the khaki figures which were darting in and out of the ramparts, and the scream of the shells as they passed overhead to explode in the centre of the city, Ypres was a city of the dead. No Flemish town could boast a prouder history. It had been harried by fire and sword at intervals ever since the twelfth century, but many of the Renaissance houses had been left standing amidst the ruins of the more up-to-date buildings.

It was the burghers of Ypres and Courtrai who, in 1302, destroyed Count Robert of Artois's army, and drove his cavalry into the dykes before the city. In 1383 the English burnt the outlying parts of the town; it was sacked by the Gueux in 1578; it was captured by Alexander Farnese in 1584; Oliver Cromwell's Ironsides in red coats had captured it shortly after the fall of Dunkirk; the French obtained possession of it before the War of the Spanish Succession and lost it three times; in retaking it they had burnt parts of it under orders from Louis XIV. As a Southern Irish Regiment, the history of Ypres was of particular interest. The Irish Brigade in the service of France fortified the city against an attack by Marlborough in the latter's task of driving the French from Flanders. Up till the 1st Battle in October, the remnants of some English Colours, which had been captured by Clare's Irish Regiment at Ramillies, were hanging in the chapel of the Irish Dames of Ypres (Benedictine Nuns).

In the midst of the routed French Army, Clare's Regiment particularly distinguished itself in this battle. Clare's, Lally's, Dillon's, and Lee's men were "the wild geese," those hardy Irish soldiers of fortune, who after the capitulation of Limerick crossed

---

[1] There were many weird pronunciations of the name Ypres. I always noted that men belonging to our 1st Battalion invariably alluded to the place as "E-prey," but the 2nd Battalion were satisfied with its more familiar name of "Wipers." Quite recently the writer was shown a letter written by one of Marlborough's officers from Flanders: "The men speak of the town as Wypirs," wrote this eighteenth-century soldier.

the sea to fight for the France they loved, and the Stuart rights.
And now, here we were again, holding Ypres against an enemy
coming from the same direction.   But the enemy was the Hun,
with his terrible devices of frightfulness.

Although the old town fascinated me, I did not go into it, as it
was being shelled.   I had seen too much shell fire for the past
week ; enough to last me for my life-time !   I knew the town
well.   In June I had rambled from house to house with poor old
Jim Marsland.   We had roamed through the Cloth Hall and the
Cathedral, and into the Church of St. Martin's, where all the
vestments were lying about, covered in the powder of high
explosive shells.   Behind the altar, Marsland had raked out the
second foundation coin, dated in the sixteenth century.   It was a
fine gold plaque, and he gave it to an old Abbé who was there
salving what he could between the shell-fire.   Graves of British
soldiers lined the ramparts south of the Lille Gate.   I returned to
our billeting line, and Macartney had dinner with me, as I had the
night off from working parties, Caulfeild and " Cherrie " having
taken the Company up to Hooge.

20th August.

We were woken up at about 7 a.m. by heavy shell-fire.   Our
area was being strafed with " big stuff," which were bursting with
reverberating explosions.   The shells came every minute, and
when they burst in the adjacent buildings and streets, we seemed
to be lifted off the ground by the vibration.   We were sleepy,
and optimistically thought that they were searching for one of
our " Heavy " Batteries.

But it was not so !   Every shell came closer and closer, and we
grew more and more uneasy.   At last one, a 16-inch, landed in
the middle of our semi-circle dug-out line.   I was thrown off my
looted bed on to the ground.   Getting up, I rushed out into a
dense red smoke, to hear nothing except a continual roar for
stretcher-bearers.   The earth and debris from some old ruined
houses were falling with great chunks of masonry all round.
Pulling on my gum boots over my pyjamas, I went out to find a
huge chasm right in the midst of our lines.   I collected all the
men of the Company whom I could, 35 in all, and doubled them
off as hard as I could down the canal bank towards the station,
realising that the only thing to do was to get the men away out
of the shelled area.   Most of them had only their trousers and
grey-backs on.   All were in their bare feet.

The Company dog, a kind of Irish terrier, came with me.
Later I was joined by Ducat, and some of B Company.   One of

his men had gone raving mad. We remained behind a large building for some time, and heard more shells exploding in the same place.

At about 9 a.m. we left our temporary sanctuary, l'Ecole de Ypres, and marched back to the company lines, via the Cloth Hall Square, the men still in bare feet and I in pyjamas! When we got back we found a shocking sight. Two more shells had landed slap into our dug-out lines, completely obliterating eight dug-outs, which, worse luck, were occupied. Sergt. Price and Sergt. Molloy, the sergeant cook, Privates Casey, Martin, Ross, Rutledge, and Reynolds had been killed, two of whom had been blown into the trees overhead, as no trace of them could be found, although we had the men digging up the earth all round the shell craters. Pte. Griffin was so badly wounded that he died later, and Pte. Prendergast of Piper's platoon had his leg off, and Pte. Johnston of B Company had his arm hanging on by a piece of skin. Four others, including C.Q.M.S. Wall, were badly wounded. Total casualties 8 killed and 6 wounded. B Company's H.Q. dug-out was completely blown up, including all Ducat's clothes. Our mess had also disappeared.

We afterwards discovered that at 6.30 a.m. a Boche aeroplane had come close over our dug-outs and had spotted the men out in the middle of this amphitheatre " drumming up their char," and the Company cookers, which Molloy had left standing right in the road opposite our lines! It was a very sad sight, all these stout fellows lying out in a row waiting for the stretcher-bearers to take them off to the cemetery. Some of them hadn't a scratch on their bodies, and had been killed by concussion. Caulfeild and Piper returned. They, with the remainder of the Company, had taken refuge in the trench which ran along the ramparts. The C.O. came round to see us. He was as ever very sympathetic, and very upset about the casualties, he brought Ducat off and gave him some of his clothes. But as the C.O. stood six foot one and Ducat five foot four it was difficult to make them fit with the exceptions of boots and puttees!

I got orders to report to the Adjutant of the North Staffords, Hobart, with regard to a working party for the night. I took up Jackson with me, and we went up via the Lille Gate and Menin Railway. We took to the C.T. on the ridge, but as it was full of water we got out of this trench, which had been appropriately called " Muddy Lane," and walked up in the open. I got my orders for the fatigue party, and brought back Sergt. Brill from A Company, as he was taking over the duties of C.Q.M.S., Wall having been wounded. Later, I took up 100 men to Hooge, and worked on a C.T. near the culvert. I finished my task at 1.30 a.m., and I was guided to a new dug-out line by Sergt. Ginn, who was waiting for me at Birr Cross Roads.

21st August.

We were in field surrounded by hedges just north of Zillebeke. Good dug-outs had been built all round the field under cover of the hedges. The Company was in reserve to the North Staffords. The casualties for the fighting at Hooge were :

Lieut. Marsland, M.C., died of wounds.
Lieut. Barnett   ,,   ,,
Capt. Daly   wounded.
Capt. Algeo[1]   ,,
Lieut. Laville[2]   ,,
2nd Lieut. Poole   ,,
2nd Lieut. Pearman[3]   ,,
2nd Lieut. Monaghan   ,,

Other ranks : killed, 49 ; wounded, estimated at 250. The casualties of the 6th Division for the Hooge attack were estimated at 70 officers and 1700 other ranks.

We received congratulations and thanks for having consolidated the new line from the Divisional and Corps Commanders. Daly was awarded the D.S.O. Several of the N.C.O.s and men received D.C.M.s Drummer Hutchinson and L/Corpl. Leonard of B Company performed very brave deeds. The latter had saved his section by throwing a box of bombs, which were exploding, over the parapet, but in performing this heroic action he was badly wounded. The Company stretcher-bearers were all mentioned in despatches.

The officers who went into action at Hooge were :

Battalion Headquarters.

Commanding : Lieut.-Colonel G. M. Bullen-Smith, D.S.O.
Adjutant : Lieut. A. D. Murphy, M.C.
M.G. Officer : Capt. J. V. Macartney, M.C., attached to D Company.
Bombing Officer : Lieut. J. Marsland, M.C.
Transport Officer: 2nd Lieut. J. K. Ducat, attached to B Company.

A Company.	*C Company.*
Capt. F. W. Prendergast.	Capt. W. S. Caulfeild.
Lieut. S. E. B. Laville.	Capt. N. Algeo.
Lieut. D. O. Barnett.	Lieut. R. L. Piper.
2nd Lieut. R. L. Stirling.	2nd Lieut. F. C. Hitchcock.

[1] Killed 30/11/17.   [2] Killed 18/8/16.
[3] Killed with R.F.C. 1 1/16.

B Company.	*D Company.*
Capt. L. D. Daly.	Capt. R. A. H. Orpen-Palmer.
2nd Lieut. H. Pearman.	2nd Lieut. T. H. Poole.
2nd Lieut. J. H. Monoghan.	2nd Lieut. G. Murray.

and the Rev. Father J. P. Moloney, M.C.

We had an unmolested day from shell-fire, shells only fell into the adjacent fields. I spent the morning preventing the men from putting their washing out in the middle of the field! Had a Boche plane come over we would have been unmercifully strafed. Caulfeild took the Company up to Hooge on fatigue, and I had a night's rest.

22nd August.

Quiet day. Only a few whiz-bangs over. We watched our aeroplanes carrying out a reconnaissance under heavy " Archie " fire over the Sanctuary Woods. At dusk I set out with forty men to carry R.E. materials from the North Staffords' battalion dump to H.12. We had to wait for the North Staffords' transport, and when their G.S. waggons came, they dumped seventy-three footboards. We had two quick journeys up the C.T. which ran parallel with the Menin Road, and finished the fatigue before midnight.

23rd August.

A Company Commander of the 2nd Battalion Royal Irish Rifles came up in the morning to take over from us. The 3rd Division were again taking over the Hooge sector. Rumours of a rest in Poperinghe.

24th August.

Quiet day. At 9 p.m. we were relieved by the 2nd Battalion South Lancashire Regiment (Prince of Wales's Volunteers) of the 7th Brigade, 3rd Division, instead of the Royal Irish Rifles. We returned to billets at Poperinghe via the Menin Railway and the pontoon bridge at the ramparts, which brought us into Ypres by the " Sally Port." We got to our billets, a convent on the Proven Road, at 4 a.m. having had a longish march.

25th August.

Our billets in Poperinghe seemed very quiet after the Hooge sector. We had our Company Mess in a large room looking out over a lovely stretch of country. Our billet was covered in saintly statues and holy pictures. I was strafed by the C.O. for not having handed over a captured trench mortar to the North Staffords. He told me it was wanted by a staff officer on the Corps Staff. I should have handed it over to the North Staffords, as they were going to have it cleaned up and sent down the line. The C.O. said I was to go up to Hooge and look for it, and take an orderly with me ! The C.O. was annoyed with me, but I afterwards found out he was hostile towards the Staff for worrying him and his officers about souvenirs, when holding a critical line like Hooge.

Smith,[1] a battalion runner, was detailed to accompany me, and we got bicycles from orderly room. We got shelled going through Ypres. At an old farm on the near side of Hell Fire Corner, we left our bikes and walked up to H.12. Here we found the 1st Battalion Wiltshire Regiment of the 7th Brigade, who were getting strafed, and having some casualties. Under shell-fire, and bringing down terrible oaths on the damned Staff Wallah's head, I looked for the missing toy, but it had completely disappeared ! I returned with Smith by the C.T. to Birr Cross Roads, and passed a terribly mangled corpse in the trench.

Returning to Ypres via the Lille Gate, we got into a barrage of shells, which were searching for our " Heavies." However, we came out unscathed.

I reported to the Adjutant on my return at 3 p.m. and he sent me up to the transport lines to examine a trench mortar which had been brought there. I found it, but it was a French one, with " Paris 1888 " stamped on the muzzle. I believe it was despatched to Corps Headquarters, as the German *minenwerfer* captured at Hooge ! At the transport lines, I met Louis Daly, who had recovered from his wounds. O'Brien drove us back to Poperinghe in the Mess cart. Outside the town we were stopped by the Military Police, as the town was being shelled. We drove on when the shelling ceased. Lieut. G. A. Todd, 3rd Battalion, joined the Battalion from the 2nd Royal Dublin Fusiliers, and was posted to D Company.

26th August.

I took the Company for a route march in the Proven direction, the men enjoyed getting out into the country. It was a lovely day, and we fell out for a halt in a field of corn stooks. We could hear the guns rumbling in the distance.

---

[1] 9954 Pte. Smith was one of the Battalion Boxing Team, he later was awarded the Military Medal and was killed at Delville Wood standing beside Colonel Murphy.

27th August.

Paraded in the morning. At 5.45 p.m. " Cherrie " and I paraded the " Company " and we marched off to the Vlamertinghe Wood. We divided the Company in two, " Cherrie " taking 11 and 12, and I 9 and 10 Platoons. The men were all very cheery, as there had been an *estaminet* opposite our billets on the Proven Road, and they had only been paid out the day before !

We passed a French Territorial regiment on the march. I never saw such a weird-looking outfit in my life. They wore long blue coats pulled back from the knees, showing dirty red trousers. Their equipment and rifles were in a dreadful state. They had no march formation whatsoever. They were followed by some broken-down waggons, and ill-conditioned-looking horses, as transport, the harness of which consisted mainly of rope !

I was made responsible for the Company Mess, catering and collecting Mess bills, a job which Jim Marsland did. I was not long installed in my position, before Capt. S. H. Dix, M.C., Leinsters and O.C. Divisional Cyclists, borrowed a bottle of whisky from me. He was killed later in the War gallantly leading the 13th Battalion Northumberland Fusiliers at Passchendaele.

28th August.

The same encampment was allotted to the Battalion. Our heavy casualties were again brought home to us when five huts were found sufficient for the Company, whereas ten had been filled before we went up to Hooge.

I took the Company for a route march. In the evening Todd and I went for a ride in the woods and along the Vlamertinghe–Poperinghe road. Todd rode a new horse belonging to D Company, and I rode the Transport Officer's " Dolly," C Company's former charger.

In the evening we had a sing-song in one of the huts.

29th August.

Took half the Company to the Divisional baths in Poperinghe, and had one myself. The men's khaki was put in a fumigating engine, where it was kept all the time they were washing ; this process was known as " Delousing " ! Clean shirts and socks were issued out to every man, and we fell in and marched back to camp.

30th August.

. Drilled the Company in the morning. Remained in camp until 6 p.m., answering for Murphy, the Adjutant. At 7 p.m., horses came up from the transport, and George Murray and I rode off

to Poperinghe to see the 6th Divisional concert, " The Fancies."
It was a top-hole show, Murray and I enjoyed it immensely.
The concert troupe consisted of nine artistes and two French
girls. The latter were known as " Glycerine " and " Vaseline."
One was a refugee from Lille, and the other was the daughter
of an *estaminet* keeper at Armentières. The most priceless turn
in the show was the singing of " I'm Gilbert the Filbert " by one
of these wenches who could not speak English ! Dunlop of the
3rd Rifle Brigade was responsible for the management of " The
Fancies."

We stopped a Divisional Headquarters car just outside Poperinghe and got a lift to camp.

31st *August.*

The Battalion practised getting in to a line of trenches which
had been dug for shelter in case the wood was shelled. The C.O.
went home on leave, and O.-P. assumed command during his
absence. Murray and I went into Poperinghe for a bottle of
" Fizz." In the evening I dined with D Company. Three
subalterns joined the Battalion, in H. G. Newport and J. G.
Young from the 4th Battalion and M. A. Higgins from the
3rd Battalion. We received news from Gallipoli of the landing
made by the 10th Irish Division at Suvla Bay. Our 6th Service
Battalion was reported to have suffered severely. Capt. D'Arcy-
Irvine, Lieuts. Gough, Figgis, Toomey, Willington, Hickson and
Griffiths killed, and Colonel Craske, D.S.O., Major Stannus,[1]
J. C. Parke (so well known in the Rugger and Tennis world) and
Little wounded. The other ranks had also severe casualties,
76 being killed. I recalled going to the Curragh Races with
D'Arcy-Irvine in January. He was an absolute topper.

1st *September.*

" The O'Mahoney " came to visit us with some members of
the Irish League, who were visiting the Front. He gave us a
long speech about Ireland, and congratulated the C.O. on having
such a fine Battalion, with such an excellent fighting record.

The men cheered him like blazes, as they had had a second
payment that morning, and had spent some time in an *estaminet*
hard by ! Macartney and I took ranges with the Bar and Stroud
on aeroplanes. Caulfeild returned from leave. Stirling and
Young dined with me. At 9.30 p.m. we got orders to find two
platoons for special duty in Ypres. Caulfeild and I started out,
leaving Piper with the rest of the Company. We reported to the
Town Major at the old prison, and got orders for Secret Service.

[1] Died of wounds received at Messines in June, 1917.

Espionage was practised about Ypres pretty freely, and we had to picket various bridges and gates which led into the city. Caulfeild took the Lille Gate sector, and I was given all the bridges on the Ypres–Comines Canal, south-west of the town, to guard. All civilians and our staff officers were to be stopped and asked for pukka identification. My hopes ran high, and I wondered if I would get the " souvenir hunter " of trench mortar fame, as I had permission to stop anybody I chose from the gilded staff to drummer boy ! A French interpreter was detailed to remain with me for cross-examining civilians and liaison with the Belgian gendarmerie. He was a pukka " B.F." and a damned nuisance. The men called him " Th'ould Interrupter." I slept the night in a dug-out beside a bridge on the Dickebusch road. The men were billeted in the ruins of an old mill some 200 yards away. Shells fell near us throughout the night.

2nd September.

Walking round in the early hours of the morning, I discovered that a large house close to my dug-out was occupied, caretakers, who had remained on, and endured a ghastly existence in the cellars. They were very decent poor people, and cooked a fine breakfast of omelette and coffee for the *officier de liaison* and myself.

I paid them well, but they were, unlike the other Belgians I had met, really kind-hearted. We had a poor regard for the Flemish peasantry ; they robbed us right and left. It was a well-known fact that the people around the back areas of Ypres lived on British rations, bully beef and tins of Maconochie especially. The men used to say : " Faith, they are so bloody mean they work their dogs ! "

At 8 a.m. my duty started. I halted everybody and demanded passes, which had been issued out the day before to all employed around the city. The identity discs and pay books of the rank and file were sufficient.

I halted Staff officers, batteries of gunners, and A.S.C. convoys to scrutinise their passes. Several instances had been brought to light of German spies coming through our lines in staff kit within the past few months, so I was, therefore, very suspicious, and I had been warned to scrutinise Staff officers' passes carefully. We were subject to heavy shell fire all evening, a 16-inch shell landed on top of a house close by and blew it to blazes. Not a brick was left standing ; the road was littered with debris. It was intended for the 42nd Battery, which was in action in an adjacent field. The shell-fire was so heavy that I forsook my dug-out and slept in a cellar of the château.

3rd September.

We left Ypres at 8.30 a.m.   I was detailed to go all round
Ypres withdrawing the pickets.   At 10.30 we got to our hutments
in the Vlamertinghe Wood.   I had two bottles of wine in my
pockets which the Town Major, a sportsman, had given me when
I reported to him to return maps and documents.   He was killed
later in the War.   No one envied him his job !

Finnegan and Murphy were the worse for drink but kept in the
ranks all right.   Finnegan was a grand soldier in the line, who
unfortunately was shot by a sniper at Hooge in March, 1916.
Finnegan once asked me to censor a letter to his father in County
Cork.   It was one of the few I ever read, but knowing it was written
by Finnegan it was bound to be unique.   It was to the effect
that he had been " in clink " for being late returning from leave,
but not to mind as when he got home again they would have
another " grand old blind together."

At 6.30 p.m. the Battalion paraded in awful rain for the canal
bank north of Ypres.   We got to our position by the Brigade
road, and No. 4 pontoon bridge.   Shelling was spasmodic only.
Allotted a line of dug-outs along the east bank in a sea of mud.
It was very dark and we slithered all over the place.   My kit
consisted of gum-boots, a blanket, great-coat, ground-sheet and
washing gear.   " Cherrie's " servant, Morgan, and Jackson slung
our ground-sheets like hammocks in a large dug-out.   I was very
tired, and after I had seen my platoon settled in I turned in
and went to sleep.   I had covered over 16 miles during the day
through mud and over the hard, uneven cobbled roads.

The 1st Battalion K.S.L.I. was the regiment we relieved.

4th September.

Breakfast at 10 a.m.   Splendid day.   We were on the east
side of the Yser Canal.   Our dug-outs were built into the bank
which overlooked the canal and led out on to the towpath.   The
canal was about 50 yards in breadth and about 15 feet deep in
the centre.   It ran due north to Dixmude from Ypres, and was
connected with the Ypres–Comines Canal at Kaai due north of
the city.   It had high banks on both sides, which were thickly
belted by bushy-topped poplar trees.   It ran parallel with the
main road to Boesinghe, which was on its western side.   The
country was typically Flemish, barren wastes, fields of rotten
corn, grass, or stubble, with dykes and ditches separating them.
The ruins of old burnt-out homesteads were studded about here
and there.   The canal was crossed by four pontoons, one large
one known as No. 4 Bridge opposite Noordhofwijk, and three

others of duckboard breadth only. The water was black and slimy. Padre Moloney and some men stripped and swam about in it. They had some nerve as it must have been very " fruity " from corpses ! One man got torn from some barbed wire which the French Territorial Division had thrown into it. O.-P. brought Piper, two of his subalterns, and myself up to La Brique to reconnoitre a new line we had been ordered to dig. We went up by La Belle Alliance, once a fine farm, but reduced by constant shell-fire to a heap of blackened bricks, and returned by Irish Farm and La Brique. O.-P.'s two subalterns had only just joined the Regiment, but he, Piper and I found the sector greatly changed since June.

At night the road behind us was shelled and our ration parties got a rough passage going to the ration dump.

5th September.

Two officers joined the Battalion in Plowman and Brassington, just commissioned from the South Irish Horse. They had been in the country since August '14 with G.H.Q. troops. Plowman, who had acted as trumpeter to Sir John French on many occasions, was posted to C and Brassington to B Company. The canal bank was shelled with gas shells without doing any damage. Enemy aircraft very active, and I watched them dropping flares and white balls on Turco Farm, ranging for gunners. At night I took the company out digging behind La Belle Alliance. In our task we unearthed some dead Turcos. I found a good servant in Horrigan for Plowman, he had formerly been poor old Jim Marsland's batman. Horrigan had wept for days after Marsland's death. He, too, like Plowman, was destined to be killed later on in the War.

6th September.

Excellent weather and the muddy towpath became bone dry. There were two old boats tied up to the banks, in which the men paddled about. Not having oars, they used shovels. All day long parties of men rowed up and down from pontoon to pontoon, while their pals from the banks threw stones and lumps of earth at them. They made fine targets.

I watched Sergt. Sweeney directing his bombing party. He shouted out, " Repeat the Heavies," and away went a hail of clods. Next thing I saw was the boat overturned and half a dozen men floundering about in the grimy canal. Sweeney then turned to me with a grin and asked if that wasn't " good registering." In the evening " Cherrie " and I dined with B Company.

7th September.

Piper got orders to sail for India to join his Indian regiment as he had completed his year's service with a British regiment. Macartney started a course for officers on the Vickers gun, and we fired many belts into the canal bank opposite. The Adjutant told me that my name had been submitted for leave in the U.K. for seven days. 2nd Lieut. A. Burns joined, and was posted to B Company. He had just been commissioned from the 3rd Hussars where he had been Squadron Sergt.-Major. He had won the D.C.M. at Le Cateau.

8th September.

Toured the Company messes with " Cherrie," who was leaving by the second train from Poperinghe and wanted to say good-bye. I was very, very sorry he was going ; we were great friends, and had been through some hectic times together. All were sorry to lose him, but most especially his platoon, No. 10. I saw him off down part of the way to Brielen. After three weeks' leave in the U.K. he had orders for India, and for joining the 57th Wilde's Rifles, Frontier Force, Waziristan. He was sad about leaving the Battalion, but was naturally glad to get away from the shells and the Western Front. He looked forward keenly to the more primitive warfare and khud-side scrapping employed against hostile Mahsuds. Piper[1] was killed in East Africa in 1917.

NEWS OF ZEPPELIN RAID ON LONDON

9th September.

Working with D Company at night with 50 men of C Company. Our task was to revet the C.T. which we had dug some nights previously towards Turco Farm from La Belle Alliance. O.-P. came round to inspect our work. I felt really " windy " throughout this fatigue as I was proceeding on leave next day ! Sergt. Ginn suggested that I should stop a jammy one and have a long leave while I was about it ! The Germans yelled across to the 1st Royal Fusiliers, " London is on fire," and " What about the Dardanelles now ? " The R.F.s, being Cockneys, strongly objected to the first remark, which happened to be the first news they had heard of the Zeppelin raid on their capital. The Fusiliers got on their fire steps, and never did I hear more amazing language than this Cockney regiment shouted across to the Huns ! Rapid fire was opened from both sides, but the Huns burst shrapnel over our front line, which inflicted some casualties on the R.F.s who were all standing to on their fire-steps.

[1] Posthumously awarded M.C.

10th September.

Prendergast and I left the canal bank at dusk. Our side of
the bank was shelled spasmodically during the day. Donoghue
came up with the Mess cart and drove us to the station in
Poperinghe, where we enquired about the trains for next day,
afterwards driving back to the transport and sleeping in bivouacs
between the horse lines. We saw some houses on fire in the
Brielen direction.

11th September.

Prendergast and I started off for the station in the Mess cart.
Our train left " Pop " at 6.30 a.m., and we got to Boulogne at
12.30, where we lunched. After some " wangling," we managed
to get on the Staff leave boat. It always left port four hours before
the ordinary leave boat. By getting on it, Prendergast and I
who were both bound for Ireland got another twenty-four hours
in our homes. At 8 p.m. we arrived at Victoria Station in a
Pullman and hurried across town to Euston, where we caught
the Irish mail for Dublin.

2nd ARMY. - LEAVE FORM

1.   This authority must be taken by officers and other
ranks proceeding on leave and produced when demanded.
     (General Routine Order No. 911.)

2.   Officers and other ranks leaving France individually
will proceed via a Base Port (Calais or Boulogne), and
unless prevented by wounds or sickness, will report to the
Assistant Military Landing Officer prior to departure.
     A similar procedure will be adopted by individual
officers and other ranks returning to France.
     (General Routine Order No. 329.)

Lieut. F. C. Hitchcock. 2nd Bn. Leinster Regt. has permission

to proceed to England from..*2" Sept. 15*..to.*16" Sept. 15*

10" September 1915   *B. C. B. Town*

Times of Trains.   *Staff Captain 17° Dy/Bde.*

HOMEWARDS.
        Train leaves POPERINGHE at 1.41.p.m.
        BOAT leaves BOULOGNE about 10.p.m.

OUTWARDS
        Train leaves VICTORIA at 5.40.p.m.
        BOAT leaves FOLKESTONE at 8.45.p.m.

12th September. Sunday.

We arrived at the North Wall, having had a rough crossing. I drove off on an outside car for Kingsbridge.

13th to 15th September.

Having had exactly seventy-two hours (three days) at home, I left for the Front.

At Victoria, Prendergast and an old friend, Trench, who was attached to the 2nd Battalion Royal Dublin Fusiliers, joined me. We got cheered like blazes by some excitable people as our leave train steamed out of the station. Embarked in darkness at Folkestone. Most of the men were in a state of morbid drunkenness, and kept singing the old campaigners' ditty, known as " Oh, Colour-Sergeant, leave me at the Base," which went as follows :

> " I don't want to go to the trenches no more ;
> I've had enough of this bloody old war.
> Oh my ! I don't want to die ; I want to go home."

We were all packed like sardines on the decks, three trains full. Trench and I went to sleep, hearing everybody talking of mines and submarines being loose in the Channel, but even this " wind," and the hard saw-dusty covered bar floor, did not prevent us from sleeping like logs.

17th September.

Woke up to find that our transport had not moved, so there had been truth in the submarine scare ! Trench and I had breakfast ashore. We were told that we could go off for the day, as the boat would not sail until 7.30 p.m. The majority returned to London, but Trench and I decided to remain at Folkestone. A few officers were detailed to march the men off to a rest-camp at Shorncliffe, where they were to stay until time to embark. Captain Prendergast was detailed to command the party. At 7 p.m. Trench and I, having dined and wined well at the Pavilion Hotel, embarked. The boat sailed at 10 p.m. We remained on deck, and were greatly intrigued with the various signals out to sea.

18th September.

At midnight we arrived at Boulogne. I said good-bye to Trench, as our trains were going to different railheads. I never saw him again. He was killed with the 2nd Dublins within seven months. He and I had been great friends in the old Cork days.

At 2 p.m. our train left the pier and we got to St. Omer at
9 a.m., where we had a long halt, owing to the lines being blocked
by a French Regular Division, which was entraining for the
south for the new " push " in the Champagne.   They were
fine-looking troops, and were all wearing their new steel helmets,
which were said to be splinter and shrapnel proof.

Got to Poperinghe at 1.30 p.m., and found Jackson in the
Mess cart waiting.   The Battalion was in billets in the town at
the convent on the road off the main " Pop "-Elverdinghe route.
Macartney was holding an officers' Vickers gun class.   D Company
were with us, and we both messed together in a schoolroom on
the ground floor.

19th September.

Paraded all morning.   Higgins, Plowman and I went to " The
Fancies " in the evening.

20th September.

Received orders for the line for the next day.

21st September.

Carried out the usual inspections before proceeding up the
line in the morning.   Iron rations, respirators and ground sheets.
We were attached to the 18th Brigade.   Caulfeild and Laville
went up in advance to take over the canal bank from the
2nd D.L.I.   In the evening I marched the company up via
Vlamertinghe and Brielen and we took over the same line as
we had been in before.

22nd September.

Plowman, Brassington, and I went for a row in the Company
boat.   As No. 1 pontoon bridge got blown up by a direct hit of
a 6-inch we quickly put into port !

Took the Company out digging, working on a new line east of
St. Jean, running parallel with the St. Jean–Potijze road.
O.-P. came round to inspect the work.   He had just got his
Majority and had been appointed second in command.   There
was great activity in sniping, but I had no men hit.   Sent
Brassington off with Sergt. Sweeney and 25 men, and followed
later taking the route La Brique and the brigade road called
" High Holborn Castle."   At dawn the canal bank was heavily
strafed and we left our dug-outs and got into the trenches
hard by.

23rd September.

The Adjutant gave me orders to draw pay for the Battalion at the Field Cashier's. I " jumped " a lorry outside the Ypres Convent on the Poperinghe road, which decanted me near our transport lines, where I got B Company's charger George, and rode to the Louvie Château near Proven. I drew 4000 francs on a chit from Murphy and rode back. I enjoyed this part of my duty, especially on the drive of the château, where one could always have a nice canter, in spite of orders to the contrary.

I rode back to the transport, where I had permission to stay the night. Squire gave me dinner and a top-hole bivouac between the horse lines under the trees. I completely forgot all about the war ! There were a certain amount of " casualties " at the Front at this period with lame horses, owing to picked-up nails on the roads. These nails were mostly attributed to the firewood used in regimental cookers. On numerous trees along the Ypres–Poperinghe road were nailed small boxes for the collection of picked-up nails.

Drawn by F. C. Hitchcock

Peace in Poperinghe. My bivouac at the regimental transport lines.

24th September.

Paid out men who were proceeding on leave on that never-to-be-forgotten Army Form N.1510 ! A new Padre arrived at the transport lines in relief of Padre Moloney, who had been wounded when our billets were strafed some days previously in Poperinghe. The " relief " had been Chaplain to our 1st Battalion when they were fighting around Hill 60. After lunch I left the transport lines for the canal bank. I " jumped " an ambulance as far as Vlamertinghe, where it stopped at the Casualty Clearing Station.

After a short delay a 3-ton lorry came along on its way to Ypres, and I " jumped " it.

It belonged to the Divisional ammunition column, and was carrying 4·2 shells up to the batteries. The shells were loose on the floor, and were rolling and banging about as we went over the uneven cobbled road. There was a real strafe going on at Ypres ; shells were bursting right along the road from the Gold Fish Château to the town.

The Convent was getting very heavily shelled, due to the fact that the enemy rightly suspected it harboured a 6-inch battery. We drove on past this building, with the shells screaming overhead to burst with a vibrating bang in its ancient cloisters.

At the water tower—a large metal tank on a brick pedestal—close to the prison, due west of the city, I got off the lorry, and turning sharp to my left made for the canal. Shells were falling all round in the adjacent fields ; houses in front of me were getting direct hits and collapsing in heaps on the road. It was too unhealthy ; so leaving the road I cut across country. I skirted the relics of an old menagerie with its shattered remains of lion cages and hobby horses, and arrived at the end of the canal at Kaaie.

The canal banks were being intermittently shelled, and the towpath had been turned up in many places by new shell craters. It was the eve of the colossal attack at Loos in the south, and to ease matters, and to draw the enemy's reserves from the big battle, the 3rd and 14th Divisions were " doing a side-show," a B.E.F. term for a subsidiary attack, and attacking on a front from Bellewaarde Farm to Zouave Wood inclusive. Our batteries had been in action for three days.

Had tea with Prendergast and Young in A Company's Mess. J. L. L. Johnston arrived from the ranks of one of our affiliated regiments of Canada, and took over a platoon in A Company. (He died of wounds commanding a company on 21/6/16.) Brassington and I took carrying parties up to Potijze. It rained heavily, and we got drenched and badly shelled. The slates which remained on the roofs were all falling from the continual vibration caused by the bursting of shells.

25th September—Sunday.

At 4 a.m. our batteries opened for the preliminary bombardment along the Bellewaarde ridge. The Battalion stood to in the adjacent trenches in case of artillery retaliation on the canal. However, the Huns did not shell the canal immediately, con-centrating all their fire over the front line and on our artillery.

Plowman and I went back to our dug-out and went to sleep,

but we were not to sleep for long, as the Huns opened on our lines, no doubt expecting to find our reserves. The bridges got strafed badly in turn, then the shelling methodically drew nearer and nearer, until the crumps landed beside our dug-outs, and the shrapnel burst in the trees directly overhead. Every second we seemed to be lifted out of our beds by a large crump, which landed on the bank behind or in the canal. In the evening we got news of the results of the attacks. The 1st Army, composed of the following Divisions, 1st, 2nd, 7th, 9th, 12th, 15th, 28th 47th, and the Guards, with the 21st and 24th in reserve, reported that they had made a successful advance on a front of 6 miles, and that the villages of Loos and Hulluch were captured. Gas was reported to have been used in the assault on the Hun first line. Thousands of prisoners reported captured. The French reported that their advance in the Champagne was materializing most successfully, and that 10,000 prisoners had been captured. The attack on the Bellewaarde ridge was a failure. Aided by a mine which was sprung, the 14th Division attacked on the north side of the Menin Road and the 3rd Division, co-operating with them, attacked south of the Menin Road through the Sanctuary Woods. Both Divisions took their objectives, but in a strong counter-attack carried out by determined and skilful bombers, all gains were abandoned by the 14th Division, who retired back to their front line at Railway Wood. The 3rd Division hung on to their position until midday when owing to a raking enfilade fire and heavy casualties they withdrew to their original " jumping-off " position, holding only a few of their hard-earned gains. It was a dismal failure, and our casualties were terrifically heavy. In retiring, the battalions of the 14th Division got practically wiped out by machine-guns. The attacking troops of the 14th Division were Service Battalions of the 60th Rifles (K.R.R.) and Rifle Brigade.

At 5 p.m. D Company got sudden orders to move up to Potijze in support to our 18th Brigade. Drummond joined the Battalion from the ranks of the Royal Engineers. He reported to the Company for duty with Corporal's stripes and wearing spurs, as he had come from a mounted branch of the Sappers in a cavalry division.

At dusk I took the Company on fatigue to the north side of Railway Wood. I led the men across to the barrier on the La Brique road, and from there struck out for Potijze across the Brigade track. The road was being badly strafed, and a battery which we skirted on the outskirts of Potijze was being shelled. On we went, two deep in pouring rain, with shells " plunking " into the turf on either side of us ; the track was a sea of mud, and we all slipped and slid all over the place. The men used terrible language and made an awful row with their shovels and picks, which clanged every minute. The Gunners came out of their dug-outs, expecting no doubt to see an army corps, but instead, through the mist, they only saw sixty grousing Leinsters.

At Potijze Cross Roads a guide met me, and directed us along the main road through the Potijze wood which was being strafed, and then into a trench which brought us to the line we had held in July. We marched on through the support line, which was being held by our D Company under Tim Laville. We then got out in the open, and followed our guide through a chewed-up, shell-pitted area. Some five hundred yards found us at our destination behind the front line of the 2nd Durham L.I. The heavy rain had stopped, but it was still drizzling. Arms were piled, equipment taken off, and we commenced our task of making machine-gun emplacements in concealed positions near Gully Farm. They were fine positions when we had finished, and guns mounted on them could be guaranteed to hold up an enemy attack along the Roulers railway. We had worked all the time under heavy shell and machine-gun fire ; both sides had been very peevish ever since the attack in the morning in this sector.

Under three hours, during which time the men had worked splendidly, we were ready to move off. I passed the word to dress along the line, and we slunk off into the darkness, halting every now and then for a Véry light to fall and burn itself out in the rank grass. We had had no casualties, which was remarkable under the circumstances.

26th September.

The canal bank was strafed at intervals all day, and we got drenched occasionally from the splashes of numerous crumps, as they landed into the canal. I saw one of our aeroplanes, which had been hovering over the Boche lines near Turco Farm, winged and brought down to earth. At 9 p.m. we got the word to fall in in battle order, and to proceed to Potijze to support the 2nd Durhams, who had telephoned to Brigade " S O S Durhams." Under orders from the Adjutant, we took every available man, Cutts only being left behind to look after our kits and the Company Mess. The Battalion fairly stepped out up to Potijze via La Brique and St. Jean. C Company were leading, and the Colonel and Adjutant strode just ahead of my platoon. Here we met Brassington and Drummond returning with working parties, and whipped them in too. However, we were stopped in the Potijze Woods, which were being badly strafed, by a Brigade runner, who said the S O S had been sent out from the 14th

Division Durhams, and not the 2nd Battalion Durhams, whom we were supporting. The Battalion about-turned and marched back to the canal bank. This march cost the Battalion some casualties, two men being killed and half a dozen wounded. How we all swore that night for being called by mistake.

27th September.

The official communiqué reported progress by the 1st Army at Loos. We were shelled all evening, and had some casualties. Murray, of my platoon, and L/Corpl. Viner, were wounded. At 7 p.m. we paraded by companies, and marched up to Potijze. Caulfeild had gone on in advance to take over the line. We were not at all sorry to leave the canal bank ; apart from the shell-fire the endless fatigues to all sectors north of Hooge had " fed us up " completely ! We would not have lost as many men had we been holding an ordinary part of the front line. Our casualties had been over the average, and some very fine men of the calibre of Corpl. O'Sullivan had been killed. Led the Company up to the front line without guides, as I knew the sector like the palm of my hand, and at 8.30 p.m. we relieved the 2nd Durhams. We held exactly the same line as we had in July, the only difference being that the advanced line had become the main trench, and the original main trench had been turned into the support. My platoon held the extreme left flank of the Battalion in touch with the Queen's Westminsters (T.F.). Crump Farm was just behind our trenches. The distribution of the Battalion from right to left was as follows : C Company, Nos. 9 and 12 Platoons in the front trench with the bombers, and 10 and 11 Platoons in support. B Company with their platoons organised in the same way. D Company in reserve and A Company in support. The Battalion front was from Crump Farm inclusive to the Roulers railway line exclusive. The line was in a particularly bad state. I put out the listening posts, about 50 yards across No-Man's-Land in a dis-used trench. Sergt. Ginn and I went out on patrol, but the mist was against us, and we returned. I then turned all available men on to strengthening the parapet which was frightfully weak.

I was on duty all night from 10 p.m. to 5 a.m., and was very tired and sleepy, but kept myself awake by detonating and clean-ing bombs, which the Durhams had handed over. Caulfeild and Plowman were the only other officers in the Company.

28th September.

Slept from 5 a.m. until 10 a.m., and then had the firing line fixed up as well as possible. Most of the duckboards had sub-merged, and had to be re-set with stakes, as the whole line was under water. Privates Byrne[1] and Coghlan made a bomb store. The C.O. brought our new Brigadier—Brig.-General J. W. V. Carroll, of the Norfolk Regiment—round the line. General or " Uncle " Harper, as we called him, had gone to take over command of a Territorial Division. No. 10 Platoon relieved No. 12. It rained incessantly throughout the night. I sat on a fire step and fired Véry lights up at intervals. The Huns did the same. It was very, very dark, and I experienced great difficulty in walking along the line to visit the sentries.

The Battalion had not been drafted since Hooge, and was considerably under strength. When the ration parties left the front line, it seemed that there was only one man left to every fire bay ! Drafts intended for the 2nd Battalion were being sent to reinforce our 6th Service Battalion at Gallipoli.

29th September.

The French reported that they had taken Souchez : 32,000 prisoners were estimated by the attacking troops at Loos and in the Champagne.

The enemy blew a mine at Hooge and attacked. Their attack was a failure, but all night long there was tremendous activity ; shells, bombs, star-shells, and bursts of rapid fire. I saw one of our aeroplanes brought down near Birr Cross Roads. Corpl. Coghlan and I went out on patrol, and on our return got some rum which we brought out to the listening posts, who were frozen, as the frost had set in. (These listening posts consisted of 1 N.C.O., 2 bayonet men, and a bomber.)

30th September.

Plowman and I " liaised " with the Queen's Westminsters, who were on our left flank. The old Stink Post sap was just the same. With them, I met Bellew, now of the South Irish Horse, who was functioning as trench mortar officer. He had looked after me well when I stayed with the 4th Royal Irish prior to embarking for France.

We sent guides off to meet the incoming Regiment at 6 p.m. While waiting for the reliefs B Company's guide got an explosive bullet in the arm which smashed the bone to pieces. It was a stray shot, as he happened to be walking behind our trench in support. Morrissey had a hard job bandaging him up.

At 8.30 p.m. I fainted in the support trench ! I had not felt well all day, but C.S.M. Morgan brought me into his dug-out and gave me a strong tot of rum, and I felt better. Caulfeild sent me down to the dressing-station in the Potijze Château to get a lift back to Poperinghe, so as to avoid the march of 10 miles to

[1] Later in the War awarded D.C.M., M.M. and Bar.

billets. When the shelling had ceased on the building and woods, the ambulances crept up with muffled lights and drove me off with some casualties to Vlamertinghe. The roads were being badly strafed all the way to Ypres, and two shells exploded in the square of Ypres as we drove through. It was a bad night, pitch dark and raining heavily. I wondered when the Company would get relieved. At Vlamertinghe we halted at the C.C.S. and I watched an M.O. extracting splinters from a man's face and chest. Another ambulance came along, and took us to Poperinghe.

I went off to the Convent, where I found that Jackson had made down my valise. I was asleep at 10.30 p.m.

The Battalion did not get in to billets until 2 a.m. as their relief had been very late. The Regiment which took over our line was the 8th Battalion 60th Rifles, 14th Division.

1st October.

No parades. The Company had come back to billets drenched through in the early hours, and the yards were lined with their wet clothes. The Convent was as cold and dreary as ever ; only a few nuns had remained after the town had been badly shelled early in September. Those who were left were kind old ladies, who seemed very glad to see us. C and D Companies were billeted in the Convent, and we had our cookers, or field-kitchens, just behind the buildings under some trees, to escape the eyes of hostile aircraft. Plowman and I rode off to the field cashier's for payment for the Company. We drew 6000 francs. Plowman rode Caulfeild's mare, Matilda, and I rode Macartney's white-faced horse, called George. We had a nice canter up the main drive to the Louvie Château, an avenue which was out of bounds to all bar the Corps Staff ! (George was killed later on by a shell.)

In the evening Plowman and I went to " The Fancies," the Divisional concert troupe.

2nd October.

Caulfeild drilled the Company on the polo ground. Later I paid out the Company. In the afternoon Plowman and I got horses and rode off to see the 6th Divisional A.S.C. train, where we met L'Estrange and his friends, who were encamped on the left side of Proven Road. They gave us tea, and then showed us over their horse lines ; one or two of their horses were down with colic, quite a common complaint with animals picketed out in the B.E.F. We popped over some jumps which had been erected for a horse show.

Capt. R. W. Gray arrived, and took over command of A Company. In the evening we all went to " The Fancies," and returned to our mess to kill the " convoy " which we had received that day from the Base canteen. We stayed up so late that the nuns shut us out from the wing of the building where we slept, so we climbed in through the windows.

3rd October.

Drilled on the polo ground. I got orders to obtain money from the field cashiers. Plowman, Brassington, Higgins, and Drummond came with me. I drew the money, and we then had a fine cross-country ride round corn-fields, hop-gardens, over ditches and dykes, and back to billets, having successfully put the wind up all the Belgian peasants north-west of Poperinghe ! We watched a Taube trying to blow up one of our observation balloons, but it did not succeed, as the balloon took to earth very speedily ! Weather excellent and the men seemed to sit out all day under the trees playing " House."

4th October.

Took the Company bombers out to the banks of the Poperinghe canal for " throwing practice." Poperinghe square and our billets were badly shelled all afternoon, and we had a few casualties. The C.O., who had just returned from leave, came round with the Second in Command, and suggested taking the men out in the country. However, the shelling soon stopped, and quite a number of the shells were " duds." All day we heard a great rumbling of guns on the Belgian front.

The three French Divisions which had broken through in the Champagne, were reported " safe ! " This announcement caused us great amusement, as we did not know that they had been lost ! We afterwards learnt that they had advanced too far near Soissons, and had got cut off for some days. The 2nd Battalion Sherwood Foresters were badly strafed at Stink Post, Potijze, at 9.30 p.m., and had many casualties, to our regret.

5th October.

C and D Companies went for a route march towards Proven, under Macartney. At night we had a gay dinner party in the Convent. Our stone-floored Mess was very cold, so we had braziers placed in the corners of the room.

6th October.

We heard that the Germans had regained the Hohenzollern Redoubt at Hulluch by a well-organised bombing attack, and would have gained more ground only for the determined resistance of the 2nd Battalion Irish Guards, who had only just arrived in the country. We all knew by this time that our offensive at Loos had been written off as a failure, and our casualties had been colossal; as bad luck would have it, the gas used by us for the first time had been caught by a sudden change of wind and was blown back in the faces of our attacking troops. We had never expected gas to be used, and we were all greatly surprised owing to the following story, which was current throughout the B.E.F. to the effect that our attempts at gas had been so unsuccessful that when experimented on a flock of sheep, the animals had been seen grazing away contentedly after the gas cloud had passed over them! The Staff were reported to have witnessed this fiasco from a few fields distant, all smothered in gas helmets of every description!

At 4.30 p.m. the Battalion paraded for the front line at Potijze. As we were falling in, one of the nuns rushed out and demanded payment from Higgins for some broken crockery which she had found in the room where he, Plowman and I had slept. This miscellaneous piece of earthenware had not been smashed by us, but by a splinter from a shell which had hit the church steeple just opposite the window of our billet! However, rather than distress the good ladies of the Convent, who had been very kind to us, Higgins "antied" up 5 francs!

At 8.30 p.m. we relieved the 8th Battalion K.R.R., or 60th Rifles, in the same line which we had held the week previously.

The bad weather had caused some of the parapets to fall in bodily, and others sagged badly, and threatened to fall at any moment. The 9th Service Battalion of the Sussex Regiment, 24th Division, were attached to us for instruction. Their Division had just arrived in the Salient from the Loos sector. I put out all the listening posts for the Company. With each post I put out two men of the Sussex. I "liaised" with the regiment on my left flank, the 2nd Battalion Sherwood Foresters, they seemed pleased to have us alongside them and gave me full details about the Stink Post show.

All through the night Sergt. Flaherty and I patrolled No-Man's-Land as it was very dark, and the enemy was not putting up any star-shells.

7th October.

Spent the day revetting the trench as well as we could, without exposing ourselves over the parapets. We also dug sump pits to drain off the stagnant water which lay in the bottom of the trench. In the evening I went down to Railway Wood to see A Company. Their line ran through the wood, and through numerous mine craters like a jig-saw puzzle, and then over the railway line where there was a sand-bagged barricade which had rows of "knife rests" in front of it. The trench at Railway Wood formed an ugly little salient before it swung back towards Hooge, less than 40 yards separated from the enemy line, and it was so close that the barbed wire entanglements put up by one side answered equally well for the other !

Stirling and Young seemed very gay, and had lots of good yarns. We found three companies in the front line from Crump Farm to Railway Wood inclusive, C, D, and A. B Company was in support. The enemy shelled Crump Farm all evening. They had spotted one of the old toughs scrounging around in it for firewood. I was on duty from 12 midnight to 6 a.m., an uneventful night.

8th October.

More ground reported lost at Loos. The C.O. and Second in Command came round the line, and seemed well satisfied.

Rumours were spread throughout the Battalion that we were moving south. These were somewhat strengthened by orders to our transport to "pack up." The 9th Sussex were relieved.

We worked all night on the revetment of the main communication trenches called Duke and Jermyn Street. The daily communiqué stated that the British and French Expeditionary Forces had landed at Salonika.

9th October.

Early in the morning Major Orpen-Palmer came round. He called me up to come round the line with him, and ordered flying traverses to be built and sniping plates let in to the C.T.s. Although jaded out for want of sleep, I understood what he wanted done. Sleep was a necessary evil in the front line, and one took it when one got the chance. I had been on duty from midnight to 7 a.m. and had retired to sleep when O.-P. came round at 7.30.

His orders were carried out at night ; 9247 Sergt. T. Flaherty and I went out on patrol. We gave a password to our listening posts, and went out some distance beyond an old disused trench. We crossed it and crept up quite close to the enemy lines. We then lay down in the wet rank grass and listened. The enemy were talking away and laughing. They appeared to be working behind their lines, as we heard the clatter of spades digging and slapping down earth. I gave Flaherty a dig in the ribs and we crept away between the Véry lights which shot up from the Huns' line. I had plans for dispersing that digging party. In my haste I fell over a trip wire ; it was an alarm with tin cans full of stones, but although I made an awful clatter, the enemy did not hear, as they were working so noisily themselves. Within five minutes Sergt. Bennett was firing a belt of 250 rounds into this cheery fatigue party ! It was dark, but I had given him the direction by the aid of a Véry light. Howls and roars went up from the Huns' line, followed by short blasts on a whistle, the Germans' signal for their stretcher bearers. Our patrol had accomplished something, and we had caught their working party. " Faith, an' they won't be laughing now," remarked Flaherty as he disappeared round a traverse.

10th October.

An uneventful day. Our supports, Daly's Company, got badly crumped with 5.9s and had casualties. I went out on patrol with Sergt. Sweeney. It was a dark night, and we lay for a long time in the muddy, shell-pitted No-Man's-Land. We heard nothing. Everything was as silent as the grave, with the exception of the rats, which were squeaking and capering around us. Now and then a star-shell winged its way aloft, showing up the enemy's barbed wire, taut, shiny grey, and forbidding-looking, immediately in our front, and beyond it their sand-bagged parapet. We remained lying out for some time ; the pitch darkness made patrolling impossible. The Hun was very quiet.

After the spout of a star-shell had died away, we withdrew to our front line. In returning across the 150 yards of No-Man's-Land we must have been heard by an enemy listening post, as Véry lights were put up in quick succession, which pinned us to the chewed-up ground. A machine-gun traversed right over us as we sprawled across shell craters, we made more ground as its fire swung round and again flattened ourselves as it traversed back. The bullets were going low, just whistling " softly like," as Sweeney afterwards said, passed our ears, and cutting our barbed wire, as we saw the sparks flying from the strands as they were cut.

We had difficulty in finding the gap in our own barbed wire to get back to the trench as it had been made in a zigzag way, so as not to be apparent to the enemy. Eventually we found it, and stumbled into our front line. O'Mahoney, who was on sentry go, said : " Pass all the word, the patrol is in." Although we had not accomplished anything, yet we had discovered that the enemy furnished good listening posts with good communication to their front line.

In the early hours of the morning a rifle grenade got a direct hit on a listening post of the 2nd Sherwood Foresters on my immediate left, which knocked out all the men. This was a real piece of bad luck, and proved to us all what an extraordinary

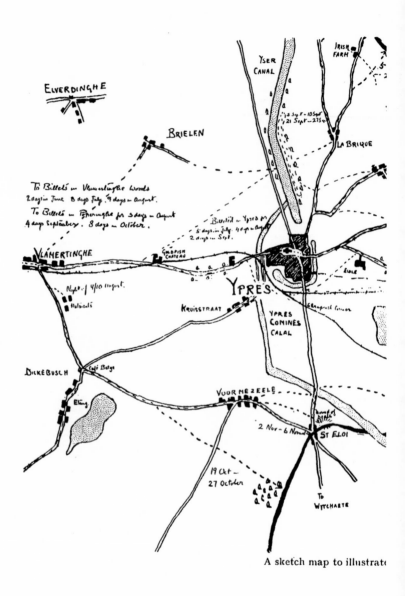

A sketch map to illustrate

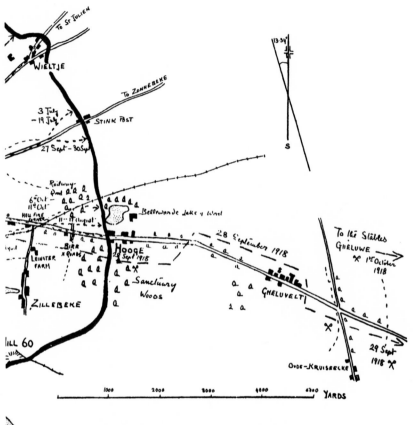

To St JULIEN

WIELTJE

To ZONNEBEKE

13·34'

S

3 July
– 19 July — STINK POST

27 Sept – 30 Sept

Railway
Pond

6ᵗʰ Oct –
11ᵗʰ Oct

HELL FIRE
CORNER — 11ᵗʰ 17 August

Bellewaarde Lake & Wood

28 September 1918

To the Stables
GHELUWE

X 1ˢᵗ October
1918

BIRR
X ROADS

HOOGE
29 Sept 1918

LEINSTER
FARM

Sanctuary
Wooods

GHELUVELT

ZILLEBEKE

HILL 60

OUDE-KRUISEELKE

29 Sept
1918 X

1000   2000   3000   4000   5000   YARDS

2ⁿᵈ Battalion's Actions & Billets in the
YPRES SALIENT during 1915.
Engagements in 1918 also marked.

varfare and open warfare at Ypres.

thing war was, that one solitary rifle grenade would wipe out a post of four men in a chance of 1000 to 1 against, whereas an hour's furious bombardment had often been known to have left a company unscathed.

11th October.

As quiet a day as I had ever experienced in the front line before Ypres. At the exact hour as stated in orders, the 1st Battalion West Yorkshire Regiment relieved us. We filed out as a frost was setting in. Heavy sniping made us wisely keep to the C.T.s, as on other occasions we always went back "over the top." I let my platoon go on in front, as I had to hand over my bomb store. Within half an hour I was following, accompanied by L/Corpl. Parker.

At Potijze I found them sitting in a ditch near the Cross Roads, eager to be off. "I'm telling ye now, 'tis no sort of a spot to be stopping at. Faith, an' ould Johnnie might put over a few of his souvenirs at any time, and mop the lot of us up, iron rations an' all." McMahon was right. I fell in the platoon, sloped arms, and so we swung off down the uneven Potijze road. There was a moon which showed the jagged silhouette of ruined houses for some distance ahead of us. The Company's rendezvous was at the Cross Roads near the Menin Gate ; we had only to wait for a few minutes before we heard the tramp of the last platoon on the cobbles, and the jingle of their mess-tins on their equipment. We got the order to move, and marched off for Poperinghe across the silent square of Ypres, " walking for all the world like a flock of ould hens on hot bricks, and expecting a shell to land on top of one of the platoons at any minute."

We passed the Square safely, and the Cloth Hall, which loomed up in the moonlight, on our right flank. How we all dreaded Ypres, even Caulfeild's charger seemed to have been infected with the Ypres fear, and shortened her usual striding steps, and turned her head from side to side, whinnying. We left silent Ypres, some of us were destined to see it again and some were not. We did not know at the time, but we were leaving the Salient for some time.

Got to our billets at the Convent before midnight, where our servants who had gone on ahead were waiting with the needful hot water for punch. The Battalion on the whole had had a quiet tour, and our casualties were below the usual average for the Potijze sector. The only thing worthy of noting was the circulation of a Battalion order to all companies to the effect that all men for patrols had to be inspected by an officer before leaving our line. A man of A Company had one night gone out on patrol under the influence of drink. When this fact was discovered the N.C.O. in charge tried to persuade him to go back, but nothing would induce him to. Instead he walked up and down in front of the enemy's wire entanglements to the left of Railway Wood, reviling the Huns in most awful language. He cursed them in the name of Cromwell, and called on all his saints, including St. Patrick, to come down and look at them! The Huns fired and machine-gunned him, but the darkness and the devil who looks after his own, saved him. He was eventually brought back by C.S.M. Kerrigan, who had felled him with one blow, a dazed, hiccoughing lump of mortality, but absolutely unscathed!

12th October.

Rode off to the field cashier's in Fusilier Wood, Vlamertinghe, on the late C.O.'s (Colonel Reeve) grey. Drew payment for the Battalion, and rode back along the main Ypres road. My mount, which was always very keen and excitable, seemed more so than ever, and bolted with me when we were overtaking a battery of Heavies. We clattered down the middle of the road, my horse's hoofs ringing on the steel-like cobbles. Just before we got to the " Pop " railway station, I managed to get it under control. I then cut across country to the Convent. To have done this at first would have been impossible, as the road was lined on either side by numerous defence lines and masses of barbed-wire entanglements.

I paid out the Company, had breakfast, and attended orderly-room with a few defaulters. After the crimes had been dealt with and orders read out, the C.O. sent for me, and told me that as Caulfeild was going away for a few weeks to act as a liaison officer with artillery, he was giving me temporary command of C Company. He said that although there were other officers senior to me in the Battalion, yet he considered I was fit to command a company, and that the responsibility would be a good experience.

I felt very proud at having even temporary command of a company in the Battalion. Later in the morning, the C.O. had a conference with the Company Commanders. He broke the sad news that we were leaving the 6th Division with the 17th Brigade, and being sent into the 24th Division as a backbone. He also informed us that we were moving to a new sector, probably St. Eloi.

He finished up by enjoining us to tell our commands that although we were joining a new brigade to teach them how to soldier, we must not overdo the " old soldier "! At 6.30 p.m. our billets were strafed, but we had no casualties.

As the C.O. had laid such particular stress on the turn-out of the Battalion before joining the new Division, I toured Poperinghe after the shelling had ceased, in search of the following : Medal ribbons, King's and Queen's South Africa. Nearly everything in the way of British Army requirements from a pair of puttees to a brass button-stick was procurable in this little Flemish town ! After searching several of the numerous little shops in the main street, I found what I wanted, and purchased a yard or so of each ribbon. I distributed the same on my return to those entitled to wear them in C Company, just over a dozen. These old toughs were highly pleased, as the ribbons they were wearing were quite unrecognisable from the constant rubbing of their oily rifle magazines. The Quartermaster issued me out with a few dozen new cap badges. These articles of dress disappeared with extraordinary regularity after the first night in billets !

13th October.

We got orders for a battalion parade as the G.O.C. 6th Division wished to inspect, and make a farewell speech to the 17th Brigade before leaving Poperinghe and his Division.

As it was raining hard, we paraded in ground-sheets. It was a great pity, as these were awkward articles to wear, and prevented good arms drill.

Riding Matilda, I led the Company to the markers on the polo ground. At the same time the three other battalions marched up and the brigade formed three sides of a hollow square in the following order : 1st Royal Fusiliers, 1st North Staffords, ourselves, and 3rd Rifle Brigade. General Congreve, V.C., then rode up, dismounted, and gave us a fine speech. He recalled the various actions the Brigade had taken part in ; how well it had acquitted itself, and how he regretted parting with us. We gave the G.O.C. three cheers, and then marched past giving " eyes right." We marched back to the Convent by the Elverdinghe road and dismissed. Whilst the G.O.C. was addressing us, Macartney's horse, George, tried to lie down with him !

Macartney, Higgins, Plowman, and I went to " The Fancies " in the evening—a special farewell show for the 17th Brigade. In honour of the Regiment, the whole troupe sang " The Dear Little Shamrock." The last time I had heard this sung was at the " Rugger " international between Ireland and Wales in 1913. After the entertainment we all went off to 4a Rue de Dunkirk, where we had supper and a sing-song with Whitehead, the " star " of " The Fancies " ! We joined forces with some of the 1st Royal Fusiliers, one of whom was M. C. Bell.[1] At 2.30 our party broke

[1] M. C. Bell was awarded the D.S.O. and M.C. later—on the Somme in August '16—he placed a white tape under our barrage and then proceeded to dress his company along it.

up and we returned to the Convent. Going across the square, we found fresh shell-holes pitted about in the *pavé*. We afterwards learnt that Poperinghe had been badly shelled while we were having supper, and we hadn't heard it !

14th October.

At 1.45 p.m. the Company paraded on the road outside billets, which we left in a spotlessly clean condition. An inspection of the Company followed, and I found that the men were well turned out. Boots and webbing equipment had all been cleaned, and there were no deficiencies in cap badges. Their buttons were all blackened, some from gas, but under orders from the C.-in-C. brass buttons were not allowed to be cleaned. We marched off to the rendezvous in the Poperinghe Square, and were joined by the other companies, who had been billeted in different streets. Weather excellent. The Battalion looked in splendid trim as it swung across the Poperinghe Square, and the physique of all ranks excellent. Two led pack-horses followed in the wake of each company with the ammunition. Colonel Bullen-Smith, D.S.O., led the Battalion riding his grey, with the pipers in front skirling some national air.

We had a short march, as our destination was Reninghelst, some five miles south-east of "Pop." All the townsfolk, and numbers of men from the new Division we were about to join, turned out to watch us going through Reninghelst, a quaint little village situated in a well-wooded hollow. Pre-war the population of this small town was 2500, but at this date it was only half the number, the shells having scared the richer inhabitants away. The people and the new troops seemed greatly impressed by the Battalion, and the pipers ahead of it. We turned off to our camping area north-east of the town, and found rows of tents, pitched by our advance party, under some trees.

15th October.

The camp was well situated, overlooking Reninghelst, from the well-timbered high ground. The white canvas had been well splashed with mud and green paint, camouflage to conceal us from hostile aircraft. Our transport was parked hard by, and the horses were picketed along the banks of the small stream. In the morning paraded in column for the C.O., who addressed the Battalion. He was very brief, and told us the reason of the transfer, and what all ranks had to do. He said he could rely on the Battalion to show the New Army what the Regulars were like in action. He reminded us that we were drawing close to the anniversary of the battle of Prémesques, where the Battalion had fought so gallantly against overwhelming odds.

16th October.

The 17th Brigade paraded for an inspection by our Divisional Commander, Major-General J. E. Capper, late the Royal Engineers. The G.O.C. addressed the Brigade, and said he was glad to command such veterans as composed the 17th Brigade. He then inspected the Battalions by companies. When he came towards my leading platoon I called the Company to the " slope." He shook hands with me, and I accompanied him round the platoons. He asked me about the men, and their length of service. At 2.15 p.m. Macartney, Daly, Gray, Murphy, and I got orders to meet the C.O. with horses and maps, as he wanted to reconnoitre the roads leading to Dickebusch. We had a fine hack round the country. The Reninghelst area was very picturesque, and had numbers of windmills dotted around on every hillock. We had no difficulty in finding the roads, which were all fringed by a guiding line of willows. I always enjoyed seeing the Adjutant, Murphy, riding. He had a grand seat on a horse, and was always well mounted.

17th October.

The C.O. sent for company commanders after orderly-room. He informed us we were being sent to the 73rd Brigade in the new Division, and he gave us the distribution of the other three regular battalions to the brigades and the reorganisation of the 24th Division, which was as follows :

17th Brigade.	*72nd Brigade.*
1st Battalion Royal Fusiliers.	1st Battalion North Staffordshire Regiment.
3rd Battalion Rifle Brigade.	
8th S.B. The Buffs.	8th S.B. Queen's Royal West Surrey Regiment.
12th S.B. Royal Fusiliers.	9th S.B. East Surrey Regiment.
	8th S.B. Queen's Own Royal West Kent Regiment.
S.B. = Service Battalion.	

73rd Brigade.

2nd Battalion The Leinster Regiment.
9th Service Battalion Sussex Regiment.
7th   ,,   ,,   Northamptonshire Regiment.
13th   ,,   ,,   Middlesex Regiment.
12th   ,,   ,,   Sherwood Foresters (Divisional Pioneers).

The transferred Brigade kept its old number, 17, and the transferred 24th Division's 74th Brigade retained its number in the 6th Division. This 74th Brigade had been composed of service battalions of the following regiments : Norfolks, Suffolks, Bedfords, and Essex.

The C.O. then read out the 24th Division's standing orders on trench and billet discipline.

Macartney lunched with me, and afterwards we went into Reninghelst. We bought some champagne at the not too exorbitant price of 12 francs per bottle.

18th October.

At 8 a.m. all company commanders reported to the C.O. as we had to accompany him up to the new line, which we were under orders to take over next day. We rode up via Dickebusch, and left our horses at the Café Belge in charge of our grooms. We then walked up to the brasserie, where we were met by officers of the Battalion we were relieving. After a long trek in a well duck-boarded communication trench we arrived in the firing line held by a service battalion of the Royal Fusiliers. My appreciation of our new line was short—" Uninteresting area. Enemy trenches on a commanding ridge looking down into ours which run through a small wood. We hold several unhealthy-looking advanced posts, approximate breadth of No-Man's-Land, 100 yards. Much mining activity in area by both sides. One redeeming feature is having the Canadian Corps on our right flank."

I then went back and reconnoitred the support line which C Company was detailed to relieve. I found the New Army Company mustered some 300 men. Burns and I returned to the brasserie, where we found our horses. They had been brought up under cover from the Café Belge. We rode past some Belgian batteries, and struck out across country for Reninghelst. " Matilda " got very upset passing some of the countless wind-mills, which were all in action !

19th October.

At 4 p.m. we struck camp and marched off as a battalion, headed by the pipers for the trenches. At Dickebusch we turned off to the right across a marsh and through some woods to our line. I remained in rear of the Company with the bombers.

The relief was complete at 7 p.m.

20th October.

Fairly comfortable in the support line. All the men had dug-outs. We were in a very picturesque bit of country ; it certainly seemed so after Ypres salient.

A light railway ran up from the brasserie to our support lines, which was used for our ration parties at night. A stream ran from the German lines on the high ground through our trenches, and we posted sentries over it to prevent the men drinking the water as we suspected it was poisoned.

Our support line was known as P.5 and P.6, and had a redoubt in the wood called S.8. I was made responsible for this redoubt, and for holding it with two platoons, Nos. 9 and 10, under Sergt. Ginn and Corpl. O'Donoghue.

We did not look forward to being strafed in this redoubt as, apart from the parapets which were excellent, the rest consisted of wood, corrugated iron, and sandbags only ! The officers' mess was quite a good one in the way of comfort, but the word protection was forgotten when being built. It was the usual verandah type !

In the evening I went up to the front line to see A Company.

21st October.

I toured the line up to St. Eloi as I was in charge of some fatigue parties, pumping water from the C.T.s and digging a drain trench under the supervision of a sapper officer called Whitfield.[1]

22nd October.

George Murray and I went up to the front line, and then along to see the Canadians on A Company's left. They were the 21st Battalion and were a fine-looking body of men. Their trenches were in splendid condition. At night we revetted the parapets of our redoubt. I also had a party of men digging out in front of the redoubt and throwing up more earth to broaden the parapets. We left them wide enough to allow G.S. waggons to drive along them, as the men said ! Got machine-gunned several times while at work.

23rd October.

Slept most of the morning to make up for the night. The sappers brought the tracks of the light railway up as far as our company dump. O.-P. came round in the afternoon and inspected the redoubt. He gave me much information about the fighting which our 1st Battalion came in for at the Mound of Death in March.

[1] Killed on 12th May, 1916.

At 11 p.m. I was thrown out of my dug-out by the vibration of a mine explosion. Pulling on my gum-boots, I went out to see lots of Véry lights and S O S rockets shooting sky high round the village of St. Eloi. The men said "only wind," so I went back to sleep, but a new army battalion on our left kept up bursts of rapid fire throughout the night.

24th October.

Spent the morning strengthening our wire entanglements around the redoubt. We could not be observed owing to the thick undergrowth.

I went down to the brasserie with C.S.M. Morgan in the evening to meet the transport, returning with the ration parties who were shoving one of the trucks along the new railway.

There was considerable rifle fire during the evening and it seemed as if the enemy had some fixed rifles laid on our company dump and on the railway line. Bullets zipped and pinged all round and I was hit on the forearm. It must have been a ricochet as it made a jagged hole in the sleeve of my great-coat, but my arm was only grazed. The men all yelled, "Jammy one, sir," but I had no such luck !

25th October.

Very wet day. The 5th Corps Commander, Lieut.-General H. D. Fanshawe, late The Queen's Bays, inspected our line. We were very interested in his rows of medal ribbons. With Sergt. Flaherty I explored the ruins of Dead Dog's Farm and Moated Grange, but all we found were a few dead cows.

26th October.

An officer of the 9th Sussex reported and was attached to the company. I took over command of the Company as Caulfeild went to Reninghelst with a party of men to represent the Battalion at the King's review.

A German aeroplane was shot down over Voormezeele.

ACCIDENT TO THE KING

27th October.

Raining hard all day. The day of the King's review, the King's horse reared during the parade and fell back on His Majesty, who was seriously injured. At 8 p.m. we were relieved by the 9th Battalion Royal Sussex Regiment. I took the Company back via Scotch Wood and Dickebusch to some hutments known as "C" camp on the outskirts of Reninghelst. I reported the

Company present to Murphy, the Adjutant, at about 10 p.m. Weather cleared on the march. Caulfeild returned with an account of the Royal review. Apparently the troops on parade were unaware of the King's accident, which occurred on a flank when they were at the slope awaiting the order to present arms at the Royal Salute. Caulfeild stated that the Prince of Wales was particularly interested in our cap badge.

28th October.

The camp presented a dreary appearance in the morning, so many huts in a sea of mud connected by duckboards. C and D Company officers slept in one hut, Caulfeild, Macartney, Laville, Drummond, Higgins, Plowman, Todd, and myself. We arranged our valises along the sides ; it rained in the night and we got very wet as the roof leaked badly.

29th October.

At 2 p.m. C and D Companies paraded as a working party for the line under Caulfeild, one man of D had had too much beer.

Sixteen G.S. waggons of the 24th Divisional Ammunition Column (Mules) arrived for our conveyance to Dickebusch, where we were decanted. Tea having been issued out from a company cooker at the Café Belge, we paraded in parties under guides. I moved off to Voormezeele with part of my platoon and No. 11 with Sergt. Hart. Here I reported to a sapper officer near the convent ruins, who brought us for a terrible trek to work on a flooded C.T. near Hill 60.

We had the very hell of a job as it was raining hard all the time. We dug large sump pits just off the C.T. and managed to drain off some of the water. I was better off than the men as I was wearing gum-boots. Looking about in the open, I came on the bodies of three British soldiers who, judging from their appearance, seemed to have been lying out for some time. We finished our task at 12 p.m. and moved off for Voormezeele. We had a terrible march back through mud and slush along the canal by Spoil Bank. To make matters worse it was a pitch-dark night.

At Voormezeele the sapper officer brought me to his dug-out behind the convent and gave me a much-needed whisky. I then struck out for the Café Belge, which we reached at 2 a.m. The Companies were forming up and getting into the G.S. waggons when we joined the convoy, fagged to the world.

Got back to camp at 3 a.m., very wet and cold. Hot tea was waiting for all.

30th October.

The Battalion had, by this time, discovered that rest in Reninghelst consisted of continual fatigues. The Battalion paraded daily, and was taken up in G.S. waggons as far as Dickebusch, where it unloaded and split itself into carrying and digging parties for destinations at St. Éloi and Hill 60.

31st October.

Companies detailed for fatigues under the R.E. sappers. At 2 p.m. we paraded and got the men mounted into waggons for the front line. We got badly bumped going along the cobbled roads, the mules being very slow. Macartney was in command of the convoy. At Voormezeele we were split up into parties and a sapper officer came along with me. He set me a task in the vicinity of Oosthoek, behind the front line. One of our parties must have been heard as we were shelled with " whiz-bangs " for some time, splinters flew about, but we had no casualties. We knocked off work at 12 p.m. In this area there was no support line, it had to be abandoned owing to being full of water. At 2.30 a.m. we got back to our camp in Reninghelst.

1st November.

Ordinary day in billets. Orders circulated to companies for the relief of the 1st North Staffords in the front line at the " Mound of Death " on the morrow. Company commanders went off on reconnaissance and returned at night with a bad account of our new line. For the past month the area round the ruins of St. Eloi had witnessed much fighting. Three mines had been exploded, and there was the usual scrapping for possession of the craters.

Our Division expected an attack, and we were detailed to hold the position. Platoon commanders were given maps, and were told to explain the situation to the men. It was during this so-called rest, which was in reality one long endless fatigue, that Headquarters issued orders that owing to the unsavoury tone in the word " fatigue " in future the term " working party " must be used.

It was pointed out that these working parties performed most important work, and that there was as much honour and glory in a " fatigue " party as there was in being the attacking troops. We were ordered to read this out on parade. I did so, and when I had finished one " old tough " was overheard to remark : " Begorra, ye can change the bloody name but the fatigue is still there."

Secret

The General Officer Commanding directs me to request. that you will particularly impress on the Officers of your brigade, & through them on all ranks, that the word "mine" is not to be mentioned at any time or in any way in connection with the trenches. The word "sap" may be mentioned as far as necessary. He regards this as of the first importance, in order that as far as possible secrecy may be maintained concerning any of our operations.

The reason for not using this word is also to be explained carefully to the men.

Further, any sandbags filled at a sap shaft are on no account to be built into the parapet or dug-outs or used for any other purpose in the vicinity of the sap. They must be removed to in rear of the support trenches. The reason for this will also be explained to all ranks, viz, that when filled these sacks will be wet and of a bluish colour, and as such will be readily recognisable by the enemy. If used near the sap shaft & recognised they will disclose to him the position of the shaft & draw shell fire.

(Sd) A. Stewart L[t] Colonel
G.S. 24th Division

13.10.15

O.C "C" Coy

all ranks.

20.10.15.

Above to be brought to the notice of

A D Whiffy Capt.
Adj' Leinster Regiment

The word "mine" was also scrapped, "sap" being substituted, owing, they said, to the Huns getting to know about our mining activity. There was a rumour afloat that it was the intention of the Higher Command to stop the rum issue and give hot coffee in lieu. Fortunately nothing materialised in this direction and we all breathed in peace once more.

ST. ELOI

2nd November.

At 3 p.m. paraded for the trenches, and the Battalion, headed by the pipers, marched to Dickebusch, which we reached at dusk. At Voormezeele I remained behind with Sergt. Flaherty[1] to bring up the bombers and their bombs. Leaving Voormezeele after darkness had set in, we took to the communication trench. However, using it was out of the question as it was under water from the recent heavy rains.

As the heavily laden bombers slid and staggered at every step owing to the duckboards tilting sideways underfoot, we left the C.T. and marched up to the trenches by road. At the barrier at St. Eloi we got into the front line, and branched off to the left.

We discovered that the line was equally as bad as the C.T. It was water-logged, and the inky darkness of the night added to our difficulties. This sector of the line was held by the North Staffords, and the fire bays were fully occupied. Gradually the line became worse, and when we got to our Company flank we found practically no trench at all. We seemed to have been in one continuous nightmare of mud. Many of my heavily laden bombers were engulfed in the trench, and had to be helped out.

Words cannot describe the state of our new line, and rain was falling heavily to complete our discomfort. Practically the whole company front was under water, and the floating duckboards would fly up and hit the unwary one in the face when stood upon. At 9 p.m. we relieved A Company of the 1st North Staffordshire Regiment. In our company front there were three mine craters to hold. The North Staffords reported the Huns particularly hostile.

All the craters were in the middle of No-Man's-Land as the mines had in every case failed to reach the lines, and both sides held the near lips by saps run for about 50 yards from the main trench. Wet up to my waist, I put out the unfortunate bombers in the listening posts. The enemy hurled bombs for some time,

---

[1] Unfortunately this very gallant N.C.O. got badly torn by barbed wire when out on patrol at a later date, tetanus set in and he died, to be deplored by all ranks in the Battalion.

1915

THE MOUND OF DEATH

N ——— S

12⁹ᵗʰ Saxon Regt

A CRATER

B CRATER (30 yards long)

C CRATER

Fallen Trees

"C" Coy H.Q.

SHELLEY FARM

Nos 9 and 10 platoons

Sheet of water pumped from Mine Shaft.

SAP HEAD

WHITE HORSE CELLARS

ROAD FROM YPRES

St. ELOI

"C" Company 2nd Leinster Regt. at St. Eloi, Ypres.

and then became silent. Having been warned of an expected
attack, we kept very much on the alert throughout the night.
There were only a dozen dug-outs in the whole line. Caulfeild and
Plowman shared one, and Burns and I another. One of our
advanced posts was very difficult to get to ; going over the open
was impossible, owing to the mud and wire entanglements.
There was, however, a fallen tree trunk lying across the trench
which was flooded to a depth of two feet. By hanging on to the
foot of a Boche corpse, which was protruding out of the so-called
parapet, one managed to get to the post without getting drowned.

Burns and I sat up for the remainder of the night, taking turns
to visit the posts every hour. A rum ration was issued ; also
smelly goat-skins which had got soaked being brought up with
the rations and the mail.

It poured throughout the night, and Sergt. Ginn kept reporting
that a dug-out or parapet had fallen in on top of one of the men,
and then we would have to muster a rescue party. It was truly
a terrible night.

3rd November.

At 6 o'clock Sergt. Ginn called me to say that the enemy were
walking about on their parapets. Burns and I went out to find
that some Germans were walking about in the mist, swinging coke
braziers to and fro to keep them alight ! Like us, they were
caked in mud. We did not fire, as they, being on the brow of the
ridge, had the advantage over us. At stand to I went round the
Company and found the men wonderfully cheery, in spite of
the terrible conditions. The rain had stopped, and it had started
to freeze hard.

During the morning gum boots were issued out to all ranks.
However, as they only came up to one's knees, and as in most
places the water came well up the thighs, they welled water at
every step. The result was that the owners often preferred to
pull their feet out of them by the aid of the suction of the mud,
and carry on in their socks !

All morning spent in trying to drain out the water. Sump pits
were dug, as the only trench pump available would not function.
Fatigue parties worked away with old biscuit tins, and baled the
water out over the parados. We all walked about in the open as
the Saxons were also walking out on their parapets. Their
trenches, although on the high ground, were water-logged, and
we watched them bailing and pumping water into the large mine
crater. The Colonel inspected the line with the Second in
Command, Major Orpen-Palmer.

I carried on, wearing boots and puttees, and I was thoroughly wet. Salvos of "Little Willies" were fired at us all day, but we had no casualties. Most of the shells exploded harmlessly in Shelley Farm. It froze hard all night. I was on duty from 12–6 a.m. and shivered all the time. Every time I visited the outposts meant getting wet, as the C.T.s could not be drained.

4th November.

Stood the Company to in the early hours of the morning, and visited all the advanced posts. Went on my rounds along the parapets in the following kit : a Balaclava helmet, a goat-skin coat (inside out, as the hairy side got soaked rubbing against the muddy trenches), waders, my webbing equipment, and a revolver. Some soldier ! The enemy shouted out " Good morning " to me. When I was in front of the largest crater, I watched six Germans coming up in the open, and getting into one of their advanced posts. Six more got out with their rifles slung, and with braziers in their hands, yelled " Good-bye " to me, and went back to their main trench. The relief started to try and fraternise with us immediately. During the morning we witnessed a very fine aeroplane scrap just behind our line. Three enemy planes which had been patrolling over our area all morning were attacked by one of our Vickers fighters. The latter, who displayed great pluck, drove off two of the enemy, and after some fine manœuvring, managed to shoot the third down. He fired a short burst of his machine-gun. The enemy seemed to waver, and then nose-dived into a small copse, which fringed the Ypres–Comines canal. We afterwards heard that the plane crashed on top of a dug-out belonging to the 3rd Division, who were on our left, killing two men of the 1st Battalion Royal Scots Fusiliers. The C.O. and Second in Command inspected our line, and were well satisfied with the amount of work we had done on the trenches. At 12.30 p.m. I counted four 17-inch shells going over our lines in the Ypres direction.

During the night there was some sniping on D Company's front. Pte. Levis, brother of 2nd Lieut. Levis of the 1st Battalion, was shot. He was a stretcher bearer in D Company.

In the early hours next morning, C.S.M. Brereton sniped two Huns to make up for Levis being killed. On duty from 3 to 6 a.m. which watch included " Stand to."

5th November.

About dawn the frost broke, and the trenches became as bad as ever. The sand-bags of the few remaining revetments bulged outwards and collapsed. The cold was intense, at " Stand to " I

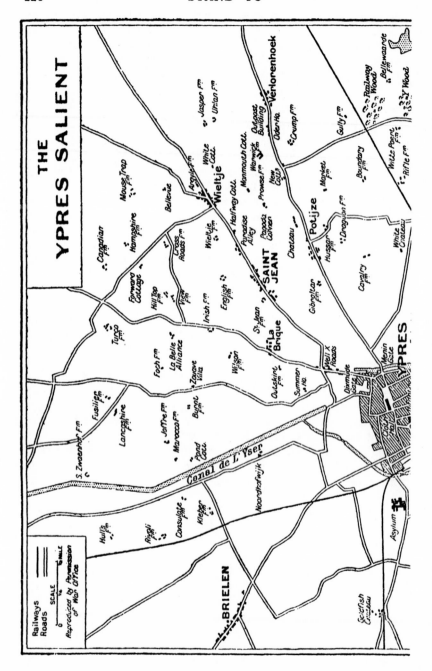

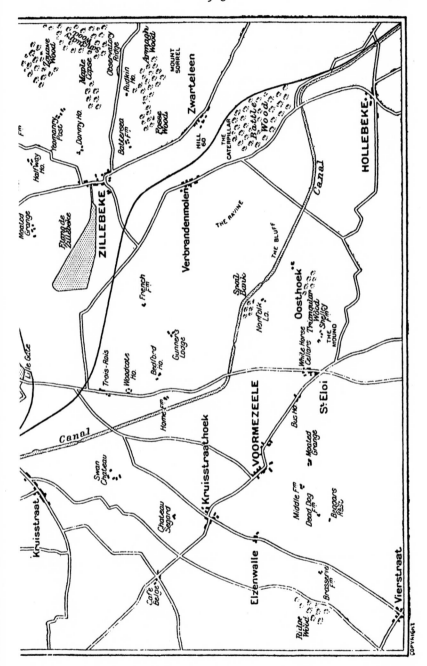

found the men so benumbed that some were unable to pull back the bolts of their rifles.

At dawn throughout this tour I went round all posts armed with a rum jar. After the N.C.O. in charge had reported his command present and his rifles clean, each man of the post filed up to me, and I issued him his "tot" in a small metal cup. I never saw the rum more appreciated than it was during this tour.

The "old toughs" who had been up all night in a water-logged sap-head would hold out their ration and say: "best of luck, sorr," or "best respects," and drain the rum in one gulp.

'07 Kelly said to me one morning after he had drunk his tot, "Begorra, 'tis wonderful, sorr. 'Tis trickling yet." And they all in turn would lick their lips, stamp their feet, and so life would smile on them again. The ration rum was excellent, and as Kelly said, when frozen through after a long wet night, one could feel the rum trickling down into one's very toes ! I asked one of the old "sweats" what he thought the initials S.R.D. which was on every rum jar meant, and he replied, "Soon Run Dry."

At 6 a.m. our line was systematically shelled with whiz-bangs. On going round one of the traverses into a fire bay I found that there had been a direct hit. Drummer Spencer was killed ; Pte. Farrell was bleeding badly from the head and had his eye out, and Pte. Richards was wounded in the ear. They had been sitting round a brazier, making tea for their breakfasts, and had, no doubt, drawn fire with the smoke. When I got to them, the poor fellows were lying half submerged in the liquid mud, with pools of blood all round. Our casualties up-to-date amounted to 7.

At 11 a.m. the G.O.C., Major-General Capper, toured our line with his galloper Murray, and expressed himself well satisfied with the work the Battalion had done on the line, and he liked the great spirit of the men. He told the C.O. that he was particularly struck with the reply of "Grand entirely, sir," from a man of D Company, who was frost-bitten and lying in a sea of mud, when he, the General, asked him how he was. This shows how the morale held up, in spite of the terrible exposure to weather, the water-logged trenches, and the continued subjection to shell-fire without sufficient cover.

In the evening, I visited C Company's H.Q., where Macartney gave me a drink, and then returned with me accompanied by Drummond, to see the Germans opposite the crater. He spoke to them in German, and to try and find out some information about them, he chucked over a small flask of whisky. It fell short, so I retrieved it and gave it to them, and they

St Eloi. November 1915,

Sketch of the village of St. Eloi, The Mound of Death, and Bus House.

clapped their hands. I saw " 129 " on their shoulder straps, and had a good look into their advanced post.

TOPOGRAPHY OF THE ST. ELOI SECTOR

The German lines ran along the top of the predominating ridge, which lay east of Ypres from Hooge to Wytchaete. Just below ran the British trenches, but never any further distant than 150 yards. At St. Eloi, at the neck of the Salient, the lines came very close together and ran astride the main Ypres–Wytchaete road, with not more than 50 yards separating them. The village of St. Eloi itself, now reduced to a small cluster of ruins, stood at the junction of the cross-roads Ypres–Wytchaete and Voormezeele–Warneton, on the highest part of the commanding ground, and was held by the enemy. Constant shell-fire had reduced the ridge to a state of nakedness. It was devoid of all trees, and all signs of vegetation. The scene which met the eyes on looking over the parapets was that of the enemy's dense wire entanglements, mostly consisting of large *chevaux de frise*, behind which the jagged silhouette of the crumbling ruins of St. Eloi stuck out against the sky, and slightly to the left, or south-east of the village, stood a large mound of earth, or tumulus, known as the " Mound of Death."

St. Eloi was a most important part of the line, and had the enemy been able to advance their line in this locality our trenches running round Ypres would have become untenable. Owing to its importance strategically, St. Eloi had witnessed many fierce battles, and since October, '14, the ridge had been occupied alternately by British and Germans. As a regiment, this sector had a great link with our records. In the early fighting, our 1st Battalion, of the 27th Division, who had just arrived from Fyzabad, greatly distinguished itself, and was mentioned in Sir John French's despatches, together with Princess Patricia's Canadian Light Infantry, for gallantry in the February and March operations. Here and there behind our line were graves of some of our 1st Battalion, and in the ruined cemetery at Voormezeele there were numbers of our officers and men buried. This fact alone testified to the fierce fighting and how heavily the Regiment had been engaged.

Here we were, the 2nd Battalion, in the same sector, just eight months afterwards, not fighting in the real sense of the word, but holding gamely to an exposed trench line under the most deplorable conditions imaginable. During this tour, a noted landmark, " The Bus," which had been lying derelict on the side of the

road to Voormezeele, 300 yards behind our line, was salved by
A Company and pushed down to Dickebusch.

An old ruined house, which it had been ditched alongside since
the early days, had been named officially " Bus House " on all the
maps. It was during this tour that we made the acquaintance of
the sector mascot, a Sapper L/Corpl., who was in charge of the
mining parties just behind my platoon's trench. He strolled
into our dug-out one night to have a chat, and we gave him some
rum. He was an Irishman and stood well over six feet.

In reply to Burns' and my questions, he replied :

" Yus, sir, I was alongside your other battalion here in March,
when they retook ' The Mound.' They left me here, me being in
charge of all the mines, do ye see, when they went off to the
Sanctuary Woods (East of Ypres) and here I've been ever since.
One week I blows 'em, and faith and the next week they blows us,
and in the meantime, I takes a promenade down to Voormezeele
and back." (At this period Voormezeele was in ruins, and just
one kilometre behind the line.) " And by the same token, this
dug-out we're in now is undermined by the Alleymen."

And with this joyful remark he took his departure. He was a
splendid type and well known for his stout heart.

Sergt. Ginn and I were out at night wiring. We connected
up the crater lips, the Germans heard us, but did not try to molest
us, as they were on the same wiring stunt themselves !

It was very strange out wiring, Germans and British working
away in the darkness, and less than 15 yards separating them.

Caulfeild walked out to see how we were getting on with our
task. He mistook the enemy party for our own, and walked
slap into them, and to make matters worse, got stuck in the
mud ! His orderly went to his assistance and extricated
him.

I received orders to proceed to the U.K. on the following day
for a course. These instructions, as can be imagined, were not
received with any mixed feelings of regret.

6th November.

Visited the sentry posts at 7 a.m. and at the bottom of the
largest crater I found Pte. Bates, an A Company bomber who
was rather undersized and comical looking and who had been
lent to us for the tour, fraternising with a German who spoke a
little English. The following was their conversation :

Bates : " What rank are you in your army ? " Saxon : " I am
a corporal," indicating stripes on his collar. " What rank are
you ? "—" Oh," replied Bates, " I am Company Sergt.-Major ! "

The German was a fine-looking specimen, and was wearing the ribbon of the Iron Cross from the second button-hole in his tunic.

I left the trenches accompanied by Jackson at 2 p.m., just a few hours ahead of the Battalion, who were relieved by the 1st North Staffs. We left behind a good fire trench for our relieving unit. It is not too much to say that the efficiency of a regiment can be tested by a comparison between the state in which it takes over, and that in which it leaves its trenches.

Having reported at Battalion H.Q., situated in a ruined house at Voormezeele, Jackson and I cut across country for Dickebusch, where we had the good luck to find a lorry belonging to the A.S.C. on the way to Reninghelst. Got into billets early, and packed my valise, and had dinner with Prendergast,[1] the Doctor, George Murray,[2] and Squire.

When we were at dinner, No. 7071 Corpl. T. Leavy, D.C.M., came along. At 6 a.m. in the morning he had left the front line for Poperinghe, where he was going to be presented with the Médaille Militaire by a French General. He had first gone to the transport lines to shave and clean up (shaving was out of the question at St. Eloi). However, at the transport he had been told that he would be late for the investiture if he waited to clean up, and rather than miss it he "hopped" on the nearest lorry at Reninghelst for Poperinghe without the necessary clean up ! His own description of the investiture was as follows :

" Begad, sorr. 'Twas grand entirely, Froggie General and all. He shook me by the hand, and to me utter astonishment, kissed me on both sides of me face, and me with the two-days' growth."

Promoted sergeant later, Leavy was killed on 7/3/16.

At about 10 p.m. the Battalion arrived in billets, tired and covered in mud, but in great spirits, although there was nothing more to look forward to than a few nights' rest in the cold, draughty, wooden huts of A camp, accompanied with endless fatigues to the front line. This last tour had told on the Battalion. We had suffered from spasmodic bursts of shell-fire which accounted for a number, but a new enemy, " frost-bite," or trench feet, had claimed more than its share of victims. About a dozen men, including Higgins,[3] had gone down the line that day with the latter complaint. The strength of the Battalion was not much more than 500 all told.

[1] Severely wounded on the Menin Road at the beginning of 1916.
[2] Killed commanding a company on the 4/6/16.
[3] Killed later on Vimy Ridge on the 31st March, 1917. Lieut. M. A. Higgins was a brother of Mr. Kevin O'Higgins, I.F.S. Minister, who was shot in Dublin in 1926.

Roll of the officers, warrant officers, and staff sergeants on the strength of the Battalion on the 6th November, 1915 :

Headquarters.

Lieut.-Colonel Bullen-Smith, D.S.O.
Major Orpen-Palmer, Second in Command.
Capt. Murphy, M.C., Adjutant.
Capt. Prendergast, Transport Officer.
Lieut. Murray, Machine-Gun Officer.
Lieut. and Quartermaster Squire.
R.S.M. Smith, D.C.M.
R.Q.M.S. Vickery.
Colour-Sergt. Phelan, Orderly-room Sergeant.

A Company.

Capt. Gray.
2nd Lieut. Stirling.
2nd Lieut. Young.
2nd Lieut. Johnston.
2nd Lieut. Burns, D.C.M. Bombing Officer.
C.S.M. Kerrigan, D.C.M.
C.Q.M.S. Bond.

B Company.

Capt. Daly, D.S.O.
Lieut. Newport.
Lieut. Todd.
2nd Lieut. Brassington.
C.S.M. Brereton.
C.Q.M.S. Kimberley.

C Company.

Capt. Caulfeild.
2nd Lieut. Hitchcock.
2nd Lieut. Plowman.
C.S.M. Morgan.
C.Q.M.S. Brill.

D Company.

Capt. Macartney, M.C.
Lieut. Laville.
2nd Lieut. Drummond.
C.Q.M.S. Hartley.
Sergt. Bennett, D.C.M., Machine-Gun Sergeant.
Sergt. McCarthy, Transport Sergeant.
Sergt. Tobias, Armourer Sergeant.
Sergt. Flaherty, Bombing Sergeant.
Sergt. Pettitt, Signalling Sergeant.

At 2 a.m. I left a sleeping hut, and went to the horse lines, where I found Donoghue awaiting me with the Mess cart.

When we got on the *pavé* of the main road, the horse jibbed, and we could not get him to move. In the end, he backed us off the road into a big dyke. Luckily we were not hurt owing to the cart having iron bands round it to keep up its awning. Jackson and I scrambled out, leaving the driver unharnessing his charge, went back to the horse lines, and got another conveyance.

This time we got a good horse with the Maltese cart. We got to Poperinghe, where I just managed to catch the " Blighty " train for Boulogne. It was still dark when I shook hands with Jackson, as we steamed out of the station at 4 a.m.

7th November.

At 11.30 a.m. I got to Boulogne, where I had lunch with a fellow in the Grenadiers who was attached to the R.F.C.

At 3 p.m. our boat sailed for Folkestone, which we reached after a not-too-smooth crossing.

1916

AT the beginning of July I received orders to rejoin the British Expeditionary Force, France, from Cork, where I had been stationed in Victoria Barracks attached to our 3rd Battalion. Cork was a very cheery spot, and I had a good many friends serving with the 3rd Battalion, in Algeo, George Read,[1] Stirling, Holland, and Ducat. There were numbers of 2nd Battalion N.C.O.s and men in Cork recovering or recovered from wounds, awaiting orders for drafts for the Front. Some of them, including C.S.M. Boyer, came over to the Mess to say good-bye to me the morning I left. Reserve battalions in the War performed a most important rôle, i.e. feeding the battalions in the field with officers and men. All recruits passed through the 3rd Battalion at Cork, as Birr, our depôt, was too small for training purposes, and for the numbers of personnel and attached.

14th July.

In the evening I sailed from Kingstown with " Tin-Belly "[2] Holland, who was also under orders for the B.E.F. Ray Stirling, who had been badly wounded with the 2nd Battalion, came to see me off. There was a large number of officers on board belonging to Irish regiments. This was the first month of the Somme offensive ; the majority of the Irish regiments had been engaged, and had suffered severely.

The long casualty lists which had appeared daily since the 1st of the month accounted for the number of reinforcement officers sailing. As our boat moved off from the pier, a band playing on the Marina struck up, " Come back to Erin," which happened to be our regimental march.

15th July.

We arrived at Euston Station at about 6.30 a.m. ; as we had to report to the Embarkation Officer at Folkestone before 11 a.m. we had only time to shave, wash, and breakfast in town. Several

---

[1] Killed 9th March, 1917.
[2] So called because he had served as a trooper in the Life Guards before receiving his commission in the 3rd Leinsters. Pre-War he had been a veterinary student.

train-loads of troops left Victoria Station for the Front. There were a number of men returning from leave in the U.K., but the majority were reinforcements. We sailed at midday, and were escorted for the greater part of the passage by a destroyer. After a calm crossing, we landed at Boulogne within an hour and a half. At 5 p.m. we left Boulogne, and entrained for Etaples and our destination, the 16th Infantry Base Depôt, arriving in time for dinner. We were allotted to Nissen huts, with straw on the floor. I put a fine bundle of straw under my valise, and slept soundly.

16th July.

Reported to the Adjutant of the Base Depôt, Capt. Featherstonehaugh, Royal Scots Fusiliers.

Hot weather. Camp very congested and accommodation for officers poor. Mess arrangements left a lot to be desired. There were several sittings for meals.

Met Galway of the 2nd Royal Irish and an old friend in McCarthy-O'Leary of the 1st Royal Munster Fusiliers.

17th July.

Training for war the daily programme. This consisted in marching off to big open area some five kilometres distant. Here there were various classes for bombing, bayonet fighting, and P.T. Those of us who had been " out before," as they called it, were excused these tortures! The training ground went by the appropriate name of " The Bull Ring." The Australians had a camp close by with a wet canteen which was greatly patronised by the officers of the 16th I.B.D.!

18th and 19th July.

Paraded all morning, drill, and short route marches. The men in our Base Depôt consisted of the following regiments : Royal Irish, Connaught Rangers, Leinsters, and Munsters. On account of the large casualties, drafts were being sent up the line to feed fighting battalions daily. Owing to the heavy demands for reinforcements from the Somme area, there seemed to be no discrimination with regard to men being sent to their own units. Two hundred men of the Connaught Rangers were sent up the line to join the Munsters, who had suffered severely in the attack on Mametz Wood. A Leinster draft of over fifty was sent to the Black Watch! Posting men of one Irish regiment to another was reasonable, but sending Leinsters to join any regiment but an Irish one gave cause for much legitimate grousing.

20th July.

McCarthy-O'Leary[1] and I went into Paris Plage on a tramcar. Palin of the 1st Battalion arrived at the Base camp. He had just been promoted captain. I had not met him before. Palin and I became firm friends in those days at Etaples. He was the first fellow I saw wearing the newly introduced gold stripes, worn on the left arm to indicate wounds in action. He had been wounded twice with the 1st Battalion, once actually with a bayonet.

21st to 22nd July.

Still at the Base, awaiting orders for the Front.

23rd July.

Palin and I were dining in Etaples, when we got orders to report immediately to camp. We finished our bottle of red wine, and returned to find orders for the Front awaiting us. We were both posted to the 2nd Battalion, as we expected, and Holland of the 3rd Battalion got orders to join our 7th Service Battalion, with which he was destined to win the V.C. within seven weeks.

As we said *au revoir* Holland said to me " I am going to get one of two things, a Victoria Cross or a Wooden Cross." It turned out to be no idle boast ; his luck was in and he gained a richly deserved V.C., for, as the Gazette stated, " he undoubtedly broke the spirit of the enemy before Guillemont."

We left camp at dawn for Etaples siding. Palin and I got in a train marked for Bailleul, Holland's destination was in another direction, and he went off with a number of fellows under orders to join our 7th Battalion.

Had a short halt on our journey at St. Omer. Here we found a party of sowars belonging to the Deccan Horse,[2] and Palin chatted to them in Hindustani.

At Hazebrouck we had lunch in a small *estaminet* close to the station, and entrained again for Bailleul, which we reached about 4 p.m. The R.T.O., arrayed in blue tabs, had orders for us regarding transport to the Battalion's billets. We got to Battalion Headquarters after an eight-kilometres' drive in an old taxi.

[1] Killed on the Somme, 6th September, 1916.
[2] A regiment which had greatly distinguished itself on the 14th July by charging against the enemy trenches between High and Delville Woods. This was the first occasion on which cavalry had been used in their correct rôle since the stagnant trench warfare had set in. The Germans bolted before them, but eventually machine-guns and barbed wire held them up. For some weeks before their " show " they had practised their horses jumping over trenches—formidable obstacles to negotiate. The Indian Expeditionary Force had been brought to France in 1914 by General Sir James Willcocks, K.C.B., D.S.O., late The Leinster Regiment.

The Battalion was billeted in a few large farmhouses, spread round the village of Godewaersvelde, near Flêtre. Palin was posted to B Company, and I rejoined C Company. The following was the distribution of officers to the four companies at this date:

Headquarters.

Lieut.-Colonel Orpen-Palmer, D.S.O.
Major Murphy, M.C., 2nd in Command.
Lieut. Burns, D.C.M., a/Adjutant.
2nd Lieut. Whitby, Intelligence, 4th Batt.
2nd Lieut. Möllmann, Lewis-Gun Officer, 4th Batt.
2nd Lieut. Plowman, Transport.
Lieut. and Quartermaster Squire.
Rev. Father Doyle.

A Company.

Capt. K. G. O'Morchoe, 5th Batt.
Capt. Newport, 4th Batt.
Lieut. McNamara.
2nd Lieut. Sharp.
2nd Lieut. O'Connor, 3rd Batt.
2nd Lieut. Magner, 3rd Batt.

C Company.

Capt. Poole.
Lieut. Liston, 5th Batt.
2nd Lieut. Handcock, 3rd Batt.
2nd Lieut. Jameson, 4th Batt.
2nd Lieut. French.
2nd Lieut. Hyde-Sander.

B Company.

Capt. Barry, 3rd Batt.
Lieut. Crowe, 4th Batt.
2nd Lieut. Brassington.
2nd Lieut. Powell, 4th Batt.
Lieut. Todd, 3rd Batt.
2nd Lieut. Siddons, 4th Batt.

D Company.

Capt. Laville.
Capt. Frend, 3rd Batt.
2nd Lieut. Thornley, 3rd Batt.
2nd Lieut. Dobbie, 4th Batt.
2nd Lieut. Smyth, 3rd Batt.
2nd Lieut. Hall, 4th Batt.

Palin and I made the strength of officers up to 33, and brought the strength of regulars up to 11.

Regimental Sergt.-Major Smith, D.C.M.
Regimental Q.M.S. Vickery.

The Battalion was well up to strength. They had just come out of a quiet sector of the line Wytschaete, and were "fattening up" for the Somme Battle. Got a nice welcome from the men of the Company.

I noticed quite a few of the Battalion stretcher-bearers wearing the medal ribbon of the newly instituted Military Medal awarded for bravery in the field. Battalion organisation was practically the same as it was at the end of 1915, with the exception of the complete disappearance of the Machine-Gun Sections. Earlier in the year, all the Vickers guns had been taken from battalions, and together with their crews had been sent to form a new corps called the " Machine-Gun Corps." The Vickers had been replaced by a much lighter automatic gun, named the " Lewis Gun." This gun was a very shoddy affair after the Vickers, and it fired magazines containing forty-seven rounds, instead of belts of 250 rounds.

The distribution of these L.G.s was one per platoon, and at a later date was augmented to two guns per platoon.

There was an important addition to equipment ; steel shrapnel helmets, after the French idea, but of a totally different shape, had been issued. They were very cumbersome and heavy, but one got used to them after a time.

The billets were of the usual French kind, a farmhouse, barns, and stables forming three sides of a square, plus a manure heap, with the accompanying smell, in the centre !

At a distance, French or Flemish homesteads looked very picturesque with their red-tiled roofs and tall poplar trees standing all round like sentinels, but otherwise they were pretty obnoxious places. I was given command of No. 11 Platoon ; my platoon sergeant was a Boer War veteran, in Sergt. Henry.

25th July.

Battalion received movement orders. At 2 p.m. we paraded, and marched off to a railway siding close by, where we entrained for the Somme. Had a long journey to Amiens via Hazebrouck–St. Omer–St. Pol–Doullens. At 1.30 a.m. we detrained at Amiens and C Company were detailed to unload the transport vehicles.

This task took us the best part of an hour, as it was pitch dark ; the drivers being kept occupied with the horses. We then dressed and marched off to join the Battalion, which had fallen out on the side of the road awaiting us. At 2.30 p.m. we moved from this siding, called Longpré, for billets at Molliens-Vidame, some twelve kilometres distant.

26th July.

We arrived at Molliens-Vidame at 7 a.m. after a good trek. It was better marching in the cool of the night than in the heat of the day.

27th–30th July.

The men were allowed a good rest before training parades started. This day only inspections were carried out, but severe training programmes were sent round from Battalion Head-quarters for the remainder of our rest.

My former batman, 8243 Jackson, had been temporarily looking
after an officer in D Company, however, Poole got him back for me,
Molliens-Vidame was a typical little French village, with nice
surroundings. The Battalion billets were quite good. Companies
ran their own messes separately. C Company were allotted a
school for their mess, and the men had a large yard at the back,
with goodish outhouses.

I slept on the floor of a small room above our mess. Four
subalterns joined in : W. J. Porter, who had been at Campbell with
me, where he had been a brilliant wing three-quarter, and A. P.
Gately, who was transferred from the Army Service Corps. He
was a cheery cove who had been a veterinary student before the
War. Also Hamilton and McCann. Palin appointed Adjutant.

Daily we carried out strenuous training programmes. The area
allotted was only a short distance from billets, but we paraded at
an early hour in battle order. The important item was practising
for the new barrage system of shell-fire. We were taught how to
advance when the barrage lifted ; to make things more realistic,
the Battalion drummers beat a roll to represent shell-fire.

We advanced at walking pace, the men carrying their rifles at
the high port. The Battalion attacked in waves of platoons on a
two-company frontage ; each wave had its special rôle, and was
followed by a party called the " Moppers-up." The moppers-up
were made responsible for clearing up all captured trenches,
destroying all dug-outs and killing or capturing all spare Huns !
At the beginning of the offensive some Divisions had bitter
experiences when capturing several lines without these " Moppers-
up." There were several instances of Germans in the front lines
scuttling into their deep dug-outs allowing the British to advance
on to their second objective, and then coming to the surface
again with machine-guns to pour a withering fire into the backs
of the attackers.

The evenings at Molliens-Vidame were devoted to boxing
contests, or a concert party organised by some officers in the
73rd Brigade. Swan, of the Northamptons, put on an amusing
turn after " Bric-à-brac." The Battalion won all the boxing
competitions. While we were billeted in this quiet little French
village, we heard a town crier with a drum going through the main
street, calling out the casualties amongst the natives of the
locality. The French always employed this method for informing
the next-of-kin during the War.

All officers were instructed in the handling of the Lewis Gun
under the L.G. officer, one Möllmann, of German extraction. He
was a fine fellow, and proved himself to be a first-class soldier.
Each brigade in the 24th Division had a distinctive sign and each

regiment had a special colour. The 2nd Leinsters wore a yellow square on each shoulder with a diamond in a company colour. A Company had a blue diamond. Green, which was the colour of another brigade, would have been more suitable for us. We always joked about a yellow or orange colour for a southern Irish regiment, but as we were a line battalion politics was a subject which fortunately officers and men gave a wide berth to.

ON THE SOMME

31st July.

At 5 a.m. the Battalion left Molliens-Vidame for Fluy, where we entrained after a short march of six kilometres in the cool of the morning. At Amiens we detrained, as there was no further railway accommodation for us. There were rumours of buses being placed at our disposal, but they never materialised, and at 10 a.m. we struck out on a fourteen miles' march.

We were the only regiment in the Brigade to march this journey. It was a long trek in the heat of the day, and to make matters worse, part of the 13th Middlesex overtook us in buses, and covered us with dust. C Company led the Battalion, and the C.O. marched ahead all the way.

We had one long halt due west of Corbie, on the right bank of the River Somme. Here we piled arms, and had a good wash in the river. Our next halt was at a little village called Vaux-sur-Somme ; here we were allotted billets. Jameson and I were billeted at the same farm.

1st August.

Bathing parades were the orders for the day. The weather was extremely hot and we kept our platoons on the banks of the Somme after we had dressed.

The men all enjoyed themselves immensely, and were much better away from the village, where there was only very bad beer for sale. Vaux was a most perfect little place, just on the river, and, except for the rumbling of guns in the distance at night, one could have forgotten the War.

2nd August.

Bathed in the morning. At 4 p.m. the Battalion paraded for an encampment north-west of Bray-sur-Somme, known as the " Happy Valley." Pte. Byrne had " drink taken," but could march. All my platoon, in fact, were unnaturally cheery, and I wondered where they had scrounged the beer. Their last pay-day had been some time back. I myself paid the Company at Molliens-Vidame, and they had only received the usual 5 francs in the French paper-money. Our march, which was long and tiring, lay along the right bank of the Somme.

Near Sailly-le-See we passed a huge " cage " of Boche prisoners guarded by the French. The country we were passing through was very uninteresting, very open, and with very little cultivation. Everywhere were the signs of the gigantic offensive which was being waged. Large aerodromes belonging to the French. Camps of Boche prisoners. Colossal dumps of ammunition and shells of every calibre. Endless lines of horses, all picketed under any available cover.

A rough track off the main road brought us to our camp, some 600 yards north-west of Bray-sur-Somme. We were in clover in our camp, officers and men having pukka bell-tents. It was quite dark when the Company fell out, but the whole sky was lit up from the colossal shell-fire on the Front, some four miles north-east of our position. Poole, Porter and I shared the same tent. Close to our lines were several " sausage " balloons, observing gun-flashes. Throughout the march Jameson complained of the heaviness of his pack, as a joke Handcock had put a weight in it which he never discovered until he took out his greatcoat when we got to our destination. 2nd Lieut. Warner rejoined the Battalion on the march.

3rd August.

Early morning inspections only. The heat being intense, we remained under canvas all morning. The camp was situated on the high ground overlooking Bray, a fairish sized town with the usual red-tiled roofs and a church with a spire. Between our camp and Bray were parked a number of ammunition columns, with rows and rows of horse lines, all picketed in the open without any shade whatsoever. There were a number of other infantry encampments all round, most of them belonging to regiments in our Division. I counted 30 observation balloons up at the same time. They were all, of course, " captive balloons," i.e. attached by a steel cable to a special kind of motor-lorry.

To the north-east the horizon presented a forbidding appearance. The sky seemed quite black from the shells. There was continual rumbling of artillery all day. Peronne, where the French were operating, was too much to our right for visibility, but at night this area was just a mass of flame from the shells.

In the evening all officers attended a demonstration of co-operation between aircraft and infantry in action, which was very interesting. A low-flying plane came over and we carried out the ground signals by means of flappers. These flappers were worked on a kind of Venetian blind system, with the reverse sides painted white. Every Battalion was given a special code name—our's was "Muriel." Lieut.-Colonel C. C. Harman, who had been Adjutant at Cork and who was now commanding a battalion of the Royal Sussex Regiment, visited us. He had just come out of the Somme Battle in which he had gained a D.S.O. He warned us of the shortage of water and advised the carrying of two water-bottles ; sound advice which some of us took.

4th August.

Poole, Porter, and I did a tour of the old Boche front line at Fricourt. This was the original line held by the Huns prior to the 1st July, the date of the first attack. We were very surprised and amazed with their old stronghold on the commanding ground north of Fricourt.

It looked as if it must have been almost impregnable, but the several mine craters told the tale of its capture. Masses of *chevaux de frise* and barbed wire were heaped up all over the area. There was an Indian encampment close by—a Punjabi Regiment—employed on the lines of communication.

5th and 6th August.

Quite a tropical heat wave. Parades before breakfast. Lazed all morning. Camp raided by swarms of flies, and all over the food. Ghastly !

7th August.

One man of the Company drowned on a bathing parade in the Somme near Bray. Our former C.O., Brig.-General Bullen-Smith, D.S.O., came to see us. He told us a good deal about Guillemont and the efforts of his (5th Brigade, 2nd Division) to capture it. His Brigade did actually enter the village. He was riding his old Leinster charger. In the evening the Brigade formed hollow square and was addressed by General Capper,[1] he impressed on us the necessity to send back information as to our position in battle and that we must dig in properly to consolidate.

8th August.

At 2 p.m. the Battalion paraded and moved off for a bivouac line at the "Citadel," where we became part of the XIII Corps reserve. We were allotted an area between a cemetery and an

---

[1] The G.O.C. actually witnessed the operations on the 18th August from an observation balloon.

Indian Battalion. Porter and I shared a bivouac. Near Fricourt we watched one of our 9.2 guns firing. It was mounted on rails and after each shot recoiled 200 yards.

9th August.

The weather broke ; it rained heavily, and the men got pretty wet. At 7 p.m. the Company paraded for a working party. Poole took us out and we buried a cable. The rain cleared, and we watched the shelling on the front.

10th August.

The Colonel borrowed my water-bottle. Orders were issued stating that only four officers per company were to go into action, and that the remainder would be held in reserve. The following remained as detailed for the nucleus : Frend, Newport, Crowe, Hyde-Sander, Hamilton, Hall, Gately, McCann, Warner, French, McNamara, Porter, and self. Some of us, however, joined the Battalion going into action. I shared Plowman's (Transport officer) tent in the horse lines. Frend and Gately went off for a month's course at the Corps School.

11th August.

D Company had 21 casualties from shell-fire when digging a C.T. through Trones Wood.

12th August.

Porter, Hamilton, and I rode into Albert. I rode Matilda. The greater part of the town had been reduced to shambles from recent shell-fire. We rode up to the church and saw the famous steeple with the leaning Madonna.

It was quite amazing, leaning right over the street. The French said that the War would end when the Madonna and Child fell. (It actually fell from Boche shelling in '17.)

We returned by Meaulte where the Irish Guards were billeted.

13th August.

John Burns wounded. Wet day. Hall and I rode to the Citadel, where I bought some wine at the canteen. We passed a regular battalion of the Royal Scots Fusiliers on their way to battle, men of excellent physique. Met " Prince " Hamilton, a Leinster on the Staff.

14th August.

[1]We all went up to make a reconnaissance of the front line area—Mametz and Montauban. It rained hard, and we had a depressing tramp in the mud. The battle area had a terrible appearance—just ridges absolutely devoid of any timber, cultivation, or buildings—the whole area was pitted with shell craters of every size. From the Briqueterie we saw the ridge, where the front line trenches ran—from Guillemont to Maltz Horn Farm. Bernafay and Trones Woods were on our left, and had been reduced to a state of burnt stumps. Guillemont could not be seen as it was hidden by an intervening ridge, but the tortured bricks of Maltz Horn Farm lay silhouetted on the horizon. There was a colossal amount of artillery fire going on. On the way back I met Willy McBride, South Irish Horse, a Kinnitty friend, in a canteen in some cellars on the side of what had been the main street of Fricourt. I got the loan of a motor from an R.A.M.C. Major, and we all drove back to our soaking camp at Bray. Hamilton became very ill and was invalided to the Base, likewise French.

15th August.

Went up to Carnoy to the Battalion. They were still employed digging the C.T., now called " Leinster Avenue," through Trones Wood. The Battalion was situated in the northern outskirts of the demolished Carnoy ruins. All managed to get cover from the cellars. I saw all C Company and Laville. It was the last time I saw him alive.

16th and 17th August.

Still encamped on the ridge north of Bray. Spent most of our time with the Lewis Guns.

GUILLEMONT

18th August.

Major Murphy took over command of the 7th Northamptons as their C.O.,[2] Mobbs, had been wounded.

Crowe, Newport, and I got orders to report at Battalion Headquarters at the Briqueterie. We left our lines and struck off across country, getting a lift from an ammunition column on the way. At the Briqueterie we found the Battalion preparing to move off for action. Each man was given sand-bags and bombs

---

[1] On the way up we watched one of our captive observation balloons (sausages) ascending in a high wind with great difficulty.
[2] A well-known man in the rugby world : he was killed in 1917.

in addition to his cumbersome " battle order." It was a sweltering day, and the men were too heavily equipped. All had been issued with a white metal plate, which attached to a string was to be worn round the neck, the disc hanging on the back between the shoulders. The Staff told us that these plates were for co-opera-tion with aircraft, and that they would be conspicuous from the air. For the most part, officers and men treated these discs as a huge joke. We all wore them properly, but the wags of the Battalion took the opportunity to scratch such remarks as " R.I.P.," " 4010,"[1] or " Kick me," on those of their pals. Jameson had " Lead the Blind " on his. Every aeroplane was fitted with a " Klaxon " horn which they sounded when they wanted to co-operate with the Infantry. We were then supposed to do the ostrich trick, i.e., bury our heads in the ground and show these discs. As might be imagined, the lives of the discs were short ; they were found to be of no practical use, and were discarded. Another issue was in the shape of morphine tablets by the regimental M.O. to all officers.

This attack was not only a divisional operation ; there was to be a general advance along the whole corps front. On our left the 14th Division, and on our right the 3rd Division, were advanc-ing, and at Péronne, the French were attacking in conjunction.

The main topographical feature of this country was the Guillemont–Maltz Horn Farm ridge. The ruins of Guillemont stood on the highest point of this ridge, predominating the surrounding country. Guillemont was, therefore, the key of the position, and once it was captured we would have command of the whole area. Three of our attacks on Guillemont had been written off as failures. The Germans fully realised its important strategic position, and had turned it into almost an impregnable fortress to bar the way of the Allies in their advance up the slopes of the Somme plateau in Picardy. I got an excellent view of the attack from the top of some old ruined walls near the Briqueterie. This place was about 1000 yards as the crow flies from the jumping-off trenches before Guillemont. It stood up on another ridge smaller and separated from the Guillemont ridge by a wide valley known as " The Valley of Death."

Before Zero hour, the leading companies of the Battalion

---

[1] The Leinsters were always known as the " Fourty Tens." The way we received this strange identification, or nickname, was that in the earlier history of the Regiment a man somewhat the worse for alcohol who stood number 50 on parade called out 40,10 after 49 when the company was numbering. Where-ever the Regiment has been stationed this number will be found written, carved, or chiselled. From the Pyramids to Ottawa, and from India to South Africa and Silesia. 4010 was once seen tarred on the bows of a battleship riding at anchor in Jamaica.

(B and D) were moving across this valley and winding up the Guillemont ridge. We were now going to witness the much talked of creeping barrage.

The men were silent, and did not volunteer any ideas about the new system of shell-fire, but I overheard my platoon-sergeant (Sergt.•Henry) telling the " toughs " when in training, " to use their imagination and follow the shells " (the Battalion drummers). This explanation seemed to satisfy all. Here to-day was the reality, and no imagination was needed. Up till now there had only been intermittent shelling ; mostly counter-battery work. Suddenly a crashing roar resounded over the whole area ; the preliminary bombardment of the Hun lines had started punctually to the second. All the British batteries were giving tongue simultaneously. Thousands of tons of shells were crashing down on the enemy's trenches on the sky line. Shells came from places unthought of and unseen, so excellently were they camouflaged ; field-guns in pits with only a covering of rabbit wire interlaced with grass and leaves to conceal them. Behind them again were rows of howitzers all staked to the ground so tremendous was their recoil every time they fired. The noise of the explosions, the whine of the shells, and the concussion produced, was unlike anything I had ever imagined. Here and there shrapnel bursts flashed in the inky darkness. Above this curtain of fire one could see numerous German S O S rockets of all colours shooting up into the sky. We passed some of our gunners on our way up ; they were all stripped to the waist, their sweat-begrimed bodies showed one the almost superhuman effort of endurance they were making under the blazing heat of the August sun at midday. How long would this furious bombardment last ? The flash of our shell bursts seemed further away, the gunners were lengthening their fuses. The barrage had lifted—" zero."

Simultaneously out got a line of forms from the British trenches, the first wave, and disappeared into the smoke. This cloud of smoke grew denser with the debris of brick and mortar from the ruins of Guillemont. The enemy was now retaliating with a vengeance on the slopes of the ridges to wipe out our supports, and the rattle of musketry or machine-guns could now be heard above the roar of the guns. Their artillery was not to be frustrated, and reaped a harvest. Laville and Handcock were killed, and our gallant C.O. Lieut.-Colonel R. A. H. Orpen-Palmer, D.S.O.,[1] O'Morchoe, Burns, D.C.M., Todd, and Magner were wounded, as well as 100 rank and file. L/Corpls. Jenkins and Egan were the first to be hit in C Company. Over 100

[1] Afterwards commanded the 2nd Battalion in Silesia and on disbandment of the Leinsters took over Command of the 2nd Battalion East Surrey Regiment.

casualties just going up that ridge without seeing the enemy. Fodder for guns indeed !

Something had happened on the right. The Highlanders of the 3rd Division were coming back, and so were the attacking regiments of our Brigade. They were not " walking wounded " coming out of the smoke—wounded do not come back in lines. " A failure ! " It had been a fine sight seeing the leading battalions advancing into action, but it was a most depressing one seeing them retiring.

Streams of wounded, walking and on stretchers, were now beginning to drift by ; men with smashed arms, limping, and with the worst of all to see—facial wounds. They all muttered of machine-guns in a sunken road, which enfiladed them and had broken up the attack. Amongst the stretcher cases were the C.O. and C.S.M. Bennett, D.C.M. The former was badly hit in the groin, and the latter severely in the head. I talked to them as they lay on their stretchers in a small hollow. The C.O., with his amazing memory, told me that he had given my water-bottle to Palin ! Swan of the Northamptons was another stretcher case. He had been badly hit, and was delirious.

THE ORDER FOR ATTACK ON GUILLEMONT

73rd Brigade. Two Battalions in the front line. 7th Northampton Regiment on left, and 13th Middlesex Regiment on right. The 2nd Leinster Regiment in support, and the 9th Sussex Regiment in reserve. First objective the German front line before Guillemont to be taken by leading units. Second objective the village of Guillemont to be taken by the regiment in support (us), who would leap-frog the front-line battalions. Our rôle was to exploit the success of the leading regiments, but as the attack had failed, we had now to cope with the task of replacing a disorganised battalion, and holding the original British front line against counter-attacks.

We were informed that everything had gone splendidly for the attacking troops, until they had got to within 30 yards of their objective. Our barrage had then to lift off the Hun lines and, when it did, up rushed the Boche from his deep dug-outs with machine-guns, and directed a withering fire on the attackers. Machine-guns which had been lying out concealed in a sunken road which ran between the advancing battalions also enfiladed the flanks of the two units.

Surprise being the greatest element in warfare, and the attacking troops being caught in an unexpected hail of well-directed machine-gun fire, were held up and then retired back across

No-Man's-Land. On our left, the 17th Brigade had captured some small posts near Waterlot Farm, and a party of the 7th Northamptons under the leadership of Major A. D. Murphy, M.C. (who was acting O.C. 7th Northamptons), captured a small post at the Quarries near the Railway Station. The 3rd Division had also failed to gain any of their objectives.

The Leinsters got orders to take over the front-line trenches from the remnants of one of the attacking battalions. The officers in reserve joined their Companies—so Newport, Crowe, McCann, and I started off across country for Guillemont. We moved through a terribly devastated area—every inch churned up by shell-fire, everywhere were shell-holes, most of them overlapping. We struck up against communication trenches, most of them were obliterated. Here and there lay huddled-up figures in khaki. It was getting dusk when we reported, at Battalion Headquarters, to Poole, upon whom command of the Battalion had devolved, as senior officer. I will never forget the scene in that small dug-out or shelter off the main C.T.

Poole was sitting on the ground, giving his orders in a clear and concise manner. Palin, the Adjutant, writing on a message form by candle-light, with two of the Battalion signallers lying on the ground beside him, and Lieut.-Colonel J. Greene (a captain in the 7th D.G.s), C.O. of the 13th Middlesex, sitting on an ammunition box, thanking Poole for having come so speedily to take over from his Battalion. I got orders to bring up bombs from the sunken road to the barricade in our front line. On my way I met John Burns limping down the C.T. He had been hit for the second time during that afternoon. I got up to the barricade on the sunken road at 5.30 p.m. It was being held by the Battalion bombers, with a gun and crew of the Machine-Gun Corps. Everything seemed extraordinarily still after the furious pandemonium of the afternoon. A solitary shell burst over us occasionally, and some went whining over our heads in the direction of our transport dumps. I peered over the barricade at the Hun lines and Guillemont, barely 150 yards away. Our stretcher bearers, Morrissey (now L/Corpl.), Reid, Dooley, and Merriman, all heroes of Premesques '14 and Hooge '15, were out searching No-Man's-Land for wounded. Occasionally one could hear the cries of some who had been missed in the torn-up and shell-pitted ground. What had been the ruins of a village some six hours previously, was now only heaps of red bricks and debris. The few trees which had been left standing were now all torn up by the roots. Arrow Head Copse on our left flank had ceased to exist. The ploughed-up yellow earth stank of lyddite and powder. From the constant firing of Véry lights by the enemy, we could judge his nervous state. There were no wire entanglements left, they too had disappeared in the bombardment. It was the picture of desolation. L/Corpl. Delaney took out a patrol to make a reconnaissance of the enemy position. I overheard Poole saying that he wanted to carry out a night attack, and had telephoned to Brigade for sanction. The morale of the Battalion, in spite of its casualties, was very high, and a determined bayonet charge that night would have wrested Guillemont from the enemy. Poole walked about on our parapets under shell and occasional bursts of M.G. fire, restoring the line.

Brigade refused to hear of an attack, and gave us orders for relief. At 9.30 p.m. the Battalion was relieved by the 1st Battalion North Staffordshire Regiment, 72nd Brigade. Having handed over, C Company got orders to move to the Brigade left flank, and support the 7th Northamptons. Here we lay for some time in another sunken road. The enemy had attempted to counter-attack, but were beaten off, and the company was not required. We got orders to take up our position for the night in the sunken road. On our way back we passed Padre Doyle, making cover for our wounded near an advanced dressing-station. Later, this fine man had his leg blown off by a shell and died. The Battalion M.O. was also wounded. We took up our position in a sunken road, which ran parallel to our front line, near Arrow Head Copse.

In the dim light we could make out a lot of figures lying in huddled-up heaps in the middle of the road. A Company of the 1st North Staffords had " caught it " when coming up to relieve us earlier in the night.

We posted sentries at intervals, a task that was rendered difficult by the dead of the 1st North Staffords, whom we stumbled over in the darkness, and got the men under what cover was available. There were numerous undercuttings in the sunken road, known as " funk holes." Whitby, Jameson, and I crawled into these and, leaving our legs exposed to the rain which was now falling, went to sleep.

19th August.

Woke up at dawn, wet and cold. Discovered that lying on either side of Jameson and myself were two dead men of the 1st North Staffords. The whole sunken road was taken up with the dead of the same regiment—at least 30. Our men had no rations, so we turned out the kits of the dead for iron rations ; got some cigarettes too. I had a strange species of fodder in my haversack—tinned lobster and crab. With the help of some bread, Whitby, Jameson, and I had a weird breakfast.

At 6 a.m. orders came to move lower down into the valley, where the Battalion was. We fell in and moved off. Everything very wet and clammy! Enemy shelling spasmodic. R.S.M. Smith came round and collected a party of our men for the burial of the 1st North Stafford dead, and a few of our own.

We got to a reserve trench some 800 yards away, where we found the Battalion. The men were walking about under cover of a thick mist, making their breakfasts. Liston went off to arrange about the burial of Laville and Handcock.

This line consisted of fire-bays, so we stretched ground sheets across from parapet to parados, and most of us went to sleep on the wet fire steps. All day we had orders and counter-orders for the front line ; being in reserve to the 72nd Brigade. At about 6 p.m. there was terrific shelling of the Front, and we expected to go up at any moment. Some of our platoons were out on fatigue, mostly carrying *chevaux de frise* from the dump at the Briqueterie to the front line. No enemy attack materialised from the intense barrage, and at 9 p.m. we were relieved by a Bantam battalion ! This was the first Bantam unit the 2nd Battalion came across in the War. It had only recently arrived on service from the U.K. and it seemed hard that the " poor little blighters," as the men called them sympathetically, should be sent into the Somme offensive.

It was a cold but clear night when we moved off at intervals by companies for an old dug-out line near Carnoy, some three miles march away. At 10 p.m. we found ourselves on the high ground on the northern outskirts of this shell-scarred village. Our " billets " for the night were to be the network of abandoned and shell-shattered trenches which were the Huns' front line up to the first day of this great Somme offensive, 1st July, '16.

This line was considered impregnable by the enemy. It had predominated our trenches which were on the lower ground. To make certain of success, on July 1st we had exploded mines at close intervals under this line as far as Fricourt. Here and there along the ridge, the line was completely obliterated by the colossal mine craters.

The whole aspect of this area must have been altered by those gigantic cavities. At any rate, it was now called " The Craters." It was getting dark when we saw the men finally settled down for the night. The Battalion always had a wonderful knack of adapting themselves to any situation, and within an incredibly sport space of time had all lit fires and were " drumming up their char," as they called brewing their tea ! To-night it was a sore-hearted and disgruntled Battalion that bedded down. Through no fault of its own it had lost a great chance. The capture of

Guillemont at the point of the bayonet was to have been the star turn of the battle. The morale of the Battalion had been excellent, and our patrols had reported that the Hun front line was only lightly held.

We were now in Divisional Reserve, and under orders for the front line, or, as the order stated, " to hold ourselves in readiness and to be prepared to move to Guillemont within an hour."

Our servants lit a fire in a bay of the trench. Poole, Palin, Jameson, Liston, Hyde-Sander, Whitby and I sat round it discussing the situation. We all decided to spend the night under the stars. There were some dug-outs, real deep ones, but the majority of them contained German dead. After some good tea with better rum, we all dropped off to sleep.

20th August.

A fine morning. Murphy returned from commanding the 7th Northamptons, and took over command of the Battalion from Poole, who resumed command of C Company.

At 7 p.m. companies were detailed to find fatigue parties for the front line. I took a party of 100 men, carrying rations to the 3rd Rifle Brigade. We dumped these with a front-line company who were dug in before Waterlot Farm. Earlier in the day, I had made a reconnaissance of the best way up with a few N.C.O.s. I had attempted to take up the party in daylight, but at the Brigade dump, south-west of Bernafay Wood, our Brigade Major stopped me, and told me not to go up until darkness set in. I, therefore, returned to the Carnoy Craters ; on the way up we had got shelled near Montauban, but had no casualties. A passing driver annoyed me by jumping off his G.S. waggon, and making a bee-line for a ditch near by, when a few shells came over—leaving his pair of horses ! I said some rude things to him, while my party halted in fours on the road.

At dark we started off again, and all went well until we entered Trones Wood. Suddenly the enemy put down a box barrage all round the wood. Luckily we had good cover in the C.T. which the Battalion had dug some weeks previously, called " Leinster Avenue." A Company had also a carrying party out under Sharp ; they were in front, and had decided to halt, so there we were jammed up in the trench. The open was impossible, owing to the fallen trees and thick undergrowth, so we had to lump it, listening to the shells raining down all round, and sniffing the smell of a number of decomposing corpses, mostly those of German gunners who had tried to hold the wood in the first few days of the offensive. I sent a message to Sharp, asking him if it was safe to push on, but he sent L/Corpl. Ronan, M.M. (A Company Stretcher-bearers' N.C.O.), to say it was quite impossible owing to the barrage in front. We were just half an hour in that stinking wood. At last we moved on, without a single casualty, to the front line, and returned at 2 a.m. to the Battalion. 2nd Lieut. Hyde-Sander got very ill, and was invalided down to the base.

21st August.

Rumours of returning to Guillemont, and more orders for working parties. However, by midday all these orders were cancelled, and instead, we got orders for a rest (" but to be prepared to return to action at short notice," ran the friendly document !). We moved off by platoons at 2 p.m. in a westerly direction. On the march we passed parties of the Grenadier and Irish Guards mending the roads. They belonged to the Guards Entrenching Battalion.

General Capper passed us in his motor car. He slowed down and we saluted him. We soon got to our destination—an encampment with pukka tents on some sloping ground due east of that scarred and desolate Albert. In the distance we could make out the figure of the Madonna hanging suspended in mid-air from the mutilated spire. Spent the evening stretching ourselves on the grass and listening to the rumbling of the guns.

After dinner, Poole, O'Connor, Jameson, Liston, and I killed a bottle of whisky over the usual talk, " The War." Poole, Liston, and I shared the same tent.

22nd August.

All day spent fitting the men with clothes, boots, and making up deficiencies in equipment and necessaries. The men looked very clean and fit ; clean clothes and underclothing were their only worry ever. All day they seemed to be washing or shaving. Weather excellent.

23rd August.

Orders issued for the relief of troops holding line in front of Guillemont by the Battalion in the evening.

The Adjutant and the four Company Commanders rode off at 5 p.m. to reconnoitre the new line. At 6 p.m. the Battalion moved off, with 500 yards' interval between companies in the following order, A, C, B, D. We had a half-hour rest on the road beyond Carnoy. In the distance we could see the shell-bursts, which were exploding farther up on our line of march.

It was getting dark when we passed one of our batteries in action south of the Valley of Death. (We made a detour of

Montauban owing to the shelling.) All went well until we got to Stanley dump, right in the valley. Suddenly, the Huns put a terrific barrage down on top of us. To make matters worse, our complete transport was there unloading rations and barbed wire. We knew that quite close at hand was the C.T. which we were to take, but in the darkness and with the shell-fire all was chaos. One shell burst right beside me and knocked out three men immediately behind me, and Sergt. Henry was wounded. Two fine old toughs were killed instantaneously, 4807 Pte. Lynch, a reservist who had been with the Battalion since '14, and 4238 Pte. McDonnell, another fine type.

I was knocked clean off my feet, but did not waste much time getting up again, owing to the shells which were raining down upon us.

Our way was blocked by A Company, who had been held up, and there we were with our transport all round us! Sergt. McCarthy, Transport Sergeant, gave the order to trot, and I then heard R.S.M. Smith's[1] voice; "This way, C Company." He gave great assistance that night, standing out under a heavy barrage directing the companies as they came up. The men were splendid, and did not budge—just stood up with heads bent, no rushing about to look for cover. Tom Morrissey and Reid were superb, kneeling out under the barrage attending to McDonnell, who was just dying. We left them there, while Gerry Liston led the Company up the shallow C.T. on the rising ground.

The C.O. met us near Battalion Headquarters and conducted the Company across the open and behind the front line to the sunken road junction. Here we entered the trench and proceeded to take over or relieve the isolated sentry posts in our area. On arrival, we learnt that Poole and Barry, who had gone on in advance to reconnoitre the line, had been wounded. We actually relieved two units, both of which were Bantam Battalions! The umpteenth battalions of the Gloucester Regiment, and Sherwood Foresters. Our men chaffed the little West Countrymen with uproarious Irish badinage. The Battalion found itself astride the sunken road with Guillemont some 150 yards away. We were in the exact line that we had held on the night 18th–19th August. A Company was on the left in front of Arrow Head Copse. We, C Company, were on the right. Both companies joined at the barrier on the sunken road where the Battalion bombers and a section of the Machine-Gun Corps were posted. C Company also found a detached post away on the right flank. Later, I was to get well acquainted with this isolated detachment. B and D

[1] Now Captain and Quartermaster, M.C., D.C.M., The Depôt, The Manchester Regiment.

Companies were in support and reserve respectively. Battalion Headquarters was behind A Company and parallel with the sunken road. On duty all night, as Liston felt very ill, but would not leave the line. I walked all night, visiting the sentries. It rained hard, and we got shelled severely every half-hour. I rested for some time on a muddy fire step, with 8464 Corpl. Broadbent. Private O'Leary, Jim Marsland's scout of Hooge days, was standing up on the fire step on sentry-go beside me. I left them in that position, and in ten minutes returned to find a colossal shell-crater in the parapet, or where it had been. Poor Broadbent was dead, and badly smashed up, and O'Leary,[1] the keen sentry of ten minutes previously, was terribly cut about the head and body —and was raving. Morrissey and Reid took him away—never did I expect to see him again. We spent the night deepening the trench, and building up the parapets. What cover suited the Bantams of 4 feet 8 inches to 5 feet did not suit the 2nd Leinsters, averaging 5 feet 10 inches !

24th August.

At 5 a.m. I met the C.O. who had come up to inspect the line. He was particularly sympathetic about the casualties. We toured the whole Company front, including the detached post. To get to it we had to cut across the open. However, as it was foggy, the Huns did not observe us. We found Jameson and his platoon under deplorable conditions, all around them were enemy dead, and the little ditch of a trench full of mud, with pieces of equipment and half-buried corpses. Jameson was cheery, but complained of being short of rations. This post on the right of the Company was at least 200 yards away from the main line. It had no C.T. or wire entanglements, but was echeloned back facing Leuze Wood. Later in the day I got in touch with the unit on Jameson's right. We were subject to heavy shell-fire all morning. C.S.M. Kerrigan got badly wounded in the arm ; also Sergt. Dignam and a few men.

I received a chit from Jameson regarding his relief (page 150). From Battalion Headquarters we understood another unit was taking over this detached post.

Shell-fire was hellish all afternoon. Box barrages were put down all round, and the earth was going up like volcanoes, completely smothering us. The heat was intense, and as we were all sweating pretty freely, we got into a filthy state. Crouching in the trench, hugging the forward side, one could feel every minute small stones and lumps of earth ricochet off one's helmet. Now and

---

[1] Years afterwards I ran across this man whom I had believed to have died of wounds, walking across the square at Fort St. George, Madras.

then one would be almost smothered by the parapet being blown in. The dirt flying about and the fumes from the lyddite added to our discomfiture. During a bombardment one developed a craze for two things : water and cigarettes. Few could ever eat under an intense bombardment, especially on the Somme, when every now and then a shell would blow pieces of mortality, or complete bodies, which had been putrefying in No-Man's-Land slap into one's trench. Shell-fire, too, always stirred up the swarms of black flies, of which there was an absolute plague on

> was told by adjutant I was to be relieved by H.L.I. before 12, but there is no sign of relief yet. Will you see the C.O. and ask whether he wishes me to evacuate without relief ?? C.S.M. Kernagan here wounded & not able to move before dark Sgt Dignam also wounded & fine down
>
> To 2/Lt Hitchcock
> from
> 2/Lt A.M. Jameson

Message from Jameson, who was killed eight days later at Delville Wood.

the Somme battle-fields. The bombardment was intense, at times it reminded me of Hooge exactly one year previously. I had been in command of the Company all day, and as part of our front line on the right of the sunken road was completely obliterated and untenable, I got the platoons to side-step to the flanks.

Our whole line was one cloud of smoke, evidently the Huns anticipated an attack as they sent all kinds of coloured S O S Véry lights up. I got our Lewis guns into position and gave the order to fix bayonets. (In such a case this is always good for the morale.) Throughout the bombardment the men were splendid, not a sentry shirked his duty.

Pte. O'Mahoney stood up on the fire step with his whole chest exposed, cracking jokes, whilst the shells exploded all round him. After the shelling ceased the platoons linked up in the centre again where we found the line completely obliterated by the still smoking craters. As it was now dark, we started digging, and connected up all the shell-holes. A Company had some men killed, but we got off lightly with a few wounded. Sleep was out of the question this night.

25th August.

By "Stand To" we had established a good line, put up parapets and deepened the trench. I was the only officer with the Company now. Liston was still with us, but was very ill, and refused to go down the line. Brassington joined me in the afternoon from the transport lines. All morning we were subject to periods of intense shelling. One fine old character, who had been continually with the Company since the Aisne, No. 7332 Pte. Cutts, was killed instantaneously. I felt very sad at seeing Morrissey and Reid bringing him away for burial. Cutts had been C Company officers' Mess cook in 1914 and '15. It was a sad task writing to his wife and giving her some details when I got out of the line. At 4 p.m. I went over to the detached post and took over from Jameson. Between the bombardments we maintained touch with patrols.

Earlier in the afternoon I had reported to the C.O. at Battalion Headquarters. He had sent for me, so that I could arrange about the relief with the incoming unit of my detached post. L/Corpl. Geard and I made a thorough reconnaissance of the C.T.s in the vicinity. The C.O. was very cheery and asked all about the men and rations.

Met the officer of my relieving unit belonging to the 20th Light Division. Strange to say, the Battalion was being relieved by one regiment, while another regiment was furnishing a platoon to relieve my detached post opposite " Lousy Wood," as we called it. This was the worst detached post I ever came across in the War— absolutely in the blue. In fact, the enemy had a post between us and the right flank of the Company. It consisted only of linked-up shell craters, all around were dead bodies. When our men got killed we buried them by filling in a shell-hole. All the torn-up ground around us was lined with the dead. We had no barbed wire, and we were not visible from any other point in our line. Up to now the shelling had taken its toll of the Company strength. C Company[1] had only one sergeant left with the Company, and one with my detached post. One always got to know and appreciate the men when under shell-fire ; during the bombardment on the previous afternoon, Corpl. Heggerty, a veteran of the Boer War, had told me his experiences in South Africa.

The morning had been very wet, but the afternoon turned out fine, and we felt the stuffy heat in our little trench very much. The flies came out in swarms, and were very obnoxious. With the original strength for my post, two Vickers machine-guns and their crews had been included. However, all their personnel had become casualties. Fortunately, Sergt. Rivers, who was with me, was a machine-gunner, so we fixed up the guns on their tripods into battle positions. Throughout the afternoon I had had the men deepening the trench, and I had no cause to regret it, for exactly at 5 p.m. the enemy put up a colossal barrage. All round my post the earth was upheaving, with great columns of black smoke and clods of earth raised by the howitzers. Luckily, the enemy had not got our exact range. A complete barrage would land 5 yards in front and then 5 yards in rear. A few shells landed on my parapets, but did no harm, but the dust and dirt was choking us. Now and then shells would land on some of the numerous corpses in No-Man's-Land, and then some gruesome pieces of mortality would be hurled into our battered trench. I had all the men kneeling down, hugging the forward side of the parapet with fixed bayonets. One sentry for the platoon and one for the machine-gunners was sufficient, as we all, especially Sergt. Rivers and myself, were walking or rather crawling about all the time. Private Moran, at one time poor old Jim Marsland's platoon sergeant, was splendid. He was a tower of strength throughout the nine hours' incessant shelling. We were all terribly fatigued. Practically no one had had any sleep since leaving our bivouacs near Albert. Lack of sleep, to my mind, is the worst strain in warfare, and how difficult it is to keep awake. I was in charge of thirty lives and two Vickers guns, holding an important isolated post, and yet at frequent intervals I found myself leaning against the parapet with a Véry pistol in my hand, dozing. A shell would pitch on the parapet beside me and I would be startled out of my semi-comatose state, to choke and cough with the dust and fumes from the cordite. My relief was hours late, but we never expected them once the bombardment started. All we expected was an infantry attack, and accordingly we all stared our eyes out of their sockets across that ghastly stretch of 150 churned-up yards, waiting to see waves of Boches advancing

[1] C.Q.M.S. Wall joined the Company, and took over duties of C.S.M. on the 25/8/16.

in the moonlight. Thousands of rockets were going up from the enemy side. If any rocket happened to be a bit more brilliant or differently coloured from the rest, we imagined it was a signal for their attack.

I did not fire my Véry pistol, as it would have given away our position. Although tired, hungry and thirsty, and with our nerves all on edge, yet we would have put up the hell of a fight. The men were splendid.

The hours were meanwhile slipping by ; it was well after midnight, and yet our relief had not put in any appearance. I now became very anxious about getting relieved before daylight, as once the dawn broke, relief in our exposed position would be impossible.

At exactly 3 a.m. I decided to go and investigate, so taking Pte. Flannery,[1] I set off for the unit I knew must be somewhere on my left. We got to an isolated communication trench, some 300 yards away, and found our relief, a platoon of Bantams, asleep in the bottom of the trench. I asked them where their officer was, and they brought me to the entrance of a deep dug-out. There he was, sitting up with a candle beside him ! I duly strafed him for not being with his men, and for not making any attempt to relieve me. I left him, and ordered his sergeant to fall in his party (about 40), and with the help of Flannery brought them all up to my post, and relieved man for man.

I told the Bantam sergeant all I knew about the line. I also handed over the two Vickers guns. As it was getting light I made no delay in getting away ; all the men were ready in their battle order, so we filed out under cover of a mist, feeling damned sorry for the little blighters for whom we had had to pull down the parapets before leaving. We cut across the churned-up " open " making for the sunken road north-east of Delville Wood. We struck the support trench near the valley, where a battalion of the H.L.I. were lying. Shells were falling here and there, " lonely like " as the men said.

At 5.30 a.m. got to the Briqueterie. As we were parched from thirst, I let the men fall out, when we discovered a water dump near Brigade Headquarters. Water was always brought up in petrol tins on the Somme. I made a dive for one along with the rest—it was water, with a terrible taste of petrol. We marched off, having asked the whereabouts of the Battalion from Brigade Headquarters. There I had met the Brigade Major—Capt. Howlett. He said they had all given my platoon up for lost or captured. At Montauban I commandeered a motor-lorry which brought us to the Citadel. Here we were dumped, and performed

[1] 9456 Pte. P. Flannery of Birr. Killed 10th June, 1917.

the remainder of the journey on foot. At 7 a.m. we arrived at Battalion Headquarters, where I reported our return, and went to the Company officers' tent. Here, Jackson had my valise spread out. I stumbled into it and went to sleep.

26th August.

At 10 Jackson woke me, and brought me a breakfast consisting of very strong tea, fried bacon and tomatoes. Palin came round to see me, and told me that the C.O. had been very worried about my platoon all night. He had attempted to get out to me, but was prevented by the barrage. It appeared that the C.O. was certain that the Boche was going to attack in front of my detached post, and had gone up and ordered C Company to stand by in order to assist me.

Heard the sad news that 2nd Lieut. H. T. B. Siddons, B Company, had died of his wounds. Also that 2nd Lieut. W. V. Whitby was wounded—numbers of old friends of C Company were gone for ever. My non-arrival had caused Jackson some concern, and for hours he and Connolly had waited in the C.T. known as Hooge Alley. They both had had a narrow escape, as a 5·9 had landed beside them, burying them completely. Division had been asking about the lost platoon of the Leinsters, and the Adjutant sent off a runner to let them know that we had all turned up.

At 3 p.m. the Battalion paraded, and, complete with transport, we marched off for a rest-area near Durnancourt. On our way we passed the 2nd Battalion The Royal Irish Regiment, moving up to the Front. We gave them a great cheer. They had several Leinster Special Reserve officers attached to them in Dudley, Turner, and Daly. H. P. Dudley, a very good fellow, was unfortunately killed some days later.

The 2nd Royal Irish were now in the 7th Division, which had taken over our area before Guillemont. We got to our destination at 5 p.m. The whole Battalion was under canvas, surrounded by fields of corn stooks. Everything seemed very peaceful. That evening heavy rain fell. I gave the Adjutant the names of two men who had distinguished themselves in the consolidation of that Guillemont trench, No. 7218 L/Corpl. T. Morrissey, M.M., and No. 8030 Pte. P. Reid, M.M., the famous stretcher-bearers of C Company. The C.O. approved of my recommendation. Reid had been very seriously wounded, having his arm shot off. One of the sergeants would also have been recommended, but for the fact he managed to get too much beer before we paraded for the rest-area. He had performed a gallant act in rescuing C.S.M. Kerrigan under heavy fire, but the C.O. would not have his name

2nd Leinster Regt. astride the sunken road before Guillemont, August, 1916.

sent in, on account of his stupidity when acting C.S.M. The Battalion had lost just 100 men in the past three days.

My platoon had also suffered. A particularly fine soldier, No. 8113 Pte. J. Hanley (of Roscrea), had been killed in the last few hours in the front line.

THE ENEMY

From their very recent dead we established the identity of the troops opposite to us holding Guillemont. They were the 73 Hanoverian Fusiliers or Fusilier Regiment Prince Albrecht of Prussia, Hanoverian No. 73. This regiment had been included in our garrison which had defended Gibraltar under General Eliott from 1779 to 1783. In commemoration of this siege, when they fought on our side, the Regiment still wore the battle honour GIBRALTAR embroidered on their left shoulders. Shortly after the War, an officer belonging to this regiment, Lieut. E. Jünger, who fought against the 2nd Leinsters at Guillemont,[1] published his experiences in a book called *Midst Thunderbolts*. I can locate his dispositions exactly opposite to ours. On the German side the situation had been far from pleasant or healthy, judging from the following extracts, and I have compared his account with mine for those days, when we were dug in at Guillemont, facing each other.

2nd Battalion The Leinster Regiment.	73rd Hanoverian Fusiliers.
23rd August, 1916.	23rd August, 1916.
At 8.30 p.m. took over the front line astride the sunken road before Guillemont. Capts. Poole and Barry wounded. Ptes. Lynch and McDonnell killed, and Sergt. Henry wounded from shell-fire on journey. Later, Corpl. Broadbent killed and Pte. O'Leary severely wounded from shell-fire, which continued throughout the night. Slight rain at intervals.	In the morning proceeded by lorry to Le Mesnil. Orders for relief of troops holding front line at Guillemont. At dusk marched from Le Mesnil to Sailly-Saillisel, thence to Combles, where occupied cellars for the night. Shelled heavily throughout journey, particularly when passing Frégicourt near the Combles cemetery.

[1] The chapter entitled Guillemont was translated and published in the Journal of the Royal United Service Institution of May, 1923.

24th August.

At 5 a.m. met the C.O., came up to inspect the Company positions. Visited detached post held by Jameson's platoon under cover of mist. Heavy shell-fire all morning, which developed into an intense bombardment in the afternoon. C.S.M. Kerrigan (mortally), Sergt. Dignam and some men wounded. Expected enemy attack and fixed bayonets. Our guns retaliated on enemy trenches from which numerous S O S rockets were sent up. Trench obliterated, all night spent digging and building up parapets. 2nd Lieut. Siddons died of wounds. A Company lost some men killed. Liaised with Sharp of A Company across Sunken Road.

25th August.

Spasmodic shell-fire in morning. Pte. Cutts killed. Casualties amongst the crews of Vickers Guns Machine-Gun Corps at the barricade on Sunken Road. 2nd Lieut. Whitby of Headquarters hit. Heavy showers of rain all day, between intervals intense heat. 2nd Lieut. Brassington and C.Q.M.S. Wall joined Company from the Transport lines. At 5 p.m. reported to the C.O. at Battalion Headquarters and ordered to relieve Jameson on detached post. Pte. Hanley killed. Some men wounded. Orders for Battalion relief at 9 p.m. Intense

24th August.

At 7 a.m. issued with steel helmets. Intense bombardment all afternoon. At 11 p.m. left Combles under intense shell-fire. Took over a sector consisting of linked-up shell craters astride a sunken road to the left of Guillemont from a Bavarian Sergeant-Major who disappeared quickly after handing over a Véry pistol. A space of 500 yards lay between Company and Regiment No. 76 in front of Guillemont trench untenable owing to shell-fire. Spent the night with servant and two runners in a shell-hole. Remained awake. Warned men to be prepared to meet a British attack.

25th August.

At dawn British aeroplane hovering over position sounding siren and directing for artillery. Subjected to heavy shell-fire. Sentries on the left flank evacuated their post at 3 p.m. Terribly hot weather. The horrible aspect of the Sunken Road—a series of huge shell-holes, filled with uniforms, equipment, arms and dead bodies. A dreadful place —the dead defenders lay amongst the living. Whilst digging funk-holes we discovered that they had been buried in strata. One company after another had crowded in and been destroyed by drum box barrage on detached post. Stood to expecting attack. Sergt. Rivers and Pte. Moran built up good machine-gun positions for our two Vickers guns.

My relief did not arrive.

fire. The Sunken Road and the ground in rear of it were full of Germans ; the ground in front was strewn with British dead.

Everywhere arms, legs and heads were sticking up, torn limbs and bodies were lying in front of our funk-holes partly covered in ground sheets to avoid the dreadful sight. " Guillemont was only distinguishable by the lighter colour of the craters, due to the white stones of the houses, now pulverised."

Before us lay Guillemont station crumpled up like a nursery toy, and beyond that Delville Wood, reduced to chips and splinters.

Men's morale excellent. No lack of rations. Sergt.-Major burnt by a Véry light, and was evacuated.

26th August.

Went in search of our relief at dawn with my runner. Discovered them at 4 a.m. and brought them up to my post. Relieved man for man, and handed over the two Vickers guns to the incoming platoon.

Got to Brigade Headquarters at the Briqueterie via Trones Wood, about 5.30 a.m. At 7 a.m. rejoined Battalion at rest at Durnancourt. Terribly fatigued. Casualties sustained by the Battalion estimated at 100 for the 3 days.

26th August.

Fusilier Knicke mortally wounded through the spine. Hundreds of Britons observed coming up to relief beyond Guillemont Station.

Two English ration carriers who had lost their way stumbled up against position, and were shot in the Sunken Road.

To capture them would mean finding an escort to send them back.

Relieved at midnight, 26th/27th August.

Wounded by shell-fire in billets at Combles.

27th August.

A showery morning. News came from the 73rd Ambulance saying that C.S.M. Kerrigan, M.M., had died of his wounds. Later in the morning his brother came along to enquire for him (R.S.M. W. Kerrigan, D.C.M., 2nd Battalion Leinster Regiment, attached 13th Battalion Middlesex Regiment), and I had the unpleasant duty of breaking the sad news. All morning was devoted to specialists' training, Lewis gun and bombing classes, and for an hour the R.S.M. took the Battalion in battalion drill. Men handled their arms well. At 5 p.m. Möllmann and I took the men of Headquarters and C Company down to the River Ancre for bathing. Men were short of towels ; some of them dried in the sun. The Ancre is a tributary of the Somme, which flows through Albert. We passed an Indian Cavalry Regiment on our way—the Deccan Horse of the Secunderabad Brigade. In the evening the pipers and drums played round our camp. Heavy rain fell all night, at times it was torrential. Porter, who had been away on a Lewis gun course, returned to the Battalion and shared the discomforts of my weatherbeaten tent.

28th August.

More rain. Battalion drill. Lent Liston a pair of Bedford cord riding-breeches, which, by the way, I never got back, as he was killed wearing them, at Vimy Ridge. Pipers played all evening. Padre Moloney, M.C., rejoined the Battalion. All delighted to have him back.

29th August.

Battalion drill, a scorching sun between the showers. Orders received to move to the Longueval area on the morrow. The Colonel came round to see us in C Company Mess tent at night, and had a few drinks with us. Palin, O'Connor, Liston, Jameson, Porter, Warner, and I were there. Torrential rain fell at night ; the whole camp was flooded. Porter and I got soaked as our tent could not withstand such rain. The straw we lay on got wet, so did our valises and blankets.

DELVILLE WOOD

30th August.

Jackson brought us a kind of breakfast ; cold tea, damp bread and butter. The cook couldn't get the fire to light properly in the rain. Some breakfast, indeed, for us going into the line, and possibly action that night, with a long march before us. However, the unfortunate men fared no better, except that their "char" was served up hot by the Company cookers. I got a chit from the Adjutant while dressing, telling me to report to O.C. B Company, to which company I was attached for the coming tour.

Reported to O.C. B Company in a downpour of rain at 7.30 a.m. Here is a list of the officers and warrant officers who went into the action at Delville Wood:

Headquarters:

Lieut.-Colonel A. D. Murphy, M.C.
Captain and Adjutant A. C. S. Palin.
2nd Lieut. H. B. Möllmann, Lewis Gun Officer.
Rev. Father J. P. Moloney, M.C., Padre.

A Company.

2nd Lieut. R. A. O'Connor, O.C. Company.
2nd Lieut. M. C. E. Sharp.
2nd Lieut. H. H. Clanchy.

C Company.

2nd Lieut. A. R. Brassington, O.C. Company.
2nd Lieut. W. P. Liston.
2nd Lieut. A. M. Jameson.
2nd Lieut. W. J. Porter.
2nd Lieut. R. E. Warner.

B Company

Lieut. Fitz-W. H. Crowe, O.C. Company.
2nd Lieut. F. C. Hitchcock.
2nd Lieut. W. M. Powell.

D Company.

Captain H. G. Newport, O.C. Company.
2nd Lieut. D. P. McCann.
2nd Lieut. H. H. Thornley.
2nd Lieut. A. J. Dobbie.

R.S.M. C. H. Smith, D.C.M.

Company Sergeant-Majors:

Sergt. Bradley "A," C.Q.M.S. Brill "B," C.Q.M.S. Wall "C," C.Q.M.S. Sanderson "D."

Transport Officer: 2nd Lieut. J. Plowman.

THE PRINCE OF WALES

We were not sorry to move from our sodden camp. The ground was flooded and most of the ancient bell-tents had fallen through their poles. Rain was still coming down in torrents. We were dripping wet marching past the Guards' billets at Durnancourt. The men were as usual in battle order, and only had ground sheets.

We had five quarter-guards to pay the necessary compliments to in the pouring rain—Grenadiers, Coldstream, Scots, Irish, and

Welsh. Our pipers played ahead of the Battalion, which brought
the Irish Guards out of the billets, who showed their appreciation
of them in vociferous terms. My burberry became useless.

Near Méaulte a Staff car passed us in the rain. On account of
the mud it had to drive slowly past. In it I saw a very boyish
face under a Guardee cap, and I recognised the Prince of Wales.
This was, to my knowledge, the second time H.R.H. met the
Regiment in the War. It was only a glimpse I got of our future
Colonel-in-Chief. Later, a battalion of Bantams passed us on
their way to rest. They looked small and miserable in the
downpour of rain.

Here we were, practically minus breakfasts, soaked through,
and on our way into action at Delville Wood, but all cheery,
cracking jokes and whistling. At 12.30 we fell out behind Fricourt.
Standing under a small corrugated-roofed shed, I devoured wet
sandwiches with Palin and Möllmann, washed down with some
whisky. The companies had piled their rifles and were surrounding the cookers. Rain still falling in buckets. The C.O. was in
great form. He always showed his 100 per cent soldiering qualities
under discomfiture, and would appear to revel in it, which I
well knew was not the case.

At 2 p.m. guides from the regiment which we were relieving
reported to each company. We paraded by companies at 10
minutes' intervals, and marched off for our destination. Due
west of Montauban we struck off for Caterpillar Valley. It was
now only drizzling rain, but the going was terribly heavy. The
valley was water-logged, and we all got caked with mud up to
our " fetlocks." Solitary shells falling ; a few exploded very close,
covering us with liquid mud, but did no other damage. This
Caterpillar Valley was a miserable place, muddy, and all churned
up by shell craters of all sizes, now filled with water. The few
trees had been reduced to blackened stumps, and not a blade of
grass was visible either in the valley or on the rising slopes. All
along was the evidence of battle ; old web equipment, twisted-up
rifles, broken limber wheels ; and here and there a horse which
had been putrefying for weeks under the blazing August sun.
No one had thought of burying them, or covering them with lime,
because it was a valley of the dead, and no one stayed in it any
longer than necessary. The light railway line which led up to
Guillemont was completely torn up, lengths of it were standing
up for ten feet in the air, with great shell craters under them.
All along the valley were abandoned stores, boxes of S.A.A. and
the familiar, long-shaped blue boxes, which contained the Mills
bombs. These derelict explosives told of carrying parties which
had been caught out by barrages, and had been forced to dump

some of their loads owing to casualties. Our guide was most
communicative on our journey, and told me all about the fighting
his battalion had had in the past week. He was a fine type of a
regular English soldier. After a long, tiring tramp along the
valley, appropriately called Caterpillar from its winding nature,
we got to a dump called Green Dump (Map reference : Longueval
Trench Map 57c, Square S., 22a, 7.2). Here the Adjutant Palin
was awaiting us with the R.S.M. at a large dump of bombs and
sandbags. Each man was detailed to take two sandbags and
two hand-grenades. This looked uncommonly like business, and
we knew we were in for " a show."

Green Dump was always a very unhealthy spot, and particularly
so this afternoon. Shells (high explosive) were falling all round,
plastering us with mud. Now and then the Huns would sweep
the valley with shrapnel. A direct hit would have done a lot of
damage to the companies halted as we were. However, we had
no casualties ; the shells just hurried us up in distributing the
extra " impedimenta."

We were all very surprised at seeing an ancient bell-tent
pitched close to the dump. Some optimist must have put it up ;
it was completely riddled with shrapnel bullets. We moved off
in single file up the ridge, stumbling in the mud, and tripping
over the endless telephone wires which stretched at random
everywhere.

We took over the support line on the crest of this ridge from the
4th Battalion Middlesex Regiment (one of the four regular
battalion regiments), a fine battalion. The 4th Middlesex[1] belonged
to the 7th Division, which was at that date entirely composed of
regular battalions. Over on our right stood Delville Wood which
was being straffed as we carried out the relief. The dug-outs in
the line were plentiful and very deep. They had, of course, been
built by the Boches, and therefore all faced in the wrong direction.
The trench itself was good, and had well-revetted parapets. Gas
sentries were posted, and we tried to dry our clothes, which were
quite sodden. B Company servants—Mullins and O'Neill, aided
by mine, Jackson—made us quite a good dinner under the
circumstances. Crowe and I met the Adjutant, who told me he
was prepared to lay odds on a " pukka " attack. Crowe, Powell,
and I slept on the steps of the dug-out, as the dug-out itself
contained some putrefying German corpses.

[1] The Middlesex Regiment was shorn of two of their line battalions, 3rd and
4th, in that disastrous year 1922 which saw the disbandment of the five Southern
Irish regiments.

31st August.

Went along to see C Company at about 9 a.m. There I met Liston, Jameson, and Porter. They were in their shirts, and had their breeches spread out on the parapet drying. Enemy shelling Delville Wood with "big stuff." Green dump came in for a strafe, and some Maoris who were on fatigue there were wounded. My platoon on the right flank of the Company got shelled. Sergt. Parsons and one man were severely wounded. At 11 a.m. the shelling became colossal on Delville Wood and R.S.M. Kerrigan, D.C.M., now attached 13th Middlesex, walked along our parapets and called out that his regiment was retiring. A few minutes afterwards, Palin came along and gave us the order to "Stand to." The only information he could give us was that the 13th Middlesex had given some ground. The front line which the 73rd Brigade held lay between High and Delville Woods. The units holding the Brigade front were the 9th Sussex and 13th Middlesex respectively. We being in support and the 7th Northamptons in reserve.

At 12 p.m. Palin came along with movement orders for the front. He told us that the Boches had got into the 13th Middlesex trenches, and had in fact bombed them back into Delville Wood. Being on the right of the Company, mine was the first platoon to move. Palin told me to go to the head of the C.T. where I would meet the C.O., who would give me further orders. The shelling was fairly heavy, and there were a number of casualties streaming back, and soon the small dressing-station in our line was over-crowded. Padre Moloney was there, but hearing I was going up to the front, he came along with me to the C.O. I met the C.O. standing up at the head of the C.T. looking across the valley on to the ridge, where Longueval stood. He had his monocle in his eye, and was leaning on a long stick. He told me to go up and report to the O.C. 9th Sussex, whom I should probably meet near some lone trees (indicating them) and take all orders from him. He said that he knew my rôle would be to bomb the Huns back.

I had about ten heavy boxes of bombs with me. As we scrambled over the top, the Padre blessed us. We had to go down into a small valley before getting to the ridge, where Longueval was situated. The enemy probably expected that we were mass-ing troops in this dead ground. At any rate, he gave it a thorough searching with shrapnel, and a systematic strafing with "Black Marias" and "Jack Johnsons." There was a C.T. but we did not use it. Besides it was full of wounded making their way back.

A fatigue party of Maoris passed us ; thick-set, brown-skinned

men from New Zealand, all carrying cork-screw wire entangle-
ment stakes. The shelling did not seem to worry them in the
least. The going was terribly heavy, and my men were laden
with cumbersome boxes of bombs. In the smoke and noise, I used
my whistle to hurry and direct the men, away in our rear I could
still see Colonel Murphy standing up like a statue on the horizon.

Men were now streaming back without arms or equipment, a
number unwounded, and in these circumstances our advance was
made " nerve-racking." It is a severe test to both officers and
men to advance through demoralized troops who are retiring in
disorder. On we went without hesitation. The men were
splendid ; no troops can touch them as regards behaviour in
action. I got orders to halt at the trench on the ridge, and so
far we had arrived unscathed.

The rest of B Company now came up under Crowe and
halted in this trench called Pont Street. Across on our right we
watched khaki-clad figures running back from the southern
edge of Delville Wood and through Longueval.

I was now detailed to bring my platoon up, and support the
9th Royal Sussex. My way lay up a slope on the top of which we
scrambled into a shallow communication trench, as we were
quite visible to the enemy, who was now sniping at us.

From the ridge one could discern khaki-clad figures in a
disconnected line, due west of Delville Wood. We made our
way direct to these, taking full advantage of all available cover.
Here I found the C.O. of the 9th Sussex. The exact position
was at the junction of Plum Street with Chesney Walk. The
O.C. 9th Sussex ordered me to advance up Plum Street with
my platoon and bomb the enemy, who had a position at the
" T " junction formed by Orchard Trench, which we knew they
were holding in strength.

In broad daylight I was ordered to advance up an exposed C.T.
with my platoon in file ! Had I been ordered to take up my
platoon in extended order over the top I would have had a much
more sporting chance of carrying out the final instruction " to
capture the enemy post in Orchard Trench."

I got my platoon into the correct bombing formation, of
bombers, bayonet men, and carriers, placing myself as No. 3 in
the line, and with bent heads we turned into Plum Street, which
was at right angles to Chesney Walk. We advanced very

During this German counter-attack the 8th Battn. The Queen's of the 72nd
Brigade, who were entrenched on the N.E. edge of Delville Wood, were subjected
to an intensive shelling. In order to avoid casualties they showed great initiative in advancing some fifty yards, where they took up a new line in accom-
modating shell-holes. Throughout the Somme offensive stress was laid on
holding the ground in preference to the holding of an actual trench which had
been such a feature in the stereotyped trench warfare.

cautiously, as 150 yards ahead of us, on commanding ground, was the Boche post. Along the left-hand side of Plum Street were the shattered stumps of trees, and when we had advanced some 20 yards only, where we came to an iron 5-barred gate thrown into the shallow trench, bombs rained down all round us. My bombers retaliated, and after a short exchange, the Boches whom we could see quite distinctly wearing their coal-scuttle shaped helmets, retired. We again advanced, but crawling on our hands and knees, as the trench was completely obliterated. Enemy snipers now started to worry us, as our screen of smoke from the bombs cleared off. Some men were hit behind me.

We were now (i.e., the head of the platoon) taking advantage of some cover from a flattened-out traverse. To cover our advance, I detailed two men to observe the Huns from some shell-holes on either side of the C.T. and snipe. They were put in position, and had only fired a few rounds when they were both shot straight through the head. Within a few seconds two more men were killed, and I narrowly missed one myself, the bullet hitting the earth beside my head, and driving some stone splinters into my neck. We were now out of bombing range and we watched the Boches climbing back over the barrier which they had erected at the head of the C.T. These we fired at, and probably hit a few. Simultaneously as the last Hun disappeared a Maxim opened on us, and I had six men killed instantly.

Advancing was now out of the question, as the trench was completely obliterated, so I withdrew my men. All the Lewis Gun Section being casualties, we brought back the gun.

In this attempt I had twelve men of my platoon killed by snipers and machine-gun fire. Crowe joined me, and we returned to Pont Street to bring up the other two platoons, leaving Powell with his platoon and the remnants of mine at Sussex Headquarters. We picked up an officer of the 13th Middlesex on our way back. During the attack in the morning, he had got cut off from his unit, but had gallantly remained with a mere handful of men in an isolated trench on the fringe of Delville Wood.

We brought the remainder of the Company up without casualties, though all the back areas were being heavily shelled by "big stuff." There were a number of stretcher cases lying about under cover, waiting until darkness set in to be carried off to the dressing station.

B Company was now allotted a line of sorts, connected shell-holes on the extreme edge of Delville Wood. On the map on page 167 can be seen Bugle Trench. In this trench we were approximately situated. We experienced difficulty in getting to this line. We all ran the gauntlet from the

enemy snipers, who were extremely vicious. One by one we ran
from shell crater to shell crater, bullets whizzing past and slapping
the earth beside us. Our dead lay all over the place. I remember
in the fold of the ground two dead men sitting up straight, their
mouths wide open, and full of horrible black flies !

It was about 6 p.m. when we manned our so-called trench and
prepared for eventualities. C Company, less Powell's platoon
attached to D Company, was now reduced to some thirty-five
strong. The enemy now began putting over gas shells, and gas
helmets were donned. Most of the shells passed over us, and fell
into the wood, but the gas hung about our area, which was in a
hollow. All the time heavy shelling was smashing up Delville
Wood. Our guns were very silent, and did not fire in the enemy
trenches during the evening.

The map on page 167, I actually carried in the action at
Delville Wood.[1]

1st September.

Throughout the night 31st August/1st September the other
companies of the Battalion had been engaged in bombing attacks,
which failed in the main object of restoring the front line. The
Huns had the advantage of knowing the ground, and had properly
consolidated their positions. They seemed to have had an endless
supply of machine-guns.

Newport wounded. Later C Company successfully attacked
under Lieut.-Colonel Murphy, and they succeeded in regaining
all the left position of the original front line. In this attack, a
stretcher-bearer—Merriman—showed great daring in rescuing a
wounded man who had fallen behind a German barricade, and
2nd Lieut. Jameson, a very white man, was killed. At 10 a.m.
A Company, who were on our left, attempted to bomb up Plum
Street, but met with no more success than I had done the day
previously. The officer temporarily commanding A Company,
2nd Lieut. R. A. O'Connor, a stout-hearted fellow, was shot
through the head when directing this operation.

At about 4 p.m. there was a sudden lull in the fighting which
seemed rather uncanny. Artillery, machine-guns, and snipers
seemed to pause, as it were, for breath.

The stillness was rudely broken by the crisp bark of a bomb.
All strained our eyes towards the ridge on the left which
C Company was holding.

A khaki figure, minus steel helmet, the only human figure
visible on this vast stretch of desolation, could be seen throwing

[1] It will be seen from the map on page 173 that the British line at this date
formed an ugly salient round the edge of Delville Wood.

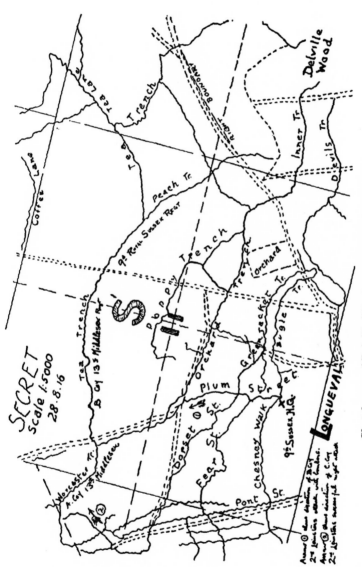

Sketch map of Delville Wood sector showing the trenches.

bombs with extraordinary rapidity into what was presumably an enemy advanced post. He fell, but quickly regained his feet and continued hurling hand-grenades.

Then he became enveloped in a cloud of smoke which screened him from view. Clearing, it revealed him once more throwing bombs. A machine-gun opened fire and steadily traversed along the front. The bomber fell to an invisible foe, having courted death for some sixty seconds of what seemed a charmed life, and disappeared into a shell-hole. " Faith an he's took the count this time," muttered an " old tough," who was, like myself, an interested spectator, with Celtic psychology.

Investigations failed to discover the name of this hero ; he was one of C Company, undoubtedly, who was trying to regain our lines after the night attack.

And so this unknown Irish warrior of a daring exploit was swallowed up in the weeping countryside of tortured Picardy.

It was a sweltering hot day, and gas from the shells hung all round the place. We had now turned our line of connected shell-holes into a useful fire trench. The men did dig in well, and C.S.M. Brill did good work. Dobbie and Powell were wounded.

The enemy certainly " had their tails well up " at the commencement of this engagement. They had gained a huge piece of ground ; they had the complete superiority of fire, both by snipers and machine-guns, and they must have known that they had caused us heavy casualties. Whether it was a coincidence, or whether it was because the Boches' intelligence was especially good, will never be known, but at any rate the 13th Middlesex, which came in for the gruelling, was the unit which had had such a terrible ordeal in front of Guillemont, just a fortnight earlier. Its depleted ranks had been filled with a large draft of young and inexperienced troops.

All afternoon enemy aeroplanes hovered over us, and the edges of Delville Wood, like a lot of angry hornets. They were obviously observing for their gunners, and making a reconnaissance of our lines with a view to another attack.

At 5 p.m. after a short preliminary bombardment, the 3rd Rifle Brigade and the 8th Battalion The Buffs attacked on our left in waves and drove back the Huns. The attack was in full view of our sector, and we watched the riflemen advancing at the " high port," and the Huns running like rabbits. All the ground which had been lost had now passed back into our hands.

This attack was a fine sight. Our infantry steadily advancing in perfect waves, their R.S.M. standing on a flank dressing them as they went by. Enemy shells were bursting, and taking their usual toll, but there was no hesitation, except for the casualties and the stretcher bearers, who dodged about in the rear picking up the wounded.

During the attack the enemy was particularly active with his artillery. The outer edges of Delville Wood and our trench came in for a rough time. However, we did not mind the shelling in the least, as we were all so excited watching the attack. The 3rd R.B.s and 8th Buffs lost rather heavily consolidating the regained line. The ration party which another regiment was supplying did not turn up, and but for Jackson and O'Neill we would not have had any food. We were drenched with gas-shells[1] all night, but had few casualties.

2nd September.

Shelled at intervals all morning. Very hot day, which brought out swarms of flies. Crowe and I on our way to liaise with the unit on our right flank came under fire from German aeroplanes, which were flying low over our area. The bullets ripped the earth up beside us. The Boches showed great flying activity all morning, hovering over our line and dropping lights which were always followed by a salvo of shells. This was the only time I saw the enemy planes at all prominent on the Somme. Later we witnessed a very fine air duel, in which two Boche areoplanes were sent crashing to earth. One fell close to Delville Wood and the other behind their own lines. The enemy shelled the outer lips of Delville Wood spasmodically during the day, and again drenched us with gas-shells. At 4 p.m. we watched a ration party which was on its way up to the northern edge of the wood, coming in for a bad strafing in Longueval. They had quite a number of casualties. Delville Wood at this date provided no cover whatsoever. There was no undergrowth left, and all the paths through the wood were taped to the square foot by the enemy artillery. Padre Moloney came round to see us. He was as cheery as ever, and blessed us all before he departed. One amusing incident happened during the day. Our Brigadier, who was up touring the line, was very disconcerted at seeing a Leinster soldier marching gaily through that charnel house, Delville Wood,[2] minus rifle, equipment, and gas-respirator, but swinging a bottle of whisky as he strode along. He called to the man and asked him where the blazes he was going with the whisky, and received the glib

---

[1] Our company donned gas masks, but not before some of us had had some whiffs of gas, and felt very wretched and choky. This dose of gas affected me very seriously afterwards.

[2] Delville Wood now belongs to South Africa, it was presented to South Africa in commemoration of the gallantry displayed there by the South African Brigade in the 9th Scottish Division.

answer that the alcohol " 'twas for th' officers." The soldier proved to be Pte. O'Neill of B Company, Crowe's servant. The Brigadier, who had a keen sense of humour, let him go on his way, and Pte. O'Neill duly reported to us, and saved our lives! At 6 p.m. a company of the 7th Northamptons under Wright arrived and took over our line. We wished him luck and filed off. Crowe went in advance, with half of B Company, whilst I remained and picked up Clanchy with A Company. At 8 p.m. I reported to Norrie at Brigade Headquarters that the last company of the Leinsters had been relieved. A few shells followed us up on our way out, but we had no casualties. The other companies lost a few men,[1] and I was terribly sorry to hear afterwards that No. 7730 Pte. O'Mahoney of C Company had been killed by a shell on the ridge south-west of Longueval. He was carrying the mess-basket on his shoulder. He was a good soldier, and I have mentioned him before as the keen sentry before Guillemont.

At about 9 p.m. we got to an old disused Boche line running along the ridge south of Mametz, known as the Pommeran Redoubt. Here we found our valises. Porter and I turned into them for a badly needed sleep in the open under a starry sky.

3rd September. Sunday.

Woke up late and had breakfast. Excellent weather. We were in Divisional Reserve, and were told we might be required at any hour to move into action, which was very hard indeed, as we had been reduced to some 9 officers and not more than 270 other ranks. However, General Capper said the Leinsters' morale made up for deficiencies in numbers.

We counted our casualties in the Battle of the Somme, and got the following list, which was severe to say the least.

Officers . Killed 7 Wounded 15
Other ranks ,, 147 ,, 418

The following were the casualties amongst the officers :

Killed.	*Company.*	*Actions at*
Capt. Laville	D	Guillemont
2nd Lieut. Handcock	C	and at
,, Jameson	C	Delville Wood.
,, O'Connor	A	
,, Siddons	B	
Rev. Father Doyle		

[1] Also killed : 7510 Corpl. Haggerty, 9367 Sergt. O'Connor, 9954 Pte. Smith, M.M. (C.O.s orderly), and Pte. Guinan (Poole's orderly).

Wounded—Battalion H.Q.		*Actions at*
Lieut.-Colonel Orpen-Palmer, D.S.O.		Guillemont and at
Lieut. Burns, D.C.M. (twice).		Delville Wood.
2nd Lieut. Whitby.		18th Aug. to 2nd Sept.
Regtl. M.O.		

Companies.

Capt. O'Morchoe	A
Lieut. Todd	B
2nd Lieut. Magner	A
Capt. Poole	C
,, Barry	B
2nd Lieut. Powell	B
Capt. Newport	D
2nd Lieut. Dobbie	D
,, McCann	D
,, Thornley	B
,, Smyth	D

Warrant Officers.

C.S.M. Kinsella	Killed.
,, Kerrigan, M.M.	D. of W.
,, Bennett, D.C.M.[1]	Wounded.
,, Saunderson	,,

We had been in two engagements, and on both occasions we had got orders for an attack, but at the eleventh hour we had been thwarted by some unforeseen circumstance.

While we were resting and licking our wounds on the Fricourt ridge, a successful attack was made by the 16th Irish Division on Guillemont and Guinchy. Our 7th Service Battalion, who were in the 16th Division, took a conspicuous part in the attack. It was actually the 7th Leinster's bombers led by Holland who captured the village, or shambles, of Guillemont. We had met some of the personnel of our 7th Battalion on our way back from Delville Wood on the previous night.

At 6 p.m. we paraded by companies, and marched back to an encampment south of Fricourt. We were not to go back into battle that night, at any rate. Here we found a draft of some eighty other ranks from the Royal Irish Regiment awaiting us. Reinforcements at this stage were not too welcome a sight, as it portended our return to action !

---

[1] Died of these wounds in 1917.

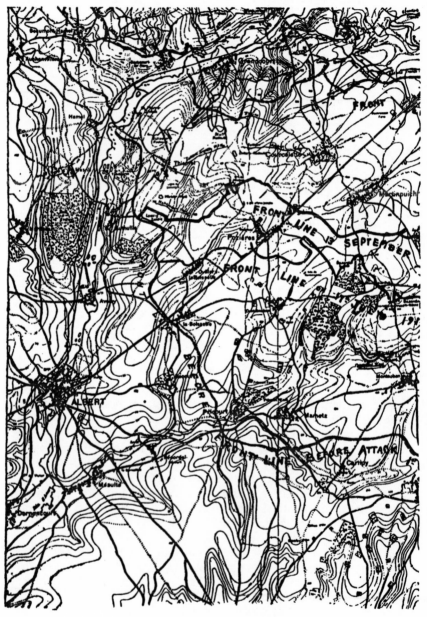

The Somme offensive, 1916, showing

ground gained in the phases of the battle.

4th September.

A wet morning. We got orders to parade at 11 a.m. for an inspection by the G.O.C. It was still drizzling when we fell in and formed hollow square. The draft was drawn up on the left flank ; they all looked very clean in new khaki ; they were nearly all old toughs who had been wounded before. Less the draft, the Battalion could only muster 9 officers and 270 other ranks.[1] Major-General Capper had a short inspection, and then said : " I deplore your severe losses, but I am proud of the Battalion. Captain Palin, officers and men : I always knew I could depend on The Leinsters, and I know it more than ever now." The G.O.C. warned us we would probably be returning to the line that night. Not too cheerful a piece of information !

The nine officers on parade were Capt. Palin ; Lieutenants Crowe, Sharp, Möllmann, Porter, Warner, Clanchy, Brassington, and myself. The C.O. had sprained his ankle badly, and was lying in his tent.

All day long the expected orders hung over us like a black cloud. They had not arrived by 10 p.m., so we all " turned in."

5th September.

Spent the morning inspecting the platoons and reorganising the sections with the new draft. Standing to for the front line. In fact, it seemed a dead certainty that we would move off in the evening. We were close to a battalion of the Grenadiers, and we watched them doing arms drill during the day in a sea of mud. Men who could handle their arms with such precision under such conditions were bound to give a good account of themselves in battle.

6th September.

Movement orders were received at 10 a.m. for REST. " Walley " Morrogh came to see us. He was now serving with the M.G.C. At 2 p.m. the Battalion struck camp at the Citadel, and marched off for Durnancourt. It was turning cold and foggy when we got on to the main road, now a complete quagmire from the endless traffic. Our march was broken by long halts on the side of the road to allow infantry and ammunition columns to pass. All troops returning to billets had rightly to make way for troops going up to the front. At 8 p.m. we arrived at Durnancourt, and took up a few separate camping areas throughout the village. We were all accommodated in ancient bell tents. The men were

---

[1] The 2nd Battalion mustered 39 officers and 1200 other ranks when it was launched into the Somme offensive.

not too tired to fraternise with the Irish Guards, who were billeted in the village.

7th September.

We struck camp at 4 a.m. and marched off from Durnancourt in the dark for the railhead. The General took the C.O. in his motor, as he was unable to walk or ride with his ankle.

Entraining took some time, owing to the transport which had to be loaded without any platform. We got to Amiens via Corbie, and detrained at Longpré.

When entraining at dawn we could hear the continual rumbling of the guns. Always the guns—they never ceased firing in Picardy in 1916. We had suffered all the horrors of war in the last month. Colossal shell-fire from guns of every calibre, gas-shells, machine-gun and rifle fire, hunger and maddening thirst ; and we had all suffered, from the C.O. down to drummer-boy, from lack of sleep, and from the heat of the day and the intense cold at night ; also from pests—the enormous blue-black flies which plagued the Somme battlefields. How they crawled into one's food after they had been settling on some exposed piece of human mortality lying on No-Man's-Land !

We had all been soaked through many times. We hadn't minded being bombed by hand grenades, but we had minded being bombed by aeroplanes at night. Our only consolation on the Somme was the fact that if conditions for us were bad, they were equally so for the Boche. The Battalion marched off from Longpré at about 10 a.m. and after a long march in the heat of the day, along seemingly endless roads belted with the familiar poplars, we got to a village called Bruchamps, which nestled down in a hollow surrounded by woods. Brig.-General R. G. Jelf halted to see us march past.

I had lunch with Padre Moloney in the local *estaminet ;* as the beer was poor we drank bénédictine, much to my sorrow later. Porter and I shared the same billet. Companies were scattered throughout the little village, which seemed delightfully tranquil after the scenes of the past month.

8th September.

Crowe read out battalion orders to the company on parade. I was surprised, and very overjoyed to hear that I was to proceed at once and take over command and payment of A Company. My servant, Jackson, was almost as pleased as I was, and packed up my valise in less than no time. I went over to A Company billets, and duly took over. The only officers in the Company were Sharp, who had transferred to us from the 5th Royal Irish Lancers, together with his batman who gloried in the name of Drinkwater, and who later in the War was awarded the Military Medal, and 2nd Lieut. Clanchy.

Sergt. Bradley was acting C.S.M. and Sergt. Kells was acting C.Q.M.S. The pukka C.Q.M.S. Bond was acting R.Q.M.S. at the time. Difficulty in finding an officers' mess cook. Jackson, however, volunteered to take on the duty temporarily.

9th September.

A Company's billets were particularly good. A large farm-house overlooking a spacious cobbled yard. The outbuildings were very good, and all formed three sides of a square. The men were comfortably accommodated.

10th September.

Morning parades. Lewis Gun and all specialist classes in full swing. The men were very happy and the Lewis Gun classes looked particularly peaceful, sitting round their guns under some shady trees. It took me a few nights to get accustomed to sleeping between sheets. Sergt. Guilfoyle joined the Company. Being a qualified P.T. instructor, he was a great asset, and took the men in bayonet fighting and put a rare jerk into them. 2nd Lieut. Warner joined the Company, being transferred from C. In the evening I received a chit from Palin asking if I would like to accompany him on 48 hours' leave to Paris !

11th September.

A batch of reinforcement officers arrived ; amongst them were Lieut. H. C. Berne, M.C., and 2nd Lieutenants Mathias, Moritz, and Cullen. The latter was posted to A Company. Capt. Frend and Lieut. Gately, who had been on a long course near Abbéville, returned to the Battalion.

I went round to meet Palin at Battalion H.Q. where he had arranged for the mess cart to bring us to Brigade H.Q. Palin told me that the C.O. had said that the leading platoon of B Company had gone into action at Delville Wood in splendid style.

O'Brien, the mess cart driver, " famous " for bringing the mess cart actually into the Valley of Death, possibly under the influence, drove us to Brigade H.Q. Here we were joined by the Staff-Captain—Norrie[1] of the 11th Hussars, who had won his M.C. in the action at Neary in September, 1914. Moll, a Special Reserve Leinster, in charge of the Brigade trench mortars, also

[1] Now Commanding 1st Cavalry Brigade at Aldershot.

two officers of the 7th Northamptons, joined us at the Abbéville station. At 7 p.m. we got to Paris, after a very comfortable journey. Two things I remember about it were the amount of whisky we all consumed, and the following notice which was plastered up in every compartment : " Mefiez-vous, Taisez-vous. Les oreilles ennemies vous écoutent." Palin and I taxied from the Gare du Nord to the Provost Marshal's office, where, in accordance with our instructions, we reported. The A.P.M. was one called Brett, and the husband of Zena Dare the actress.

Having signed our names in a book we left and made a bee line for the Hotel Continental to park our haversacks. It was a good thing for us that Palin knew Paris so well. We went to the Folies-Bergères that evening, where we met the two Northamptons, Gurney and Wright.

12th September.

At the American bar in the Place de l'Opéra, where we drank rainbow cocktails. I was complimented by the old barman for " holding so many for one so young ! " He said two of those special brands of his were sufficient for most people. Palin and I again went to the Folies-Bergères in the evening. Bar ourselves, and the few who had come with us from the Division, there were practically no other British soldiers in Paris.

13th September.

Strolled in the boulevards, looking into a shop window at some French decorations—Croix de Guerre, Médaille Militaire, etc. The owner came to the door, and asked us to buy them. However, Palin told him that we had to win medals in our army, not buy them !

14th September.

Gurney and Wright lunched with Palin and myself at the Café de Paris ; as this was our last day in the French capital we celebrated the occasion by eating frogs. At 6 p.m. we left our hotel for the Gare du Nord and the Battalion. We slept in the train, which was full of French officers.

15th September.

Arrived at Abbéville, where we breakfasted. Got back to the Battalion in time for regimental sports. Inter-company tug-of-war was the chief item. As Battalion H.Q. claimed the services of the Transport, they walked away with the Battalion championship. There were sack and boot races. Padre Moloney running in the former caused much amusement. There was also a race for men in marching order. Sergt. McCarthy, the transport sergeant, won this event in fine style.

16th September.

Took the Company out for an advanced guard scheme. In the evening went for a long ride, exploring the neighbouring villages. The country was lovely, crops in full bloom.

17th September.

Battalion route march with an advanced guard scheme. My Company, which was leading, furnished a van-guard to the Battalion. It was a splendid morning, and the country was very open, and lent itself to the scheme.

Night operations for the Company. We carried out a night attack across a newly cut cornfield. When we returned to billets, I found movement orders for the following day. We had all enjoyed our rest, and it had done us all a world of good. There was practically no crime in the Battalion during the rest. I had only two cases of drunkenness.

18th September.

Paraded at 5 p.m. for the rail-head. We vaguely heard that our new destination would be near Bethune. The evenings were getting short, and it was quite dusk when we got to our rail-head—only some six kilometres distant—and entrained. The men got tea served out from the company cookers, and the officers went into an *estaminet* near by for coffee and omelettes. The rail-head was called Longpré-les-corps-Saints, not to be mistaken for the other Longpré just outside Amiens. Here we met some of the 7th Battalion, including Gerald Farrell, who had just left the "War" on the Somme under Lieut.-Colonel H. W. Gaye. 2nd Lieut. Heming joined the Battalion from Sandhurst.

19th September.

After a long, uncomfortable journey with tedious halts, we drew up at a railway siding somewhere close to Bethune. Here we detrained into a wet and cold morning at 4 a.m. feeling very miserable. The usual delay took place over unloading the transport, my Company being detailed for this hectic task.

It was dark when we marched off for billets in Bruay. As dawn broke, a most depressing countryside revealed itself. In place of the lovely green fields of Bruchamps were coal mines, and all their hideous accessories. The very road along which we were

marching, was made of cinders. Shared my horse with Sharp.
At 7 a.m. we got into Bruay, wet, tired, and hungry. Had a room
in a miserable billet with Plowman overlooking the railway
station, and all round were smoking factory chimneys.

20th September.

Inspections only ; men all very smart, having recently been
refitted with brand new khaki and boots. Met Massey, who had
been at Sandhurst with me ; he asked Porter and myself to dinner
in his R.F.C. Squadron Mess. He now sported a Military Cross
and Bar. We had a cheery night, and met an old Nenagh friend
in one Waller, who was O.C. the Squadron. We did not return
to billets until the early hours.

As we were leaving, orders came in detailing various pilots for
reconnaissance patrols over the lines at 5 a.m. The R.F.C. were
always early birds.

VIMY RIDGE

21st September.

At 7 a.m. Palin, Frend, Mollmann, Brassington, and I went off
on a " Cook's Tour " (i.e. to inspect our new line) in motor buses.
We were joined by the Brigadier and Howlett, Brigade Major,
Norrie, Staff Captain, and Company Commanders from all
regiments. The country through which we were passing was
opening out. Gradually we left the mining area and the smell of
smoke for pleasanter scenes—large fields, where the harvesting
was in full swing.

When we got to Villers au Bois, which was right in the midst
of the 9th Divisional area, the roads became bad, and our cumbersome buses made slow headway. It was not until 11 a.m. that
we pulled up on the western edge of Carency, after a tedious
journey. Here we " debused," and met guides from the units
we were relieving. The village, Carency, was just a mere shambles,
and lay in a valley between the famous slopes of Notre Dame de
Lorette and the southern end of Vimy Ridge. Carency, it will
be remembered, was the scene of some of the bitterest fighting
which ever took place between the Frogs and the Boches, bar
Verdun, in the War.

The state of Carency alone testified to this. The French attack
in May, 1915, had been successful in wresting the famous heights
of Lorette from the Germans, but it is said to have cost our Allies
over 90,000 casualties. General Pétain had commanded the
French, and exploited his success up the valley towards Souchez
(the French call this action the 2nd Battle of Artois). From

Givenchy, at the end of the valley, the enemy had observation of the main road which ran through Carency. This accounted for the large canvas screens which were stretched at intervals right up to "Daly's" as camouflage. At "Daly's" (the name for the supporting battalion's headquarters) our guides led us off the road into a deep communication trench.

A lot of the trench notices were still in French, and all the trenches were marked as "Boyau 29," etc. This C.T. seemed endless, as we walked over miles of duckboard tracks. We were on the western slope of Vimy Ridge (or the right bank of the Souchez River). Across the valley on the Lorette slopes, the ruins of the Church of Ablain St. Nazaire stood out white against the dark and forbidding heights. We were now in Zouave Valley, and when we got to within a kilometre of Souchez we turned to our right up the ridge. When I got on the crest of this colossal ridge, I found the Company Commander, whom I would relieve in a few days, awaiting me. His regiment was a Service Battalion of the Argyll and Sutherland Highlanders in the South African Brigade, 9th Scottish Division. His front consisted of sap-heads running out to the lips of a number of big mine craters, which lay in the middle of No-Man's-Land. The line seemed very tranquil. Our return journey did not take long, and we were landed back at our billets in Bruay at about 5 p.m. Massey of the R.F.C. came to have dinner with Porter, Plowman, and myself, and we had a very gay evening.

22nd September.

The Battalion paraded at 6 a.m. and we marched off for our new billeting area—Camblain l'Abbé. It was a long march, and I made use of my horse. My groom was Donoghue, an excellent fellow, who managed to put a lot of my kit in my saddle-bags. Saddle-bags were a great asset on service ; one could always clean up on arrival at billets, and not have to wait for the transport to bring one's valise around. It was a perfect morning, and we got to our destination for lunch.

Our billets were hutments, with beds made of rabbit wire. When the men had all settled down and the Company cookers had arrived, we went into the village, where we got the usual French lunch at a local *estaminet.* In the evening the C.O. had a conference for the Company Commanders. He explained the defence scheme of Vimy Ridge, and then touched on some details regarding trench warfare. "We are going to worry the Boche and have the offensive spirit all during our tour," were his final words.

23rd September.

At 9 a.m. B Company moved off, and I followed with A Company, keeping 500 yards interval. We kept 100 yards interval between platoons in case of shell-fire. It was a lovely morning.

On the outskirts of Carency I gave my horse to Donoghue, to bring back to the transport lines which were situated at Petit Servins. At midday we got to our line, which ran along the crest of Vimy Ridge, and relieved the Argyll and Sutherland High-landers. Everything went off without a hitch, and the relief was completed under half an hour. The Highlanders had been a fine battalion before the Somme offensive, but they had been decimated in the capture of Trones Wood, where they behaved so gallantly. They were splendid-looking men, and numbers of their officers and other ranks wore a South African ribbon or two. A fair sprinkling had even fought against us in the Boer War, and some of these men sported the South African ribbons! Fighting so splendidly for us now, I suppose they felt they might as well show it was not their first campaign. All their officers had been promoted from the ranks, and were all South Africans. This was the first occasion on which we had ever carried out a daylight relief, and it could not have been done had the trenches been shallow, or the Germans had good observation.

However, contrary to the usual site for British trenches, we were actually on the top of the ridge, and, if anything, had the advantage of the Boche regarding visibility. My company front lay in a very interesting sector. The trenches were very dry, and well built, and on the right of my front were five large mine craters, called, from left to right, " Gunner," " Love," " Momber," " The Twins." We held the near lips of these craters by " T " head saps, known as 4, 5, 6, 7, 8, running out from the front line. There was sufficient accommodation for the men in numbers of small, but deep, dug-outs, and a few disused mine shafts. My Company Headquarters was in a lane called Heaton Road, on the reverse slope of the Ridge. It was bomb-proof, but the Company Mess which adjoined it was of the verandah type. B Company, under Brassington, was on my left, their right flank resting some two fire bays on the left of Sap A.1. The regiment on my right was the 1st Battalion Royal Fusiliers, of the 17th Brigade. A regiment of the Saxon Corps was opposite to us. They seemed very tame.

Toured the Company front many times, so as to get thoroughly acquainted with it under these ideal conditions. The sap-heads were very important and particularly interesting. It was all very weird ; here we were on the near lip of a large mine crater, the enemy holding the opposite lip, with, as the "toughs" said, "a few yards of air between their rifles' muzzles and our own."

24th September.

A quiet morning, one or two rifle grenades fell into my left sector, but no harm was done. The enemy seemed particularly inoffensive, and we started being somewhat hostile. The C.O. appointed Lieut. A. P. Gately (who had just returned from a long course) Battalion Bombing Officer. We commenced by sending over salvos of rifle grenades on the enemy's advance posts at the craters. We kept this up throughout our tour; we never knew if we caused any casualties to the Huns. However, we did a lot of material damage to his line, and no doubt lowered his morale.

25th September.

The Saxons attempted to fraternise with the sentry group in Sap 8. L/Corpl. Hudson, i/c of the post, let them, until he discovered the number of the regiment on their shoulder-straps and then commenced firing. The Adjutant sent me instructions (page 183) with regard to the finding of a "crater-jumping party."

26th September.

We carried out a trench-mortar strafe in the early hours. There was an attack further down on our right. The enemy retaliated with a vengeance. Went round at "Stand to" accompanied by C.S.M. Bradley, to see that all the men bar the sentries were under cover. The enemy fairly shook up Zouave Valley with their trench mortars. I watched them from my dug-out entrance. Colossal great bombs waddling across through the air, with their long timber tails waving—to explode with a deafening roar, which re-echoed through the valley. News came through of the award of bars for the Military Medal to L/Corpl. Morrissey and Pte. Reid, for their bravery on the Somme fighting, they having won the medal for bravery at Hooge in '15. The medal was bestowed on No. 7974 Pte. Merriman. The Brigade trench mortars carried out a strafe on the Huns in front of my sector in the evening. I spent some time watching their shooting. Their best gunner was an old C Company man, and had been in my platoon—8212 Brown, who hailed from Templemore.

27th September.

Capt. P. Lynch, M.C. (with bar), 2nd Lieutenants Haddick and Sikes joined the Battalion. The former took over B Company

OC. A Coy   O.R.H.22

        The attached is an extract from
Div Letter a1- 23.9.16.
        At a suitable place close to in
rear of the front line each company will
arrange for a small emergency dump of stakes
wire, sandbags and shovels. The position of
these dumps is to be known to all ranks and
the stores in it will only be touched in the
event of emergency. Notices are being made
and will be sent up tomorrow. O.C. Corps will
inform me of the position selected for these
dumps by before 12 noon tomorrow
        During the night in future each
company in the front line will detail "A
crater-jumping party" of 1 N.C.O & 6 men.
These parties may be employed in the front
line for routine work during the ordinary
hours but they must be kept together and
they must fully understand that it is their
duty, in the event of a mine being sprung,
to at once rush out and seize the near
lip of the crater. Each man of these "crater-
jumping parties" will have two bombs in
his pockets and an extra bandolier of
S.A.A.
        Crater jumping parties should be
detailed from the support platoons and
they will withdraw after morning
"Stand to"
                              act'Adm Capt
                              Adj' Leinster Regt

25/9/16

from Brassington ; Haddick was posted to C Company, and Sikes to A. I will never forget the latter reporting to me without any equipment, revolver, or kit ! He was as irresponsible as ever, so I sent him to a platoon with a very fine sergeant for instruction. Our heavy artillery carried out a shoot in the afternoon opposite my line. The C.O. told me to evacuate one of my advanced posts in case of shells falling short. Some of the shells did fall short ; one went slap into the C.T. called Uhlan Alley, and made a devilish mess of the duckboard, " A " frames, and corrugated-iron sheets, which were revetting the parapets. It was really quite funny, as the sappers had only laid down the " A " frames that morning as a pattern for us to copy ! We luckily had no casualties. I sent out patrols all during the night.

28th September.

The C.O. came round my line in the morning. He told me to send out a reconnoitring patrol at dusk towards Gunner Crater, and find out if the German sap-head was occupied or not. He then gave me instructions for a local bombing attack. We picked on the following for this small operation : Sharp, Corpl. McNamara, and four other ranks. Detailed all concerned at once, so as to give them every opportunity of observing No-Man's-Land while daylight lasted. At 11 p.m. on a beautifully fine night, Sharp led his bombers over the parapet. For about ten minutes everything was very quiet. But suddenly the silence was broken by the sound of bombs. The enemy sent up numerous Véry lights from their main line. I, from my position on the left of L/Corpl. Hudson's post (Sap 8), could make out our men quite clearly. After half an hour, the expedition returned. Sharp reported that the German post was surrounded by masses of knife rests, that they got direct hits right into the Hun post from less than fifteen yards' range, and that there was no sign of the enemy ; also there was no retaliation whatsoever.

29th September.

L/Corpl. Feery of the Lewis Gun Section shot a Boche who exposed himself opposite Sap 4 near Ersatz crater. Major-General Capper inspected my line. He seemed very upset, and I learnt that he had received news that very morning that his son had been killed with the Gunners on the Somme. News came of some very belated honours for the Battalion, Capt. Poole, C.S.M. Boyer, C.S.M. Bradley, and a few men being the recipients of the Military Medal for bravery at Premesques in October, 1914 ! Shortly after this action in 1914 Poole had been promoted on the field from C.S.M.

30th September.

Received official news of another big push on the Somme, of the capture of High Wood and Flers, and of the use of " tanks." " With the assistance of tanks, Flers was captured," ran the message. What on earth were tanks? They, or what they might be, was the topic of conversation all day. Padre Moloney, who came round to see me during the day, suggested armoured cars. He wasn't far wrong. It was not until some days had passed that we really discovered what these tanks were.

During this tour, I made good friends with a Machine-Gun Corps officer called Davis, a cheery character who volunteered to remain in the line with his gun crew, instead of remaining in a " cushy " dug-out on the heights of Notre Dame de Lorette. He had invented a special stand for his Vickers gun; taking off the tripod, he had the gun fixed on a long shaft with two legs. This enabled him to sit on the parados and have the gun mounted on its six-foot stand in the trench for firing.

1st October.

At 11 a.m. I was relieved by the 7th Battalion Northampton-shire Regiment. When all the platoons had moved off, I proceeded to Battalion Headquarters and reported to the C.O. that the relief was complete. To my knowledge this was the quietest tour in the front line the Battalion had ever experienced. I had not one casualty in my company. Accompanied by C.S.M. Bradley, we set off for Carency, where we were allotted billets in the cellars. In taking a cut across country, we struck the " Cabaret Rouge," and got to Carency for lunch.

Appointed to the acting rank of Captain as I had completed the period in command of a company on active service necessary for the a/rank, i.e. twenty-one days. 2nd Lieut. Haddick was invalided to the base.

2nd October.

In good billets. Men comfortable in bomb-proof cellars. A and B Company officers' quarters alongside each other. The latter consisted of wooden-framed dug-outs with a good lot of cover on top, situated north of the village near the railway line. Battalion Headquarters situated at Daly's. Orders issued for a raid on the enemy's trenches by the Battalion. I was told that I was to take over the front line, which I had just vacated, for two days. The raid would be made on the Boche trenches just opposite Sap A.1, and it was only natural that we wanted the line to be held by Leinsters, and not by another regiment, while the raid was in progress. The object of the raid was to obtain

To :- Lt.Col. A.D. Murphy, M.C.,
    2nd Bn. The Leinster Regiment,

27.9.16.

I wish as Colonel of the Regiment
to express to yourself, Officers,
N.C.Os. and men of the 2nd Battalion
my admiration of their gallant behaviour and deeds in the late Push
on the SOMME. Nothing could have
been finer than the courage and
dash shewn by the Battalion and I
notice with regret the heavy losses
suffered by all ranks. These
heayy losses shew the undying
spirit of all ranks. The dash and
gallantry of the 2nd Battalion in
the Push on the SOMME will be for
ever a feather in the cap of The
Leinsters. I deeply deplore the
heavy, heavy losses suffered by all
ranks but trust the relatives of
the fallen ones will have their
grief modified by the knowledge
that these losses brought about such
a splendid victory.

I trust you will convey to the
Battalion my admiration of their
gallantry and assure them I watch
their doings with the greatest
interest and sympathy.

(Sd).G. Upton-Prior, Colonel,
                Maj-General,
The Prince of Wales's Leinster Regt.

Copy of a letter which appeared in Battalion Orders on 1st October from
Major-General Upton-Prior, Colonel of the Regiment.

identification of the troops opposite—which could only be done properly by capturing prisoners.

3rd October.

Much talk about the coming raid. Called on a battery of gunners who were in position just east of the village.

I had now got to know a good deal about my company; the recent quiet tour in the line had helped me enormously in getting to know the men. They were a fine body, well drilled, disciplined, and of splendid physique. The N.C.O.s, especially the sergeants, were highly efficient. Their names were C.S.M. Bradley, M.M., Sergeants Kane, Nihill, O'Neill, McNee, Guilfoyle; Corporals McNamara, Murray, McDermott, Moynighan, Honour, McSweeney; Lance-Corporals Masterson, Yates, Campion (N.C.O. i/c of company signallers) and last, but not least, C.Q.M.S. Bond. C.Q.M.S. Kells was attached from C Company.

In the evening explored the railway line north of the village, and got under the heights of Notre Dame de Lorette. One would have thought that these heights where the woods lay in thick patches had been impregnable. However, they fell to the fierce onslaught of the French in May, 1915. C.S.M. Hartley was posted to A Company vice C.S.M. Bradley, M.M., who went as instructor to a Corps school.

4th October.

Dinners were served early to the Company, and at 1.30 p.m. we paraded for the front line, and marched off with five minutes' interval between platoons. As C.S.M. Hartley had gone on in advance to take over stores, Sergeant Kane took over his duties and accompanied me back to Vimy Ridge. When we had got well up the C.T. we found that Zouave Valley was being badly strafed by trench-mortars; the C.T. had had some direct hits. We watched No. 3 Platoon (2nd Lieut. Sikes) going up the crest of the hill without using the C.T. as they were in dead ground; as bad luck would have it, a mortar landed close beside the platoon. One man fell, and we saw the stretcher-bearers rushing to his assistance. Sergt. Kane and I were only a few hundred yards away; when we got up we found that Sergt. Guilfoyle, the P.T. instructor, who had only joined us at Bruchamps, had had his leg blown off. We completed the relief very quickly, and the Company of the 7th Northamptons moved off. It was the same line which I had vacated on the 1st October.

The trench mortar strafe had died down, and we had a peaceful evening. The night was fine, and the Battalion scouts were patrolling in view of the raid on the morrow. I take the following morbid extract from battalion orders, particularly as it appeared on the eve of the impending raid, regarding burial-grounds which have been placed at the disposal of the Regiment whilst we are in this sector.

BURIALS

The following is a list of selected burial-grounds with map references :

Right Section

Cabaret Rouge, Souchez	S.14.c.
Carency (extension of French cemetery) . .	X.21.a.2.7.
Ecoivres	F.14.C.

Left Section

Ablain St. Nazaire (extension of French cemetery)	X.3.C.2.4.
Bois de Bouvigny (extension of French cemetery)	R.25.a.2.4.

Back Area

Les 4 Vents (extension of French cemetery) .	W.9.b.1.2.
Chateau De La Haie Station . . .	W.18.a.3.8."

So it appears that we are made honorary members of the French cemeteries, or "rest camps" as the men call them whilst in the line on Vimy Ridge.

5th October.

Quiet morning regarding enemy activity, but we were all busy with the preparations for the raid. I had to furnish a covering party of an officer and twenty men, and detailed 2nd Lieut. Clanchy with his platoon for this duty, and an N.C.O. (L/Corpl Hudson) and ten men for carrying the "Bangalore Torpedoes."

"Bangalore Torpedoes" were a new trench warfare device. They were aluminium tubes of about 6 feet in length, filled with ammonal, and were worked by an ordinary fuse. They were to be used for demolishing the enemy's wire entanglements if not successfully cut by artillery bombardment, to allow the raiders to get into their trenches.

However, there was little chance of the Boche wire being thick, as our trench mortars had been cutting it for some days, and L/Corpl. Delaney and the Battalion scouts had been cutting it nightly with wire clippers. The torpedoes would only be used as a last resort, and they were always cumbersome articles to work, and if used, the chief element in the raid, "surprise," would be lost, and the Boches put on their guard. These "torpedoes" were invented in Bangalore, S. India, by a gunner officer. The raiders were found by B and D Companies, and were divided into two parties under Lieut. Gately and 2nd Lieut. McCann respectively, with 14 other ranks in one party, and 13 in the other. The raiders carried rifles with bayonets fixed, bombs, and knobkerries (the latter made from entrenching tool handles). At 7 p.m. I sent out my covering party in front, and to the right of Sap A.1; and at Zero, 8 p.m., the raiders left Sap A.1 in single file.

The C.O., Captain Lynch (the directing officer), myself and a number of stretcher-bearers, telephone operators, and orderlies, took up our position at the head of Sap A.1.

When the enemy opened rifle-fire, we judged that the raid was in "full swing." A few of our own wounded crawled back, but they didn't prove very informative. There was now a great deal of bombing, which showed they were meeting with opposition.

Then some more wounded came back, and were closely followed by a small party escorting one wounded (slightly) Hun. Within a half-hour from Zero all the raiders had returned to our lines. Our casualties were 6 men wounded. The raiders had great scrapping in the Hun trenches, and accounted for at least 6 enemy killed. It was a most successful enterprise, and the Battalion received congratulations from the First Army Commander. The prisoners on being given some whisky, became very communicative, and talked of machine-gun and trench-mortar emplacements, reliefs, and casualties. During the raiders' return, there was a great deal of trench mortar activity on my front by the enemy in retaliation. All King Street, Coburg, and Uhlan Alleys came in for a hot strafing. About midnight, the Company of the 7th Northamptons, which was to relieve my company, arrived. When all my platoons had moved off, Davis of the M.G.C. came along to see me at my Company H.Q. He had done good work that night on the right of my line opposite Ersatz crater. C.S.M. Hartley and I then left for Carency. We struck out for the main Souchez–Carency road, and I reported to the C.O. at Daly's. Major Howlett was still there, and they were discussing the raid and the prisoner. It appeared that the Boche was quite pleased at his capture, as he had a wife and ten children! He was of the Landstürm class, and evidently not over-keen on fighting.

6th October.

In billets at Carency. In the morning Brassington and I explored the heights of Notre Dame de Lorette, and got on to the ridge where Ablain St. Nazaire, or its ruins, stood. Numbers of

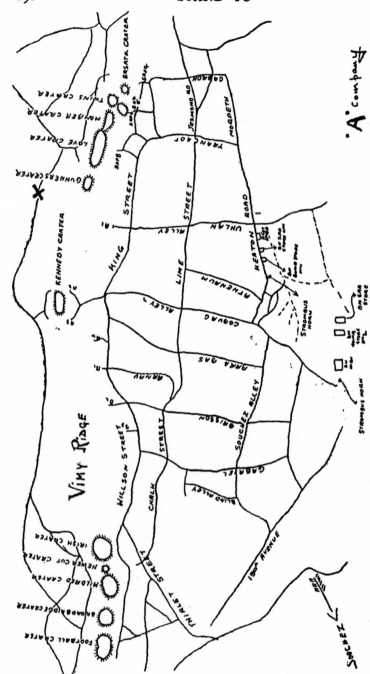

Trench map of Vimy Ridge showing trenches held by 2nd Leinsters in September and October, 1916. Where the Battalion made a successful raid on the German trenches is marked with a cross.

skulls and bones lay strewn about in the high withered grass on the heights of Notre Dame de Lorette, and in the Zouave Valley. We came across several colossal graves which, according to the wooden crosses, contained some fifty French and German soldiers, all buried together. These graves testified to the terrific struggle in May, '15 for the possession of the key of the Carency sector. From this vantage point we had a wonderful view of the lines further north, and it was an exceptionally good day for visibility. Down on the plains we could see the various clusters of red-roofed houses, which we identified as the villages of Angres and Liévin. On account of the coal mining, the country was very artificial, and the landscape was spoilt by the numerous pyramid-shaped crassiers, puits, fosses and factory chimneys.

We watched one of our heavy batteries in action, and some Boche shells bursting near it.

Gately went down the line with some bomb splinters in his eye.

7th October.

At 2 p.m. the 8th Service Battalion The Buffs relieved A and C Companies in our cellars at Carency. Platoons marched off independently for rest billets at Petit Servins. Company commanders' horses having come up to Carency, Brassington, Möllmann and I rode back together. Petit Servins was a very poor little village. The officers' quarters were not good, but the men fared better. A and B Companies were billeted in the outbuildings which formed a square of a large farmhouse. This farm was about ten minutes' walk from the village. It had a long avenue, belted with poplars on either side. At the back there was a large field which was allotted to both companies as a parade ground. Officers' billets and company messes were scattered throughout the village. Sharp and I shared the same billet.

8th October.

Spent the morning in the Company lines. All the men were busy with the usual "clean up" which always followed a long tour in the trenches. There was a pronounced change in the weather; the mornings were very cold, and the evenings were getting dark much earlier.

9th October.

2nd Lieut. Brassington was attached to the Royal Flying Corps, and left the Battalion. Paddy Lynch, Mouritz, and I rode off to the railhead—some 8 kilometres away, to see him off. Brassington's mount, "Dolly," bolted with him on the way, but he soon got her under control. At the railhead there were a number of Boche prisoners working on the lines and roads. We gave Brassington several drinks at a handy *estaminet* before he departed.

10th October.

The C.O. went on leave to his home in Tipperary, and Captain Frend took over command for the few days. Waller of the R.F.C., whom I had met in Bruay, passed through Petit Servins in a tender, and I brought him in to lunch.

11th October.

Morning parades and specialist training on our parade ground behind the château. The men turned out for football in the afternoon. Divisional band gave concerts in the B.E.F. canteen hut. The Military Medal awarded to Sergt. Young, D Company, for bravery on the Somme.

12th October.

Day spent in short parades. Sharp, Möllmann, and I went for a hack in the afternoon towards Bouvigny; from here we had a fine view of the Loos sector; on our way back we crossed our defence lines and numerous gun emplacements. Company commanders got orders to proceed up the Vimy Ridge on the morrow, and inspect a line which had been allotted to the Battalion for our coming tour.

13th October.

Lynch, Möllmann, Crowe, Sharpe, Moll (of Brigade trench mortars), and I rode up to Vimy Ridge on a reconnaissance tour. We left Petit Servins at 9 a.m., going via the cemetery and Villers au Bois.

We had a fine gallop up from Cabaret Rouge. We lost our way and went too much to the right by Mont St. Eloi, but eventually we got to the end of a C.T. Here we left our horses with the two grooms who accompanied us. Toured the front line held by the 1st Battalion North Staffordshire Regiment. Knowing that my Company was to take over the right sector of the front line, I paid particular attention to it. Had a drink with the Company Commander of the North Staffords, a Major, and left, and rode off for billets.

14th October.

Battalion paraded at 9 a.m. in the village where a fleet of buses were drawn up for our conveyance to the outskirts of

Carency. A wretched morning, and the rain was coming down in torrents. A and B Companies, who were again detailed to hold the front line, started off with Battalion Headquarters. We went past Brigade H.Q. at Villers au Bois. After a long weary tramp in the rain on the muddy Cabaret Rouge, we got to our line, and by midday had relieved A Company of the 1st N. Staffords.

15th October.

B Company was on my left, and the unit on my right, with which I immediately liaised, was a battalion of " Terriers "— called the London Irish.

The sector which the Battalion was now holding was on the extreme right of the line we had held on the previous tour. Battalion H.Q. was situated in Zouave Valley. There were no mine craters to hold in my sector, but there were a number of advanced posts running out into No-Man's-Land from my main trench. I found that these posts were not practical, and that only two men in the required sentry group of 1 N.C.O. and 6 men could use their rifles effectively. I got to work at once, and dug " T " heads to all these saps—giving perfect fire positions to all the men of each post. They had indeed been death-traps. The sentry groups were crammed into them like sardines, and one direct hit with a shell or a well-thrown bomb would have knocked out every man. The C.O., who had returned from leave, expressed great satisfaction with the Company's work on the new line.

16th October.

B Company were strafed at intervals all day with trench mortars. The front line companies in this sector had to detail sentries for an extra duty ; every platoon furnished one sentry with a whistle to give warning to the remainder to look out for " Minnies." When a whistle blew one looked up to see where the mortar was wobbling to. If towards us we edged off to the next few fire bays. These sentries were undoubtedly responsible for saving many lives. T.M.s could always be seen coming across, and one invariably had time to take cover. However, these sentries and their reliefs made the duties harder for the men. I had to find gas sentries as well for the platoons, and a Company H.Q. sentry over the " Strombus horn."

The Brigadier, accompanied by Norrie, toured my line in the morning.

17th October.

B Company were again strafed by " Toc Emmas," and Lynch had several of his men buried by them in Boot Street. C.S.M. Hartley and I brought over half a dozen men with shovels to dig them out. Three men were dead from suffocation. We never expected to get them out alive, as we were digging for at least half an hour. Every few minutes our rescue work was interrupted by T.M.s which were directed at the section of the line where we were working. Several times we were within an ace of getting at the unfortunate victims, when a T.M. would be signalled. We would all dive for cover, and return to find the cursed " Minnie " had landed slap in the same spot, and had obliterated the entrance of the dug-out where we were working.

The rescue party were splendid, working away in their shirt-sleeves, trusting to myself to warn them with my whistle. Our party must have been seen by the enemy, but strange to say they never opened rifle-fire, but went on strafing Boot Street in a systematic manner. The unfortunate men who were buried had not a scratch on them when we finally dug them out, but life was extinct. They were all men of the last draft (joined at Fricourt, Sept. 4th), and had originally belonged to the Royal Irish Regiment. I told C.S.M. Hartley to salve their equipment, which was the usual khaki webbing, in order to exchange for a few leather sets which I was trying to get rid of in my company.

18th October.

2nd Lieut. Clanchy left my company on attachment to the Brigade Trench Mortars. Very sorry to lose him, as he was a cheery soul, and had a stout heart. However, he was not strong, and not fit for the strenuous life of a platoon commander in the trenches.

19th October.

B Company was " Minnied " at intervals throughout the day. It turned to rain, and the line became muddy. Clanchy's departure left me short of officers, and the " watches " were lengthened in consequence. During my " watch " at night, I always walked up and down the trench, and usually on the parapet, which saved one slipping about in the dark on the greasy duckboards. I used to come back by degrees from the far end of the line ; stopping at each sentry post or sap to chat to the night sentries. In this way I got to know a good deal about the men ; it helped to keep the sentries awake, and helped me to kill the long tedious hours as well. At intervals along the line, the trench suddenly opened at the mouth of a sap running out to an advanced post.

In my front line I had several mining saps. They were in an advanced state, and had galleries right under the enemy line. All day and night sappers passed backwards and forwards along the line. At night fatigue parties furnished from regiments in reserve came up to carry away the " spoil." All the spoil from the mines had to be taken well away, as the earth, which was always of a bluish colour, would have been spotted by enemy aircraft, and consequently they would have had warning of our mining activity.

One of my Lewis guns jammed very badly with Pte. Rolands, and I went down to the H.Q. Lewis Gunners, and got Corpl. Cunningham to come to the rescue. Cunningham was a fine N.C.O., and won the Victoria Cross six months later in our attack on Vimy Ridge, but the poor fellow never lived to receive it, as he died of wounds. He was surounded by the enemy when his Lewis gun jammed. Using it as a great bludgeon he felled about six Huns and the remainder fled before him as he followed them up with bombs. He was mortally wounded in saving what the official wording of his exploit stated " a critical situation."

20th October.

At 8 a.m., Jackson called me, saying that the G.O.C. was waiting for me at the dug-out entrance ! (This dug-out was not the usual kind as found in Ypres, but was a pukka dug-out, made by the French, with numbers of steps and separate rooms.) I was naturally in bed, having been up half the night, but to make matters worse, was actually in pyjamas. I jumped up, and with the aid of Davis, the M.G. officer, who had attached himself to A Company, dressed in the following kit : a Burberry which came well over my knees, a tin hat, respirator, and Davis's gum boots with the pyjama legs tucked into them. I hadn't time to put on breeches. In this kit I mounted the steps to find Major-General Capper and his galloper, Murray, awaiting me.

I saluted, and said I had only just turned in, as I had been on the last " watch." The General wanted to inspect my line, so up we went. He objected to the positions of some sniping plates and rifle racks. He visited all the advanced posts and questioned the sentries.

The G.O.C. left me on the flank of my company on his way to see Paddy Lynch. The Company seemed to please him ; all sentries were alert, and the N.C.O.s answered his questions smartly. I was glad that it was over ; as all the time I was in terror lest the General should spot my pyjamas ! Murray evidently spotted them by the vent at the back of my " mack " which I had forgotten about, as he appeared to be very amused over something.

21st October.

B Company's trenches strafed with "Minnies." At 2 p.m., Paddy Lynch rang me up on the telephone to say that his H.Q. dug-out was blocked at both entrances by M.G.-fire, and that all the Company officers and signallers were trapped inside. I instantly sent a fatigue party with picks and shovels to rescue them.

22nd October.

Quiet day for A Company. B Company strafed at intervals with T.M.s. Patrols out at night.

23rd October.

Nightly Davis toured B and A Companies' lines with his machine-gun and crew. He always fired a few belts. He may have killed some Boches, but at any rate he cut a lot of the enemy's wire entanglements. As he fired, one could see the sparks flying from the enemy's wire. Paddy Lynch and I usually accompanied him on these tours.

24th October.

Rain falling, duckboards very slippy. Went down to Battalion H.Q. in the evening. Zouave Valley was very muddy. Passed numbers of skeletons on my way down the sunken road, which the C.T. led into, all undoubtedly French soldiers who had been killed in the big offensive of May, 1915.

Here and there French equipment lay strewn about, with parts of uniform and ammunition clips for the *mitrailleuses*. A rusty and twisted rifle barrel stuck into the ground, surmounted by the familiar *képi*, indicated the grave of some unknown *poilu*. Skulls and bones bleached white lay strewn throughout the rank grass. Twisted French rifles and equipment lay rotting everywhere. A skull was lying on the top of Uhlan Alley communication trench. Some wag had stuck a derelict *képi* on it in grim humour. A very macabre sight for those ascending the ridge for the front line! In the valley on the far side of the Lorette Heights, stood the ruins of the famous *Sucrerie*. When there was a wind in the valley, one always heard its loose and twisted wreckage of iron rattling and moaning. This, and Zouave Valley, formed an angle at the apex of which lay the now demolished village of Souchez.

The British line ran round the outskirts of its ruins, but the line was approached by long C.T.s on either flank, as the area where the village lay was " out of bounds." The reason for this order was due to the fact that the shambles were known to be plague-ridden. This of course was due to the swarms of rats which infested the ruins and its cellars.

As the French had not buried all their dead after their great offensive, they were left to decompose in the sun, and the majority of them provided a feast for the rats. I saw many rats on the ridge and in the valley. They were a colossal size, almost as big as dogs. Rat-chasing was a great recreation when in the line on Vimy Ridge. In the billeting areas for the Vimy Ridge there were numerous French cemeteries. A very large one lay just midway between Villers au Bois and Carency. This had been filled from the advanced dressing-stations. There were a few regimental *drapeaux* hanging over the entrance gate. They were all badly torn and frayed, and on one of these tricolours was pinned the Croix de Guerre.

Complete battalions had been wiped out of the French Army List during the terrific struggle for Ablain St. Nazaire and Souchez.

The French Foreign Legion had particularly distinguished themselves in this attack and it was here that Lieut.-Colonel J. F. Elkington,[1] D.S.O., Royal Warwickshire Regiment, displayed such conspicuous gallantry serving as a legionary in this celebrated corps which won for him the Médaille Militaire and reinstatement in command of his old battalion by the King which he had been deprived of during the Retreat from Mons.

The French casualties during the operations for the few days had been estimated at 90,000. If the casualties for the various sectors in the Allies front from the North Sea to the Alps were compared, the Souchez sector would not be found very far behind those of Ypres or Verdun.

25th October.

Canadian officers came along to reconnoitre the line as they were relieving us on the morrow. The Canadian Company Commander who was taking over my front had lunch with me, and killed an amount of whisky ! In many ways I was sorry to be leaving this area ; my company had been very comfortable, casualties had been practically nil, and the weather had been very good. The dug-out which was used as Company H.Q. was the finest one I ever occupied in the trenches.

This dug-out accommodated as many as 6 officers and 10 men, Sharp, Clancy, Sikes, Cullen, Davis (the M.G.C. voluntary

---

[1] In the Hall of Honour of the Foreign Legion Headquarters at Sidi-Bel-Abbas, Algeria, the writer was within recent years shown a portrait of this distinguished soldier, whose career constitutes a record in the Foreign Legion, by the C.O., Colonel Rollet.

attached!) and myself.   The men were our 6 batmen, 1 cook
(Pte. Stafford), 1 runner (Pte. Gallagher), L/Corp. Champion and
Pte. Hart, company signallers.   The gas alarm sentry over the

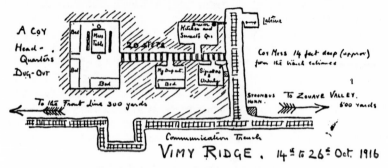

"A" Company Headquarters' dug-out, Vimy Ridge.

Strombus horn was found from one of the platoons.   With the
exception of the first tour in the trenches at Ypres in June, '15,
this was the longest period I ever did in the same frontage.
Relief orders issued.

26th October.

After "Stand down" the weather broke; it became a wet
drizzling morning, and a thick fog descended over Zouave Valley.
At about 9 a.m. the enemy opened a systematic strafe on
B Company with "Toc Emmas."   They had several casualties
before their relief at midday.   One trench mortar got a direct hit
into one of their fire bays, knocking out all the occupants and
completely obliterating the trench.   One of the unfortunate men
got a terrible wound in the leg ; in fact, it was almost severed but
for a piece of skin.   2nd Lieut. Mathias showed great resource
cutting through the skin with a pocket-knife, and managed to get
the casualties evacuated on a stretcher, although in full view of
the enemy.   At 12 o'clock, platoons of the relieving Canadian
regiment filed into the line, and relieved my company.   When
my last platoon had filed out I left my H.Q. (rather reluctantly)
and went along to report relief complete to the Adjutant.   At
H.Q. I met the C.O., Adjutant and Padre, who were just vacating
Battalion H.Q.   Led by the C.O. we started off for our billeting
area along the valley, and up the Carency ridge.   A long tramp
through those endless C.T.s brought us out at "Daly's."   Here
our horses were awaiting us, so we mounted and galloped off
across country to Camblain L'Abbé.   Strong rumours of a
Divisional move to a new area had been floating around for days,
and when we were stepping out along Zouave Valley, I turned

round to have a last look at the Vimy Ridge, now almost enveloped in a thick mist. For trenches I had spent the happiest time in the War on the Ridge. So we left the Vimy Ridge, which looked so grey and forbidding in daylight, but so totally different at night.

Going up through Zouave Valley at night towards Souchez, one could almost imagine one was approaching some big town with all the lights from the dug-outs. One never realised how many dug-outs there were cut into the edge of the Ridge until revealed by their lights when darkness set in. Right up from the valley they were built tier upon tier, until the support line was struck at the top. The Battalion returned from the line by 2 p.m., and hot dinners were issued. Two new officers joined from Cork, who proved to be stout fellows, in 2nd Lieuts. Lauder and Foley, both belonging to the 3rd Battalion. Rain fell all evening. The Battalion was accommodated in a number of wooden huts, which had formerly been built and used as billets by the French. These were the same billets that we had used on the night of the 22/23rd September. Paddy Lynch and I shared a small room in one of these huts, which had two most awfully uncomfortable beds made of rabbit-wire. He and I went into Camblain L'Abbé and procured some very bad " fizz " at a local *estaminet*. At 6 p.m. the C.O. had a " pow-wow " with Company Commanders. He said that we were under orders to move to a new sector immediately—Loos. The C.O. gave us a short lecture on trench warfare, and I find the following remarks in my note-book : " Trench warfare too casual ; posting of sentries must be carried out by N.C.O. on duty. One N.C.O. on duty by day and night per platoon ; latrines no excuse for absence." Detailed to proceed next morning with Porter (intelligence officer) to Loos, and make a reconnaissance of the new area. 2nd Lieut. Lauder posted by my company.

27th October.

Morning spent in the usual routine of the first day in billets. Rifle inspections only and the rest of the morning in " cleaning up," men having hair-cuts, equipment and boots cleaned.

LOOS

28th October.

Having spent a most uncomfortable night in the cold, draughty hut, I got up early for the journey to Loos. Porter joined me at Brigade Headquarters where we had been ordered to rendezvous. Here we met the Acting Brigadier, Lieut.-Colonel R. Pigot,

D.S.O., M.C., of the 3rd Rifle Brigade, the Brigade-Major, Howlett, and the Brigade Intelligence Officer, Egerton-Young, of the
9th Sussex, also accompanied us. Our journey by bus was very
tiring, a bus is always a bad mode of conveyance, but given
uneven cobbled French roads in a war area, it is doubly so.

A long journey of over three hours through most uninteresting
mining country, brought us to a little *estaminet* which stood at
some cross-roads, 600 yards south-west of Maroc village.

Here guides were waiting, and we were conducted across some
waste ground, pitted with shell craters, and studded with covered
gun emplacements. At Maroc, a village whose roofs had suffered
severely from shell-fire, we took the communication trench,
which brought us to a support line at O.G. 1.

Here I met the O.C. Company of a Welsh bantam unit, and had
a good view of the front lines beyond Loos from the high ground.
Far away over miles of barren wastes lay Hulluch. Then the
lines swung out in a salient before the ruined village of Loos
with all its shattered houses.

Our new area was in what was called the right sub-sector of
the Loos Salient. One could liken the Loos Salient to half a
plate, with the enemy trenches looking down into ours from its
outer edge. Hulluch on the extreme left, then the shambles of
Loos and its Tower Bridge, now reduced to a wreckage of twisted
iron girders, and the Loos Crassier shooting out towards the
Boche lines, where Hart's and Harrison's craters lay midway in
No-Man's-Land. The trenches then curved down across Hill 70,
coming to an abrupt turn at the famous Triangle to straighten
themselves out towards the Double Crassier—huge mammoths
of waste slag and charcoal, which started at the top of Hill 70 to
run for some 1000 yards through German and British lines—on
the extreme right and neck of the Salient. I could easily discern
the British trenches, the chalky nature of the soil showing up the
parapets very plainly. Here and there little puffs of white smoke
circled up from our front line. These I was told were rifle grenades
and " aerial darts " which the enemy showed particular activity
with in this sector. I returned to Maroc where Porter met me.
Here we were asked to lunch by the O.C. Reserve Company of
the Royal Welch Fusiliers, who was most hospitable.

We departed for our bus, and rejoined the Battalion, which
had just arrived at Noeux-les-Mines, having passed through
Bully, Les Brébis, and Mazingarbe.

29th October.

Paraded at 8 a.m. and moved off in torrential rain for Loos.
Our route was right through a dense coalfield Mazingarbe–Les

Brébis–Grenay and Maroc. At Les Brébis I nearly rode down an excitable Froggie, who was gesticulating in the middle of the street. Dismounting at the cross-roads, where the *estaminet* was, I led the Company up the road, and into a long C.T. at " The Hole in the Wall." This spot derived its name from a large shell hole in the red-bricked wall, which ran parallel with the trench. A long tramp of some two miles brought us to a reserve line called Duke Street, immediately behind Loos. Here I took over from a Bantam Company, and C.S.M. Hartley and I were somewhat amused in trying to stuff eight hefty Leinsters into a dug-out earmarked for double that number of Bantams !

30th October.

Detailed to furnish large working parties nightly. The dug-out line which I was holding had been the German 3rd line before the great Loos offensive in September, 1915. The dug-outs were very fine, but, of course, all faced in the wrong direction. During the day I explored the ruins of Loos and its environments. I saw the ruins of its church just by the square, and on my way to liaise with the O.C. 9th Royal Sussex, whose Battalion Head-quarters was situated in the cellar of a small and very dismantled house called " Hatchetts," I passed " the Heroine's house," now a demolished heap of bricks and rafters. The Heroine was a French woman, who went to the assistance of our wounded under fire, when we captured Loos in September, 1915.

31st October.

Went to see the O.C. 12th Service Battalion Sherwood Foresters, the Divisional Pioneer Battalion, which was responsible for the Loos village defences. Ran him to earth after a lot of walking about in subterranean passages. His Headquarters were situated right under the Loos shambles. This was a marvellous dug-out, and had of course been originally made by the Germans. I was in reserve to the 9th Sussex, who were holding the left sub-sector trenches, but my whole Company was out nightly from 7 p.m. to 2 or 3 a.m. on fatigues which I had orders to supply permanently while in Duke Street. One party went to the 9th Sussex, and two parties went to the Sappers. Palin, Möllmann, and Lynch came up to see me.

1st November.

I went into Les Brébis with Möllmann for a bath in the Divisional baths. It was a good walk, and half the journey had to be accomplished on the most tiring of all things to walk on—

duckboards. I did not get back to Duke Street until dark. Slight artillery activity all evening.

2nd to 3rd November.

I turned out the platoons for improving our parapets, and making the cook-house more shell-proof.

Terrible plague of rats in the vicinity ; dug-outs, especially the cook-house, full of them. Killed one with a brick.

4th November.

Strolled around Loos and found a number of graves belonging to men of our 7th Battalion, near St. Patrick's dressing station. Went down to H.Q. to see Palin at about 10 p.m., taking Jackson with me.

5th November.

Went up to " Hatchetts " to superintend the loading of one of my carrying parties with duckboards, cork-screw stakes, and coils of barbed wire.

6th November.

Porter came through my trench leading the Battalion Lewis Gunners. They were also going on fatigue ! At 9 a.m. I led the Company off to South Street via " Whitehall " and the Crucifix Dump. The C.T.s were all very deep. I relieved Gurney's Company of the 7th Northamptons. Here we were in support to B Company, which was holding the front line. We were not sorry to have left Duke Street, the dug-outs were filthy, and infested with rats.

I remember when we were there 8645 Pte. Corbally had a bad attack of malaria one night. I gave him several glasses of whisky, and lent him my great-coat. This treatment cured him all right, but next night several men complained of having malaria !

7th November.

This support line quite comfortable and Company Headquarters dug-out was good. Two Keeps, or defended localities, called St. James's Keep and Traverse Keep, branched off it at right angles. South Street, besides being a support line, was a C.T. for the front line. There was a deal of traffic through it, and at night with working and ration parties it became very congested.

Had to furnish ration parties for B Company nightly, and also to find a platoon every night to hold a trench which ran near B Company's Headquarters. The Regimental Transport sent a few limbers with the rations as far as the Loos Square, when darkness set in. Here the various ration carrying parties would await them. The Loos Square was usually a most unhealthy place to loiter in, as it was invariably under shell-fire. My right flank rested against the Loos cemetery, which had suffered severely from shelling. The ground was all pitted by craters, and most of the tombstones were smashed. Strange to say, there was a large Crucifix, over 7 feet high, standing up absolutely un-scathed, amongst the churned-up earth. Our rations were left nightly at Crucifix Dump.

This night I had to go down to Battalion Headquarters at Maroc and I got a lift back to Loos in one of our G.S. waggons, sitting beside the driver, McCarthy. As we drove on there were some sudden outbursts of machine-gun fire and one of the horses became very restive and broke out in a muck sweat. It appeared that this mare had had a bullet through the withers up at Ypres and ever since had been very " gun shy."

8th November.

At dark I visited Paddy Lynch in the front line, escorted by my orderly, Gallagher.[1] Found Lynch visiting his sentry-posts, and together we toured the line. What a ghastly one it was ! Half of it had been abandoned, as it was supposed to be under-mined. The original support trench functioned as the front line, and was held by a system of sentry groups with two dangerous sap-heads jutting out like a pair of horns on either flank towards the enemy. " Barricade " was the name of the post on the left, and " Russian Sap " of that on the right flank.

B Company front ran right across the bottom of Hill 70, with the Boche lines only some 100 yards away on the high ground. The enemy had perfect observation into most of our line from his " O.P.s" on the Double Crassier. Davis, the M.G.C. officer, had attached himself to Lynch's company, and I met him touring the line with his section. The new sector had made a bad impression on me. It seemed that in case of an attack the front line would have to be sacrificed, as there were not enough men in my Company to support the isolated sentry groups.

9th November.

My Company, less a party of 8 bombers who were required by Battalion Headquarters for holding the Crassiers, proceeded to the front line at 2 p.m. and relieved B Company. Regarding the line, I see the following entry made at the time in my note-book : " The trenches are in a bad state, and very wet. The

---

[1] Killed 27th March, 1918.

Germans have full advantage of positions, especially *re* observation, both from Hill 70 and the Double Crassier." Here is a copy of a sketch made at the time by Paddy Lynch :

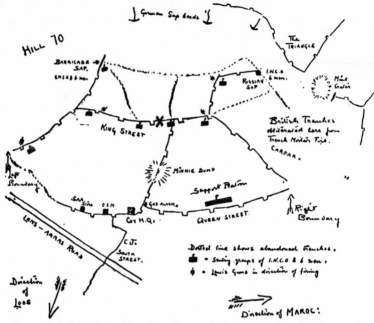

Copy of sketch of the Loos trenches made by Paddy Lynch who was killed on the 27th December, 1916, at the spot where I have marked with a cross in King Street.

10th November.

Had my first experience of " aerial darts " in the early hours of the morning. Going the rounds of my sentry groups at about 4 a.m. a salvo of these aerial darts landed close to Company Headquarters. My S.A.A. store got a direct hit ; 50,000 rounds of ammunition and 10 boxes of Mills bombs went sky-high. When visiting Russian Sap at about 4 p.m. I spotted a Boche moving about in The Triangle. I took a rifle from the sentry and aimed at him. I registered " an inner " all right as I saw him throw up his arms as he disappeared into his trench. Corpl. Honour, who was in charge of Russian Sap, saw him fall.

Hostile snipers were particular offensive during the day ; they seemed to be firing from the top of the Crassier, but we were unable to locate their positions. During the Battalion's stay in the Loos sector, these Crassiers were a constant source of annoyance. They provided outlets for all kinds of Boche " hate." They were under-tunnelled, so that trench mortars could be pushed out on rails to fire and return under cover, and there were numerous and perfectly concealed machine-gun and snipers' nests along the sides.

Of the countless number of sentry posts found by the 2nd Battalion in the War, that on the Double Crassier must undoubtedly have been the strangest.

Right on top of these two colossal slag heaps which shot out parallel across Hill 70 from Lens for some 1000 yards towards Maroc, were sentry posts. The nearer, or left Crassier, was included in the Battalion's front, but the right Crassier was held by the Canadian Corps on our immediate right. Two large mine craters, which had been blown midway in these Crassiers some twelve months previously, separated the German and British sentry groups, which were situated in " T " head saps. Our advanced post, or sap-head, was approached by a long and shallow communication trench, dug into the slag along the crest beside a railway line. The Crassiers at their highest point must have averaged 40 feet. I sent Lauder and Corpl. McNamara out on patrol at dusk ; they got up to the enemy wire, and explored our disused front line. Davis came round with his Vickers gun when the patrol came back, and started firing. I also fired a few belts from different places in the line, and practised the "Morse code." Davis then took over the gun, and was in the middle of a belt, when he got a bullet slap through the wrist. It was a fine " jammy one," but it gave him a lot of pain. We bandaged him up ; I gave him a stiff peg, and off he went to the dressing-station. I have never heard about, or set eyes on him since. Some day I may have the luck to meet him. He was a " rare plucked 'un." But on the other hand, he may have been killed later on in the War, as undoubtedly the majority of the best fellows were.

11th November.

We officially heard that the Victoria Cross had been awarded to Lieut. J. V. Holland, 3rd Battalion attached 7th Battalion, for his gallantry in the capture of Guillemont. This was the first V.C. awarded to the Regiment in the War, and we were all delighted. I wrote and congratulated him, and I also wrote to the mother of 8212 Pte. Brown, at Templemore, consoling with her on the death of her son. " Dusty " Brown had been killed on the 27th October by a trench mortar. The dead soldier had been in my platoon in 1915. I felt that nobody would write to the poor woman and give her any details, as her son was not serving with the Regiment when he was killed.

At dusk I had a fatigue party deepening the C.T. to Russian

Sap ; it had only been four feet deep, and we were always exposed to the Boche snipers on the Crassier.

12th November.

At 9 a.m. platoons of the 7th Northamptons arrived to take over the line, and 11.30 a.m. found my Company billeted in Upper Maroc, so-called after the French North African Colony Maroc, or Morocco in English. In the numerous cellars there was ample accommodation for the whole battalion. Maroc village was very typical of a modern town in an industrial district ; every house was identical with the next, and it was laid out in set squares. However, the enemy bombardment had altered the dull similarity somewhat, as here and there a house was completely demolished. Shrapnel had removed a number of the red tiles or slates, which left the jagged rafters exposed to view.

13th November.

Had my Company Headquarters and Mess alongside Battalion Headquarters, and nearly opposite the little chapel. An unfortunate incident occurred in the Company cook-house during the evening. L/Corpl. Yates, one of the bombers, was examining an old bomb, when it exploded in his hand. Fortunately, he was not killed, but he lost all the fingers of his right hand, and a few off his left. I never thought that hand wounds could look so ghastly. The unfortunate N.C.O. suffered terrible agony, and I was with him while the M.O. extracted pieces of bomb splinters from his face, and bandaged up his hands. Yates had served continuously with the Battalion since September, '14. Needless to say, there was a court of enquiry appointed by the Adjutant to investigate into the case, and I was detailed as president. The documents had to be rendered in triplicate—always the same " red tape," even within rifle fire !

Coming from the dressing-station, I saw a very gruesome sight. I happened to go into a wrong house by mistake, and in front of me in the dim light I saw the dead body of an officer of the Sappers stretched on a table awaiting burial. As I looked I was horrified to see a rat jumping down off the corpse. The house was being used as a mortuary by the R.A.M.C.

14th November.

The word " Rest " in this new sector was a " camouflage " name. This " Rest " proved to be a continual fatigue. Every night, even the first night of the rest, when we had only returned from the front line in the morning, my whole Company was split up on various fatigues to and from the trenches.

15th November.

A new horse was allotted to me as a company charger. He was a fine upstanding chestnut of 16.2 hands, which had just arrived from Remounts. Whilst out of the line, I invariably went for a morning hack with Donoghue, my groom. When out riding shells frequently fell close to us.

16th to 18th November.

Usual fatigues furnished by my Company nightly. The evenings became much shorter, and we felt the trying conditions of winter in the trenches descending upon us. The C.O. anticipated water-logged trenches, as Battalion Orders were full of instructions regarding sock changing, gum boots, and cases of frost-bite. The Staff fixed the number of days to be spent in the front line at three, for support three, and seven in reserve, so the tours in the Loos sector were cut and dried until Xmas at least.

19th November.

In heavy rain paraded the Company, and marched off for the trenches. At 11 a.m. I relieved the 7th Northampton Company under Gurney, which had been lying in support at South Street. The trenches were extremely wet, and in several places in the long C.T. the duckboards were floating about.

20th to 21st November.

Paddy Lynch informed me that conditions were bad in the front line. The C.O. came round and decided that as the men couldn't cook their food properly in the line, it would have to be done in the support trench, and he decided to use an old house close to Crucifix Dump. Here A and B Mess Cooks were installed with their dixies, and all cooking paraphernalia. Sergt. Brady,[1] of A Company, was placed in charge. When the food was ready it was placed in special dixies, surrounded with straw, and carried up to the front line. The actual carriers were found from the support company, so this was another of the numerous duties which the support company had to fulfil.

It was a splendid scheme, as it insured the men getting hot and well-cooked food when stuck out in isolated and water-logged sap-heads. On the very first day of their installation in this old ruin, the cooks allowed their fires to give forth volumes of smoke, which curled up through the rafters. This drew several salvos of whiz-bangs, which exploded all round the derelict building, but no damage was done.

---

[1] Killed 6th November, 1917.

22nd November.

After company dinners, platoons moved off at intervals to the
front line, to take over from B Company. I was not surprised at
the appearance of the front line, as it had been raining for some
time. However, things were far worse than I had anticipated.
The trenches were flooded, and in many cases the parapets had
fallen in completely. I was unfortunate in the first night of my
tour, as a salvo of aerial darts landed in South Street, where the
Lens–Bethune road met the trench, just as my ration party was
passing. 7394 Pte. Conroy was killed, and 9888 Pte. Ahern and
Pte. Hewitt were wounded, both seriously. Ahern was lamed for
life, and Hewitt nearly lost his eye. I was very sorry about
Conroy, and only a few hours previously had been chatting to
him as he had been on sentry duty outside Company Headquarters.
Conroy had always been a good soldier in the line. The casualties
were all time-serving soldiers, men whom I could ill-afford to lose.

23rd November.

McCann came round to see me in the morning. He had just
been awarded the Military Cross[1] for the raid at Vimy Ridge.
My men in Russian Sap had a bad time all day with trench
mortars, which fairly plastered the ground around the sap-head.
I was in the sap at night, when it was being subjected to one of
these " Minnenwerfer " strafes. As it was dark, one couldn't see
them, but a lot of sparks seemed to follow their track. I was
particularly sorry for the sentry group having to remain in that
isolated post, standing in water, and every few minutes getting
smothered with earth from the trench mortars which were
falling all round. Corpl. Chalmers,[2] one of the Battalion bombing
N.C.O.'s, afterwards opened a " dud " trench mortar which fell
near Russian Sap and discovered it was full of broken razor
blades and nails.

24th November.

Worried by snipers throughout the day. We located one
sniper's position, behind one of the derelict railway waggons on
the top of the Crassier. During the morning my company line
was toured by the Acting Brigadier, Lieut.-Colonel Lucas, D.S.O.,
M.C., The Buffs. He was accompanied by Colonel Kay and the
Brigade-Major. The latter told me he was most anxious to
secure a Boche prisoner for identification. He said that the only
thing our own Intelligence people knew about the troops opposite

---

[1] Finished War with two bars to his M.C.
[2] Killed in May, 1917, as Battalion Bombing Sergeant.

our Division was that they were Bavarians. He then said to me, "Will you tell the men of your company that I will give £5 to the first man who produces a live Hun?" I did not like the idea of telling this to the men, as the award would only make them take unnecessary risks in endeavouring to get a prisoner.

I told the N.C.O.'s and men who usually went on patrol, to be very careful indeed regarding risks in trying to obtain the prize. It was not through any lack of the offensive spirit that I did not jump at the Brigade-Major's offer. No Boche, dead or alive, was worth a fiver, though the actual identification might be valuable !

My company scouts under Corpl. McNamara were quite keen enough without being bribed. In the evening our Stokes and trench mortars situated in Carfax Road, just behind the Russian Sap, carried out a strafe on The Triangle, with the result that my right flank was subjected to a terrific retaliation.

In this new sector there was an addition to the numerous duties of an O.C. company in the line—a log book of daily occurrences, enemy activity, working parties, improvements to the line, etc., to be kept. I had taken it over from Paddy Lynch, who had in turn taken it over from the 7th Northamptons. In scanning the back pages I found the following weird statement, which was signed by a Company Commander of a Bantam Battalion : " Wiring: during the tour my company have placed out a number of knife rests in the vicinity of Russian Sap, but they have always disappeared immediately, and I am forced to believe that the enemy takes them away." How we laughed over this entry, which I outlined in pencil.

Espionage was practised successfully by the enemy in our Divisional sectors at Vimy Ridge and at Loos, towards the end of this year. One day a daring Hun got as far as the Lorette Heights dressed as a sapper officer. He made a thorough reconnaissance of our machine-gun emplacements and departed. That night, practically every machine-gun position got a direct hit from shell-fire.

To guard against a repetition of this ruse, General Headquarters decided that it was advisable to have pass-words for fighting troops, so every twenty-four hours a pass-word was issued from Brigade, who selected it. The new word commenced from the evening "Stand to," and our Brigade, the 73rd, chose the names of the officers commanding battalions at first—Greene, Mobbs, Murphy, etc. On the fifth and following nights, ordinary words such as " Rabbit," " Apple," etc., were introduced.

Some of the " old toughs," however, found some difficulty in remembering the absurd words which followed, and on one of the dark nights of this tour, seeing a man approaching me, I called out, " Halt, who goes there ? " only to get the following unusual reply, " Begad, I was a rabbit last night, a spud the night afore, and I'm damned if I know what I'm meant to be at all to-night."

It was 8645 Pte. Corbally. He apologised profusely when he recognised me. I told him the pass-word, and went on my tour laughing. Corbally was a treasure.

The Loos sector was famed for Boche trench-mortar activity, a form of frightfulness which was loathed by all ranks. For these strafes the Huns took advantage of the Double Crassier for cover. The Crassiers were under-tunnelled, and contained nests of these dreaded mortars. They had so many emplacements to fire from that our Stokes guns could never register on them with accuracy.

The trench mortars never made any warning noise, but one could always see them in the air, so we again employed " warning sentries " with whistles, as we had done on the Vimy Ridge. Going up to Russian Sap one morning, I overheard a man yelling out : " Look out, boys, here come the lads with the rubber heels." I asked the man what he meant, and he replied : " Sure, them trench mortars do steal across so soft-like, sorr, they do be on top of us before we know where we are." From this time onwards, T.M.'s were always known throughout A Company as " the lads with the rubber heels ! "

Here is a roll of the officers serving with the 2nd Battalion during the end of November, 1916 :

Lieut.-Colonel A. D. Murphy, M.C.
Capt. A. C. S. Palin, Adjutant.
2nd Lieut. W. J. Porter, Lewis Gun and Intelligence Officer.
Lieut. J. Plowman, Transport Officer.
Rev. J. P. Moloney, M.C., R.C. Padre.
Lieut. Ransford, R.A.M.C.
Lieut. and Quartermaster Squire.

A Company.	*B Company.*
A/Capt. F. C. Hitchcock.	A/Capt. P. S. Lynch, M.C.
Lieut. M. C. E. Sharp.	Lieut. F. W. H. Crowe.
2nd Lieut. C. Sikes.	Lieut. L. S. Mathias.
2nd Lieut. H. J. Cullen.	2nd Lieut. C. J. H. Mouritz.
2nd Lieut. W. D. Lauder.	2nd Lieut. M. A. Foley.

C Company.	D Company.
A/Capt. H. B. Möllmann.	Capt. J. R. Frend.
Lieut. W. P. Liston.	Lieut. H. C. Berne, M.C.
2nd Lieut. R. E. Warner.	Lieut. C. L. P. Heming.
2nd Lieut. N. D. Prendergast.	Lieut. C. F. Stewart-Moore.
2nd Lieut. C. Coffey.	2nd Lieut. D. P. McCann, M.C.
	2nd Lieut. E. P. Hall.

25th November.

A quiet day, bar the usual enemy trench-mortar activity in the evening. Corpl. McNamara took out a patrol at night.

I was sitting in the Mess dug-out at 11.30 p.m., reading some orders which my runner, Pte. Devoy, had brought up from Battalion Headquarters, when Corpl. Murray came down to see me. He seemed very excited, and was carrying an empty and much-blackened dixie in his hand. Knowing that he was N.C.O. i/c of Russian Sap, and hearing mortars exploding in that vicinity, I immediately thought there were casualties. However, Murray started off : "Beggin' your pardon, sorr, but there's a mutiny beyont in the Russian Sap. I spilt the rum issue, and I'm afeard to go back to them !" At first I wondered if the brave corporal had drunk the issue himself, and was trying to pull my leg. However, I gave him half a bottle of "John Jameson" to make up for the spilt rum. I also offered him a separate tot, but he refused it, saying he was a teetotaller. This statement I could hardly credit, so next day I told my C.S.M. who said it was a fact that No. 9412 Corpl. Murray was a teetotaller, but that he was the only one in A Company, and he believed, in the Battalion. This good N.C.O. was unfortunately killed later in the 3rd Battle of Ypres.

26th November.

Battalion relieved at 10 a.m. by the 7th Northamptons, and we proceeded to Maroc upper. I had hardly got settled into billets before I got a chit from the Adjutant, detailing me to find fatigues that very night.

The end of November was marked by the issue of box respirators, to replace the smelly and sticky anti-gas or P.H. helmets. The new respirators were a vast improvement, though, strange to say, they had been in existence for some time without being definitely issued. Our Machine-Gun Section possessed them as far back as 1915. Special parades for box-respirator drill were the orders daily while in billets. It took a few days to get the men accustomed to these new articles, and the drill, like all drills " by numbers," commenced! To give confidence in the new issue, we were told to make the men talk to each other, and give words of command. One morning all my platoons were formed up in squads on the middle of the main road behind our billets doing respirator drill. A hostile plane came down, and as all the men had their masks on, it cleared off unobserved, to call up its gunners. A salvo of shells landed behind us suddenly, and we all made a bee-line for our cellars.

The C.O. invited me to dinner at Battalion Headquarters Mess, which was situated beside the Maroc Church. Those who sat down to table were Padre Moloney, Palin, and Porter. The C.O. told me that the Mess had had a direct hit on it when he was sitting in that very morning, and he told me a lot of yarns about his experiences on the Somme. It was a very cheery evening.

During this rest, I went down to see Plowman at Petits Sains several times, and lunched with him. In the evening I often rode back with him to Maroc, as he had to come up with the transport.

Capt. van Cutsem of the 4th Battalion joined the Battalion on the eve of its departure to the front line. He was given command of D Company, and Capt. Frend was appointed second in command of the Battalion. On the last night of our rest, one of my fatigue parties, which was working for the tunnelling company, got shelled, and Pte. Corbally was seriously wounded.

1st December.

It was terribly cold during the night, and froze hard. At 8 a.m. the Company paraded for the line. There was a thick frost and the roads were like glass. I moved off by myself down the main road of Maroc, intending to take the communication trench north-east of the village, where there were no longer any buildings to afford cover, and where the whole Maroc–Loos road was under direct observation of the enemy from Hill 70 and the Double Crassier.

However, when I got to the C.T. I found that there was no way into it without jumping, as it was very deep, so I walked on out into the open. I had gone about 200 yards when a sniper opened on me from the Double Crassier. There I was well away from the C.T. and no available cover handy. I ran across to the C.T. with bullets tearing up the ground beside me, the frozen surface of the road added to my difficulties. When I got to the C.T. it was six feet deep at least. The sides were very steep and frozen; also the duckboards looked horribly slippery. I hesitated a few moments before jumping in, but a few close shots made me think that a broken leg would be better than being killed, so in I leapt.

That sniper was a wretched shot, as I was never out of 500 yards' range, but his hands may have been frozen. Mine were not, and with my heavy equipment I was quite breathless when finally landing in the bottom of the trench. He fired at least six rounds at me.

At 9 a.m. I had taken over the same front line from the 7th Northamptons, and telephoned relief complete to the Adjutant in code, owing to the enemy being able to tap our wires.

2nd December.

At "Stand To," C.S.M. Hartley came round to tell me that poor old 8645 Corbally had died of his wounds in St. Patrick's Dressing Station, Loos. Poor old Corbally! Always with the ready answer. Always the clean soldier, never wanting in his place in the line, devoted to the Regiment ; he thus passed out of history as D. of W., F. and F., 2/12/16 (Official Casualty List). I was sad !

Weather very good, and my line was quite dry everywhere. Things had gone smoothly up to date, but the end of the tour for my company brought some exciting incidents and a few casualties. At 11 p.m. Lieut. H. C. Berne, M.C., who now belonged to B Company, arrived up from support with two N.C.O.s and reported to me. Paddy Lynch and I had a bandobast about inter-company patrols, he and I having previously patrolled for each other. On the first evening of my tour Berne, accompanied by two N.C.O.s, had been out in No-Man's-Land. This night I escorted Berne and his N.C.O.s to the bottom of the Russian Sap. It was now midnight, and although there was no moon, it was not too dark.

After I had watched the patrol disappearing into the darkness, I proceeded to tour my company front and the Barricade Sap. Returning towards Russian Sap, I was accosted by a breathless man, who was looking for me. He was Corpl. McCray, M.M., who had accompanied Berne on patrol. He informed me that both he and the other N.C.O. had missed Berne, and that the last he saw of him was near the Boche wire, and that this was with the aid of a stray Véry light, as they were some 30 yards away from him.

I immediately proceeded to my Company Headquarters and telephoned to Battalion Headquarters. Palin was in and I spoke to him, giving him the facts, and suggested taking out a strong search party. The C.O. then came to the telephone and said : "Send out a strong party with fixed bayonets, and make a thorough reconnaissance of enemy wire and No-Man's-Land." Also that I should "keep a sharp look-out, and be prepared to meet all eventualities." I detailed my support platoon, which lay in Queen Street, for this duty, and within an incredibly short space of time my men were scouring No-Man's-Land. We could find no trace of Berne, although the platoon advanced down No-Man's-Land in extended order, with one flank resting on the Boche wire, and the other on the line of our advanced and disused trench. After an hour's fruitless search, I reluctantly gave orders to the platoon to return to our trenches, and abandoned all hopes of getting Berne or his body. Strange to say, the Boches did not attempt to disturb or hinder my platoon when patrolling. I have not the slightest doubt that they heard us—thirty Micks on a still night do not need special listening posts to hear them! Berne was certainly snaffled extraordinarily quietly, and everything pointed to him being caught in the wire by one of their listening posts. I toured my front, and warned all sentry groups to keep a special look-out.

3rd December.

During this tour we got exceptionally heavily strafed by "Minnies" at Russian Sap and Carfax ; our Stokes retaliated on the Triangle. I was visited by the acting Brigadier.

In the evening Lynch arrived with his company, and took over my line, and as per the usual programme, I returned to the support line in South Street.

4th December.

Quiet day. Turned in early to make up for sleep lost on the previous night. However, I couldn't sleep, owing to a rather heavy trench-mortar bombardment on our front line. Then Lynch rang me up, saying he was being heavily strafed, and that he anticipated a raid ; also that he had got on to our artillery, but could get no support. I immediately stood my company to. Later the bombardment became intense, and I saw various-coloured S O S lights shooting up into the darkness from B Company's sector. However, the numerous calls to our artillery asking for retaliation were without avail, as our covering batteries were carrying out reliefs at the time.

Countless rockets went soaring into the sky without getting any response from the gunners.

2nd Lieut. Lauder and Corpl. McNamara of my company were at this time in the front line. They had proceeded up to B Company shortly before the bombardment, intending to patrol for Lynch. Later Lynch rang me up, saying he was being raided, and that Russian Sap had been cut off by a box barrage.

It was now about 3 a.m., so I decided to go up to the front line, and judge the position for myself.

Palin arrived up from headquarters and taking my servant, Jackson, with me we set off for B Company. We got up to the front line just after the raid. Lynch was busily employed re-organising his sentry posts, and everything was restored to normal. It appeared that a strong raiding party, estimated at 100, had entered B Company's line at the base of the Russian Sap at about 2 a.m. B Company's post retired to the junction of King Street, fighting fiercely.

In this scrap, the post was ably assisted by 2nd Lieut. Lauder and Corpl. McNamara. Our men put up a most determined resistance, but not without loss, as 2nd Lieut. Mouritz and his servant, Pte. O'Neill, were suddenly pounced on by another party of the enemy when coming along Carfax, and fired on. The officer was killed, and O'Neill badly wounded. B Company then sent their platoon, which lay in support, to reinforce this post, and they drove the Boche out of their line.

The enemy left two of their dead, and a colossal amount of explosive material behind them. Everything was silent when I got up to Russian Sap. At the junction of Carfax and King Street trenches I got out of the trench with Jackson, and I was later joined by Pte. McAuliffe of B Company.

We wandered out towards the head of Russian Sap, which had now been abandoned, to see if there was any trace of dead or wounded Germans. Hearing groans, we proceeded in their direction. Lying huddled up in a shell-hole on our side of Russian Sap was a groaning Boche. He was in great pain, and together we carried him back to our line. I actually carried him part of the way on my back, as I was most anxious to get him to our line alive for identification purposes. When we got him into the trench we gave him some water, and I had him carried down to Paddy Lynch's headquarters. Here we attended to his wound, which was a bad one in the foot. We had to cut his boot with a razor down to the toe, as it was the usual half-Wellington pattern worn by German troops.

I remember how surprised we were at finding straw in his boots. The prisoner was a fine-looking man of about twenty-two years of age. He couldn't speak any English, but seemed grateful to us for what we were doing. We had a lot of trouble with O'Neill, who was also lying wounded in the dug-out, as when the stretcher-bearers left the prisoner, O'Neill made a dive at him!

O'Neill had passed through a terrible ordeal during the raid. He had been alone with Mouritz when the Boches suddenly pounced on them. Mouritz having been killed and O'Neill severely wounded in the arm, feigned death at the bottom of the trench. Backwards and forwards the Boches trampled on him during their occupation of the Russian Sap area. (O'Neill will be recalled in the whisky episode at Delville Wood.) The finding of Mouritz's body testified to the gallant show which they put up ; there were six bullet wounds in Mouritz, and there were five empty cartridge cases in his revolver, which lay beside him.

Lynch was full of praises for the pluck shown by 2nd Lieut. Lauder and Corpl. McNamara ; and for his subalterns, Crowe and Foley, who had also done remarkably well.

The smart repulse of this raid was considered a feather in the Battalion's cap, and brought high praise from the Divisional Commander. From the prisoner who was interrogated on the following day, we learnt that the raid was on a large scale, and that over 100 men had taken part in it. Training for the raid had been taking place for over a fortnight on a facsimile of our trenches and Russian Sap, and there were sappers with the raiding party whose job it was to blow in our dug-outs. It was indeed a good show ! Two officers, and not more than twenty men holding up 100 raiders equipped with every device imaginable, including explosives to blow up our mine shafts.

This German prisoner ironically cost me £5, as when we found him I told McAuliffe I would see he got the promised booty. However, the method of his capture did not appear to come within the rules for the reward, so I personally wrote out a cheque to McAuliffe for £5.

The Boches were denied even the satisfaction of capturing a prisoner. They did, indeed, get one of our men who was wounded in the leg, and carried, or dragged him, across No-Man's-Land. When they reached their own wire they left their prisoner, saying that they would return with a stretcher. The minute they left him the " prisoner " proceeded to crawl back to our lines. His luck was in, for our guns, which had up to that time been silent, started putting down a barrage on the Boche front line. This probably put the " wind up " them. At any rate, the wounded man got back to us without being molested. The enemy left helmets, revolvers, bombs, and boxes of explosives behind them when they decamped, most of which we salved after the raid. Oddly enough, that very morning the C.O. had written to me, sending a scheme for a proposed raid on the enemy trenches.

5th December.

Returned to South Street at about 4 a.m. and turned in. Later in the morning I witnessed the following procession going through my support line on their way to the dressing-station.

Dec 4th

Dear Hitchcock,

Will you look over rough notes & let me know by bearer what you think of the general scheme. Also make any alterations, suggestions or additions.

Mine are merely hints & do not bind you at all.

But I must inform BHE of our plans & arrange with R.F.A. and T.M.s etc, so send this back as soon as you can so that I can make out a proper draft

The artillery barrage is doubtful and I shall not insist on it

Send this back tonight as I have no 2nd copy,

Yours,
A D Murphy

7.10 pm

A letter which I received from Lieut.-Colonel A. D. Murphy, M.C., on the 4.12.'16, with regard to a proposed raid on The Triangle, Loos.

Stretcher-bearers and the German prisoner on a stretcher, followed by Pte. O'Neill, with his arm in a sling.

From Lauder, I ascertained the exact details of the bravery shown by Corpl. McNamara, and I sent in a recommendation for this N.C.O. for the C.O.'s consideration.

6th December.

Battalion relieved by the 7th Northamptons, A and C Companies proceeding to billets in Lower Maroc, and B and D Companies to Les Brébis, where they lay in Divisional Reserve. On my way round inspecting my platoon's billets, I overheard an old tough giving forth a " hymn of hate " towards the Boche, in most blood-curdling terms. It was Pte. Coleman, a soldier of some fourteen years' service. I asked him what was wrong, and he replied : " Sure, aren't the Jarmans after breaking me only pipe on me when I was above on the Crassiers." It appeared that when Coleman was in the advance sap-head on the Double Crassier a Boche sniped at him, missed, but shot his pipe out of his mouth.

Coleman was one of the cold-shoers in the Company. Frequently Company commanders were instructed to send in the numbers of cold-shoers under their command, always a demand for farriers.

7th December.

The C.O. told me that two squadrons of the 5th Royal Irish Lancers were being disbanded, and that the men were being sent to infantry units. The " Dandy Fifth " were billeted near Bethune, and came into the 24th Divisional area. He told me that the men had been given the option of joining regiments in the Division, and that all had volunteered for the 2nd Leinster Regiment. We were very much under strength, as since leaving the Somme we had only had a small reinforcement consisting of ex-Royal Irish Constabulary men. He said that practically all the Lancer N.C.O.s and men were on time-serving attestations. The C.O. was looking forward to the prospect of getting these men, the majority of whom were Irish. His hopes, however, were badly shattered. We did not get the promised draft of the 5th Lancers, but instead, got a draft from the Dorset Regiment !

The Higher Command decided that we didn't need any strengthening, so the draft of 5th Royal Irish Lancers, amounting to approximately 160 other ranks, went to the 13th Service Battalion the Middlesex Regiment. This was an injustice to us, and to the Lancers. Of the Irish cavalry regiments, the 5th Lancers and the 6th Inniskilling Dragoons were particularly representative of our country. The 5th drew their recruits mainly from Dublin and the South of Ireland.

8th December.

The Colonel, Palin, Möllmann, and I went on a " back area tour " organised by Division. We left Les Brébis and reported at Divisional H.Q. at Nœux-les-Mines. We visited the " Q " Department, and saw the R.E. Section. General Capper had a " pow wow " in his Headquarters which we all attended.

Palin, " Molly," and I were given lunch by the Divisional veterinary officers.

9th December.

It was during this period in rest that a very strict order was circulated regarding the removal of doors and rafters from the village of Maroc for firewood by the troops. This order originated from Corps H.Q., and it hit us all particularly hard.

The winter had settled, and our billets were dreadfully cold. Shrapnel having long since robbed the Maroc houses of their tiles, we had to resort to ground sheets, stretched from rafter to rafter. A Company's servants were scroungers of the first order, and not the risk of the severest penalties would keep them from getting firewood—even had it meant looting the A.P.M.'s very bed ! Later in the year, when the snow was lying thick on the ground, these " toughs " set out one evening for fuel.

They were stalked by my C.S.M., who told me afterwards that he went into a house and found two of them sitting on top of its tileless roof, handing down rafters to O'Leary, who was standing below. They were cracking jokes about " the landlord being a decent man and that he wouldn't mind," when the Sergt-Major, who had been watching, unobserved, stepped in. However, I took no action in the matter. All I cared about was that we all had hot food, and any comfort that was going ; as it turned out, some five months later, Maroc was a shambles. It happened to find itself on the fringe of that great offensive, " The Battle of Arras," and the fighting for Hill 70, and accordingly it disappeared " off the map." Several officers joined from the 3rd Battalion at Cork, amongst them were Lieut. Nye and 2nd Lieut. Macready. Nye was posted to D and Macready to my company.

10th December.

I made a habit of going for a hack every morning when in reserve, and this morning I was riding off gaily towards Les Brébis, across the usual track, when an anti-aircraft gun suddenly opened fire on a Boche Taube from inside an old ruin which I was passing. My horse jumped slap into a disused trench with fright.

At Battalion H.Q. I met R.S.M. Smith, D.C.M., who had just

been awarded the Military Cross,[1] a good honour for a warrant officer. He thoroughly deserved his new decoration. I visited B Company and had a drink with Lynch. The C.O. asked me to lunch at Battalion H.Q.

11th December.

Issued out with leather jerkins, sleeveless leather coats, to wear over our jackets. Complete preparations had been made to meet the winter and the water-logged trenches which we all anticipated. Battalion orders stated that a gum boot store was being arranged in Maroc, where men could change or leave the boots when going up the line. During this rest, the C.O. came up to visit my company. He asked me some details about the capture of the Boche prisoner, and said that he had heard that I was responsible for it. He also told me that Porter and L/Corpl. Delaney had found the bodies of two dead Germans whom B Company had killed on the night of the raid. 2nd Lieut. Mouritz was laid to rest in the small military cemetery south of Maroc. He had put up a splendid show, and we were all rather surprised, as he was a particularly frail-looking chap, but he had a stout heart. We all attended his burial.

12th December.

The Battalion relieved the 7th Northamptons in the line. B Company took over the front line, and I took over the support trench, "South Street." Weather good, and the line was dry.

13th and 14th December.

Quiet. No shell-fire. Supplied usual fatigues nightly and a platoon in close support in Queen Street to B Company.

15th December.

Relieved Lynch's company in the front line, one very important alteration had been made—Russian Sap, that ghastly death-trap, had been filled in two nights previously by Lynch. This, indeed, was a blessing, and we could hold the line equally as well without it, as it ran off at a tangent on our right flank. By abandoning it, the line was not made the least bit more vulnerable.

The Machine-Gun Corps in rear had brought a new scheme into operation of covering us with a barrage. It worked splendidly, and we had a few tests—an S O S call, and inside sixty seconds we had a barrage of bullets sweeping up and down No-Man's-Land.

---

[1] The Military Cross, which was instituted in December, 1914, could be awarded to captains, subalterns, and warrant officers. For the latter discharged on pension, it was worth an additional sixpence per day.

After the raid on B Company the C.O. had a consultation with Lynch and myself regarding the advisability of abandoning this exposed sap-head. Having heard our views, which agreed with his own, he placed the matter before Brigade for sanction. The day before it was filled in, the G.O.C., Major-General Capper, who was tall, investigated Russian Sap; with bent shoulders, he wallowed out in the shallow and muddy communication trench, to find a perfectly collected sentry, head and shoulders above the parapet, looking out towards the enemy, oblivious of any danger. The G.O.C. told him not to expose himself, and asked : " Have you not got a periscope ? "

The sentry eyed the General, and replied : " Sure, what good would it be, sir ? Aren't they just after breaking two on me ? "

Major-General J. E. Capper was a well-known figure in the balloon world before the War, having been Commandant of the Balloon School. His brother, Major-General Sir Thomas Capper, was the famous commander of the 7th Division, which had saved the situation at Ypres in October, 1914, and who died of wounds in the Battle of Loos in 1915.

16th December.

The Germans were carrying out numerous raids in the Loos sector at this time. They had special storm-troops set aside for this purpose, and they moved along the Front complete with their trench mortars to raid the various battalions in our Division. We nicknamed these raiding troops " The Travelling Circus."

During the day enemy snipers showed great activity, especially at Barricade Sap. At night I erected quite an amount of barbed wire along our front.

17th December.

Received a chit from the Adjutant regarding my recommendation for Corporal McNamara. Full details were required by the Corps Commander, who considered it was a case deserving of the D.C.M. Paddy Lynch came up to see me, and together we toured the line. Going up the Barricades Sap, a sap-head which could be enfiladed by the Boche, we were sniped at from the top of the Double Crassier. We dived for cover behind a traverse, and there we had to remain, whilst the sniper cut the earth and sand-bags up all round us. We located the sniper near one of the derelict coal trucks on the Crassiers.

18th December.

Sikes wounded.[1] He was returning from Barricade Sap when a sniper got him in the hand, and at the identical spot where

[1] Wounded severely, Messines Ridge, June, 1917.

Lynch and I had got sniped on the previous evening. Since the Russian Sap was filled in, the enemy had turned their attention to Barricade Sap for the purpose of strafs with snipers and trench mortars. At midday I was relieved by a company of the 7th Northamptons, commanded by King. After relief, I set off for Duke Street, accompanied by C.S.M. Hartley. As Duke Street, the reserve line behind Loos where my company had spent the first tour, was near St. Patrick's Dressing-Station, I went to see how Sikes was getting on, and when darkness set in, saw him off in a motor ambulance. He had stopped what was called " a jammy one."

19th December.

At an early hour I went into Les Brébis to have a hot bath prior to a front-line tour.

20th December.

Weather cold, but fine. Our front line seemed to have quietened down considerably since we arrived in the sector. The Boches had certainly not got it all their own way, and they were " learning to behave themselves," as the men said. Our previous tour had almost been a record one for peacefulness. Macready and I explored Loos, whilst we lay in reserve in Duke Street. We were amused at finding some clever caricatures of British Army types, drawn by a German soldier on the white-washed walls of one of the houses, and, of course, Highlanders had been depicted. Loos had been in the enemy's hands from the beginning of the War until September, 1915.

21st December.

Snow fell, and weather became intensely cold.

22nd to 23rd December.

Still occupying reserve line in Duke Street.

24th December.

Christmas Eve. Relieved 7th Northamptons in South Street. A bitterly cold morning and snow was lying thickly on the ground. Rathbone,[1] whom I took over from, like a good sportsman, had left some whisky behind on the mess table for us. The whole area looked miserable, and the uncovered rafters of Loos sticking up so forlornly caked with snow, took away all the Christmas feeling of the snow.

---

[1] Killed on 21st March, 1918.

25th December—CHRISTMAS DAY.

I had told my C.Q.M.S. to send me up two cases of whisky for this tour, and they arrived all right. We presented the C.S.M. and all platoon sergeants with a bottle each for themselves and their N.C.O.s. Padre Moloney celebrated Mass in the trenches. The men built a small altar in a large fire bay, with sand-bags, and all attended with the exception of the gas sentries. All the Company officers, Macready, Cullen, Lauder, and myself were present, with the exception of Sharp, who had been attached to B Company in the front line. The service lasted for some 25 minutes. It was undoubtedly the most impressive I have ever attended.

We were about 120 strong, crowded into some large fire bays, hard by to Crucifix dump, holding our steel helmets and listening with bowed heads to the Padre. The whole area was covered in snow, and it lay thick on the parapets and parados. An occasional enemy shell whined overhead, to explode in the Loos shambles. The whole atmosphere seemed in keeping with a Christmas Day in the trenches.

P7078

O.C. " A " Coy.

With the intention of showing the enemy that we have no intention of fraternising with him, and also with a view to taking advantage of any slackness on his part during Christmas, a special programme will be carried out by the Artillery, T.M.s and Machine Guns during the following hours :

24th Dec.

    4 p.m. to 4.15 p.m.
    7 p.m. to 7.15 p.m.
    10.15 p.m. to 10.45 p.m.

25th Dec.

    1 a.m. to 1.15 a.m.
    9.10 a.m.   Artillery only CODE B.
    12.30 p.m.   ,,   ,,   ,,
    4.10 p.m.   ,,   ,,   ,,
    7.30 p.m. to 7.40 p.m.
    8 p.m.   Artillery and T.M.s.
    9 p.m. to 11.15 p.m.

26th Dec.

    1 a.m. to 1.30 a.m.
    10.15 a.m. Artillery only.
    11.45 a.m.   ,,   ,,
    2.10 p.m.   General Strafe by Artillery.

(1) In order not to interfere with our patrols which may be out during the intervals no firing (except in case of emergency) will be carried out except in the hours laid down in the above programme.

(2) Rifle grenades will be active during the day.

(3) Any attempt on the part of the enemy to show himself, is to be met immediately by fire of *every possible description*.

(4) The above programme will not affect any fire called for by observers who see good targets especially as regards para. 3.

Watches will be synchronised at 2.15 p.m. to-day over the wire.

CODE : APPLE.

A. C. S. PALIN, Capt.
Adjt., 2nd Bn. Leinster Regt.

24/12/16.

I received the above order on Christmas Eve. The programme was carried out according to schedule. It shows what the enemy had in the way of a Happy Christmas !

Had a very cheery lunch and dinner in our Company Mess, with a few guests, one of whom was a Sussex officer called l'Estrange. Macready went up at night to reinforce B. Company, as Paddy Lynch was short of officers.

26th December.

Sergt.-Major Kerrigan, D.C.M. (2nd Battalion The Leinsters, attached 13th Middlesex), came to see me. He told me that the draft of 5th Royal Irish Lancers had joined the 13th Middlesex, and that they were splendid men.

27th December.

A terrible tragedy in the battalion. Captain P. Lynch, M.C. (and Bar), and Sergt. McCormick were killed by an aerial dart. Paddy was giving orders regarding the relief to his A/C.S.M. —McCormick—in King Street trench, when a solitary aerial dart got a direct hit on the parapet behind them. Seeing Lynch's body being carried away by the stretcher-bearers, I pulled back the ground sheet which was covering him to have a last look. The whole top of his head, from his eyes, had been blown away. I removed one of his collar badges, which I gave to 2nd Lieut. J. J. Kelly when he joined, to send to Lynch's people. Sergt. McCormick was still breathing on the way to the dressing-station, but died as soon as he got there. He had been terribly mauled about the chest. It was sad, seeing these two brave men being

carried away—one dead and the other delirious. Lynch's death
affected me more than any other casualty in the War.

At 2 p.m. I relieved B Company in the front line. I could see
from the demeanour of the men that they were all terribly upset
by the loss of their commander.

An Aerial Dart fired from
a trench Mortar.

What killed Captain Lynch and Sergt. McCormick and many officers
and men in the Battalion at Loos.

The Colonel went away for a few days to attend an Army
Conference. Pte. O'Neill of B Company, who had gone down
wounded, awarded the Military Medal.

In the evening we watched one of our aeroplanes being shot
down over Lens, behind the enemy's line.

28th December.

At 2 p.m. I left the front line to attend Lynch's funeral. Every
company sent representatives. From the mortuary a party of
about 50 officers and other ranks followed the bier, which was
borne on a wheeled stretcher, Father Moloney marching in front,
in his surplice. We had only to go some 700 yards up the main
street of Maroc to the cemetery.

With one of his N.C.O.s I helped to lift Lynch's body into
the grave, which was almost alongside that of Mouritz. Lynch
was buried like all at the Front, his body being sewn up in a brown
army blanket.

After the funeral, Palin asked me to tea at Battalion H.Q.
on my way back to the front line, where I returned with a heavy

heart. It was now thawing hard, and the melting snow was flooding the trenches, so that I got wet over my knees.

29th December.

Palin rang me up on the telephone to say that No. 9432 Corporal McNamara had been awarded the D.C.M. We were all very pleased, and I sent for the N.C.O. to congratulate him, and, of course, gave him a few drinks. The account of his gallantry appeared later in the Gazette, describing how he had rescued bombs and S.A.A. from under the very noses of the Boches, and how he had led the counter-attack, following the enemy back to their own wire, inflicting casualties.

The thaw had made conditions in the trenches deplorable. They became full of icy slush, and in many places the duckboards were floating. The nature of the soil made things doubly bad, and we all got caked in a chalky mud. Later in the day the rain came, and then my line was in an appalling state. Sadly, I watched our parapets collapsing bodily into the trench, assisted by the usual trench-mortar vibrations.

In spite of the conditions, I found the men all in excellent spirits, and I overheard them talking about the Christmas dinner which they were looking forward to when we got out of the line. In fact, this had been the main topic of conversation throughout the tour. They had heard that I had ordered C.Q.M.S. Bond to procure a brace of pigs and barrels of beer—in fact, one " old tough," No. 7211 Ahern, a stretcher-bearer, had come forward as a volunteer to kill the pigs !

Sock-changing and rubbing the feet with whale oil had been carried out during these last few days, and always under the supervision of the platoon officers. There is no doubt that this continual sock-changing and massage with whale oil minimised cases of frost-bite to a great extent. The statistics proved this, and we had not that awful wastage of men continually dribbling back to the dressing-stations that there was in '14 and '15 with frost-bite. It was also proved that if the individual carried out orders regarding sock-changing and massage, the chances were 80 to 1 against his getting frost-bitten. Frost-bite, under these circumstances, was regarded from a disciplinary point of view, and became a crime.

On this last day of the Battalion's tour, Lieut.-Colonel Kay of the Divisional Staff came round my line, and he talked to the C.O. about a proposed raid on the Triangle by the Battalion.

30th December.

A wretched morning. Men got soaked through. However, they were all in good spirits, as we were due for relief at 11 a.m.

The line this morning reminded me of the trenches round St. Eloi in November, '15.

At midday my relief, the 7th Northamptons, arrived, and we filed out in the slush for our march to Les Brébis.

31st December.

Our new Brigade Commander, Brig.-General W. J. Dugan, C.M.G., D.S.O., late The Worcestershire Regiment, a brother of Major Dugan of our 1st Battalion, inspected A and B Companies. He addressed us and referred to his connections with the Regiment, and that he came from Birr. Afterwards he presented Corpl. McNamara with the D.C.M. in front of the Company. Busy making all arrangements for the morrow for celebrating a belated Christmas.

I was lent the Division concert-hall to use as a dining-hall for the dinner. My N.C.O.s, especially C.Q.M.S.s Bond and Kells, were, to a great extent, responsible for its success.

The end of the year saw a few changes amongst the officers. Lieut. Nye and 2nd Lieut. Foley were invalided down the line. All company commanders were asked to give their opinions and suggestions for Army Headquarters on the men's leg wear for the trenches. We were asked if we thought that breeches and gaiters, or boots of German pattern, might be substituted. Puttees, it was feared, caused trench feet. I was all for retaining our kit. Coming out of the line, men could take off their puttees and walk about in slacks, which they couldn't do in breeches, and puttees only stopped the circulation to aggravate frost-bite when put on too tightly.

1917

1st January.

AT 12.30 p.m. marched the Company over to the cinema hall for the Christmas dinner. Turkeys, bacon, and plum puddings were in abundance. Each man was rationed with two pints of beer, as I wanted them to eat their food. The C.O. and Adjutant visited the Company during the dinner. When the feast was over we paraded and marched back to billets.

Into a small compound which surrounded the C.Q.M.S.'s billet I led them. Here we unkegged two barrels of beer, and distributed it evenly amongst all. By a mistake a few bottles of port were brought out and left on a table. I watched one " old tough " making a " B " line for it. He opened one and, pouring out the entire contents into his dixie, raised it to his mouth. He made an awful grimace after a gulp and ejaculated : " Port, be Japers ! " emptying his dixie on to the grass !

When the beer was finished, all the men went off happily, and then tots of whisky were issued out to the N.C.O.s.

Capt. N. Algeo, who had been wounded at Hooge in August, '15, returned to the Battalion, and took over command of D Company from Capt. Van Cutsem. Algeo was a really gallant soldier who, unfortunately, was killed at the end of 1917. He richly deserved recognition for his bravery at Hooge, but decorations were few and far between in those days.

2nd January.

The C.O. had a company commanders' conference. He said that the Battalion had been detailed to carry out a raid on the enemy's trenches at The Triangle on a large scale, and that he had selected two platoons from A and D Companies each, as the actual raiders. The platoons would consist of one officer and twenty other ranks.

The C.O. detailed me to command the raid. The actual strength of the raiding party was 5 officers and 80 other ranks. The C.O. then selected the 4 platoon commanders as follows :

A Company	D Company
2nd Lieut. Lauder.	Lieut. Heming.
2nd Lieut. Macready.	2nd Lieut. Hall.

Capt. Algeo was placed in command of Reserves in case of a counter-attack.

The C.O. gave the approximate date of the proposed raid, and said that the raiders would not return to the line with the Battalion, but that we should remain in Les Brébis, and train daily for some nine days. The main feature of this raid was that it was to be a daylight " show." This was an entirely new departure, as hitherto one of the raiding axioms was to attack at night. Another very important variation was that there was not to be any preliminary bombardment ; therefore, one of the greatest principles of warfare—surprise—would be the chief factor throughout the preliminaries.

RAIDS AND THEIR OBJECTS

Up to this date, raids had been a great form of midnight activity employed by the British and Germans since the middle of 1916. Raids consisted of a brief attack with some special object on a section of the opposing trench, and were usually carried out by a small party of men under an officer. The character of these operations, the preparation of a passage through our own and the enemy's wire, the crossing of the open ground unseen, the penetration of the enemy's line, the hand-to-hand fighting in the darkness, and the uncertainty as to the strength of the opposing forces—gave peculiar scope to gallantry, dash, and quickness of decision by the troops engaged.

The objects of these expeditions can be described as fourfold :

I.   To gain prisoners and, therefore, to obtain information by identification.

II. To inflict loss and lower the opponent's morale, a form of terrorism, and to kill as many of the enemy as possible, before beating a retreat ; also to destroy his dug-outs and mine-shafts.

III. To get junior regimental officers accustomed to handling men in the open and give them scope for using their initiative.

IV. To blood all ranks into the offensive spirit and quicken their wits after months of stagnant trench warfare.

Such enterprises became a characteristic of trench routine.

After a time these raids became unpopular with regimental officers and the rank and file, for there grew up a feeling that sometimes these expeditions to the enemy trenches owed their origin to rivalry between organisations higher than battalions.

Information regarding the identification of the opposi...ᵤ troops, their strength, how they held their line, and the exact locations of trench mortars, machine-guns, and their emplacements, and the positions of sap-heads in order to anticipate mining activity, was always being called for by corps and Army Headquarters. Rivalry between formations is excellent, but when overdone, can be most dangerous. The rivalry that existed in France in 1916 and 1917 over raiding operations had, indeed, been carried to an extreme limit.

However, rivalry was not the cause of this proposed raid on The Triangle. It was actually a reprisal for a most successful German raid, which had been brilliantly carried out on a unit in our Division with the last tour. In fact, the way in which this raid was discovered was unique in itself.

The G.O.C. was sitting in his Headquarters when his galloper rushed in to tell him that the German wireless had been heard reporting " a brilliant minor operation at Loos and the capture of 50 English prisoners."

The General immediately detailed brigades to repeat situation reports for their units, and he got the following returns from all :

> X Battalion
> Wind S.E. Situation Normal A.A.A.

N.B.—Situation reports were a daily routine in trench warfare. At "Stand to" morning and evening, front-line companies had to render these reports. The direction of wind had to be given as an anti-gas measure.

Having scrutinised all the situation reports, the G.O.C. was nonplussed, so he decided to tour his front-line sectors, accompanied by his Staff.

They toured the 17th Brigade sector, which was north-east of Loos, and immediately discovered an unoccupied front line which terminated at a newly erected barricade, and farther on, a dead man. The G.O.C. then went off down the C.T. to find the Battalion Headquarters of this sector.

The C.O. was very surprised ; as far as he knew everything was normal in his front line. The G.O.C., now reinforced by the Battalion Headquarters, returned to the front line for further investigations. At the head of the C.T. he paused to peer across No-Man's-Land, and the following large notice in English stuck up in the wire entanglements met his gaze :

> " SAY
> What about those
> 50 Rations ? "

A MOST SUCCESSFUL BOCHE RUSE

Shortly afterwards the following facts came to light about this raid. A German patrol crept up to an advanced post of the Regiment concerned and caught the occupants unawares. These they snaffled quietly and returned to their line. The Boche commander sent out a large raiding party on the spot. This party proceeded into the front line via the advanced sap-head, and walked boldly down the main fire trench mopping up every sentry quietly. When all the sentries within a certain area had been accounted for, the Boches built up the barricades of sand-bags, and then started the mopping-up of all the dug-outs in their vicinity. For this they were full of resource. In English, they yelled down the shafts of the deep dug-outs the word "GAS." The sleepers, startled, donned their box respirators, and came out of their dug-outs to man their fire bays, only to be grabbed at and dragged across the 150 yards of No-Man's-Land without being able to fire a shot. When their shouts were not heard, the artful Boches fired Véry light pistols down the entrances, which had the desired effect. In addition to the large party captured, some sappers belonging to the 3rd Australian Tunnelling Company, who were mining in the line, were taken.

So skilfully and silently did the raiders carry out their work that the companies on the immediate flanks stated that they heard nothing to warrant any suspicion.

After the C.O.'s conference I had a company parade, and detailed the forty men required for the raid from the four platoons. The N.C.O.s of A Company were as follows :

Sergts. McNea and McSweeney.
Corpls. McNamara, D.C.M., Murray, Honour, McDermott, and Masterson.

3rd January.

At 9 a.m. the Raiders, consisting of 5 officers and 80 other ranks, paraded. Having drawn picks and shovels at the Q.M.'s stores, we proceeded to a small field behind Brigade Headquarters which had been allotted to us as a training ground for the raid. It was only about 2 square acres, but was quite sufficient for our needs. It had possibly been used as a training ground, and there were some old practice trenches and a large mine crater.

The night previously I had spent much time studying the

numerous aeroplane photographs and maps of the German Triangle which the C.O. had given me.

In a fresh part of the ground we measured out a replica of the area to be raided, and had it spitlocked. When this was finished, both parties were extended along the line with their tools and dug in for two feet. This task occupied the greater part of the morning, as it had to be carefully done according to the maps. When it was completed, one had only time to explain the general scheme to the four platoons before moving off for the men's dinners.

The enemy's line chosen for our raid, as its name implied, resembled a triangle, with its apex pointing towards the British trenches. Our intentions were to raid the complete triangle, establishing bombing posts on the extreme flanks of the parties beyond, and including the base line. Both parties had then to work in towards each other, systematically mopping up all dug-outs, sap-heads, trench mortars and, of course, all spare Boches. Before this inward movement took place, however, the flanks of The Triangle beyond the base line had to be consolidated. The small sketch opposite will show The Triangle and the proposed flank bombing posts at A and D.

From the initial day we carried out the practices in the exact formations that we would maintain on the field.

The raiders were all split up into small parties of an officer or N.C.O. and ten men, and all these separate parties had their own functions. Success in raids depends entirely on every man having a definite rôle, and knowing it thoroughly. Thus the importance of a perfect training behind the lines can be realised. When a man knows his job he has confidence in himself. Should he not know it, he is liable through ignorance to get " windy," and cause alarm amongst his companions, turning the raid into a failure.

The actual dispositions and functions of the various parties working in order from the left-flank party of A Company to the right-flank party of D Company were as follows :

" A " COMPANY

Left-Flank Blocking Party. 2nd Lieut. Lauder, Corpl. Honour and 10 men. Duties : To establish a bombing post beyond and including the base of The Triangle and hold same against all opposition. Shovels and empty-sandbags, in addition to bombs, to be carried by all ranks.

Main Party : 2nd Lieut. Macready, Sergt. McSweeney, Corpl. Masterson and 10 men. Duties : To gain and keep touch with left flank and support party, and " mop up " enemy trench.

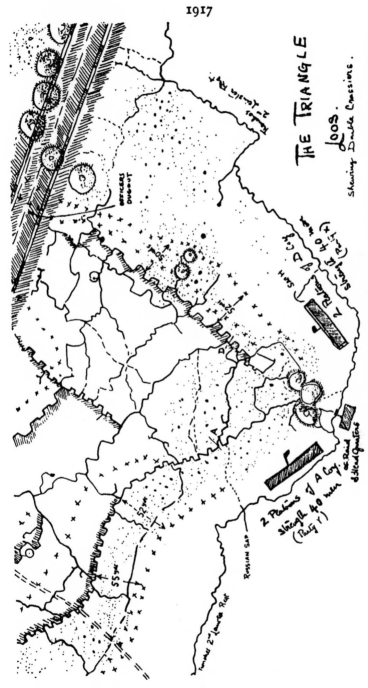

Trench map showing The Triangle, Loos, which was selected as the objective for a daylight raid by the 2nd Leinster Regt.

Support Party. Sergt. McNea, Corpls. McDermott and Murray, and 8 men. Duties: To cover trench party from enemy parapet with rifles and prevent a counter-attack coming over the open. To keep parties supplied with bombs and to provide reinforcements as required.

Headquarters. O.C. Raid (self), Ptes. O'Leary and McGrath (runners). To take up a position in the apex of The Triangle as quickly as possible, establish touch with all parties and keep the directing officer (in our front line) informed of movements.

Liaison Party. Corpl. McNamara and 6 men. Belonging to Headquarters party, but jumped off from a different position, joining in enemy trench.

"D" COMPANY

Main Party. Lieut. Heming, 2 N.C.O.s, and 10 men. Duty: To clear and mop up enemy front trench.

Support Party. 2nd Lieut. Hall, 1 N.C.O., and 8 men. Duties: To cover trench party from enemy parapet and to keep them supplied with bombs, etc. To provide reinforcements as required.

Post B. 1 N.C.O. and 6 men. Duties: Connecting Post to gain and keep touch with left party.

Post A. Bombing Post for right flank, duties the same as for the left-flank Blocking Party.

Total strength: 5 officers, 80 other ranks.

Dress:

Drill order. Steel helmets. All officers and N.C.O.s i/c of parties to carry sirens and revolvers. Officers as usual to wear their webbing equipment. Box respirators to be carried.

During the practices no details were left out, and the flanking bombing parties carried their shovels and empty sand-bags as they would on the pukka "show." The "Acme" sirens were also carried, in order to get all ranks accustomed to them. These sirens the C.O. purchased in Béthune, and they were identical with those used by the officials on the French railways. As there was not to be any preliminary artillery preparation, the success of this raid was to depend entirely on its surprise element. Therefore, the actual assembling of the raiders in their jumping-off positions, prior to the advance, without being observed by the enemy, was to be the crucial point. Practice in the assembly was practically impossible, but the other details became almost a drill movement.

The chances of the assembly in the jumping-off positions being observed by the enemy from the top of the Double Crassier, which overlooked all this sector, were about even money. However, it would take some five minutes for enemy sentries on the Crassiers to give the alarm, and by that time we would nipped been across No-Man's-Land and into The Triangle.

4th January.

All morning training for the raid. The C.O. came down to watch the work. Two new officers joined the Battalion, in 2nd Lieut. G. L. F. MacKay and 2nd Lieut. H. J. de Courcy. The former came from Sandhurst, the latter belonged to the Special Reserve. MacKay, who was a qualified signaller, was attached to Battalion Headquarters, and de Courcy was posted to my company (de Courcy was killed on 18/1/17 at Loos and MacKay was killed on 11/4/17 on Vimy Ridge).

5th January.

Carried out the usual training. South-east of our training ground were numerous mines and quite a number of Boche prisoners were employed working on the various slag heaps.

During one morning's practice we were obviously seen by a enemy "Taube," and got shelled. This shelling scared the prisoners working on a neighbouring crassier, and we watched their guards, found from some Yeomanry unit, having difficulty in restoring order.

The Battalion, less the raiders, left their Les Brébis billets for the line.

6th *January.*

Usual training for the raid. Revolver practice for all who were to be armed with revolvers on the raid. North-west of Les Brébis there was a small range, and on several afternoons we carried out revolver practice. Some of the N.C.O.s were very good shots.

7th January.

General Capper arrived to watch us carrying out our rehearsals. Afterwards we formed up and our G.O.C. told us exactly what he wanted done, and added that he knew the 2nd Leinsters would do it.

8th January.

The C.O. came along to watch the training. During one of the rehearsals all officers and N.C.O.s fell out in order to see how the men would carry on. They were not a bit " flustered," the oldest soldier in each party carrying on splendidly. The C.O. expressed his satisfaction with the training, and then formed up, as he wished to address all ranks.

He gave us his usual sound advice, and said he expected us all to give a good account of ourselves in the German line. He finished up by saying that rum would be issued before operations, but in tea. The men seemed very disappointed at the last statement, as they always preferred it neat. Before the C.O. moved away I asked him if he would alter his decision regarding the rum if I personally supervised the issue. He agreed, and I informed the men that the Colonel had given his consent for the rum to be issued neat. After I told them, one " old tough " was overheard to remark to another : " Begorra, Mick, we can now have it in its bare feet ! "

We then commenced live bombing practice, and I got every man to throw a live bomb with the pin out. This was a risk worth taking, as it gave the men confidence in allowing a bomb to fizz for a few seconds, which was necessary for dug-out bombing. The men got quite accustomed to this after a few attempts, and I had no casualties.

9th January.

All the officers who were to accompany the raid went on reconnaissance tours with their senior N.C.O.s. I took Corpl. McNamara with me to the Double Crassier. Here we were some 30 feet high and some 300 yards away from the German Triangle. From this vantage-point we studied the network of trenches which spread itself out before our gaze. I remember being very perturbed seeing the dense mass of German wire entanglements opposite to D Company's sector. However, several gaps had been made in these entanglements by Bangalore torpedoes, which had been placed out by Porter and the Battalion scouts, in spite of interruption by some Boche bombs. McNamara and I stayed on the Crassiers for some time observing The Triangle. Heming was taken over the lines in an aeroplane ; his pilot flew low over Hill 70 and The Triangle, and enabled him to get a bird's-eye view of the lie of the land. This was the first and only time that I had ever been on the Double Crassier. There were several excellent " O.P.s," and from them one could see the enemy's trenches perfectly. In places one could see right into them.

Watching these exposed places, I spotted an occasional Hun

dodging quickly round a traverse. From these " O.P.s," L/Corpl. Delaney, M.M., and his snipers, inflicted many casualties on the enemy. The officer's dug-out on the Crassier was supplied with electric light, so he, at any rate, got some advantage from the coal. At 6 p.m. I proceeded up to Maroc and dined at Battalion Headquarters. Afterwards, I accompanied the C.O. up to The Triangle in order to examine the enemy's wire and make a reconnaissance of the jumping-off positions.

We were in the Battalion's right sector, and C Company was holding the front. We came across Möllmann (O.C. C Company) touring his line. It was a clear night, which suited us for moving round No-Man's-Land. A small party was digging assembly trenches just in front of our abandoned front-line trench, which ran from C Company's left flank towards old Russian Sap near Carfax road.

These trenches were to be jumping-off positions for half the A Company raiders. It was a difficult task, as the party was working close to the enemy lines, and as we did not want the show given away before dawn, the fresh earth had to be disposed of and the new line camouflaged in case of an argus-eyed Boche Taube. The enemy wire entanglements appeared rather formidable in front of D Company, and the C.O. got a battery of Stokes' mortars on to the job.

We left the front line at midnight and I walked back to Les Brébis by myself. I felt quite optimistic about the raid, and the men were all in fine fettle.

THE RAID[1]

10th January.

On Active Service one always found that there were numerous duties and details to be attended to up to the very last moment before a " show," and this morning proved to be no exception. Inspections of the men, their rifles and equipment, supervising the issues of revolver and rifle ammunition and bombs being detonated. In every case I had to see that the Army Books 64 (the soldiers' active service pay-book) were collected, for if they fell into the enemy's hands, they would have been a complete source of identification of the Battalion. The morning, therefore, passed without suffering from the nervous tension which one would have felt had one's thoughts been unoccupied. At 12.30 we paraded and marched off by platoons from Les Brébis in our battle order for Maroc. The men were in great spirits and in the pink of condition. On the main road from Les Brébis to Maroc there

[1] See orders in Appendices.

stood a Calvary on the left-hand side, and I noticed that most of the men crossed themselves in true Catholic fashion when passing it. At Battalion Headquarters we fell out. The men had had their dinners in Les Brébis, but the C.O. had invited the officers to a cold lunch, which suited the occasion. I, at any rate, had no appetite whatsoever, and I remember toying with a tinned pear !

After lunch I supervised the rum issue to officers and men, taking a tot myself. The A. Company platoons moved off some thirty-five minutes before D's platoons, as they had to go up via Loos and South Street to get to their jumping-off trenches. I then paraded my Headquarters party. Prior to moving off, Padre Moloney came along and blessed each one of us individually. We took the C.T. in rear of the cellars which were used as our Battalion Headquarters, and passing a strong reinforcement of stretcher-bearers, an ominous sign, filed up to the front line in front of The Triangle. My Headquarters consisted of Corpl. McNamara, Ptes. O'Leary, and McGrath (runners) and six men. I met the C.O. who was superintending the assembly of D's platoons in their jumping-off positions. No details had been forgotten ; and ropes had to be thrown into the craters after zero in case of men falling into them.

Special stuffed mats were issued to D Company for use in negotiating uncut wire entanglements, and Bangalore torpedoes were all ready if required. At 4 p.m. all A Company's parties were reported in position.

I now took up my position in the left sap-head with my runners, to wait for zero. A Boche sniper on the Crassiers worried D Company in their assembly. However, the C.O. called up the Stokes guns and a few shots silenced him. As the raid was to be a surprise, we had no preliminary bombardment, but on our flanks at Hart's Crater, and on the Canadian front, heavy box barrages were put down as a bluff. One of our aeroplanes was manœuvring over Hill 70.

I sat in the sap-head, pulling at a cigarette and looking at my watch. At zero, 4.20 p.m., our advance signal, a Véry light, was fired, and we scrambled over our parapet. I got a glimpse of Macready's party away on my left, tearing across No-Man's-Land. The route for myself and my Headquarters party was around the left lips of the craters, and we advanced at a steady jog as the going was rough. Leaving the crater lips we then swung out towards the left, owing to some large *chevaux de frise.* We came under rifle-fire when nearing the objective.

Then, to my horror I found that we were unable to get into the Boche trench at the selected point as it was filled up with coiled masses of barbed wire ! no aeroplane photographs could reveal this fact. (Our actual assault on the enemy trench is to this day idelibly impressed on my mind.) Having been baulked of my original objective, I made my way along the Boche parapet, with Privates O'Leary and McGrath, easily negotiated some low entanglements and "crows'-feet," and jumped into The Triangle at its apex in company with Corpl. McNamara and some of his party. There is no doubt that we greatly surprised the enemy occupants at this point. I landed right on top of a Boche sentry standing by a periscope, occupied, not in reconnaissance, but in reading a newspaper!

I never saw any man take off equipment with such rapidity as this sentry. He, a typical young Hun, stood with his hands up, livid with fright, yelling "Kamerad." Another Boche, probably his relief, simultaneously appeared on the scene as we assaulted their line. He, however, was of a different type, and levelled his Mauser at me on the parapet and fired. Corpl. McNamara sprang at him and knocked him over, but in doing so, unfortunately received the discharge in his left forearm. These two prisoners were sent back instantly under escort.

My first duty was to establish liaison with the flanking parties, so I at once proceeded to get in touch with Macready's party. Judging from the noise, a good deal of bombing was going on in Lauder's direction, which showed that the enemy fully realised that he was being raided, and resented the new tenants of The Triangle. Some 20 yards along the trench a patrol from Macready reported that the left-flank party (Lauder) had established their post, and that two prisoners were captured. All this time, my party was being subjected to rifle-fire from the numerous dug-out entrances, which were scattered along the trench.

Systematically we bombed all these dug-outs, a form of retaliation which was most effective, and, having silenced them, and leaving a few of my party to guard them, I moved towards the right flank (having retraced our steps via the apex we had entered). I remember that at this period my revolver, a Smith and Wesson, jammed, owing to some dirt getting into it, so I put it back in its holster and armed myself with a brace of bombs.

At the apex I came across a private of D Company called English. He reportèd that D Company had been unable to penetrate into the Boche line, owing to the wire being uncut and strong opposition. I was, therefore, on the right flank of the raiders, but we were all in the trench, well covered by the D Company's support party of nine men under 2nd-Lieut. Hall.

The Triangle by this time was very much alive, and we had properly roused a hornet's nest. I now sent a verbal message by O'Leary back to the supervising officer in our crater sap-head to say that " A Company had made good their objective." All this time the enemy was busily sending up S O S rockets, green and red flares, while the ordinary Véry lights kept going up in frantic haste all along his line. My party was now somewhat reduced in strength, as I had to order Corpl. McNamara to return to our lines as he was wounded, but wished to fight on, and a few of my men were on patrol between Headquarters and Macready. I now decided to hold the right flank by a bombing post and keep the enemy (who were putting up a strong opposition) back until it was time for the withdrawal. O'Leary returned and put up some good work with bombs.

Owing to the smoke I found myself severely hampered in the trench, so I climbed up on the parapet close to the support party in order to be able to supervise the raid. This was a good position for control, and I could make out some of our men belonging to Macready's party, and I got a perfect view of the network of Boche trenches which formed The Triangle.

As was always the case in trench raids, the defenders were left in a state of uncertainty as to the exact spot that was being raided, and their artillery could give them no support in firing on the attackers, not knowing the disposition of their own troops. Therefore, from the Boche point of view, everything was chaos in The Triangle, and our raid was almost over when the methodical Hun pulled his rudely awakened senses together and commenced organising his bombers to drive us out.

Slowly the Boche was creeping along towards my Headquarters from the right, or Crassier flank, but we held him at bay completely until the withdrawal. From the top of his parapet we hurled a number of Mills bombs—some, I know, with effect. At this point I was joined by 2nd Lieut. McCann and Sergt. Sullivan of D Company, who were not amongst the raiders, but came out to join us in the fray. Although the Huns could not retaliate on my command with their guns, they subjected our front line and S O S lines to a terrific strafe with shells of every calibre.

Our own artillery put down a smoke barrage beyond the base line of The Triangle and on both our flanks, which effectively prevented my men from being worried by direct machine-gun-fire from the direction of the Double Crassier and Hill 70.

Out of this dense cloud of smoke rose like fountains the Boche green and crimson S O S rockets and Véry lights. However, as the latter entered this smoke-screen, they were blanketed and burnt themselves out. Machine-gun fire swept anxiously along our parapets in tremendous traverses, seeking a target. The Boche was absolutely nonplussed. His wire, his " Minnies," his machine-guns, and his cunning, were of no avail. He could not locate a target, owing to our smoke-screen.

Throughout the operation one of our aeroplanes co-operated with us. It flew low over the Boche lines, identified eleven new enemy batteries, and worried all their machine-gunners on Hill 70. To a certain extent the plane[1] acted as a decoy to the Boche machine-guns when we were in our jumping-off trenches preparatory to the charge.

Dusk was now coming on, and the time for our withdrawal was close at hand. To my knowledge we had captured four prisoners, and had, therefore, established perfect identification of our opponents. I did not consider that any further mopping-up of the Boche trenches would result in anything, so at 5.10 I blew my siren, the agreed signal for the withdrawal, and heard my left party answer in acknowledgment. The directing officer sent up a coloured rocket from the front line, which was the signal to our gunners of withdrawal.

This rocket soared up to a great height before bursting into innumerable balls of various colours. Almost simultaneously, our gunners, who had been standing to, replied with a colossal barrage, which smothered the Boche support trenches.

Our artillery had registered to a nicety on their proposed objectives, and they were now obtaining direct hits all along the enemy's line, sending his parapets shooting into the sky like great fountains. Under cover of this intense barrage we effected our withdrawal without being molested by direct machine-gun fire. A huge bonfire had been lit behind our lines on the high ground in Travers Keep to serve as a beacon to guide us back from the Boche lines.

Nothing had been left to chance by the C.O. as, in the darkness and melée, some of the men might have gone off in the wrong direction. The R.S.M., Smith, M.C., D.C.M., had supervised the lighting of this fire, and drew an amount of shell-fire on his party for their trouble. Leaving the support party, whose duty it was to remain on the Boche parapet and cover our withdrawal, together with my runners, we made our way back to our jumping-off position. We experienced no difficulty in our withdrawal, as there was no wire left.

Stumbling round the broken edges of the craters and across the churned-up ground, with shrapnel bursting all round us, we scrambled back into our crater sap-head.

The Boche was subjecting our front line to a terrific strafe— a retaliation with a vengeance! Great volumes of earth were shooting up all round us. When we got behind the cover of the

---

[1] The pilot was awarded the D.S.O. for his work on this date.

advanced sap-head, we were in a state of utter exhaustion, and sank into a sitting position on the bottom of the trench. The strain, responsibility, and worry over the raid, and the preliminary training for the past eight days, all seemed to react on me at this moment, and for some time I felt that I had not the energy to walk back to Battalion Headquarters. Shells were still bursting all round us, and it was now quite dark. After waiting in the sap-head for some ten minutes, and after all the parties had returned to our line (the support party under 2nd Lieut. Hall were the last to leave as their rôle was to cover our withdrawal), in company with my runners, I proceeded down the long communication trench.

We struck oil on our way, as we were given a most refreshing cup of tea by a M.G. Corps crew in a reserve line dug-out— a marvellous " corpse reviver."

Before leaving the front line I had been informed that four more prisoners had been captured, but that Sergt. Day had been killed and that Heming and some men of D Company had been wounded negotiating the enemy's wire entanglements.

The rendezvous for the raiders on their return was at Battalion Headquarters at Maroc. Here the roll had been called by the R.S.M. The men were being issued with an extra tot of rum. I now dived down into the cellars which accommodated Battalion Headquarters, and reported to the C.O.

He congratulated me most heartily, and said that he was delighted with the result. Padre Moloney, the headquarters P.M.C., had prepared a good meal ; we all, with the C.O., sat down to it. I now got full details of Macready's initiative and dash ; Lauder, having established his bombing post, and the flanks thus guarded, Macready, in the face of strong opposition, dived down into a deep dug-out with some of his men, and captured four prisoners. They at first showed fight, but after three had been killed, the rest surrendered, and crawled out in front of him up the steps of their lair.

The C.O. told me that he had seen me walking about on the Boche parapets through all the smoke directing the raid, and that I was " just like a factory chimney moving about, with the shells bursting all round." He said it was extraordinary that I was not hit. The C.O. told me that D Company experienced great difficulty in crossing the Boche wire, and that in doing so had met with stout opposition. Only a few men got into the trench on the right flank, and that one of them, Sergt. Day, had been killed. His body could not be recovered. Unfortunately D Company had a number of casualties, including Heming. Lauder and Macready were full of praise for their men. Where they had all fought so stoutly it was difficult to single out individuals, but Sergt. McSweeney,[1] Corpls. McDermott, Honour, Masterson, and Privates Farquhar and FitzGerald were names they mentioned. One, Pte. Swan, had been killed in the Boche line, but his body had been brought back to our line when they withdrew. After the refreshments, which took away all feelings of reaction, I went into the adjoining cellar, where the Brigade Major—Major R. Howlett, D.S.O.—was interrogating the prisoners in German.

I stayed for some time watching the proceedings. The eight prisoners belonged to the 9th Bavarian Corps. They were all of fine physique, and a couple of them were wearing the black and white ribbon of the Iron Cross attached to the second button of their tunics. One or two of the prisoners were more communicative than the rest, but except for their complete identification being established from their shoulder-straps and letters (which was most important), there was little to be gained from them.

Before returning to Les Brébis, I visited the dressing station. The doctors were all very busy with casualties incurred during the raid. I saw several men on the operating table having bomb and shrapnel splinters extracted from their faces and limbs. Corpl. McNamara's arm had been bandaged up and he seemed very cheery. Heming's wounds were much more serious than I had been led to believe, and I watched him being carried into a waiting ambulance on a stretcher. By this time the Boche prisoners were being herded together by their escort preparatory to moving off to one of the big camps near Béthune. They looked very sorry for themselves in their mud-stained field grey. One or two were minus their Brodrick caps; several of them were perfect Boche types, with shaven heads and glasses.

Sharp, who had been in charge of a party near our old Russian Sap, whose rôle was to meet any counter-attack which might materialize on the left flank, joined Jackson and myself in our tramp back to Les Brébis. Jackson had not been included in the actual raiders, much to his regret. I did not want to risk him being killed and also, selfishly, I felt that if I was to come back he would still be there to look after me. On the outskirts of Grenay we " jumped " a motor lorry, which dropped us close to our billets.

I visited the men, who were by this time in the greatest of spirits. The two A Company platoons were all accommodated in the same billet, which consisted of two large rooms. Both Macready and Lauder were present, and we watched them settling down to a late meal, and of course some extra beer, which they all had thoroughly earned.

This done, we moved off for our company mess, which we had

[1] 9602 Sergt. McSweeney killed 27th August, 1917.

only left at 11.30 that morning. When I got into the mess-room,
I found that it had been all gaily decorated with flowers and
bunting, and stretching all round the room were banners, with
" Welcome Back," Vive les Irlandais." The Company servants
told me that Madame had been making these all morning. She
was an optimist undoubtedly, and had certainly been anticipating
the success. Madame was a charming old lady ; her husband
was a *poilu* entrenched before Verdun. She was a thorough
believer in the *entente cordiale.* Her little house had been used
as a mess for various regiments since the commencement of the
War.

We had a top-hole dinner, and needless to say, we all wined
very well. Those present were Sharp, Macready, Lauder, Cullen,
and de Courcy.

The raid had been a great success. We had shaken the enemy's
morale, as apart from capturing the eight prisoners, we had
killed at least 20. Complete identification of the Bavarian
troops had been established, information which was being ur-
gently required by the Corps Commander. Further, a thorough
reconnaissance of The Triangle, especially of its apex and left side,
had been made ; positions of his mine-shafts and dug-outs had
been noted, and last, but not least in importance, the raid had
occupied the enemy position according to schedule for 45 minutes,
in spite of strong opposition. The Triangle was a centre of
resistance, and consisted of a labyrinth of trenches strongly
organised, in which were machine-gun emplacements and
trench mortars (" Minnenwerfer," hence the British nickname
" Minnies ").

From its rear and left flank this stronghold was covered
respectively by machine-guns from the direction of Hill 70, and
the east end of the Double Crassier. It was heavily wired on
both flanks and at its apex by dense masses of *chevaux de frise.*
In fact, these iron knife rests were all staked together in rows of
sixes in depth. Hitherto The Triangle had never been entered by
British troops, though many attempts had been made to raid it,
especially by troops of the 16th Irish Division. All attempts
had been written off as failures with much loss of life on our side.
The Triangle was deemed an impregnable position, and I doubt
if its prestige would have been lowered but for the skill of Lieut.-
Colonel A. D. Murphy, M.C. Thus the 2nd Leinsters was one of
the first British regiments to carry out a daylight raid in France.
The Boche raid on B Company on the night of the 4/5th December
was more than avenged, and as a battalion we had completely
upset the morale of the Bavarian Corps " *sturmtruppen* " (storm

troops) and their "Travelling Circus." Our casualties were by
no means severe in this operation : 4 other ranks were killed.
One officer, Lieut. Heming (afterwards died of wounds), and 18
other ranks were wounded, out of a total of 5 officers and 80 other
ranks engaged. In this account it would be unfair to close
without making special reference to the part played by the
Battalion scouts in connection with the raid. Led by 2nd Lieut.
W. J. Porter, and ably assisted by L/Corpl. Delaney, M.M., the
scouts had previous to the 10th January carried out patrols
nightly in the vicinity of The Triangle. They had reconnoitred
the ground carefully, and had obtained valuable information.
Also they were instrumental in making the gaps in the enemy's
entanglements, a daring operation, especially when functioning
the cumbersome Bangalore torpedoes under the very noses of
the enemy.

Thus in trench raids, or minor operations, as styled by General
Headquarters, the Battalion had always come out on top, as per
the following tabulated list :

Date.	Sector.	Raiders	Prisoners captured from 2nd Leinsters.	Prisoners captured from Germans.
5 Oct. '16	Vimy Ridge	Leinsters	Nil	1 Saxon.
4/5 Dec.	Loos	Germans	Nil	1 Bavarian.
10 Jan.	Loos	Leinsters	Nil	8 Bavarians.

This does not show the number of the enemy killed or wounded,
or our own casualties. The particular object in raids was to
capture live prisoners, as they provided definite information as
to their units. Their identification could always be established
by their shoulder straps, identity discs, or papers. Throughout
the winter the Germans had intermittently been harassing
battalions in the Loos sector with their "Travelling Circus."
However, the enemy was not to have it all his own way, and our
raid was the forerunner of a sequence of British raids, which were
all successfully carried out.

During the night the Battalion received many complimentary
messages from General Horne, 1st Army Commander, Corps,
Division, Brigade Headquarters, and also messages of con-
gratulation from various units in the Loos sector. I particularly
remember those from the Canadian troops on our right, and from
the 3rd Rifle Brigade, who had been old comrades of ours in the
VI Division.

11th January.

Battalion detailed to furnish a corps guard ; the C.O. selected the men from the raiders of A and D Companies, and Lauder was selected as the guard commander.

The C.O. gave me permission to take a few days' rest with Plowman at our transport lines. My company was this day returning to Maroc village, where they would lie in reserve for six days preparatory to going into the line.

At night I went up to Maroc to see the Adjutant, and returned to Les Brébis with Plowman, who had a spare horse. It was a pitch-dark night, and very wet, and ·we got mixed up with a relieving battery. Eventually we got extricated and got back to Les Brébis where I remained for the night.

12th January.

Two new officers arrived, in Capt. Heys-Thompson and Lieut. Hodge, both belonging to the Special Reserve. I gave them lunch in my old company mess. Donoghue arrived with my horse and I rode off back to the transport lines at Petit Sains. (Three months later Hodge was killed in the attack on Vimy Ridge.)

13th to 15th January.

We were within easy distance of Béthune, and thanks to the numerous motor vehicles which passed our billet, which lay on the main road, we were able to " lorry jump." Béthune was one of the largest towns in this coal mining district of the Artios. It was a perfect jewel of an old town with quaint streets. All the long winding streets led on to a large cobbled square. Béthune was of historic interest, as one of Marlborough's objectives in the War of the Spanish Succession.

Occasionally the Boche strafed Béthune with some of his naval guns ; usually they registered on the rail-head, but some of the restaurants which were situated off the square showed signs of shell-fire. Plowman had a very gay mess, consisting of the Brigade Transport Officers. Two squadrons of the 5th Royal Irish Lancers were billeted in our vicinity, and we met some of their fellows. I remember one in particular, O'Connor.

While I was on this rest I got a chit from Palin asking me to submit my recommendations at once for the raiders for the C.O's. consideration. I forwarded the following names, giving brief accounts of the gallantry displayed by the individual concerned : 2nd Lieutenants Macready and Lauder ; Corporals McNamara and McDermott, and Privates O'Leary and English. Also the name of Sergt. Sullivan, D Company, who, although not actually included in the raiders, had rendered yeoman service in the withdrawal. Porter came to lunch with me, and described a successful raid carried out by the 12th Royal Fusiliers of the 17th Brigade. They had snaffled three prisoners. While I was at Petit Sains, two mules were sent to our transport to replace two sick horses. This was the first occasion that the 2nd Battalion had mules in its lines.[1] I was greatly amused one morning watching Pte. Comerford trying to groom these " old hairies." The mules were in the same stall, and when Comerford got between them they closed in on him, and there he was wedged, giving forth volumes of oaths. All the men of the transport were busily employed making " standings " for the horses with broken bricks owing to the muddy nature of the lines.

16th January.

As the Battalion was returning to the line the following morning I ordered my horse for 8 a.m. I had had a very happy time with Plowman, and the rest did me a power of good. After breakfast, accompanied by Donoghue, I set off for Maroc. There had been a thick frost, the roads were like glass, and as the horses' hoofs were not cogged, we slithered about over the icy surface. At Grenay I dismounted, and sending Donoghue back with the horses, proceeded up to Maroc on foot. Here I found the Company in the usual cellar billets in the shambles of this " Garden City." As usual, they had been finding the nightly fatigues.

17th January.

Woke up to find snow on the ground. A bitterly cold morning, and we were all petrified in our airy billet.

Paraded, and moved off with five minutes' interval between platoons, for the front line. Relieved a company of the 7th Northamptons, commanded by King, in our usual area. I had difficulty in finding reliefs for all the sentry groups, owing to the low strength of my company. According to my notes in a Field Service Book, I see that on arrival in the Loos sector from Vimy Ridge, my trench strength was 5 officers and 115 other ranks, and that these numbers were reduced to 5 officers, 1 C.S.M., 4 sergeants, 7 corporals, 8 lance-corporals, and 65 other ranks at this date. Total : 5 officers, 85 other ranks. During this tour there was a good deal in the daily papers regarding suggested peace proposals from the Kaiser, and that the Pope had been asked to arbitrate. We did not take it very seriously !

[1] Line Battalions had horse transport in France and New Army Battalions invariably had mule transport.

18th January.

On watch from 4 a.m. to 8 a.m. I remember looking over the parapets with Sergt. Nihal at the first streak of dawn. The ground was white, and the Double Crassier looked strangely forlorn in its mantle of snow. Everything was very still, and for some time we stared at the Boche lines, and at the derelict coal trucks on top of the Crassiers.

We discovered that the enemy had dogs in their front line, probably a raid warning device! We were subjected to a "Minnie" strafe around the vicinity of Company Headquarters during lunch. The earth and our dug-out vibrated with the concussion of each explosion, which put out our candles, although we were some 20 feet underground! Had a sad fatality in my company in the evening.

I was sitting in my Headquarters dug-out, when Ahern, the stretcher-bearer, rushed in to say that 2nd Lieut. de Courcy was killed. He had been officer of the watch, and was on his way to visit the sentries of Barricade Sap when an aerial dart landed beside him. The force of the explosion blew his body down the entrance of a mine shaft which he had been standing alongside. Death, of course, had been instantaneous. De Courcy had hardly completed 32 hours in the front line ; such was war ! As Lauder was absent at Corps Headquarters with the regimental guard, we were now reduced to three officers, Sharp, Macready, and self, for the tours of duty. The tours were, therefore. very long, as we had to split up the time from "Stand to " at 6 p.m., to 7 a.m., at "Stand down," into three watches. I felt very cold in the early hours going the rounds, accompanied by Jackson, after a 4½ hours' duty. Two cadets were attached to my company for a few days' instruction. I attached them to my two platoon commanders. They were fine big men, and had belonged to the 9th Scottish Division ; they were wearing white bands round their caps. During long night tours of duty, I always made a habit of firing off a few magazines from each Lewis gun, to satisfy myself that they were in perfect working order—this always helped to keep the sentries awake ! I received a chit from the Adjutant informing me that the 17th Brigade on our left were going to carry out a raid shortly after dawn on the morrow.

A RAID IN KENNEL COATS

19th January.

At "Stand to " I warned the Company of the intended raid, and prepared to meet all eventualities, i.e. all Lewis guns ready, and sentry posts fully prepared to meet a counter-raid, but all under cover bar the sentries and N.C.O.s on duty, as our gunners were going to carry out a demonstration in our sector, and we would probably come in for all retaliation.

The actual locality where the raid was taking place was north-east of Loos, and under two kilometres away from my trench as the crow flies. Two units, the 8th Battalion The Buffs and the 8th Battalion Royal West Kents, were working in conjunction. There was to be no preliminary bombardment, as it was to be another surprise raid.

At Zero, which was 7 a.m., we descried a line of figures all dressed in white (their steel helmets had been painted white, and they wore long white coats such as hunt servants wear, so as to be as inconspicuous as possible against the snow which lay thick on the ground) advancing towards the Boche lines. When they got up to the enemy wire entanglements they became enveloped in a smoke-screen, which completely hid them from our view. There was then a terrible din of bursting shells and bombs, but the stuttering of German machine-guns could be heard above all other sounds. Later on, when the smoke cleared, we saw some of the raiders straggling back to their lines in groups. The raid was a success as far as Boche prisoners were concerned, as there were over a dozen captured, but the losses on our side were very severe, 50 per cent being casualties. The raiders experienced great difficulty in withdrawing and getting in their wounded. Some were left out in No-Man's-Land bleeding to death in the snow, and became targets for the infuriated Hun.

My line was not subjected to any kind of retaliation, so I returned to my headquarters for breakfast after witnessing this slaughter. My relief orders arrived as my company had now completed its front-line tour. Bar de Courcey being killed, I had no other casualties for the three days, although at times I had been heavily strafed by " Minnies " of all descriptions. All around my advanced posts and Company Headquarters were numerous fresh shell craters, which all showed up in the snow.

We were all in the Loos Salient at this period, concentrated on this raid warfare. C.O.s and O.C. Companies in the Division daily and nightly planned raids and anti-raid measures. My thoughts were always concerned with the latter, as my company was much under strength, and I was responsible for an awkward and straggling line. I happened to hit on an original plan for my Lewis-gun posts as follows : Off my communication trenches, I dug a short line up to the back of my parados. Here I made a " T " head for the sentry group, with pukka fire positions. From this sap the sentry group had as good a position as it would have in the actual fire bay in the main trench, if not better, and, besides, it insured complete command of the trench in front and below them. Had the enemy raided and effected an entry into our line, he could never have surprised these hidden groups as he formerly could have done on our isolated posts established every fifty yards in the main trench. With the new scheme functioning had the Boche got a footing in our trench he would have received the surprise of his life when bombed from an unexpected quarter, or fired at from behind the parados.

The following is a diagram of the first of these hidden Lewis-gun posts, which I had made off " Jermyn Street."

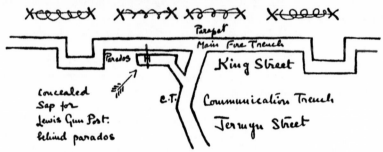

A concealed Lewis-gun position.

Undoubtedly these posts guarded against being surprised on the flanks by a strong patrol, or raiding party, which might enter our line unobserved.

The C.O. expressed his approval of this scheme when he saw the above example, and I believe that the idea was taken up by some regiments in the Brigade.

After lunch B Company, commanded by Major Freeman, who had just joined the Battalion, relieved me, and we returned to the support line in " South Street." Freeman had been serving with the 21st Division, which lay off in the Hulluch direction. This division was commanded by Major-General D. Campbell, who had, as a subaltern in the 9th Lancers, won the Grand National on The Soarer in 1896. Accordingly we were very interested in " Soarer " Campbell, as he was called.

20th January.

At the first streak of dawn my company runner, Devoy[1] (a Birr man), arrived with a chit from Palin, stating that the 13th Battalion the Middlesex Regiment would carry out a raid on the enemy's line in the vicinity of Hart's Crater at 7 a.m.

As the left flank of my company was only some 500 yards from

---

[1] Killed in June, 1918.

the theatre of operations, I naturally expected to come in for a considerable amount of artillery retaliation, also owing to our position as supports in the neck of a salient, my company lay in the immediate rear of the 13th Middlesex.

Warning all platoon commanders to put all their men in the deepest dug-outs, and leaving the gas sentries only on duty in the trench, we waited for Zero. Before Zero, I took up a good position in a fire bay, from where I could have a perfect view of the proceedings. At Zero, two parties left the Middlesex lines in file, and made their way across the short stretch of No-Man's-Land, still covered in snow. The parties got up to the enemy's wire without having a shot fired at them. Here, however, they experienced their first difficulty, for the wire as usual had not been properly cut. The right party turned to their left and wandered about on the horizon looking for the expected " G " in " Gap," which did not exist. I could see the progress of the raid perfectly from my vantage-point, as the raiders were all clearly silhouetted out against the sky. There was then some bombing and erratic rifle shots, and a great cloud of smoke. Into this the raiders vanished. Then one of the numerous coloured Boche S O S rockets soared up into the sky above all the curtain of smoke and the fun began, though it was all hidden from our view in " South Street." The enemy was now subjecting my line to some shelling. The men were all well under cover, there were a few direct hits registered on my trench, but none caused any casualties. The raid was a success, as three prisoners were captured and the casualties were only slight, but amongst them was an officer, by name Williams, missing, believed killed. It was a pity his body was not recovered. I later heard from R.S.M. Kerrigan, D.C.M., 2nd Battalion, attached to the 13th Middlesex, that the raiding party contained a large number of the men recently transferred to the Middlesex from the draft of the 5th Royal Irish Lancers, and that 2nd Lieut. Williams was killed.

It had been a surprise, as some of the enemy were found eating their breakfasts. In the evening two officers joined the Battalion —Capt. Jennings, a regular who had fought at Gallipoli with our 6th Battalion, and 2nd Lieut. Oulton. The former was attached to C Company and came along to see me ; I gave him a drink, and sent him on his way with a guide. Oulton, or " Zulu " as I nicknamed him, as he wore the '06 Natal Rebellion ribbon, was posted to my company, and a jolly nice fellow he was.

21st January.

Very cold, with hard frost at night. Finding usual fatigues for front line. Enemy very tame all day. No shells near us.

22nd January.

Received my relief orders for the morrow, which cheered me up. My company had a most hospitable reputation, and we had many mess guests who rolled in to see us, especially when in the quiet support line. These guests mostly came from the corps and oddments of the Division—Sappers, the Machine-Gun Corps, Brigade Trench Mortars, the Inspector of our anti-gas appliances —and I have specially noted that one morning I received a visit from the Divisional Camouflage Officer ! (a new and marvellous appointment). I always noticed that our mess whisky disappeared with greater rapidity when we were entrenched in " South Street " than in the front line, which no doubt was considered too unhealthy for calling purposes !

23rd January.

At 10.30 a.m. I was relieved by Rathbone of the 7th Northamptons, and my platoons independently returned to Maroc. The weather was still bitterly cold, and we found our roofless billets more miserable than ever.

24th January.

I received orders to report to the C.O. at 10.30 a.m. in Les Brébis. The C.O. said that as several senior officers had joined the Battalion recently, he had no option but to give them companies to command. Capt. Jennings and Major Freeman had just joined, and Capt. Saunders was on his way up from the Base. To the last named I was to hand over command of A Company. The C.O. thanked me for my work, and added that the discipline, smartness, and fighting powers of the Company were of a very high standard, which reflected to my credit. He said that he was sending in my name for an appointment with the Canadian Corps near Béthune, and that I would be able to retain my acting rank of Captain. However, I said I preferred remaining with the Battalion as a platoon commander, and it ended at that.

25th January.

I find that according to my Army Book 152 (correspondence), at this date I was finding the following fatigues :

For 173 Tunnelling Company R.E.

1 N.C.O. and 5 men. Sunken Road G.36 C.4.0 at 9.15 p.m.
1 N.C.O. and 5 men. Relief ditto at 2.15 a.m.
1 N.C.O. and 7 men. Relief ditto at 9.45 p.m.
1 N.C.O. and 30 men to be at Brigade Bomb Store, Loos, for 119 Trench Mortar Battery at 7 p.m.
1 officer and 50 men for R.E.

The C.O. had a " pow-wow " on or about this date. I find that I made the following notes :

1. Rum issue to be under an officer's supervision.
2. More dug-outs required for men in saps (advanced posts).
3. Cigaries required to keep men in sap-heads warm.
4. Officers' servants must know the front line.
5. Officer on duty to carry a Véry pistol. A and B Companies stand to alarm and S O S light. GREEN.
6. Officer of watch to look at rosters of sentry groups and ask sentries questions.
7. N.C.O. on duty to report " all correct " to C.O. when visiting.
8. Our wire entanglements getting very meagre in places.

This day the 21st and 22nd Battalions of the Canadians carried out a large raid in the snow, capturing 100 prisoners, south of the Double Crassier.

26th January.

Enemy shelled the western edges of Maroc with 5.9's, also one of the big mine-heads towards Les Brébis. We watched the civilians who were working there bolting for cover. The Boche got some direct hits on top of one of the cone-shaped slag heaps, which created a great dust and smoke, making them look like volcanoes. At this date the Battalion pipe band, which had been formed from the Company pipers after we left the Somme, played round the square of Les Brébis. They were very smart indeed. The band consisted of six pipers, a big drummer, and four side drummers. The big drummer was 8944 Pte. Hutchinson, D.C.M.,[1] of B Company, and two of the pipers were Privates Moran and Farrell (both of my old C Company platoon). The band was always surrounded by a crowd of admiring children, and they had a perpetual audience in the shape of the Divisional Quartermaster's stores, storemen, and transport. All the Divisional " Q " branch was situated off the square opposite the church.

27th January.

Grant Saunders joined the Battalion, and in accordance with instructions I handed over the command of A Company to him.

Algeo, Macready, and I had arranged to dine at Les Brébis. However, Algeo couldn't come, so 2nd Lieut. J. J. Kelly, who had joined A Company that morning, came in his place. We had a very cheery dinner, but we had a long tramp there and back in the snow. I remember that when we were on our way down, our

[1] Killed 13th August, 1917.

artillery started giving tongue, and that I had nearly walked slap into the mouth of one of our guns, so completely was it hidden and camouflaged in one of the numerous cellars of Maroc. I was much amazed at seeing a shell actually leave a gun. This is quite possible if one stands right behind the gun when it is firing, and when the weather conditions are good. For some time I stood and watched the projectiles leaving the guns (18-pounders) and twirling up to what seemed to me their culminating point, to disappear into space.

28th January.

Grant and I toured Maroc. This was a bitterly cold day, and we all had to wear our great-coats in the Mess. Got orders to relieve the occupants of " South Street " next morning. Kelly took some photographs of the Double Crassier. He had a small Kodak ; a camera was a forbidden article, and at this period an offender (if discovered !) was liable to be tried by F.G.C.M. Kelly[1] had been a great friend of Paddy Lynch.

29th January.

Returned to trenches, relieving the 7th Northamptons in South Street. Freezing hard all day. Grant and I made a very thorough inspection of South Street and its environs.

I remember that we were all having dinner (about 7.30 p.m.) when L/Corpl. Campion, the N.C.O. i/c of the Company Signallers, came in to tell me that the Colonel wanted to speak to me on the telephone. I dashed off to the signallers' dug-out, which was close by. When I got on the line I remember the C.O. said : " Is that you, Hitchcock ? I've rung up to tell you that Macready, Lauder and you have been awarded the Military Cross,[2] and that Corporals McNamara and McDermott, Privates O'Leary and English have been awarded the Military Medal. Will you give my very heartiest congratulations to all ? " I went to break the good news to all concerned, though Lauder and McNamara were absent. I had been previously detailed to bring up a party at 9 p.m., to B Company, and wire part of their front line, but we had an hour to " jamboree " and I left at the correct time, having killed numerous whiskies !

---

[1] Kelly was killed two months later when commanding A Company in the attack of Vimy Ridge.

[2] All the above decorations were awarded "for Conspicuous Gallantry in Action" and they came under the heading of " immediate rewards." The full details of services for which the Military Cross was awarded in each case appeared in the Gazette of March 3rd, 1917. The details of services acknowledged by decorations which did not come under this category were not given in the Gazette.

I finished my task within two hours, and on my way to South Street had some "night caps" with Major Freeman at his Company Headquarters.

At the request of the R.A.M.C. I went to see a man of B Company who was dying of some awful feet wounds at St. Patrick's Dressing Station.

30th January.

C.S.M. Hartley came round and gave Macready and myself an inch or two of M.C. ribbon, which he produced from his Army Book 64. He said he had got it at the Q.M. stores some days previously, so evidently he had been anticipating !

The ribbon of the M.C. is a particularly nice one, being white, purple, and white. Besides the awards, several men who had heavy terms of imprisonment hanging over them, and were working them off in the trenches, were recommended by me, with a view to their sentences being remitted by the G.O.C. Without exception, all these sentences were wiped out.

31st January.

The following chit from the Acting Adjutant shows how I was occupied on this date :

O.C. A Company.

A considerable number of knife rests will be put out in the vicinity of Barricade Sap. These are being made up and will be delivered at a selected place on the Lens-Bethune Rd.

You will detail one platoon to carry knife rests to the front line.

Secondly, one platoon to place knife rests in position. The work will be under the direction of Lt. F. C. Hitchcock, M.C, who will report here at 3 p.m. bringing with him the platoon commander doing the work.

Detail instructions showing hour of parade will be sent later.

No working party will be required from you for the right Coy. to-night.

JAS. PLOWMAN,[1] Lt., a/Adj.,

31-1-17.   2nd Leinster Regt.

The wiring, however, did not proceed according to schedule, owing to the fact that a few trench mortars exploded near one of the carrying parties. For hours I waited at Barricade Sap with

[1] Died of wounds, 29th April, 1918.

my wiring party for the carrying party to appear with the knife rests. The C.O. arrived, and was very annoyed at the delay owing to their non-arrival. He strode off towards South Street in the dark (he had come up over the open), and stumbled into some cumbersome knife rests, which had been thrown slap into the trench ! The C.O. had the working party formed up minus its officer, and sent up to me. Before dawn I placed out a number of these iron knife rests, but could only employ two men, as dawn was breaking, and we showed up clearly in the snow.

1st February.

We lost our Adjutant, Capt. A. C. S. Palin, who was invalided to the Base. Plowman assumed his duties, and in turn Sharp relieved him as regimental transport officer. I missed Alyn Palin ; he was always so cheery under adverse circumstances. This was a very sad day, as at " Stand to " we heard that Möllmann had been killed by an aerial dart the previous night.

A Company was now in the front line, but I managed to get down to the funeral. Möllmann was buried in the Maroc cemetery, very close to Paddy Lynch. After the funeral I called in at Battalion Headquarters and heard the joyful news that I was getting leave in a few days.

I had a long chat with Padre Moloney, who was as cheery as ever outwardly, though I knew he was very upset over Möllmann's death. He was a great man, with a heart of gold. The men adored him.[1]

Heard that the Battalion had been specially mentioned in dispatches by Sir Douglas Haig, for the raid. There were some other regiments also mentioned for successful raids, including the 1st Royal Inniskilling Fusiliers and the 21st and 22nd Battalions of the Canadians. The dispatch stated that during the month of January the British had captured 27 officers and 1228 men in raids and local attacks. We were amused with the account in the French *communiqué* regarding the " coups de main " by the " 2éme Regiment de Leinster."

---

[1] In the capture of Vimy Ridge, in which the Battalion was destined to fulfil an important rôle, there were two outstanding incidents in the amazing feat of Corporal Cunningham, which gained the 2nd Leinsters their first V.C., unfortunately a posthumous decoration, as the gallant N.C.O. died of his wounds, and in contrast a highly amusing episode. After the Battalion had captured its objectives, Colonel Murphy was astonished to see a man patiently leading a captured German horse back through the enemy's barrage in a blizzard of snow. The C.O. called to the man to know what he was going to do with the horse which was in the last stages of exhaustion and starvation. " Sure, Sor, I do be bringing him back for Father Moloney to ride," declared the captor in all seriousness and seemingly oblivious to the fact that the horse was not fit to carry one's boots, let alone the Padre who rode at least eighteen stone.

2nd February.

The C.O. accompanied by the Acting Adjutant, Plowman, toured our front. For this tour we had two sections of the newly formed Cavalry Machine-Gun Corps attached to the Company, and they were distributed along King Street. Its personnel was found from all the various cavalry regiments; the officer in charge belonged to the 4th Hussars.

This was the last occasion that I saw the C.O.[1] and it has left a distinct impression on my mind. He, Plowman, Grant Saunders, and I stood at the junction of King and Jermyn Streets, talking for some time. We must have been spotted by a sniper, as there was the familiar " slat " as a bullet embedded itself in the parados immediately behind us.

The Colonel seemed quite unconcerned, and went on talking, with his monocle in his eye and his steel helmet tilted over at an angle on the side of his head.

In the early hours of the morning I was on watch. Up and down the trench I tramped, accompanied by Jackson. I was feeling very ill, as I had caught a bad chill at Möllmann's funeral. It was bitterly cold, and I smoked innumerable cigarettes to keep awake. I did not know it at the time, but this was to be my last tour in the trenches for ever.

I was proceeding home on leave next day, and when I was to return to the B.E.F. open fighting would have taken the place of trench warfare. Peering across No-Man's-Land at the first streak of dawn, I recalled a day in the middle of December when a thick mist had enveloped our sector, so thick that I had difficulty in recognising the men at " Stand to."

This thick mist hung over our area until midday, and we had taken full advantage of this natural screen to strengthen our wire entanglements. With C.S.M. Hartley I had explored No-Man's-Land whilst Macready and McNamara examined the Boche wire. Half-way between Boyau 30 and Barricade Sap I came on a rusty Webley revolver lying beside a skeleton (probably that of one of our officers killed in the great Loos offensive of September, 1915). Macready and McNamara made a close investigation of the Boche obstacles unobserved. The only sounds they heard coming from the Boche trenches were a few coughs from an enemy sentry. I had the revolver cleaned up and brought it home when I came on leave, and gave it to my father who carried it for protection in Ireland in 1920–22. Heys-Thompson left the Battalion.

[1] Lieut.-Colonel A. D. Murphy, D.S.O., M.C. Killed on 6th November, 1917, aged 27

3rd February.

At " Stand to " we heard that Jennings, who had only just taken over command of poor old Möllmann's Company C, had been killed in the early hours by a trench mortar.

Orders came for our relief at 2 p.m. ; as I was going on leave this day, I left the trenches at 11.30 a.m., accompanied by Jackson. It was a fine, sunny morning, and in spite of a severe chill, my stock went up as we went down the long communication trench—South Street.

I called in at Battalion Headquarters in Maroc to get my leave warrant for the journey. Coming towards Grenay I passed the G.O.C. and his galloper Murray on their way to tour the line. This was the last day of the Battalion's tour in the Loos sector front line trenches. We were not at all sorry at the prospect of leaving Loos ; although it was termed a " quiet sector " when the Somme and now the Ancre battles were waging, yet it was an unlucky one from the point of view of casualties, especially amongst the officers.

Officers had simply poured through the Battalion since July, 1916. This period covered the actions on the Somme, but our death-rate was never so high amongst the officers in proportion to other ranks killed as it was for two months at Loos.

The casualties, with dates and causes, were as follows :

Rank and Name.	Company.	Date.	Cause.	Killed or Wounded.
2nd Lt. Mouritz	B	5.12.16	Shot, hand to hand fight	Killed.
2nd Lt. Sikes	A	18.12.16	By sniper	Wounded.
Capt. Lynch, M.C.	B	27.12.16	Aerial dart	Killed.
Lieut. Heming	D	10. 1.17	Shrapnel in raid	Died of wounds.
2nd Lt. de Courcy	A	18. 1.17	Aerial Dart	Killed.
Capt. Möllmann	C	21. 1.17	Aerial Dart	Killed.
Capt. Jennings	C	3. 2.17	Trench Mortar	Killed.

A company officer's life with the 2nd Leinsters worked out under 6 weeks.

Got down to Les Brébis for lunch with Squire. Afterwards had a bath and got my kit cleaned up for leave. " Zulu " Oulton had kindly lent me his British warm for leave, and I lent him my great-coat in exchange, in which he was destined to be killed in the attack on Vimy Ridge.

Egerton-Young, the Intelligence Officer, met me in my perambulations, and brought me back with him to Brigade Headquarters.

Here I met our Brigadier, General Dugan[1]; he was full of praise for the Battalion.

At 8 p.m. I got into the leave G.S. waggon, which was to convey the leave party to Béthune station, in the square of Les Brébis. Leaving Jackson, and with my haversack and a small flask in the way of kit, I proceeded on my journey. After a bitterly cold and jolting drive in the G.S. waggon over the uneven cobbled road, we got to the Béthune station. It was a moonlight night, and things could have been worse. As the train was not due to start until the early hours of the morning, I went into the station café just opposite. Here I found a number of fellows congregated, awaiting the leave train. We had a very cheery dinner, and afterwards, as it was quite late, we all lay down on the floor and went to sleep, having arranged with the stationmaster to call us when the leave train arrived.

4th February.

At 6 a.m. we took our seats in the train for a cold, tedious journey to Boulogne, where we arrived at 5 p.m. As the leave boat was not sailing until next day, I took a room in the Folkestone Hotel, which was very full of leave people. Here I met the Earl of St. Germans of The Greys, and some fellows in the Cavalry who had been at Sandhurst with me, and whose regiments were in camp outside Boulogne.

5th February.

I had developed an awful cold, and wasn't feeling very leave-like when we embarked for a rough passage. I crossed over to Euston Station, and took the Irish mail. I missed the train connection for Birr and Ballybrophy, and had to travel on the mail coach, which plied between these towns, in the middle of the night. It was bitterly cold sitting up on the box-seat, being driven by " Peter," a great character. He had fought with the 5th Lancers in South Africa, and had also been a hunt servant in the Ormond Kennels before he became driver of the Royal Mail with its pair of horses. I have always been indebted to Peter for having taught me to light a pipe under all weather conditions. He told me that no man could be called a man until he could drive a pair of horses and at the same time light his pipe in a " howling gale," and he proceeded to show me how to do it. (Years afterwards, when passing through Ballybrophy, I enquired for Peter, but was told he was dead. " The motor cars killed him," declared my informant.)

I had taken the precaution to wire my father for a car to meet

[1] Now Major-General Sir Winston Dugan, K.C.M.G., C.B., D.S.O., Governor of South Australia.

me at Birr Station, and Tom Lahey turned up with a young horse which he was breaking in to shafts, and which landed me at home in time for lunch on the second day of my leave.

I had crossed over to Dublin with the band of the Irish Guards, who, complete with the regimental mascot, an Irish wolfhound, were carrying out a recruiting campaign in the south and west of Ireland.

I had by this time developed a particularly hostile chill, which turned to pleurisy. As I had to take to my bed, I was not fit to return to the B.E.F. When I recovered, I was medically boarded at The Curragh, and passed for " home service." Then followed a brief period attached to the 3rd Battalion at Cork.

Here training for war went on at full swing under the directions of Lieut.-Colonel R. G. Currey who had been severely wounded at Gallipoli.

It was a happy contrast practising bomb-throwing with Crowe, Macready, Corpl. McNamara, D.C.M., M.M., L/Corpl. Morrissey, M.M. and Bar, and others, with whom I had thrown so many in anger and under such different conditions to the meadows around Mayfield and Victoria Barracks.

With Crowe[1] I attended a Gas Course held at Island Bridge Barracks, Dublin.

Some months later I was appointed by the War Office to the 7th Officers' Cadet Battalion, at Moore Park, Fermoy, as an instructor. In June I got orders to attend an investiture at Buckingham Palace, when His Majesty the King presented me with the Military Cross. Bellew of the South Irish Horse received his M.C. at the same investiture. It so happened that the Huns had a gigantic air raid on London that night.

In July the Cadet Battalion was inspected by Field-Marshal Sir John French,[2] the late C.-in-C. of the British Expeditionary Force.

Amongst the instructors at Fermoy were the following :

The Adjutant was G. W. Nightingale of the 1st Munsters who had won his M.C. and a Legion of Honour with the 29th Division at Gallipoli. Under a tornado of lead he had supervised the

---

[1] Crowe later returned to France where he was wounded (for the third time) by a bomb, and unfortunately blinded.

[2] Shortly before he died in 1925 this famous soldier told me the following story : When at Viceregal Lodge, Dublin, it was invariably his custom to go out for a ride every morning in Phœnix Park. One morning on his return he was accosted by an English press representative who managed to evade one of the sentries in order to gain an interview. He approached Lord French, saying, " I have just seen you riding unescorted in the Park, are you not taking a great risk with all these gun-men waiting to shoot you ? " The Field Marshal replied, " Well, I was quite safe as I was riding a good horse and being Irish they would not shoot as they might hit the horse by mistake ! "

landing of his regiment along a narrow gangway from that veritable Horse of Troy—the River Clyde. Another Gallipoli hero was Forshaw, V.C., who had won his decoration bomb-throwing with his Territorial battalion of the Manchesters.

T. A. Bradford, a Territorial Durham, with a D.S.O., had two very distinguished brothers ; one was a lieutenant, acting Brig.-General, V.C., who belonged to the D.L.I. and who was killed at Cambrai, whilst the other brother had won a V.C. in the naval attack at Zeebrugge where he had been mortally wounded. A unique distinction for a family to boast both Naval and Military V.C.s.

W. E. Caldbeck and E. F. Radcliff were 2nd Dublins. Emerson a 2nd Royal Irish Fusilier. W. D. Magill, who had fought in South Africa and in the '06 Natal Rebellion, had been severely wounded with the Prince of Wales's Volunteers. D. A. Bulloch of the 1st Devons. Major J. H. G. Baird, M.C., of the Bedfords who was my company commander. There was R. G. W. Callaghan of the Connaught Rangers. H. H. Lake, who had fought at Mons and Gallipoli, and C. B. Callander, M.C., were 2nd Munsters. R. V. C. Bodley, M.C., of the 60th Rifles and K. S. Gladstone of the 8th R.B. were amongst the Greenjacket contingent. The C.O. was Lieut.-Colonel A. G. Bruce, D.S.O., of the Royal Scots Fusiliers ; he had been wounded at Mons and at Neuve Chapelle. Last but not least was G. de M. H. Orpen-Palmer (O.-P.2) who was musketry officer. He had lost an eye with the 2nd Leinsters at Premesques in '14, and at the time, although blinded in both eyes, he managed to rescue another wounded officer, Capt. Whitton,[1] and to carry him back to our lines in safety.

Some years afterwards I met a sergeant in the 1st Royal Fusiliers who recalled the fact of seeing Leinster officers stumbling into their entrenchments. The blinded one, he said, was being directed by the one he was carrying.

[1] Now Colonel F. E. Whitton, C.M.G., the well-known military historian.

6th August.

Orders for the Front.

8th August.

Sailed from Dover, via Victoria, that amazing railway terminus of the War years.

Although it was the middle of the summer, there was a decided chill in the air. Victoria Station presented its usual war-time appearance, and was full of soldiers returning to the Front from leave. Heaps of webbing equipment and packs were scattered everywhere, and the familiar clanking of steel helmets and rifle butts on the stone platform could be heard above all the station sounds. All round were the usual leave-train sights—Tommies saying good-bye. Everyone seemed very morbid, and no wonder. The War was just entering into its fifth year. The men returning were not new to the game, they were a seasoned-looking lot, and some of them had been wounded a couple of times. I was returning for the third time to the Expeditionary Force, France.

There were a number of officers in the train. We duly reported to the embarkation officer, Dover, and as our boat did not sail until 3 p.m., went into the town for lunch. It was raining hard, so the weather was in keeping with one's spirits.

Embarked at 3 p.m., and after a choppy crossing, arrived at Calais. There were a few destroyers in Dover Harbour, and booms barred all the entrances; in fact, it had a most formidable appearance. One of the destroyers accompanied us on our route, but it was only visible occasionally, owing to a thick mist which had enveloped the Channel. There were some few lorries drawn up alongside the wharf to convey us to our various base camps. Into these we scrambled with our valises, and set off on a short but jolty journey.

The 16th Infantry Base Depôt was situated on the high ground overlooking the old historical town of Calais. We were accommodated in tents, around which deep trenches ran at intervals through the camp for use in case of a Boche air raid.

Recently, Calais had been receiving a fair amount of attention from enemy bombing planes, and a lot of damage had been inflicted in the town. The camp had had some direct hits and numerous casualties. On the southern fringe of the camp were two cages (a cage is a camp for prisoners, enclosed in barbed wire entanglements). In one of these were a hundred Boche prisoners, and in the other was encamped a Chinese Labour Corps unit, complete with their wives !

In one of the Boche air raids a direct hit was obtained on the latter camp, and a number of " Chinks " were laid out. The following night the enraged " Chinks " retaliated on the Hun prisoners ; having crawled under the barbed wire, they set on the sleeping prisoners and " did in " a number before the sentries were aroused.

9th to 10th August.

Spent all my time in Calais and had all meals at the Officers' Club. There was only one parade, an anti-gas one, which consisted of going through a long chamber into which gas had been turned, so that we could test our new respirators.

The weather was excellent, and besides walking about the narrow cobbled streets of the town, we strolled down to the sea-shore. Here had been a great *plage* pre-war, and there were numerous bandstands and derelict bathing-boxes strewn all over the place. I also explored the ramparts overlooking the harbour. Nightly our searchlights swept the skies from all angles, but no hostile planes were signalled while I was there.

11th August.

Left the camp at 8 a.m. for the military siding, under orders to rejoin the 2nd Battalion. At Ebblinghem, a small village some 12 kilometres east of St. Omer, on the main road to Hazebrouck, and which at this date functioned as the railhead, I received orders to report to the 29th Divisional Reception Camp, close by. On my way to the camp I passed several Leinsters, one of whom was 7900 Pte. O'Leary, my old A Company runner. I forthwith engaged him as my servant, as Jackson had been wounded shortly after I had left the Battalion in 1917 and was in the U.K. The Divisional Rest Camp consisted of reinforcement officers and men on their way to join their regiments, and a certain number of officers and men sent down for a rest from the line. The only other Leinster in the Mess was Macready, and I shared a tent with him and a fellow in the Lancashire Fusiliers. It was a happy coincidence meeting Macready, who had only just arrived from Portsmouth.

12th August.

At 11 a.m. Macready and I jumped a lorry going to St. Omer. After a jolty journey over the well-worn and burnished *pavé*, our driver dropped us on the outskirts of the town. This was my first visit to St. Omer, although I knew every square foot of its railway station. St. Omer, a perfect jewel of an old-world town, with a cluster of Gothic churches, lies nestling in the hollows of the downs on the River Aa. From a distance, its numerous towers and lofty steeples attract the eye. Going through a network of numerous narrow streets, one enters its Grand Place—a spacious cobbled square opposite the market-place. Apart from its ancient history as a fortress, which lay in the path of another British army, under the greatest of generals—the Duke of Marlborough—St. Omer had more recent interest for the British Expeditionary Force. It was in this old city that Sir John French had established his General Headquarters when the original six divisions had completed their transference from the Aisne to Flanders in October, '14. Here also the famous Field-Marshal, Lord Roberts, V.C., had passed away within sound of the guns on the 14th November, '14.

In the middle ages St. Omer had been under Spanish rule, and until it was annexed by Louis XIV, after the defeat of the Spaniards at Cassel by the French. It was then fortified by Vauban, and parts of the old bastioned trace remain to this day. Due east of the town lay the Forêt de Clairmarais. It was from this wood that Napoleon got the timber to build a fleet for the invasion of England.

Our General Headquarters had remained at St. Omer until the spring of '16, when it moved to Montreuil. A large house standing in the main cobbled street, and entered under one of those large archways called the *porte cochère*, brought one into the C.-in-C.'s old Headquarters. It had now been turned into an officers' club run by the British, and a very useful asset it was, but a most unpopular institution with the local inhabitants, who were thus deprived of any chance of profiteering on the British officers from the trenches. On the side of the club overlooking the street was a memorial plaque to Lord Roberts, who had died within its precincts.

We had dinner in the club at a most reasonable price, and returned to Ebblinghem on a lorry bound for Hazebrouck.

13th August.

I went in to St. Omer with Macready and cashed a cheque at the Banque de France, which was situated in the square.

14th August.

Went into St. Omer with Webb of the Royal Dublin Fusiliers and had dinner in the Club. Here, I ran up against Morgan, who had been in the same company with me at Sandhurst. Morgan was in the R.W.F. and attached to the R.A.F. We had a drink together ; reading through the casualty list at a later date, I was very sorry to see his name amongst the killed.

25th August.

An old friend, Parrie, of the Hampshires, joined the reception camp. He had been on a musketry course with me in February, '15, in Dublin. Went into St. Omer with Macready.

16th August.

There was practically no work in the camp. Short musketry parades and rifle inspections only were the orders of the day. Webb and I went for a long walk in the country in the evening, harvesting was in full swing, and the countryside all covered with corn stooks presented a very prosperous appearance. When I returned I found orders to join the Battalion awaiting me. I had now spent almost eight days between the Base and Ebbling-hem.

17th August.

At 10 a.m. Macready and I set off for the Battalion, which was out on rest in the vicinity of Hazebrouck. On our way up in a lorry, I particularly noticed that the bridges were all labelled " For Tanks," or " Not for Tanks," signs of the coming offensive ! At this date troops were not allowed to billet in Hazebrouck, as it was shelled fairly regularly. Up to the German offensive in March, '18, the town had been in the safe area, but now it was well within range of the enemy artillery and got strafed daily. It had been completely evacuated by the civilian population, who no doubt had fears of a repetition of Ypres. We found the 2nd Battalion lying up in bivouac in a field on the north-west outskirts of the town.

I duly reported to the C.O., Major (Temp. Lieut.-Colonel) H. W. Weldon.

The composition of the 29th Division :

G.O.C., Major-General Sir W. de S. Cayley, K.C.M.G.

86th Brigade.

2nd Battalion Royal Fusiliers	.	7th Foot.
1st Battalion The Lancashire Fusiliers	.	20th ,,
1st Battalion Royal Dublin Fusiliers	.	102nd ,,

87th Brigade.

2nd South Wales Borderers	. .	24th Foot.
1st King's Own Scottish Borderers	.	25th ,,
1st Battalion The Border Regiment	.	34th ,,

88th Brigade.

2nd Battalion Hampshire Regiment	.	67th Foot.
4th Battalion Worcestershire Regiment		
2nd Battalion The Leinster Regiment	.	109th ,,
Pioneer Battalion 2nd Monmouthshire Regiment	. . . . .	Territorials.

Divisional Artillery : L Battery Royal Horse Artillery.

As can be seen, the 29th Division consisted entirely of regular battalions, and was the only one at this date so composed, with the exception of the Guards Division in France. The Guards and the 29th Divisions shared the honour of being the *corps d'élite* at this period. At the beginning of '18 there had been an alteration in the organisation of infantry divisions, which had in February been reduced from 12 to 9 battalions, plus a pioneer battalion to each division.

The reduction was entirely due to the shortage of man power in Great Britain. This released the odd battalions in divisions to make up what, on paper, looked like additional Brigades, but very weak ones at that. However, as the British had taken over more ground from the French, and held at this date a front of 125 miles in length, it was necessary to have more divisions.

The failure of recruiting in Ireland had rendered it impossible to maintain all the Irish battalions, and thus the system of allowing the regular Irish battalions to absorb their service one was introduced. This had the outstanding merit of preserving nationality and regimental *esprit de corps*.

The 2nd Battalion, therefore, absorbed the 7th Battalion when they were both serving in the 16th Irish Division.

It was most unfortunate that the new organization had hardly been completed before the enemy launched his colossal attack in March, with all his numerous divisions just released from Russia, which country had absolutely collapsed. On the disbandment of the 16th Division, the 2nd Leinsters had been specially picked for the 29th Division, which they joined in April near Hazebrouck.

In addition to absorbing the 7th Battalion, the 2nd had been reinforced by four platoons of the 6th Service Battalion the Connaught Rangers. The Battalion was, therefore, well up to strength when I rejoined it.

2nd Battalion.

Roll of the officers serving with the Battalion, 17th August, '18 :

Battalion Headquarters.

Lieut.-Colonel Weldon.
Major Frend, D.S.O., 3rd Battalion.
Captain Whitehead, M.C., 7th Battalion, Adjutant.
Lieut. Sharp, Transport Officer.
2nd Lieut. O'Connor Mallins, Connaught Rangers, attached, Intelligence Officer.
2nd Lieut. McMahon, 3rd Connaught Rangers, attached, Signalling Officer.
Lieut. Kirkpatrick, M.C., 4th Battalion, Lewis-Gun Officer.
Lieut. Nye, Assistant Adjutant.
Captain Morris, R.A.M.C., attached.
Rev. Father Doyle, M.C., Padre.[1]
Lieut. and Quartermaster Mahoney, Royal Irish Regt., attached.

A Company.

Lieut. Hyde-Sander.
Lieut. Whittington, 3rd Battalion.
2nd Lieut. Moore.
2nd Lieut. Shelly, 3rd Battalion.
2nd Lieut. Barker, M.C. 3rd Battalion.
2nd Lieut Wylde, 3rd Battalion.

B Company.

Captain J. Farrell, D.S.O., 5th Battalion.
Lieut. McNamara.
Lieut. Keating.
Lieut. Mathias, 3rd Battalion.
2nd Lieut. Morrison, 3rd Battalion.
2nd Lieut. Igoe, 3rd Battalion.
2nd Lieut. Hutchinson, 3rd Battalion.

C Company.

Captain V. Farrell, M.C. 5th Battalion.
Lieut. Hickie.
2nd Lieut. FitzSimon.
2nd Lieut. Woods, M.C., M.M.
2nd Lieut. White, 3rd Battalion.
2nd Lieut. Holden, 3rd Battalion.

D Company.

Captain G. Farrell, 5th Battalion.
Captain Tomlinson, R.M.F., attached.
2nd Lieut. Johnston.
2nd Lieut. Scott, 3rd Battalion.
2nd Lieut. Midgely, 3rd Battalion.
2nd Lieut. Moran, 3rd Battalion.
2nd Lieut. O'Sullivan, 3rd Battalion.

Regimental Sergt.-Major H. Knight, D.C.M.

[1] Another Padre called Doyle, had been killed with us before Guillemont on the 18th August, 1916.

Three of the companies were commanded by the brothers Farrell, late of the 7th Battalion. This Battalion had fought gallantly, and it was unfortunate that it had had to be disbanded. It was raised in Fermoy by Colonel A. H. Wood, who had commanded the 2nd Battalion Connaught Rangers.

Except in the Transport lines there was only a mere sprinkling of the old toughs throughout the Battalion.[1] Sergt. McCarthy was still there, and was now wearing the ribbons of the D.C.M. and Belgian Croix de Guerre; also Ptes. Hosford, McCarthy, Pledge, Wallace, and last but not least, No. 6081 Pte. Cummins.

Cummins was still employed as storeman, and a splendid fellow he was. He was going on for twenty-one years' service with the Regiment, and had been with the Battalion since the Aisne, '14. He had the Boer War medals and also the M.S.M.

I was posted to C Company, commanded by Val Farrell. Had the 29th Divisional sign, a red triangle, sewn on my jacket just below my shoulder-straps and a diamond in the regimental colours, blue and green, on the back below the collar.

18th August—Sunday.

The British offensive had started in Flanders, and we got orders to hold ourselves in readiness, as our 87th Brigade was attacking in the Outtersteene Ridge. Being Sunday, there were church parades. C and D Companies supplied carrying fatigues for the front line, ammunition, rations, and barbed wire, to the 1st K.O.S.B.s who were consolidating their new positions.

19th August.

When I rejoined the Battalion I found that they had been parading daily for an inspection by two very distinguished Allied Generals. Battalion orders omitted to state the Allied country to which these Generals belonged. At 2 p.m. we were drawn up *en masse* in an enclosed field, just off the main Haze-brouck–Cassel road. Our Corps Commander, Lieut.-General Sir Beauvoir de Lisle[2] of polo fame, Major-General Cayley, and the 88th Brigade Staff, were present, and a Union Jack had been

---

[1] The 2nd Battalion had suffered severely in the attacks at Vimy Ridge, Messines, Third Ypres, and in the March Retreat with the 5th Army where the officer casualties alone amounted to 7 killed and 15 wounded. Amongst the number of N.C.O.'s killed in 1917 were Sergeants 9715 Brady, 9602 McSweeney, 7103 Melsop, 5403 Boylan, Morrissey the stretcher-bearer's brother, 8843 Murray, 8731 Chalmers, Corporals 7974 Merriman, M.M., 9412 Murray, 9443 Boyer, and 9454 Dilworth of the Transport, the tallest man in the regiment.

[2] Sir Beauvoir de Lisle originally belonged to the Durham Light Infantry, and was transferred as a Major into the Royal Dragoons in 1903, which regiment he commanded three years later.

hoisted, ready to be broken at the General Salute. After many false alarms, in which, in each case, the Battalion was called to attention and the slope, the pukka car arrived some twenty minutes late, and stopped outside the field. Then into the parade ground were heralded two Japanese Generals by a number of Brass Hats. When they reached the saluting base, the C.O. gave the order to present arms, and the buglers sounded the General Salute. Automatically the distinguished visitors put up their hands.

However, they were unable to decide when this attitude should be abandoned. The Battalion had meanwhile ordered arms, and had received the command to stand at ease. But the punctilious little men of Japan still stood rigid, with their right hands motionless at the peaks of their caps. Another embarrassing minute followed until a Brass Hat stepped forward and withdrew the saluting arms to a position of rest. There was a quiver in the Leinster ranks; but discipline told. Our distinguished visitors were only some 4 ft. 7 ins. high; they were covered in decorations and big stars; each had a small sword, and they wore high Blucher boots, which were heavily spurred. When we were forming up to march past in close column, one old tough was overheard to remark to his neighbour, " Be japers, Mick, fancy doing all this for two Heathen Generals."

The inspecting Allied officer afterwards wrote to our Corps Commander, expressing his appreciation of " the privilege of seeing this magnificent battalion belonging to such a famous Division as the 29th."

20th August.

I was detailed to take charge of the nucleus, consisting of a dozen officers and some 200 men at Hazebrouck, the Battalion having proceeded up to the front line at Outtersteene. The nucleus scheme had been introduced into the B.E.F. about May, '17, when a distinction had been made in the " effective " and " trench " strengths in a battalion. The idea was that in case of severe casualties, or even annihilation, regiments could be quickly reorganised on the nucleus, which usually consisted of 2 officers and 35 other ranks per company.

At 2 p.m. we marched off to a support line in the vicinity of Strazeele. 4 p.m. found us taking over a line which ran through some standing crops and stubble. The countryside had a most peaceful aspect on this lovely evening, and the peasants were all busily employed attending to their crops. We received a great welcome from these poor people (composed of old men, women, and children), as on the previous tour officers and men had

helped them to gather the harvest. They would have been in
terrible difficulties over the saving and cutting of their crops but
for the British Army.

I saw several mowing machines being worked by pairs of our
" heavy draughts," and driven by their own A.S.C. drivers.

At 8 p.m. McNamara, Hickie, and I got orders to report to
Brigade Headquarters immediately, as we were required as
liaison officers in an impending attack.

Dusk was drawing on as we set off for 88th Brigade H.Q. We
each took an orderly with us ; Flaherty being mine.

As we went on, the country became more devastated. Shelled
out homesteads and roofless houses were very prominent. The
ridge on which the Brigade H.Q. were established was absolutely
devoid of any vegetation or trees.

We passed Estaminet Corner, a noted spot for Boche strafes.
Reported to a Staff Captain at W.18 D.7.5, who told us that we
were not required, as the attack was postponed.

Forthwith we returned to our support line, and on the way we
were overtaken by Sharp,[1] and the Battalion Transport. There
was slight shelling in our vicinity, but no damage was done.

21st August.

Excellent weather. Received orders to proceed to the transport lines, as I was required as prosecutor on a F.G. Court Martial.
At dusk I set off and after a long trek got to my destination at
10 p.m.

22nd August.

The Court Martial was a wash-out, but I remained at the
Rear Battalion H.Q.s, as they were called, until after lunch.

At 3 p.m. I returned to the support line or zone. Macready had
his dug-out blown in on top of him, and he was evacuated to
the Base.

23rd to 26th August.

Still in the support zone. Parties found daily for various
fatigues. Weather broke on the 26th, and our line became a
quagmire. However, as it turned out, it did not matter, as we got
orders for relief. At 6 p.m. we moved off for the same field in
which we had previously bivouacked. Went to see the 29th

[1] Sharp was riding a beautiful mare with which he had been most successful
show jumping. He won the Brigade, Division, and Corps open jumping competition and he was later selected to represent the British Army at the Calais Horse
Show, where he was first in the British Army and third amongst the Allies. He
put up a capital show, particularly as our cavalry were strongly represented.

Divisional concert troupe in a local barn. Enjoyed the show, but the thought of spending the night in a rotten old bell tent rather damped one's hilarity. It rained in torrents throughout the night.

27th August.

Marched the Company to the Divisional baths. Weather good.

28th to 29th August.

Weather good. Company parades only.

30th August.

Woods, FitzSimon, and I got horses from the transport lines and rode off to Staple after lunch in order to get some money from the field cashier. On the way we passed an encampment of the British West Indies Regiment. We were particularly struck with the smart way in which these native sentries handled their arms.

Being unsuccessful in running the field cashier to earth, and being short of cash all round, we pooled our remaining francs and managed to get beer and omelets at an *estaminet*, having tied up our horses to the door. On the way back, my horse, which was once Louis Daly's company charger, picked up a stone. I took it out with difficulty, and as he was going very tender on it afterwards, I walked back. When we returned to the transport, I went through the horse lines, and discovered a few old friends of '15 days still there, notably Matilda, who was badly blemished about the hocks, having got into barbed wire some months previously during an air raid.

31st August.

Someone produced a rugby football, and we were greatly amused with the old toughs whom we tried to teach " scrumming down."

1st September.

Battalion got sudden orders to go off in pursuit of the enemy, who were reported to be retiring along the Divisional front, at midnight. Final movement orders were somewhat delayed, but the first streak of dawn, precisely 4 a.m., saw the Battalion " embussing " for the front. Left in charge of the Battalion nucleus, strength 4 officers and 140 other ranks, in our bivouac line. FitzSimon and I, being short of rations, went to a local farm to obtain some eggs. Coming back we passed a poor peasant woman who was crying. She had just been wounded in the arm by shrapnel. She presented a pathetic appearance with her children round her, screaming with fright. She was attended to in one of our dressing-stations. At night several " Taubes " came over, and we were subjected to a bombing strafe. This was my first experience of being bombed, and a most unpleasant one it was. No damage was done to our lines, but in a neighbouring transport, several horses were knocked out. 2nd Lieut. Scott, who was suffering from a severe attack of dysentery, became very ill in the middle of the night. I aroused some R.A.M.C. people who were billeted some distance away, and got them to bring along an ambulance, and had him evacuated.

2nd September.

Received orders to be prepared to move off towards Strazeele in the evening. I was O.C. the Brigade nucleus, and had parties of over some 140 men each from the 4th Worcesters and 2nd Hampshires. Two G.S. waggons from the Division Ammunition Column were placed at my disposal for the men's packs. At 6 p.m., we struck camp and paraded. The numbers were some 10 officers and 450 other ranks.

It was a lovely summer evening, and in the dusk we marched off for our destination. Our route brought us along a fairly straight road, which was belted at intervals by the familiar Flanders willows. The G.S. waggons being drawn only by pairs of mules experienced great difficulty in keeping up.

Near Strazeele, FitzSimon and I returned to find the waggons. We had not far to go before coming to them. Climbing up beside the drivers, we followed on in the tracks of the nucleus. We passed Strazeele and took a turn to our right, along a narrow road which should have brought us out at the back of Botha Farm. As we proceeded, the going became terribly difficult, with shell craters studded about all over the place. Finally, we came to a spot which was absolutely impassable, owing to two colossal craters, which had obliterated the whole road. To turn was out of the question, as there was no room, one side of the road being lined by a dense mass of barbed wire, and along the other side ran a large ditch.

We then unyoked " the hairies " and harnessed them on to the rear wheels of their respective waggons, which they proceeded to haul back. The darkness added to our difficulties, but we eventually managed to turn the waggons at a wider place. We retraced our steps, and making a *détour* of Strazeele, got round to Botha Farm. In my experience, I have always found that in circumstances like this mules are more practical than horses. The stubborn mule rarely gets excited, and pulls steadily. Had we used horses for the above transport, we would have had a terrible time ; they would have started plunging about, and there would have been terrible confusion in the darkness. Eventually we got round to Botha Farm. Strazeele had been practically razed to the ground, but here and there an abrupt piece of whitened masonry had been left standing up amongst the wreckage, as if fate had decreed they should stand as a memorial stone to the ruthlessness of modern warfare.

We pulled up where the road was crossed by the trenches. Here parties from the three regiments were waiting to draw their packs. We hoped to use Botha Farm for the night, but found it already occupied by the 1st K.O.S.B.s. of the 87th Brigade. Shelly, O'Sullivan, FitzSimon, and I spent the night in some adjacent dug-outs.

3rd September.

Daylight revealed a desolate and churned-up countryside stretched out before us, from the high ground on which the shelled-out ruins of Strazeele stood. The war-scarred town of Bailleul was directly to our front some 4 kilometres distant. Meteren was on our left and Merris on our right. The line we were occupying had originally been built by the British as a defence line.

The exact spot where my dug-out lay was in a reserve battery position in the defence zone. There were several large dug-outs which had been fitted with beds made of wire netting. Between the gun-pits, fire trenches had been constructed, with pukka machine-gun emplacements. With an excellent field of fire, this line would have been a most formidable position had we wanted it. The actual gun-pits and dug-outs were all admirably camouflaged, which fact probably accounted for the line and even the duckboards, connecting the emplacements, being left intact, although in the midst of a devastated area.

At 3 p.m., in accordance with orders I had received from Brigade Headquarters, I paraded and moved off for a new destination called Verity Cross Roads.

Our march took us through a terribly denuded area ; the country was undulating, and from the top of every fresh rise on the torn-up road a further stretch of desolation spread itself out before us. We crossed the trenches, or " grouse butts," which had recently been held by the Battalion ; FitzSimon indicated his platoon's actual frontage. We passed through the relics of many old hop-gardens ; the shells had caused terrible havoc amongst them. Here and there a few solitary poles still stood up in the void amongst the shattered ones. Merris had been almost razed to the ground, bar the church walls, which had withstood the bombardments. We were now passing through a sector which had seen the 2nd Battalion engaged with the enemy just four years previously. In October, 1914, the Battalion had wrested this area from the enemy in the III Corps advance.

Another kilometre brought us to the shambles of Outtersteene. This village had a terribly battered appearance ; whole houses had been knocked down. The narrow road over which we had to advance was obstructed with furniture, timber, and masonry. There was a sickly smell of decaying bodies in the air. Outtersteene had been occupied to the last by the civilian population, and many of them had been caught in the bombardment. Several of the poor people had returned, and were searching their dismantled homes for belongings.

One poor woman struck a very forlorn figure sitting by the ruined church weeping. Absolutely destitute, her home had disappeared, and for all I know, probably some of her children. One old man was going about carrying a large oil painting. I expect it was the only article he had salved from his demolished house. It was extraordinary how some particular article was often left completely intact after a " strafe." A guide reported to me near this village, and conducted me to a spot some hundred yards south of Verity Cross Roads, where we were to bivouac. Tarpaulins and waterproof sheets had been dumped here for our use, and straightway we set to work and fixed them up in the midst of the churned-up earth. Dusk was closing in when the camp was finally pitched. It was a lovely evening. My camping-ground had previously been a Boche ammunition dump, and all round the field were piles of new shells, which they had been forced to abandon. Right down one side of the field were the remains of the ammunition column itself. Our guns had caught them, and had caused terrible havoc, judging by appearances. Twisted-up waggons, broken wheels, and dead horses lay in huddled-up heaps. There were parts of German uniforms flapping from the boughs of the trees above us. The stench from the decomposing bodies was appalling. Lucky for us the wind blew in the right direction ! Throughout the night we saw the flames of burning houses, which the " Jerries " were destroying in their retirement. (After the end of '17 the enemy was always alluded to as " Jerry " by the B.E.F.)

4th September.

Finding fatigue parties for clearing up the wreckage on the roads. The actual cross roads were like a quagmire, owing to a stream becoming dammed up by the shell-fire. This often happened in France, especially in the Ypres sector, where incessant shell-fire often altered a water-course.

We dug large sump pits and drained off the water, and had all the bivouacs splashed in mud to camouflage them from hostile aeroplane observation. We got "wind up" over the drinking water, and had to have it boiled. A great " push " was taking place this day on our front. The 29th Division had been allotted a sector running from the left of Hill 63 to the right of Ploegsteert Wood inclusive.

When the rations arrived at dark, we got news of the result of the attack. Hill 63 had been captured by the 2nd Battalion at dawn. This gain was of great tactical importance, as Hill 63 commanded the large piece of country which stretched as far as the River Lys, which was in the hands of the Boche. The enemy had laid great stress on the importance of this vantage-point, and with innumerable nests of machine-guns and " minnenwerfers," screened behind dense masses of barbed wire entanglements, awaited our assault. The position was considered almost impregnable, in fact our Brigadier had described it as " insurmountable," with the terrible wire. Its capture was a great achievement for the Battalion, and the result was that the enemy had to retire along the front, as his positions were rendered untenable owing to this predominating point being in our possession. The attack cost the Battalion some 180 men killed and wounded. Most of these casualties were caused when the companies encountered the wire entanglements. Further south, the 1st Royal Dublin Fusiliers had captured the famous Ploegsteert Wood. This was another difficult task, as the Boche had heavily wired the wood, and so turned it into a most formidable position. They lost some 100 killed and wounded in their attack. The nucleus of the Division had by this time been concentrated at Verity Cross Roads. More bivouacs were being hurriedly pitched to accommodate all.

5th September.

We received news of the capture of Messines from the Boche. General Birdwood, G.O.C. of the Australian Corps, was in the vicinity of Verity Cross Roads during the day, but we did not see him.

6th September.

Fine weather ; received our rations in good time.

7th September.

Struck camp and paraded for Meteren. I was not sorry to see the last of Verity Cross Roads. If ever there was need for

chloride of lime it was at Verity Cross Roads. Our route to
Meteren lay due north on a line parallel with Bailleul, which was
only three kilometres away as the crow flies.

In a field north of the Bailleul–Meteren road we found the
Battalion already bivouacked. Bell tents had been pitched for
the officers' accommodation. C Company used a room in a ruined
house as a mess, and the same old shambles provided an Orderly
Room for Battalion Headquarters. I heard that 2nd Lieut.
Woods, M.C., M.M., had greatly distinguished himself in the last
" show " ; also Val Farrell. Woods asked me to word a recommendation for the latter's gallantry to send in to Orderly Room.

8th September.

I was President of a Court of Enquiry which assembled on the
" illegal absence " of one of the men. The weather broke, and we
had torrential rain, accompanied by strong gusts of wind. Woods,
FitzSimon, and I were playing poker in a bell tent when the
force of the wind completely lifted the canvas from its moorings
and it collapsed on top of us. There we were, all tangled up in the
debris with our cards scattered in the mud. We extricated
ourselves from the crumpled-up tent and got drenched, much to
the amusement of the men.

9th September.

Woods[1] was attached to the Brigade Trench Mortar Battery,
and left the Company, much to our regret. He was a cheery
soul and a fine soldier.

Many lorries passed us going down the line ; they were full of
victims of the mustard gas. Highlanders were prominent among
these casualties. After lunch FitzSimon and I got horses from
the transport, and went for a long " hack " in the Cassel[2] direction,

[1] Shot in Ireland in 1920.
[2] Curiously enough it is the hill of Cassel which figures so humorously in
a nursery rhyme which records the strange evolutions of the luckless Duke of
York in that inglorious campaign for British arms—the war of the French
Revolution—on its steep gradients :
> " The brave old Duke of York,
> He had ten thousand men.
> He marched them to the top of a hill,
> And he marched them down again."

Cassel Hill ever presented a rich prize to the German hordes, and on several
occasions they came to within close proximity. The Mont des Cats which was
only some ten kilometres distant was actually occupied by Uhlans until routed
by the 5th Royal Irish Lancers in October, 1914. In this action Prince Max
of Hesse, the Kaiser's nephew, was mortally wounded. He was captured and
tended in a Trappist monastery by Captain O'Brien-Butler, who was M.O. to
the " Dandy Fifth," and who had been a well-known performer over the formidable banks at Punchestown. The German Prince gave his gold watch to this
gallant Irishman, who himself fell shortly afterwards, but the watch was returned
to Germany after the War.

passing Flêtre and Caestre. We saw several dead horses lying on the edge of the cobbles. At Caestre we passed long convoys of supply lorries, which belonged to the Australian Corps.

We turned back on the outskirts of St. Sylvestre Cappel. It turned out a wet evening.

10th September.

I was orderly officer, and mounted Regimental quarter guard. It rained in torrents all day, and I paid out the Company in the dirty and sticky 5-franc notes in the evening. Visiting the prisoners in the guard-room with Sergt. Murphy, B.O. Sergt., I came across a man of B Company, who was awaiting trial by a F.G.C.M. He told me he thought he would be shot, as he was charged with a most serious crime—cowardice. He said he had been a certain company commander's runner at Hooge '15, and that if he could only get in touch with him he would no doubt speak on his behalf for his work in that action. I promised to write to the officer, who answered my letter by return of post. He enclosed a good chit for the accused, and said that the man had performed a brave act as Hooge as a runner, coming through a hail of machine-gun fire and shrapnel with a message.

11th September.

At 3 p.m., the Battalion paraded, and moved off in rain for Hazebrouck. We took a by-road on the left, just past the shambles of Meteren, and marching via Strazeele, got into billets in Hazebrouck at dusk. Dogs were very conspicuous on the line of march ; they had formerly been enemy messenger dogs, and had been captured by the men on Hill 63. General Plumer, G.O.C. II Army, passed us in his motor on the march. Passing a Field Ambulance west of Meteren, I met Ransford, who used to be our Regimental M.O. in the Loos–Vimy Ridge days.

12th September.

Rained heavily all night, with the result that we all got soaked in our practically roofless billet.

13th September.

Farrell went on leave and handed over command of the Company to me. I tried to make our mess-room more comfortable at the expense of the many evacuated houses in the street. There was a large, but rather shattered greenhouse belonging to a château in the vicinity. FitzSimon and I brought our servants with haversacks and got some grapes.

14th to 16th September.

Drill and training parades; also a battle order inspection. Heard from my brother[1] that his squadron R.A.F. had moved to Toronto. Parrie, of the 2nd Hampshires, and Lambert, a friend of FitzSimons, of the same regiment, came to dine. There was a battalion attack scheme in the blob formation, and the Brigadier attended it.

17th September.

Training all morning; after lunch our Brigadier, Freyberg, V.C., gave a lecture to all officers and N.C.O.s in the Battalion on the " company in attack."

18th September.

Company training, one hour devoted to drill and one to a company in attack scheme, which I had worked out the previous night. My line of skirmishers rose a hare, much to the amusement of all ranks.

FitzSimon and I dined with the 2nd Hampshires. They ran a battalion mess, which was a much better system than messing as we did, by companies. Lambert was our host, and an excellent one he was. Their C.O., Westmorland, sang some songs.

19th September.

2nd Lieut. Holden received notice of his appointment to the Indian Army (on probation). In the evening Hickie, FitzSimons, and I saw him off at the Hazebrouck Station. After months of idleness, the Hazebrouck railway was commencing to function again, but as a railhead only. The station buildings were only skeletons, and the glass-covered roof had been shattered to pieces. Holden was brother to the Regimental Sergt.-Major of our 1st Battalion. Unfortunately, within a very short time after his arrival in India he was killed in one of the numerous frontier " scraps " in Waziristan. Some new subalterns joined the Battalion, one being Coade, who was mortally wounded later at Ypres. FitzSimon and I dined with Woods in the Brigade Trench Mortar Mess.

20th September.

Rumours of a colossal " push " about to take place at Ypres. It was a foregone conclusion that the Division to which we belonged was bound to take a prominent place in the " slaughter."

---

[1] Rex had a very bad crash shortly afterwards in the Royal Canadian Flying Corps, smashing several ribs which penetrated one of his lungs.

In fact, the 29th Division was being held in hand as storm, or shock troops, like the Guards Division by the C.-in-C. Since August the Division had not been employed for holding the line. All battalions were well up to strength, their *élan* was magnificent ; in fact the prestige of the Division was second to none. Lieut. Macdonnell, 3rd Connaught Rangers, joined the Battalion. (Killed on 14th October, 1918.)

21st September.

Very busy all morning, kit inspection, etc. Orders received for a move. At dusk we evacuated our billets. Leaving the little company mess-room, I wondered what the real tenants, who might return any day, would say when they saw a lot of extra furniture in their home, and if their next-door neighbours would recognise their own particular pieces and reclaim them ! A really good statue of a horse, which I had looted from a château close by, was left on the mantel-piece.

At about 8 p.m., the Battalion paraded, and we marched off in a lovely summer night for Hondeghem, some 4 kilometres north-west of Hazebrouck. The men were in great fettle, singing and whistling ; in fact a few were quite hilarious, and produced lighted Chinese lanterns, which, needless to say, had a short life !

At Hondeghem we entrained in the trucks of the narrow-gauge railway. We had a chilly journey in open trucks to Watou, our destination, where we detrained in the early hours of the morning. The Battalion was played into a camp of Nissen huts by the pipers. This action did not tend towards our popularity with the units of our brigade who were occupying the next lines !

A résumé of the ten days in Hazebrouck billets : While we were " fattening up " as we called it, for another offensive in Hazebrouck, we had several variations from the usual routine of drill, inspections, and attacks in the " blob " formation.

Daily at 9 a.m. the Battalion formed up in the deserted square of the town for ceremonial drill. Open order, slow marching taking place to the time of the drums which occupied the bandstand in the " place." These parades did the men a world of good, but the use of the town square was later forbidden for drill purposes.

Inter-brigade boxing tournaments were the chief events of the evenings. Our chief representatives were L/Corpl. Delaney, Pte. Fleming, and Pte. Tormey ; these men pulled off all their events.

One evening there was a battalion concert in a local *école*. Corbett Cradock, who was serving with some unit billeted in the vicinity, came along and sang " Phil the Fluter's Ball," and a very fine old "tough," No. 5649 Pte. Coghlan, sang a song of some ten verses, all about a bottle of beer, the chorus of which was "Now leave down that, for it doesn't belong to you."

Another attraction in Hazebrouck was the Variety Show given by the 29th Divisional Troupe.

Gradually and cautiously the civilian population was returning to Hazebrouck, while we were billeted there. The town had been subjected to some heavy strafing, but considering everything it might have been in a more shattered state. The railway station and main road leading to it would have to be completely reconstructed.

22nd September.

FitzSimon and I jumped a passing lorry, and went into Watou for dinner. We called on the 1st Battalion Royal Irish Fusiliers, 36th Ulster Division, who were billeted near the town, as I wanted to see an old friend, Capt. R. L. Emerson, who was with me at Moore Park, Fermoy. Unfortunately, he was away, but I met several fellows whom I had known as cadets at Moore Park, and the Cadet Battalion Regimental Sergt.-Major Tynan—a splendid type, whom I had known well.

23rd September.

Val Farrell returned from leave and took over command of "C." The 29th Division had just been transferred from the XV to the II Corps. The II Corps was in General Plumer's 2nd Army, and on this day all C.O.s and O.C. Companies of the 88th Brigade were summoned to an adjacent hut to meet our new Corps Commander, who had come round to visit us. When we had all filed into the hut, our new Commander, Lieut.-General Sir C. W. Jacob, Indian Army, came and shook hands with us all, and asked us our length of service. He had a great personality, and I was very impressed with his charming manner. He informed us of the following facts: The impending attack at Ypres by the II Army, the approximate date, etc. He showed us the Divisional boundaries and objectives, all marked in coloured pencil on the familiar map "Sheet 28." The Belgian Army would co-operate on our left and the right flank of the attacking troops would pivot on St. Eloi.

He impressed on us the need for the use of the rifle and bayonet, and recalled the awful phase which our Army had passed through in '16 and '17, owing to the troops being so frightfully weak in musketry. Many Divisions, through excessive use of hand grenades, had lost confidence in the rifle as the infantryman's weapon. He said in the coming attack it was proposed to almost completely eliminate bombs. He told us of the battles which culminated in the sanguinary struggle about Passchendaele in '17, and the loss of the ridge, owing to the slackness in musketry training at the period. A half-hearted German counter-attack completely demoralised a division, which had retired without making the semblance of a fight. One volley of rifle fire was all, he said, that was required to stop the Boche.

The General said that as practically all the landmarks had disappeared in the Salient, we would have to pin great faith on our compasses. Owing to the sodden state of the country, and the few lines of communication, he stated that he had arranged for our ammunition to be dropped near the advancing troops by aeroplanes when signalled for by ground flares, by the infantry. Turning to Brig.-General Freyberg, V.C., he asked " How did that experiment work in your Brigade the other day ? " " Oh," replied the Brigadier, " a box of S.A.A. fell on top of an advancing platoon, and one man was killed."

The Corps Commander concluded by giving us his wishes for luck, and hopes for good weather. The C.O.s of the Brigade at this pow-wow were Lieut.-Colonel St. John, D.S.O., 4th Worcesters, Lieut.-Colonel Westmorland, D.S.O. (and bar), 2nd Hampshires, and Lieut.-Colonel Weldon, 2nd Leinsters.

In the evening the Battalion took on the 2nd Hampshires at soccer. This game was rather spoilt by a B.F. in an aeroplane " stunting " low over the ground. One side of the touch line was held by Micks and the other side by Hampshires. The latter kept yelling, " Go it, Tigers," much to the amusement of our old toughs, who, never at a loss for something to say, yelled out a chorus of " Go on, the Lions." The result of the match was a win for the Leinsters.

24th September.

At 2 p.m., the Battalion paraded, and by companies we marched off to a siding of the narrow gauge railway which was situated in the midst of a young oak wood. Our way led through close country, and it was very warm. We passed long rows of horse lines, carpenters' shops, stores, and endless bomb and S.A.A. dumps, all well concealed by the foliage from aircraft observation. We entrained in waiting open trucks, which conveyed us to a point due west of the shattered relics of the old Vlamertinghe Château. Here, in an open field, we detrained, and moved off for the main highway with ten minutes interval between platoons. We swung off to our left, and past the gutted-out town of Vlamertinghe, over the burnished cobbles towards Ypres. The right flank of the road was screened by high canvas, which was stretched from poplar to poplar. The enemy trenches were nearer Ypres than they were in 1915. We took over a line of dug-outs from the 2nd S.W.B.s which ran at right angles to the road in front of Goldfish Château. I remember having seen the Belgian Army making this line in the early summer of '15. We had reduced our kits to the minimum ; our valises had been left behind with our great-coats, and in a cold, but hefty dug-out, we went to sleep.

25th September.

I took up two sergeants—Young and Joyce, M.M.—to the front line at Hell Fire Corner via the Sally Port, to make a reconnaissance of our new front line, and our objectives in the pending attack. There were a number of officers on the same stunt, walking about all over the place. In fact, my party walked right up to the front line over a duckboard track in the open. Bar the railway cutting, I was unable to recognise any old features or landmarks, so completely was the place altered. To return to the Salient after three years' absence like this gave one a good idea of what modern shell-fire can do.

While we were in the front line a 4th Worcester patrol returned to the trench with four German prisoners. They all looked of good physique, but had surrendered without a fight. Having had a good look at the Boche lines, visibility being excellent, we returned along the shell-torn railway line past the Lille Gate with its battered and historic portals.

26th September.

Went up to Ypres in the afternoon to take over billeting accommodation for the Company, accompanied by O'Leary. It was a lovely summer day. We strode along over the old familiar cobbles, screened from enemy observation by the canvas that was stretched between the scarred poplars which belted the edge of the road. Passing the ruins of the convent, I noticed a number of camouflaged gun-muzzles sticking out of the debris, concealed from hostile aircraft by a canopy of rabbit wire interlaced with grass and leaves. A brace of our aeroplanes were droning overhead, busy in reconnaissance. Small white puffs of smoke—aerial shrapnel—followed in their trail, and showed up clear against the blue sky. At the water-tower—a landmark which had retained its identity throughout the four years of Hun frightfulness, though now leaning over on its brick pedestal like a drunken trooper—we branched off to our right through the shambles in the direction of St. Nicholas Church at the Lille Gate. It had long been reduced to crumbling walls ; its spire had completely disappeared. Like the spires on the Cloth Hall, it had no doubt been used for a ranging mark in tests for proficiency pay for countless Boche gunners, or for schools of their shaven-headed and bespectacled N.C.O.s trying to qualify for commissions !

Neither O'Leary nor I had seen Ypres since the days of '15, and in awe we gazed on the shell-ravaged ruins. With the exception of a large husk of masonry which towered above the tortured city from the vicinity of the Cloth Hall, nothing was left. There was no shelling going on, and the deathly silence palled on one. Ypres had a stillness of its own which had a depressing effect. All over the place were shell craters, some old and some freshly made ones. The former were all full of black stagnant water.

I recalled a day in August, '15 when a company of the 6th D.C.L.I.[1] of the 14th Division actually billeted in the Cloth Hall. A salvo of " Jack Johnsons " put the place down around them, and numbers were lost in the fallen masonry. The dead which were recovered were all stretched out in rows in the Grande Place, to await burial. Our Battalion Headquarters had just arrived and was established in a dug-out under the ramparts (absolutely shell-proof) on the right of the Sally Port.

Having inspected the allotted accommodation, corrugated elephant huts, I reported to the C.O., and asked him if I could take over some adjacent cellars, which were at least splinter-proof, instead. Heavy shell-fire tends to lower the morale, and should be guarded against, especially for troops taking an important rôle in a coming offensive. I then returned to the Poperinghe road to guide the Company up. At the convent I met the leading platoon under FitzSimon. One always marched in an attitude of tension, with ears cocked, going through Ypres—awaiting the ever-expected roar of an approaching shell. The men were silent, nothing was to be heard but the clank of hobnailed boots against the uneven cobbles, and the jingle of the mess-tins and accoutrements against the web equipment. Forming two deep, we wormed our way along a beaten track, and platoons filed into the convenient cellars, which were all sandbagged outside to keep out splinters. C Company was at the very same spot along the ramparts where we had got heavily shelled on the morning of the 20th August, '15, after Hooge, and had eight men killed and many wounded. Farrell and I shared a dug-out, standing in the middle of the amphitheatre. We slept on stretchers. There was very little shell-fire during the night.

---

[1] After the War the bodies of 40 men belonging to this regiment were discovered entombed under a huge mass of stone debris in the cloisters.

27th September.

Spent most of the morning in an " O.P. " on top of the ramparts behind the amphitheatre. Took compass bearings on the few remaining landmarks—Stirling Castle, the rise where Hooge had been, and the Bluff. What a difference the countryside presented, compared with the days of '15, from this vantage-point. No vegetation, no foliage, just stretches of wastes of rank, bleached grass intersected by dykes, trenches and a railway cutting which went diagonally across the front. Beyond, all colour gradually transformed into a dull brown, which carried on to the rugged sky-line. What appeared to be a number of uneven and twisted stakes in the distance were the relics of Sanctuary Wood. The wooden road, which made a detour of the hollow below Hooge, showed up in its whiteness. It had been made by the British in '17, but was now in German hands. From these old mediæval ramparts, which had defied even modern artillery, I scanned the country and the ridge which the Battalion was to advance over next morning. (Reference " O.P.," sheet 28, I. 14, B. 1. 5.) Immediately below me lay the dark stagnant waters of the moat, choked with weeds and rushes.

THE 4TH BATTLE OF YPRES

At 9 p.m. we paraded and marched off by platoons for our jumping-off lines, situated on the ridge immediately beyond the moat. Filing through the Sally Port, we crossed the moat which was spanned by a single duckboard track and hand-rails. Well below us was the black water which gleamed in the darkness. There was always something sinister about the moat at Ypres with those war-scarred ramparts frowning down upon me. The duckboards swayed as the men in their battle paraphernalia swung across them.

The men were very cheery and soon settled down in the assembly trenches which ran up towards the rear of the large *école* on the right of the Menin Road. The Battalion pipers, complete in their saffron kilts, arrived, as we were to be played into action on the morrow, and the " toughs " showed their appreciation of them in vociferous terms. The officers of C Company settled down in an isolated dug-out, which stood out in the open waste. We all prowled about for some time before retiring. A few shells fell close to us, and we had two men killed in the Battalion cookhouse. Dixies were being returned after teas, and a solitary 5·9 got a direct hit. We overhauled our revolvers and studied the

various signals for Véry lights, which were, according to my
Field Message Book :

Red light	.	.	. Contact aeroplane.
White do.	.	.	. For S.A.A.
Green do.	.	.	. Capture of objective.
Green-Green-Red	.	.	S O S.

I then emptied a new tin of St. Julien tobacco into my haversack,
having filled my pouch, and not wanting to carry extra weight.
Stretching myself on a bed made of wire netting, I went to sleep.

THE ATTACK

28th September.

The order of battle for the Great Flanders Offensive : General
Plumer's II Army, comprising the II, X, XV and XIX Corps,
were to advance from Ypres in co-operation with the Belgian
Army, and a French division under the supreme command of the
King of the Belgians. The II Army was lent to King Albert for
the Flanders offensive. At dawn the II Army was to advance
from the jumping-off trenches round the Salient, pivoting on
the XIX Corps, which was on the right flank at St. Eloi. The
left flank would rest on the Ypres–Potijze road in touch with the
Belgian Army, whose front extended up the sea. The actual
frontage allotted to the 29th Division lay astride the Menin
Road. The 86th Brigade was to capture the first objective, the
Hooge Ridge. Here it would be leap-frogged by the 88th Brigade,
whose objective was Gheluvelt. The 87th Brigade was in reserve.
At about 2.30 a.m. I was awakened by a terrific bombardment,
and left the dug-out to watch the strafe.

It was still dark : Ypres looked like an immense furnace ; the
whole sky was lit up by flashes of every kind of imaginable shell
from Belgian, French, and our own guns. The dawn gradually
broke and rain began to fall. The men were in the best of spirits
making their tea and were much amused at the attempts of the
pipers to " tune up " in the roar of the barrage. I issued the rum
out to the complete Company, and gave an extra tot to the
stretcher-bearers—Byrne, M.M., Pte. McKnight, etc., who were
bound to have a day of it.

The cursed rain was now coming down as it always did for all
the British operations in the Ypres Salient. Having had a short
spell of fine weather, we were all in hopes of a fine day for the
attack, as rain had such a terrible effect on the sodden and
churned-up Ypres terrain. However, it was not to be. Boche
retaliation was slight, a few shells exploded near us, still our

bombardment went on. Soon the barrage was lifting for zero for the Boche line, and we knew that the 4th Worcesters had left their jumping-off position.

Signals came for our advance. Giving orders was useless in the din, the men knew what to do and we moved off. C Company followed immediately in rear of the Battalion Headquarters. We advanced up two-deep across the open, breaking on to the duck-board tracks when the ground was bad. Shells landed close, one into Headquarters Company, killing one man and wounding Pte. Pledge. Throughout our advance to Hooge enemy shelling was spasmodic; the only real shell-fire was just before we got to Leinster Farm, but the Menin Road and the Roulers railway got heavily shelled. A few 5·9s landed on the latter with a reverberating crash as we were crossing it, without doing any damage. The hard substance of the railway was perfect for high-explosive. Through the mist we caught glimpses of the pipers in fours on the Menin Road marching parallel with us. We closed in with them near Birr Cross Roads and caught the strains of "Brian Boru." Here and there small batches of prisoners were streaming back out of the mist from Zillebeke direction, escorted by men of the 4th Worcesters and the 86th Brigade. They all looked of fairly good physique. The going was now very bad indeed, the south side of the Menin Road being caked with mud and pitted everywhere with slate-coloured shell craters full of water. It was raining steadily in our faces as we moved up the rise of that desolate and shell-ravaged region, not even the rank grass was to be seen on that denuded ridge—just mud, brown, clinging mud, and shell-holes overlapping themselves in the water-logged area. C Company's advance lay through Zouave Wood—just stumps of trees and their fallen shell-splintered trunks. The Company arrived on the commanding ridge at Hooge before its scheduled time, having wormed its way by platoons in snake formation around the many swamps. Our exact disposition was at the Jackdaw Posts. Here I met Webb with his company of the 1st Dublins reorganising at this point. Above the thunder of the guns could be heard the unmistakable muttering of machine-guns which told that "Jerry" was putting up some opposition. We were all very wet; most of us had been bogged up to our knees, struggling through the liquid mud. The Dublins had a few prisoners whom they had snaffled when mopping up the dug-outs around Stirling Castle. The whole Allied front was just one mass of flame; from St. Eloi to the sand-dunes the guns thundered. While we were waiting for the Battalion to come up, a contact aeroplane appeared out of the mist and hovered over us, flying very low, sounding its Klaxon horn. Battalion Headquarters arrived with the pipers, who had practically blown themselves to a standstill with only one wounded! The companies were now reported "all correct," but the Leinsters had to wait until the Worcesters had got sufficiently far ahead before we could advance any farther.

Some of the men took shelter in an old derelict tank, and Farrell, myself, and the C.S.M. occupied a very dilapidated dug-out, and studied our maps under head-cover.[1] News came of the capture of Gheluvelt. This objective had been reserved for the 4th Worcesters especially on account of the great gallantry displayed there by the 2nd Battalion during the 1st Battle of Ypres, 31st October, '14.

We formed up as a battalion in mass, just east of Hooge, on the north side of the Menin Road. All hostile shelling had now ceased. From our vantage-point we had a good look round the desolate area. Nothing was left of Hooge; only the colour of the ground was slightly red from the bricks. Not one of the old landmarks was left, and the Salient from this ridge looked as featureless as the Sahara. It was impossible to make out the Bellewaarde Lake, or where Château Wood had been; even the mine crater had disappeared. The earth had been so churned up that the small water-courses had been altered. The only thing that could be seen was the long straight road stretching away behind us towards Ypres and the four solitary tanks spread along the ridge. They had been ditched and knocked out in the 3rd Battle of Ypres, July 31, 1917.

The tank near Railway Wood had been bogged in a crater and looked grotesque rearing up on its stern. Although the country was so terribly altered from the time I saw it last, I had the satisfaction of looking back on it at my ease, and more or less in safety, remembering the days I had hugged the very same ground from the bottom of a trench in mortal terror. Hooge commanded a huge stretch of country, and I could well understand the importance the enemy attached to holding it. We could see men of the 9th Scottish Division advancing on our left towards Zonnebeke, and we watched over 400 Boche prisoners being marched back over the Bellewaarde Ridge. There was a continual rumbling of guns going on in the Belgian theatre of operations, and we wondered if the Forest of Houthulst had been captured. The Germans had fully realised its strategic importance and had turned it into an impregnable fortress of reboubts. The Forest of Houthulst had been held throughout the War by the enemy; the Allies

---

[1] We were in the exact locality which was held by our 1st Battalion in the 2nd Battle of Ypres, and close to the spot where Major Conyers, Captains Gould-Adams, Bates, Goodbody, and Lieuts. Westmacott and Blatchy had been killed.

had never penetrated its fortifications, though they had reached
its edges in the bitter fighting of the 3rd Battle on 26th October,
'17. During the wars of the Spanish Succession, the Duke of
Marlborough declared that " he who holds the Houthulst Forest
dominates Flanders."

A torrential rain was now driving in our faces, and we got
soaked to the skin as we moved off from Hooge, C Company
leading, with platoons on a wide frontage, in snake formation, on
the north side and parallel with the Menin Road. FitzSimon
was detailed to guide the Battalion's right flank with a compass.
The going was very heavy over the bleached rank grass. There
were numerous shell craters and disused telephone lines mixed
up with the rusty strands of old wire entanglements.

The whole area was intersected with trenches of every description, which had to be negotiated ; consequently the advance was
tedious. The Lewis gunners had a hard task carrying the weighty
Lewis guns. Earlier in the day I had helped one of the crew to
carry his spare magazines. Here and there we passed an old
derelict field-gun, or a recently abandoned one in its muddy pit.

Where the edge of Inverness Copse had been, we passed British
graves of 1914, and I particularly noted 2nd Worcestershire
Regiment and 2nd Battalion Connaught Rangers printed on
the wooden crosses. They were all dated October and November,
1914.

Along the Menin Road on our right flank we could see our
Brigadier riding with his staff. We now got orders to close on the
road, as no enemy were in sight. We formed up and moved off
in fours towards Gheluvelt. As we marched we heard that the
Messines Ridge had been captured by our troops. We passed a
few Boche transport waggons complete with horses ; these were
quickly annexed by our people for rations. Abandoned guns,
also left at the last moment with smashed sights, were ditched
along the roadside. Several shells burst over us without doing
any damage, and the column of fours was not broken. There
were some large heaps of broken stones piled on the side of the
road, and in some places the road had been freshly mended. The
enemy evidently had very optimistic plans for holding Ypres for
another year at least ! On the western outskirts of the Gheluvelt
shambles at exactly 11.30 the Battalion halted and fell out.
Immediately out came the mess-tins, and " drumming up the
char " commenced.

Several of C Company used an old " Pill Box " close at hand for
lighting their fires, and I took the opportunity of drying myself in
the sun, which had at last come out. I took off my equipment, jacket
and shirt, and wrung the latter out. It was absolutely sodden.

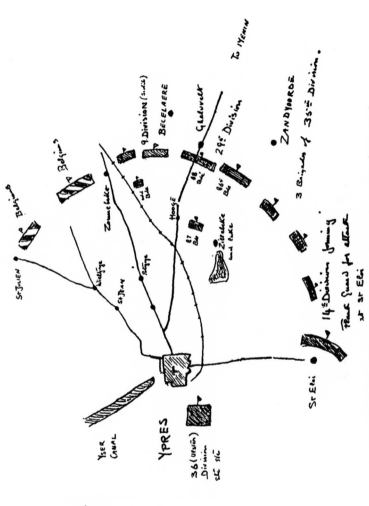

The 4th Battle of Ypres.   Situation at 11 a.m. on 28th Sept., 1918.

While eating our lunch I studied the " Pill Box," as it was the first time I had ever seen one of these famous fortifications, and I was very interested. The name " Pill Box " aptly describes what these " strong points " were like. This particular Pill Box resembled a miniature Martello Tower (so very common on the southern coasts of England and Ireland). It stood only some 6 feet off the ground on deep foundations, and had a small wing extending at the back where the entrance was. Its walls of about 3 feet in thickness were built on a steel framework, and being made of reinforced concrete were capable of withstanding a direct hit from a 5·9. They were always impregnable to the ordinary barrage of field artillery. There was room inside for a garrison of about fifteen men. A bench had been made for a machine-gun emplacement just below a narrow horizontal slit close to the ground to enable the gunner to get a wide traverse.

The Pill Box system of holding the front line in Flanders had been introduced by the German 4th Army Commander—General von Armin—in June, 1917. Our troops first came in contact with them in the Messines Ridge attack at this date, and later with often disastrous results in the 3rd Battle of Ypres. The water-logged soil in the Ypres sector made defence of deep trenches impossible, so the problem of holding their ground was solved by erecting the Pill Boxes. They were echeloned in depth with great skill, and always managed to stop or break up our attacking troops with either frontal or enfilading fire. Their only vulnerable point was at their entrances. A special method of attacking or dealing with these strong points had to be introduced—two parties working in conjunction. One party kept the Pill Box under heavy rifle-fire and a bombardment of Mills bombs (fired from rifles with the special cap attachment device), and the other party crept round the flank to a selected point. When the latter were in position they fired a Véry light. Simultaneously both parties rose to their feet and rushed the Pill Box. Another method was to attack under cover of a smoke-screen. However, the latter was not always available. Our troops quickly adapted themselves to Pill Box fighting, but at first, mainly owing to their surprise element, we were baffled, and suffered heavy losses.

While we were eating our lunch on the side of the road, several salvos of whiz-bangs burst over us without doing any damage. We suddenly discovered the reason—dense volumes of smoke were issuing out of the Pill Box and had drawn the enemy guns. We were slightly perturbed by the shell-fire, bar the old toughs, who were making their tea inside the Pill Box! The Company moved with its pack animals farther along the road, and into a rugged and churned-up patch of ground nearby, just below a

great cement-faced dug-out which stood on the south side of the
Menin Road and which had functioned as a German Battalion
Headquarters that very morning.

Farrell received orders to push on and leap-frog the unit who
were in front of us. He told us what we were about to do, and we
passed on the information to the men. We were to exploit the
success. The Battalion advanced under a hot sun, which helped
to dry our wet kit, astride the Menin Road. B Company was on
the left, or north of the road, and C was on the south side. My
platoon's left flank rested on the Menin Road in touch with B
Company.

We advanced down the forward slope east of Gheluvelt in snake
formation, and got into extended order when passing through the
4th Worcesters, who were lying prone in extended order behind
folds in the ground. We expected to bump up against the enemy
rearguards at any moment, as the Worcesters had been subjected
to machine-gun fire from the hedge in our immediate front. An
enemy Taube, with its fish-like tail, hovered over us as we advanced, its Maltese cross showing out clearly on its silvery body.
It fired several bursts from its machine-gun at us, but the bullets
went whistling high over our heads like a covey of partridges.
It did not carry out its flight unmolested, as it masked the fire
of our Vickers guns situated near the cement building on the east
edge of the obliterated Gheluvelt (the recently evacuated enemy
Headquarters), who must have hit its pilot, for it suddenly came
down to earth on the rise in rear of our right flank. When within
some 200 yards of the low thick hedge which skirted the road
running across our front, we were fired on by machine-guns
which we could not locate. Taking advantage of all natural and
artificial (shell craters) cover, we stalked forward. We wormed
our way up the Menin Road itself, running from tree to tree,
on the left we were in touch with Morrison's platoon of B Company
under D. J. Keating which was trying to make headway under
machine-gun fire. The enemy fell back gradually from their
position along the hedge at the cross-roads, but as the road they
had been holding ran diagonally across our front, there were still
some of their machine-guns firing on the right when we got
possession of the left flank.

We now exchanged shots with some of the Boche snipers. Up
to this stage there had been only a few casualties, the men having
made the most of the cover and broken ground; we had no
artillery support, as our batteries had not yet come up. The
traffic on the one and only line of communication had become so
congested that they were delayed. North-east of these cross-roads
the enemy had a large dump of stores, timber, wire, and tools,

and a number of huts. A narrow-gauge railway ran along the road across our front, with three or four trucks full of coal. All these various objects afforded the enemy good cover for their snipers and machine-guns, whom we had great difficulty in locating.

The right flank platoon of C Company tried to work round the " Jerry " position, but were held up by a Pill Box, which bristled with machine-guns. It was like disturbing a hornet's nest. I saw a few men falling, and there was a roar for stretcher-bearers. Sergt. Joyce, M.M., was killed, and some men were wounded. I could see them kicking in the long grass. Then some of my men gradually worked their way over to the abandoned coal trucks, and under cover of these engaged the enemy. (One man, Flaherty, actually climbed on top of the coal and commenced sniping.)

There was a continual " slat " and " ping " from the bullets as they either hit the coal direct or ricochetted off. Flaherty silenced several snipers, and did fine work.

While we were being held up at these cross-roads, we heard the unmistakable throb of motors behind us : on looking round we saw some of the Motor Machine Gun Corps coming up on their cycles along the middle of the Menin Road. We yelled to them to halt, but the first cyclist took no notice, and rode on.

The driver managed to get over the cross-roads, when he was bowled over on to the highway by machine-gun fire from a range of less than 100 yards. His companion jumped out of the side-car, turned his gun on the enemy and silenced them. He then picked up his comrade, who was lying wounded on the road, put him in his carrier, turned his bike, and rode off back through our lines. This was one of the bravest acts I have ever seen, and we gave the hero a rousing cheer. Later the officer i/c of this Machine Gun Corps section came up on foot, and I told him about this gallant act. The man was recommended for bravery, but I never heard what he got.

When it became dusk we moved forward on to the road ; in the ditch alongside, we found one wounded and three dead Germans. They were all lying beside their guns, knocked out by our snipers. One of these had been a hero. Earlier in the evening we spotted him firing his gun ; then we saw him tearing off back in a crouched-up attitude, under a volley of rifle-fire. He returned later via a very shallow communication trench, under heavy sniping, to his gun with a box of ammunition. Flaherty got him crossing the road, and we found him dead on the middle of it, with the unopened box of S.A.A. beside him, and his gun a few yards in front. It was strange seeing these two very brave acts performed on the same day by a man of each side. The wounded German was in a bad way, and was taken off by the stretcher-bearers.

I heard groans and feeble calling from the shallow trench in front, and another wounded German was located. Being a fine night, I moved up the road towards Kruiseecke, but not a sound was to be heard. I then went over to liaise with B Company, which had established itself in the vicinity of the wooden huts. Here I had a chat with Coade, who was mortally wounded a fortnight later at Ledgehem.

Rations and rum came up, and were issued out. I supervised the rum issue. Pte. Coughlan drank my health. At midnight we advanced; it was very dark. Platoons advanced in snake formation, my platoon being on the left flank of the Company. We had to swing in to our right, owing to the saturated state of the ground near the Menin Road. There were also some patches of barbed wire. Expecting to find the enemy holding the rise, we moved cautiously. After advancing some 300 yards over broken and marshy ground, I was suddenly pulled up by direct machine-gun fire at short range. We all lay down or jumped into the nearest shell-holes, but L/Corpl. Richards and that great old "tough," Pte. Coughlan, who had delighted all with his songs at the Hazebrouck concert, were killed when returning fire with their Lewis gun. In getting into a shell-hole just behind me, I felt a thud in my back, which knocked me sprawling on my face. I wasn't hit, but narrowly missed being so. FitzSimon's platoon, which was advancing on the right flank, ran into another machine-gun nest, and had several casualties, and one man missing. Advance was now out of the question, as we could not see more than 6 yards ahead owing to the darkness. On the rising ground, some 200 yards from the cross-roads, I split the platoon up into parties of four, and occupied a chain of shell craters stretching from the edge of the Menin Road to FitzSimon's platoon on the right. Old and new shell-holes were studded about in the long rank grass; filling the spare sandbags which all the men carried, we built up parapets and a battle position for our only Lewis gun. Throughout the night the Boche machine-guns kept up an endless chatter, and it was fortunate that we had built up cover.

29th September.

The morning broke with a thick mist enveloping the country. In fact it was a typical raw Flanders morning. Dawn revealed the Company's position in the improvised rifle pits, which were just like grouse butts. Not having had the chance to dry our clothes properly after the drenching we got the day before, we were all very cold indeed. I took off my Burberry, which I had been wearing rolled strapped to the back of my web belt, and to my astonishment found it riddled to pieces ; two bullets must have gone through it, so thoroughly was it cut about. My haversack had had a bullet right through it from end to end, and everything in it in the shape of shaving gear, etc., was smashed. My luck had been decidedly in on the night 28/29th September, 1918.

At dawn Pte. Hurley, who had been missing after the " scrap " in the night, walked into our lines with his captors as prisoners ! He had received good treatment from the Boche Machine-Gunners, who kept him in their dug-out on the ridge. After a night's argument with one of his captors who spoke English, he managed to entice the party (4) to surrender. Pte. Hurley got a month's leave for his effort, in accordance with the regulation that any soldier who had been captured and managed to escape was to have one month's leave in the U.K.

At the first streak of daylight we retrieved the Lewis gun which poor old Coughlan had been firing ; it had to be wrenched out of his iron-like clasp.

The Brigadier came round our posts ; he was attired in Tommies' uniform, complete with ground-sheet ! I did not recognise him at first. What a contrast to our former immaculately turned-out Brigadier-General Jelf, who was as smartly dressed before Delville Wood as he was on parade.

Throughout the early hours of the morning, we were sprayed with enemy machine-guns, which traversed backwards and forwards. We watched B Company on our left, north of the Menin Road, trying to advance with a line of skirmishers out in front. They took advantage of all the folds in the rugged ground, but could make no headway against the enemy machine-guns which fired from a commanding ridge in their front.

As B Company's skirmishers stalked forward, I watched a company of the enemy forming up on the high ground, and in front of a small wood ; they then disappeared. B Company had several casualties, and I saw a few of their men tumbling over like shot rabbits in the long grass, and stretcher-bearers running in their direction. At about 6 a.m. we, C Company, advanced, and made good the small ridge in front unopposed. Coughlan was still lying there stretched, with L/Corpl. Richards,[1] who was in a sitting attitude, right in front of what had been the Boche machine-gun nest.

[1] L/Corpl. Richards had been wounded in my platoon at St. Eloi on 5th November, 1915.

We watched more Boche massing on our left front, but we dispersed them with Lewis gun fire. We had a few casualties in this forward movement.

We now dug in on the new ridge, employing the same system as before, consolidating shell-holes; we were in a fine commanding position. At 10.30 a.m. the 2nd Hampshires advanced through us, and later we watched them clearing a wood down in a hollow by a stream on our left front, where they had some casualties. Since we had passed Hooge we could have counted the shells we had seen on our fingers, but now the enemy started a systematic strafe, and it seemed as if he was firing off his ammunition before carrying out a further retirement.

Our artillery had so far not put in an appearance, and practically all day the enemy shelled away undisturbed. Our gunners could not get up, so impossible was the state of the Menin Road; across country was out of the question for heavy guns, owing to the water-logged state.

Ammunition was sent up by mules, and also the Brigade trench mortars under 2nd Lieut. Woods, M.C. The mules were placed under cover in a fold of the ground just in front of us. However, they suffered severely from shrapnel which burst over our area spasmodically all day, and a good few of them had to be put down. The cross-roads got heavily shelled with H.E. all morning, and all the wooden huts were turned into matchwood. S.A.A. mules were caught at these roads coming up, and suffered severely. Their drivers had a rough time. A few direct hits put the coal waggons on fire; they blazed away all day and on into the night. The Hampshires utilised their prisoners as stretcher-bearers, and all day long they went up and down the road with the wounded. It looked strange seeing four figures clad in long field grey great-coats carrying a wounded khaki figure on their shoulders. They had to run the gauntlet of their own barrage at the cross-roads, but they behaved well indeed, and took their time with our wounded.

A battery of R.F.A., the first of our guns we had seen during the " push " coming up, came in for a terrible mauling. Two teams were caught by direct hits, and we watched wheels and limbers being blown sky-high with great fountains of earth. The other two teams managed to canter out behind our right flank, and took up a position. This was a very thrilling sight.

The enemy had certainly selected the most vulnerable point on our lines of communication. At about 5 p.m. we got word that the enemy was preparing to counter-attack on our right. This was in the 87th Brigade's area, and we watched the 2nd S.W.B.s moving up through some very broken ground on our right flank.

I walked over to watch, and I saw two Germans quite plainly looking over the red-tiled roof of an old farm, using field glasses. Shots were now being exchanged, and we on the high ground were swept by machine-gun fire from both flanks. We had several casualties, but we all walked about as the rifle and machine-gun fire was only spasmodic.

We turned our shell-holes into cover for the night. Sergt. Jenkins, M.M., O'Leary, and I shared one water-logged crater ; we passed a most miserable night in a torrential downpour of rain. I dozed a bit, as I was, like the rest, very tired, not having slept since the short night of the 27/28th September. All night long the cross-roads behind us were lit up by the coal waggons, which blazed furiously, being stoked up every now and then by another Boche crump. We, in my shell-hole, had alternate fits of dozing, shivering, and cursing ; hungry, wet, and cold.

30th September.

Heavy rain was falling when dawn broke, and we were drenched through, and chilled to the bone. At 9 a.m., having had some lukewarm tea and sodden bread, we formed up on the edge of the Menin Road under orders to exploit the success ; our objective being the village of Gheluwe, which was to be taken from the flanks. While forming up, we were surprised to hear the clatter of hoofs and jingle of bits behind us, and a troop of French cavalry rode past in half-sections towards the ridge just in front. The troop halted and the officer i/c, holding out a map, asked me to indicate on it the Boche positions. I told him they were holding Gheluwe. I was not impressed with the cavalry, the troopers were heavy, and carried colossal paraphernalia, as well as being armed with the three weapons, lance, sabre, and carbine. They were ill-mounted on weedy-looking horses of about 15.2 hands high, which were certainly not up to the weight they had to carry.

In spite of their own personal discomforts, our men gave them an enthusiastic ovation. C Company, wearing their ground sheets under a driving rain, moved off in their wake. We saw the cavalry disappearing over the rise, but shortly afterwards their remnants returned through us. When they had got over the crest in front, the enemy had directed a withering fire of machine-guns at them, and being exposed on the open road, they suffered severely. I noticed a number of empty saddles, and several troopers being kept propped up on their horses by their comrades riding on either side. Before reaching the rise, C Company swung off to the right, and deploying, advanced towards the ridge on the flank, some 500 yards distant. We advanced on a wide

front, with sections in snake formation. FitzSimon was on the
left, I was in the centre, and Farrell, with Company Headquarters,
was on the right. Our advance was uneventful as far as the ridge,
except that we rose a hare going through the high grass ; startled,
it ran right across our front, and disappeared into the thick
undergrowth.

The Boche was shelling with H.E., but his range was short, and
the shells falling in the marshy hollow in front, sent up fountains
of earth skywards. When we got on the ridge, we came suddenly
under machine-gun fire, and bullets spattered around our feet,
kicking up little sprays of grass and soil.

Crossing over a muddy and exposed lane, I edged over to the
right flank where Farrell was ; he had worked his way along a
hedge, and was established in an old, but large shell crater, surrounded by pollarded willows, on the forward slope of the ridge.
It was a splendid vantage-point, and the whole low-lying country
lay stretched out before our gaze. On the left we could see the
western outskirts of Gheluwe, and troops (B Company) moving
towards it. The wide stretch of desolate country, intersected
with small ditches, was studded with isolated red-roofed houses,
and a line of abandoned gun pits. Away in the distance we
could see the spires of Menin. It rained in torrents throughout
the day, and my Burberry, which was like a sieve from machine-
gun bullets, was useless.

Farrell and I put in a miserable time in the shell-hole, lying up
against its forward grassy edge, with our feet on an old and
partly submerged duckboard in the water at the bottom. Conditions were pretty unhealthy. Occasionally hostile machine-
guns traversed across our post, and the bullets zipped and
ricochetted off the dwarfed poplars round us. Several of the men
exchanged shots with the enemy, who was holding the houses
below us. We could not locate them, as they were sniping
through the roofs, having removed a tile or two, but we saw
several during the day dodging about behind buildings, and I
spotted one putting his head over the gable end of one of the
houses. All the platoons, less FitzSimon, were now up in the
same alignment and C.S.M. Devaney installed himself in a dug-
out just in rear, where he managed to make some tea for us.

Some 300 yards behind us lay A Company in the shell-holes
which earlier in the day we had vacated. The only comfort I had
was my pipe, and luckily my tobacco kept dry. Pte. Rice, M.M.,
the company runner, was nearly shot by one of the platoons. To
keep dry he had attired himself in a German great-coat !

At about 5 p.m. the 2nd Battalion S.W.B.s made good headway on our right flank under a smoke screen. Farrell went off

to try and find Battalion Headquarters. He told me to get in touch with FitzSimon and form up the Company. I walked across to where FitzSimon was supposed to be, the rain was still falling. I found his platoon holding some large craters in front of some ruins on the extreme edge of Gheluwe. FitzSimon had, according to his men, been wounded in the stomach at about 11 a.m. He had shown lots of initiative in getting as far as he had. Later on, he received the Military Cross for his work. When I was falling the Company in, Farrell appeared, and led us off towards Gheluwe.

At the Gheluwe cross-roads, two patrols, under N.C.O.s., were sent out to see whether two old huts were being held by the Huns, as we wanted to billet in them. No enemy were reported, so keeping two platoons with him at the cross roads, where there was a fine Boche stable, Farrell sent me off to the other building some 500 yards to the left front with the other two platoons. Before setting off, I moved round outside the far end of Farrell's hut, and ran into him. Thinking, in the dark, that I was a Boche, he nearly fired at me. Colonel Westmorland, of the 2nd Hampshires, came along to get in touch with us. He was wearing Tommies' kit and we were very intrigued with his canvas gaiters.

At 10 p.m. I moved off with my two platoons for the outpost ; we advanced cautiously, with scouts in front, as Boches were reported to be in the vicinity. I was guided to two large wooden stables, which lay beyond a thick hedge.[1] I occupied the right-hand one ; placing a sentry post behind some old gabions at each end of the building where there were large folding doors.

The enemy were close at hand, and I could hear quite plainly the click of a machine-gun breech-block, which was situated in the next field. I told the men to keep very "doggo," as our presence was obviously unsuspected. We scraped away the manure, and lay down for a rest. However, we were very soon disturbed, as a machine-gun in traversing along our stable wall hit Pte. Duffy badly in the thigh, through the wooden side. He gave such a roar ! Duffy, the Lewis gunner, had been one of my old platoon, No. 9 in C Company, in May, 1915. I found there was cover thrown up outside the stable all round, sufficient to stop a bullet, and that all the men were safe in the stable if they lay down. Duffy was carried off by the S.B.s. Strange to say, he was the first man hit in my platoon at Hooge in August, '15. I had a fine body of men with me, Sergt. Hackett[2] was the

[1] Just beside the stable was a ring made by horses being lunged. The presence of stables was often detected on aeroplane photographs by these lungeing rings appearing on the negatives.
[2] Mortally wounded at Ledgehem 14.10.'18.

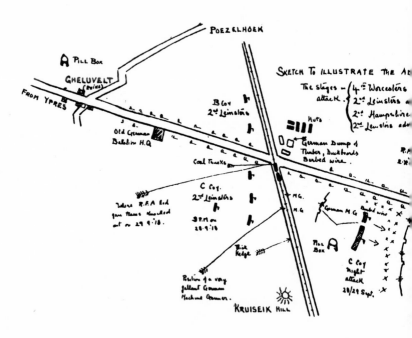

POEZELHOEK

A PILL BOX

GHELUVELT (ruins)

FROM YPRES

SKETCH TO ILLUSTRATE THE A[...]

The stages — { 4ᵗʰ Worcesters
attack. { 2ⁿᵈ Leinsters a[...]
{ 2ⁿᵈ Hampshire[...]
{ 2ⁿᵈ Leinster adv[...]

B Coy
2ⁿᵈ Leinsters

Huts

Old German Batalion H.Q

German Dump of
Timber, Duckboards
Barbed wire.

R.[...]
2.[...]

Coal Trucks

C Coy.
2ⁿᵈ Leinsters

M.G.

Where R.F.A had
gun teams knocked
out at ~ 29.9.18.

M.G.

German M.G

Barbed wire

3 P.M on
28.9.18

Pill Box

Thick Hedge

Position of a very
gallant German
Machine Gunner.

C Coy
night
attack

28/29 Sept.

KRUISEIK HILL

The 4th Battle of Yp[...]

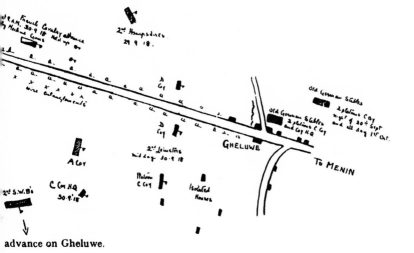

THE 4ᵗˢ BATTLE ᵒꜰ YPRES ᵒꜰ ᵗʰᵉ 88ᵗ BRIGADE

Gheluvelt. 28 Sept 1918.

attacked through Worcesters, 28ᵗ Sept at Kruiseik Cross Roads.

through Leinsters and attacked on left flank. 29ᵗ Sept

Gheluwe and occupied a line of outposts in the village on 30ᵗ Sept

French Cavalry advanced
4ᵗ P.A.M. 30.9.18 Held up on
by Machine Guns

2ⁿᵈ Hampshires
29.9.18.

Wire Entanglements

B Coy

Old German Stables
2 platoons Coy
night of 30ᵗ Sept
and all day 1ˢᵗ Oct.

D Coy

Old German Stables
2 platoons C Coy
and Coy H.Q.

GHELUWE

2ⁿᵈ Leinsters
A Coy
mid day 30.9.18

TO MENIN

C Coy H.Q.
30.9.18

Platoon
C Coy

Isolated
Houses

2ⁿᵈ S.W.B.

advance on Gheluwe.

senior Sergeant, and several old toughs, like "Jocksy" Reay, were present. I told the men to go to sleep.

1st October.

Having rested for some five hours, I got the men up at dawn, and made them dig in round the stable under the mangers. They worked well with their entrenching tools, and when they had gone down some 3 feet 6 inches we stopped. In these trenches the men made fires and cooked their breakfasts. They all had plenty of rations, as they hadn't had time to eat them before. O'Leary made me a splendid cup of tea.

I withdrew the sentry groups at dawn from their night positions, placing a sentry at either end of the stable, but looking through a crack in the open doors. The men spent most of the morning cleaning their rifles and the four Lewis guns, but the latter at different times, thereby keeping three ready in case of any developments.

Hostile machine-guns traversed across our hut all day. It was as well that I had taken the precaution to dig in, as the side (north) was like a target after 15 rounds rapid! I kept up communication with Company Headquarters with a signaller armed with two enamelled plates from the back or south side of the stable. One of our contact aeroplanes hovered over our hut during the day, it dropped a box of S.A.A. near us for another regiment. I believe this box stuck in the ground, and had to be dug out!

At 4 p.m. the enemy opened a barrage on Company Headquarters, and obtained direct hits on Farrell's hut. He immediately evacuated it, and got all his men into a neighbouring trench (a Boche reserve line, which was heavily wired), but not without losses. (Two men being killed and two wounded.) The shells seemed to brush the roof of our stable so low did they go, but they all burst behind us on Farrell's position. This strafe was followed by another form of hate, and for over an hour we were drenched with gas shells.

We quickly donned our gas masks and, fortunately, had no casualties. At 8 a.m. I got orders, delivered by a runner wearing respirator, to return to Company Headquarters, as we were being relieved. In the dusk we moved off for the cross-roads and rejoined the Company.

At about 11.30 p.m. the 2nd Hampshires arrived, and we moved off for the Battalion through an area reeking of gas. Farrell led the Company along a track running north, but parallel with the Menin Road. Near the ridge we switched on to the main road, passing many dead horses which had belonged to the French cavalry.

We found the Battalion lying up in bivouac on the same ground which we had left on the morning of the 30th. Farrell and I shared a very airy bivouac, which hardly kept out the heavy rain which fell throughout the night. We had no food, and cooking was out of the question, as we were forbidden to light fires which might draw shell-fire. Several salvos of shells did burst near us, but we were all much too fagged to worry about them.

2nd October.

After a terrible night, in which I was actually doubled up with cramp and pains in my legs and feet, we tumbled out of our " bivies " into a cold but fine morning. Rum was issued. Throughout the four days' fighting the Battalion had not suffered many casualties,[1] but the hardships had been very severe. From the morning of the attack the weather had been of the vilest description, and we were all suffering from exposure and fatigue.

For its share in this great and successful offensive the Battalion added " YPRES, '18 " to swell the list of honours on the colours.

Rumours began to circulate of the Battalion returning to the outpost line. However, this seemed highly improbable, as apart from being thoroughly fatigued, the men's feet (and likewise officers) were in a shocking condition from the waterlogged ground. None of us had had our boots off since the night of the 27th/28th September, and when we had removed them on the previous night, our feet swelled up, and we couldn't get them on again. Some shells fell close to us, but we had no casualties. I salved the back plate with sights from the light machine-gun which had shot L/Corpl. Richards and Pte. Coughlan. It had " Berlin, 1917 " stamped on it. The barrel had been splendidly camouflaged. A Boche anti-tank gun was lying about. It was the first of these weapons I had seen ; it was about 5 feet in length, its calibre was 12 bore, with a colossal bolt. Its cartridges were longer than Véry lights. The evening was fine and we turned in for a long night's sleep very early.

3rd October.

Orders came for the relief of the Division which was now suffering *en masse* from exposure to the awful climatic conditions.

The II Army had everywhere gained its objectives, which included all the heights of Flanders ; 4800 prisoners and 100 guns had been captured by General Plumer's Army, and another

---

[1] 19 men killed, Lieuts. Mathias, Morrison, Toolan, FitzSimon, and 129 N.C.O.s and men wounded, amongst those killed was L/Corpl. Organer, D.C.M.

4000 by the Franco-Belgian forces co-operating on our left. A big wedge had been driven into the Boche position. He had suffered heavy losses, and his morale had been decidedly shaken.

The 36th (Ulster) Division took the place of the 29th in the outpost line, and we watched them going up. Further advance was out of the question until a pukka line of communications had been built up across the devastated, waterlogged, but historic stretch of flats in front of Ypres. Company paraded for our billeting area in the Vlamertinghe Woods.

Although during our advance we had been but slightly shelled, yet our back areas, especially the Menin Road, had been heavily strafed. There was full evidence of this along the route, particularly at Hooge, where there were numerous transports, all put out of action, lying derelict on the side of the road, or thrown off it into the crater swamps below. Teams of dead artillery horses, transport animals, S.A.A. mules, and "heavy draughts," were heaped on top of each other in the ditches off the wooden track which made a detour of the Menin Road by the north from Hooge to Hell Fire Corner. The traffic here had been terribly congested, there being only the one road for the supply of rations and ammunition. When the enemy shelled the transport, they just had to remain where they were, as the muddy swamps on either side forbade deployment. The last I saw of Hun Kultur in the Salient was the reflected glare in the sky at night from the burning houses around Menin, which the enemy was destroying in his wake. Going through Ypres, we were very amused at the quaint sight of two army bell-tents pitched beside the tortured Cloth Hall, accommodation for the Military Police ! Our camp, called Tavistock, lay alongside that of a French Brigade. I was glad to turn in quickly into my valise spread on a rabbit wire bed in a hut.

4th October.

Heavy rain fell all day. We received a draft of officers and men belonging to our 6th Service Battalion, which had been disbanded on returning from the East. R. G. Lewis, Warburton and Staines were amongst them.

5th October.

I was detailed to attend a machine-gun course assembling at Le Touquet, on the 7th. At 5 p.m. the Battalion paraded and moved off for Ypres for another offensive. It was raining heavily when they paraded and marched off.

6th October.

At 11 a.m., accompanied by O'Leary, I set off for Proven, from " Dirty Bucket Camp." I lunched on the way in Poperinghe at "Skindel's." The Poperinghe Station had not commenced to function as a railhead, so we jumped a passing motor, and got to Mendinghem, a wooden encampment on the outskirts of Proven. Here a base had been established for troops coming up to the Ypres sector, and the Mess was full of officers on their way to reinforce the II Army. At dinner I met Capt. Redway, of the Royal Irish, who was on his way to join our 2nd Battalion. He was wounded going into action at Stacegem some 10 days later.

7th October.

We had an early start from Mendinghem, and a long tedious railway journey via Hazebrouck, St. Omer, Calais, Boulogne, and Etaples, where we detrained as dusk was setting in (7 p.m.). A number of officers joined the train on the journey at these various places. At Etaples we all secured the local "gharries," and drove off to the Lewis Gun School, situated at Le Touquet, some 3½ kilometres south of Etaples.

8th to 22nd October.

Having duly reported to the Adjutant of the school, one McDermott, a Leinster, I was told off to one of the numerous squads in course of formation. McDermott had won the D.C.M. at the Modder River with the Guards, and later was transferred to our 1st Battalion, and had been R.S.M. in 1914. The C.O. of the School was an Irish Guardsman, the majority of the officer instructors were Territorials, and the sergeant instructors of squads were all found from the Artists' Rifles, a Territorial unit. The hours of instruction were very long, and only occasionally varied by short schemes dealing entirely with the tactical employment of Lewis guns. Towards the end of the course, we carried out a firing course on the ranges with Vickers, Lewis, and with captured enemy machine-guns. The weather during the two weeks length of this course was good. The country round was picturesque—miles of tossed-up sand-dunes, with patches of pine woods fringing the hillocks, and beyond all, the blue waters of the Channel. However, the surroundings, although picturesque, were damnable for us, who had to manœuvre through them up to our "hocks" in the sand, carrying either a Lewis gun or cases of the numerous magazines. The sand was a terrible drawback and made work for the Lewis automatic guns particularly difficult. Their shoddy intestines got choked, and consequently contracted every imaginable stoppage when firing with ball on the range. Before the termination of the course there was a written examination on the tactical handling of the Lewis gun,

and on forward anti-aircraft work. I came out amongst the
first dozen in a field of fifty.

In addition to the Lewis gun course, there were also courses
on the Hotchkiss gun for cavalry, and a light trench mortar course
(Stokes) for infantry. The camp consisted of hutments and was
situated on the edge of the Le Touquet Golf Course (famous pre-
war as a fashionable resort). Paris-Plage was within a stone's
throw, and practically every evening I went into this seaside
town across the sand-dunes and had dinner with a few of my
friends, usually at the " Sea Gull " on the esplanade, where we
got champagne at a reasonable figure. I had been in Paris-Plage
before—with McCarthy-O'Leary of the 1st Munsters, just previous
to the Somme offensive in which, some weeks later, he met his
death. For variation we tried Etaples occasionally, but it was a
dull place, and crammed with troops.

While I was at Le Touquet the s.s. *Leinster* was sunk by a
Boche submarine in the Irish Sea. Hundreds of troops were lost,
amongst them two men of the 2nd Battalion who were returning
from leave. Louis Daly was on board, but fortunately was
rescued. Towards the end of the course the morale of all went up,
owing to the combined advances of the Franco-British armies
along the whole front. We all thought the War would be over by
Christmas.

22nd October.

The course broke up, and with a number of others I left for
Etaples, where I spent the night at the Officers' Club.

23rd October.

Left Etaples early. O'Leary, who had been very ill, did not
accompany me, but was admitted into hospital. I was very sorry
indeed ; I never saw him again, and he died a few years afterwards of a disease contracted on service. I had a few letters from
him later, when in India. O'Leary, M.M., had served me well. He
had had just fifteen years' service in the Regiment when invalided
out.

At 7 p.m., we got to Mendinghem, having been taken past the
station by mistake, for several miles. It would have been all
right for us (five) but for our valises, which, of course, we could
not carry. I commandeered a passing motor, which brought us
to our camp in time for dinner. Here I met several old friends—
Lieut. D. C. Bullen-Smith,[1] M.C., 1st K.O.S.B., Capt. G. C. Robb,

[1] Son of Brigadier-General Bullen-Smith, C.M.G., D.S.O., who commanded
the 2nd Leinsters in 1915–16.

Royal Irish Rifles, who had been at Campbell with me, and Don Johnston, R.G.A., of Frankford. I also met several other very cheery fellows—amongst them Lieut. MacBryan, 1st K.O.S.B., and a gay spark in the 1st Lancashire Fusiliers.

24th to 29th October.

This Proven camp accommodated the 29th Divisional nucleus. The camp had originally been used as a hospital, and the huts were large, but rather too well ventilated for the coming winter !

We remained six days at this place ; daily we got orders to travel by various trains, which never turned up. All touch had been lost with the divisions, and the adjutant of the camp could not inform us as to the whereabouts of the 29th. One morning we were sent off with our regimental details to another camp, near Rousbrugge-Haringhe on the Yser. However, there was not the accommodation or rations there for us (strength 8 officers, 500 men), so we trekked back to Proven ! To kill the time, Bullen-Smith, MacBryan, the Lancashire Fusilier, and I, played poker most of the day in a local estaminet in the Proven village.

30th October.

Paraded at 5 a.m., and marched to Poperinghe, where we had orders to entrain for the Division, which was now known to be beyond Lille. Every unit in the 29th was represented in these details, including a party belonging to the famous L Battery, R.H.A. I was in charge of the 88th Brigade nucleus, in which were 50 Leinsters and the same number of Worcesters and Hampshires. We were compensated for our early start by marching in the cool of the morning. The men carried full battle impedimenta— steel helmets and gas respirators, as well as their complete equipment. We passed the Louvie Château, with its long poplar-edged drive, along which Plowman and I used to canter (though strictly against orders) in the summer of '15. The Château then functioned as Corps Headquarters.

We overtook many families of refugees returning to " Pop," and to the numerous little wooden houses dotted along the edge of the road. Poperinghe, especially its square, presented a very battered appearance. The Hôtel de Ville, and the house which " the Fancies " had used as a theatre, seemed to have suffered the most.

Bullen, MacBryan, and I had breakfast at " Ginger's," and entrained for Hazebrouck, where we spent the remainder of the day. We lunched at a newly formed club in the square— reconstruction, indeed, had got well ahead !

The men were marched to some factory buildings, where they were rationed. At 9 p.m. we entrained for Lille, our route lay across the Lys plain, all devastated by the April '18 fighting. Skirting Bailleul on the south, we passed through Armentières, and across the L'Epinette line, where we were entrenched (2nd Battalion) in May, '15. However, owing to the darkness, it was impossible to recognise any of the old familiar landmarks which might have remained. We pulled up on the outskirts of Lille in the small hours, having had a slow, dark, and jolty journey over the newly laid rails. Here the Divisional nucleus split up for brigades for various destinations. Guides met us, and limbered waggons came for our kits. We now set off on a long march, which brought us through slumbering Lille.

We trekked for miles, right through the heart of this big city, which had just been relieved of the Hun yoke, over its wide *chaussée*. The city was in darkness. We branched off north-east, stepping out along good roads, tracks, and under and over recently demolished bridges. Very fatigued, we arrived at Croix, a small mining village midway between Lille and Roubaix, as dawn was breaking. I found where C Company was billeted, and spent a few hours asleep on the mess floor. Heard that G. W. Moore and J. H. O'C. Macdonnell had been killed in the attack at Ledgehem.[1]

31st October to 3rd November.

Our billets were fairly comfortable, though officers' quarters were very scattered. The inhabitants seemed pleased to have the British Army around them, but the four years of Boche occupation had left them very depressed and dejected. They had been subjected to severe rationing, in addition to the many forms of Hun frightfulness.

Val Farrell, who now wore the D.S.O. as well as the M.C., had been appointed Second in Command of the Battalion, and Capt. Barry, 3rd Battalion, who had joined the Battalion when I was at Le Touquet, had taken over command of C Company. Second Lieut. Staines had also joined the Company. Major Frend, D.S.O., was attached to the 2nd Hampshires. The Battalion received a draft of over 100 men from the Base, amongst whom was Pte. Colman (one of my bombers on the Double Crassier).

The Brigade fell in for ceremonial drill on one of the " German " parade grounds. In the evening I went for a hack on Matilda, on the cinder track alongside the main Lille-Roubaix road, where

---

[1] Officers wounded were Captains Redway and Van Cutsem, Lieuts. Hyde-Sander and Coade, and 2nd Lieuts. Wylde, Barker, M.C., Flannery, and Smith.

I had a nice canter. This was the last time I rode Matilda, one of the best mares I ever rode.

5th November.

Heard that the Austrian Empire had crumpled up.
Usual morning parade, " P.T." and slow marching.

6th November.

Battalion paraded at 9 a.m. for " The War," and moved off in a drizzling rain, which, as the day wore on, became steadily worse. The C.O. had gone on leave, and command of the Battalion had devolved on Farrell. Barry was acting as Second in Command to the Battalion, which left me commanding C Company.

It was the anniversary of Colonel Murphy's death ; the men had not forgotten him ; all day long on the march, and later in billets, I heard them talking about him. The journey was long and fatiguing, the first part of it being over the uneven cobbled roads through Roubaix and Mouscron, typical mining centres. In spite of the weather, crowds turned out at these places to see us marching through ; women in shawls with ragged children, then men in blue blouses and peaked caps, the traditional costume of the French industrial worker. Our march was lengthened by having to make detours where several large bridges had been demolished by the enemy in their retirement.

The march became very depressing ; as we drew clear of the towns, we struck off across a most desolate and derelict country, the cobbled roads giving way to muddy tracks. The Battalion now marched with 200 yards interval between companies. We had the usual ten minutes to the hour halts. I remember a very happy incident during one of these halts. I was lying down in a wet ditch, just in front of the Company opposite a very dilapidated cottage. Suddenly the door opened, and an old woman in her clanking sabots came out across the road in the rain towards me, carrying a chair. Smiling at me, she left it on the side of the road. This was the sole bright spot on this miserable march.

We passed through the billets of the 1st Battalion Royal Irish Fusiliers, 36th Division,[1] where I again missed meeting Emerson. The further we advanced, the more desolate the landscape seemed. At one point we came on a particularly revolting sight—half a dozen bare-footed women tearing off flesh from a mule, which had been killed some days previously in the advance. They had pulled the skin off the quarters, and with knives and

---

[1] Village of Luinghe, S.E. of Mouscron.

forks were cutting off chunks, and putting them into handker-
chiefs. They were ravenous with hunger.

We billeted in a meagre little farm, the men being accommodated in damp and smelly barns in an adjacent farm. The
peasants were poor, scantily clad, and hungry-looking, and the
children were delighted with the pieces of biscuit given them by
the men.

Cold bad coffee was all we could obtain in the way of refresh-
ment until the cookers (field kitchens) and limbers arrived.
The transport experienced great difficulty coming across the
muddy tracks. At night Barry returned from Battalion H.Q.
situated in a local farmhouse surrounded by a ring of poplars,
some 500 yards away. He brought orders for an attack to be
carried out by two platoons C Company against the enemy lines
on the Scheldt the following night. I was to command one of
these platoons. Anticipating an armistice, special instructions
were added to our orders from G.H.Q. for these operations, and
were headed : " Prisoners under White Flag," in accordance
with Field Service Regulations. C Company had orders to furnish
an advance party of an officer and one N.C.O. per platoon, to take
over the line on the Scheldt. I was detailed for this duty, and the
following were my instructions (according to my field message
book) : " Report to H.Q. 2/16 London Regt. (T.F. at U.D.6.35
(Moen), where guides would be supplied to take me round the
outpost line. Inspect cellars for accommodation of Company,
strength 100. Reconnoitre bridge and its approaches from
Bossuyt U.24.C. Take over all posts on near and far side of
Scheldt. Number of posts and how accommodated. If dumps
of S.A.A. get map reference. Obtain all information regarding
enemy and position."

7th November.

At 9 a.m. I collected four N.C.O.s who were to accompany me
on my reconnaissance of the front line at Bossuyt. One of the
N.C.O.s—Corpl. Bates—had been in my old platoon at Ypres
in '15. Owing to the swampy nature of the country we had to
make a wide detour via Ruddervoorde, before reaching Saint
Genois. On the way we passed General de Lisle, and he reined up
his horse and talked to me. A climbing muddy road which ran
past a battery of 60-pounders, in action, brought us to the deserted
village of St. Genois. Here, owing to a twisted signboard, I took
the wrong road. Nearing a small straggling hamlet, lying in a
slight hollow, where shells were bursting, I discovered my mistake,
so we retraced our steps and cut across fields of beetroot. It
was a desolate countryside, the only living things to be seen being

the familiar Flemish spectacle of a peasant ploughing with his old white Percheron, completely oblivious to war. We cut across a sunken lane, which, judging from the abandoned khaki great-coats and webbing equipment that were lying about, had been held by us in the advance. Several shrapnel shells burst over us. The going was very heavy, and the N.C.O.s with their cumbersome kits were nearly exhausted when we drew up at Battalion H.Q. of the 2/16 London Regiment T.F. (Queen's Westminster Rifles), situated in a derelict farm building on the southern out-skirts of Moen (map ref. U.6.D.3.5).

The village was being subjected to heavy shelling, and there were groups of inhabitants watching the " crumps " bursting, with great curiosity. (Moen was new to war!) I was supplied with a guide, and we headed off across a swampy stretch towards a thick clump of trees, which surrounded the Château, where Company H.Q. was situated. A fairly heavy bombardment was going on, and the Boches were searching Bossuyt, the Château and its approaches. Several H.E. crumps landed un-pleasantly close in the marshy soil, making great unheavals of earth.[1] We entered the Château grounds by a back entrance and, passing through the stables, came out in front of a beautiful mediæval castle, with grey turrets, and surrounded on three sides by a moat. I found the Company Commander of the Territorial unit down in the dark, spacious kitchen, the only safe place. All its windows had been barricaded up with sandbags on the outside, as protection against backbursts. The châtelain had decamped when the fighting started, leaving his furniture and china for the use of either Briton or Boche. With difficulty I learned the dispositions of the Company we were about to relieve from this O.C. Company, who was suffering from influenza. The line was held in a system, with three platoons in the piquet line finding sentry posts and one platoon in support with Company H.Q. in the Château. As we talked, shells were screaming incessantly overhead, and " plunking " into the moat with tremendous reverberation. A guide led me down the main pavé drive, which was all pitted with recent shell craters, and obstructed by fallen trees.

Turning to the right, we went down the main road along the domain walls, and then branched to the left down a side track towards the Scheldt. We found the right, or No. 1 piquet, accommodated in an adjacent cellar, and we then proceeded to reconnoitre a bridge and inspect the sentry group. As it was still

[1] From this intense but spasmodic shell-fire, and owing to the rumours of the enemy's expected withdrawal in this sector, we gathered that he was " emptying guns " preparatory to retreating.

light, we hung closely to the ruins on our right, approaching the canalised river.[1] Here we found the " bridge," a single duckboard track resting on airtight metal floats. We descended on to this " young pontoon," and crossed the unfordable Scheldt, a sluggish-moving river of nearly twenty yards in breadth. Cut out of the bank on the far side was a post of 1 N.C.O. and 6 men. This was the only post held on the far side in our sector, but on the right was another group found by the 2nd Durham L.I., of the 6th Division. Thus, by a strange coincidence, the 2nd Leinsters were destined to see the end of the war beside the Division they went to France with. I then reconnoitred the other positions, and returned in the falling light to the Château to meet the Company just arriving. I took out No. 1 piquet, and conducted its sentry group across the Scheldt, and returned to the Château for the platoon under Sergt. Bateman, M.M., finding No. 3 piquet, leaving No. 2 piquet to get to its position, under its N.C.O. guide, which was in some cellars behind or south of the church. No. 3 piquet was in a farmhouse on the far side of the Bossuyt canal, which ran into the Scheldt. The road bridge had been completely demolished, so we had to cross the canal by a footbridge which ran on top of the lock gates. This footbridge had had several direct hits, and where there should have been foot-space were several great chasms. However, the men negotiated these by swinging themselves across by the iron hand-rails, a difficult feat, especially for the Lewis Gunners. Having conducted this platoon to its position, I returned to the Château at about 9 p.m., and reported all the piquets correct, and then returned to command the piquet in the farmhouse which I had just left. The village was being shelled as I went through it carrying some rations. In the darkness I fell over some heaps of masonry, which lay across the road, and stumbled into a few fallen trees! My piquet furnished one sentry group on the near bank of the Scheldt.

8th November.

We were spasmodically shelled throughout the night. When going the rounds at dawn, the sentry group reported that something had approached their post at about 3 a.m., but when challenged had run away, and then they had heard splashing in the river. A dog, most probably!

From a gable end window in a loft over the stables, I obtained a top-hole view of the enemy's country. I spent some time

---

[1] The canalisation of the Scheldt had originally been designed by Louis XIV's fortress-builder, Vauban, in 1706. Like the other Flander canals, it was to serve the double purpose of a means of communication, and a line of defence.

during the morning in this O.P. with my map, studying the locality, as we were to attack over it during the night. The wide stretch of ground formed into an island by the loop of the Grand Courant with the Scheldt did not appear to be held by the enemy. He was holding the farm buildings, mostly by machine-guns on the far side of the Grand Courant, which ran behind a line of willows. Only occasional shelling throughout this day, but machine-guns were very offensive traversing backwards and forwards, and bullets ripped and slat against the bricks.

The men were all very comfortable in the cellars, and scrounged any amount of " spuds " from the garden. The biggish farm had rather a battered appearance, and shells had wrought havoc with the rooms. Crucifixes, broken mirrors, ladies' lingerie, and books, lay scattered all over the floors.

At 9 p.m. we left the farm under orders for the advance. We closed down with the rest of the company to the pontoon in front of the Château. Only a few shells whined over us. We passed a pontoon section of R.E.s in the street ; they were about to make a pukka bridge over the Scheldt, but were too late for us !

It was an extremely dark, and bitterly cold night. We crossed the insecure pontoon with difficulty, the current had made a decided curve in it and the centre duckboards were submerged in the water.

By the time the last platoon was to cross, it was in a precarious state. I sent the men over singly, telling them to step out, as when they hesitated on the duckboards down they sank. One man stopped, and I saw him sink in up to his knees. He let go the L.G. magazine panniers, and they went splashing into the water ! I was the last to cross, and then the Company was all correct with its eight Lewis guns on the far side.

This was a creditable performance considering the darkness, the insecure pontoon, that the men were wearing great-coats and carrying their complete cumbersome paraphernalia.

Thus the Company left Bossuyt, the last stationary position occupied by the Battalion during the Great War. We extended, and lined the tow-path, and a patrol was sent out in front. There was no sign of the enemy, and we advanced towards the Grand Courant, the ground being little better than a morass. I was detailed to " mop up " a farm building beyond the Courant. We approached this white-washed farm and found the door locked and the galvanised iron gate to its enclosed yard fastened. Going round to the far side, I discovered a wire fence. With my batman I climbed this fence, and jumped into a stagnant manure pond. Down I went, wallowing up to my waist into this slimy, smelly water, my servant being somewhat luckier. We crawled out soaked, stinking like polecats, and cursing like blazes to the inner door of the farm, to find chalked across the door the words " Good-bye, Tommy " (in English)—the last pleasantry of the retiring enemy.

We advanced in file, with a covering party in front, and just before entering a small village—Quesnoy—we joined up with the rest of the Company. Company H.Q. established itself in a dirty little cottage, with L.G. posts in front. An N.C.O.'s patrol was sent out in front to reconnoitre the village, and in returning bumped into one of these L.G. posts. The gunner, Pte. Penrose, fired a burst on his challenge being unanswered, and so the Battalion had its last casualties[1] in the war—Privates Kane and Bousfield being unfortunately killed, and two men wounded.

We took up our position in another farm, and very nearly surprised some Jerries having a meal, as they decamped leaving most of their repast on a table in the cellar. It was freezing hard, and being soaked through I was chilled to the bone, so I took off my clothes, bar my shirt, which stank most dreadfully. Sergt. Rochford lent me his great-coat, which, as he was a tall man, fitted me admirably. I found a pair of civilian boots with elastic sides in the farm. Thus attired, with sergeant's chevrons on my arm, I visited the outposts. The remainder of the company slept in a straw barn.

9th November.

Barry handed over the Company to me, and I was issued with a new map showing the Brigade boundaries. At 9 a.m. the Battalion advanced through our outposts. B Company were very amused at my kit. I hurriedly got into my wet clothes, which Geoghan had been trying to dry. C Company advanced in rear of B. In the advance we passed a poor woman nearly distracted ; crying, she showed me all her cooking utensils which had been pierced with holes for spite by the enemy—a perfect example of Hun Kultur. Near here we passed several dumps of enemy shells. The day was very fine, and I got passably dry. Crossing a railway, with its bridge completely demolished, we got into Celles—here we got an enthusiastic reception from the inhabitants, and from every house there flew Belgian and French flags.

---

[1] The official death casualties incurred by the 2nd Battalion The Leinster Regiment from the Aisne, September, 1914, to the Armistice, were 88 officers, and 1085 N.C.O.s and men killed or died of wounds ; the wounded were estimated, at 117 officers and 8,947 N.C.O.s and men.

There were several great mine craters across the main street.
Night found us comfortably billeted in a large farm (D.16.d.8.1).
There had been no sign of the enemy ; he was obviously carrying
out an orderly retirement. The Brigadier came round to see my
sentry groups. I was in support to B Company, who had seen the
Huns moving a gun back over the ridge in front. It was in this
billet that we found several leaflets in German and French to
the effect that the gallant soldiers of the Fatherland, after holding
and defying the world for 4¼ years, were now to carry out a
strategic retreat.

The inhabitants told us that the Huns were terribly dirty,
and crawling with vermin, and that they had been very undis-
ciplined. On the previous night, two Jerries had had a " scrap,"
and had discharged their rifles, with the result that a little girl
was wounded in the leg.

10th November.

Advanced at 9 a.m., companies got orders to rendezvous at
Arc-Ainières. While on the march the Brigadier had galloped up
and yelled out : " The War is over ! The Kaiser has abdicated ! "
We were typically Irish, and never cheered except under adverse
conditions, such as shell-fire and rain. Somewhat crestfallen
the Brigadier rode slowly off to communicate his glad tidings to
an English battalion, who, no doubt, took the news in a different
way. " And th'ould Kiser hopped it and faith and so he might,
wasn't he the quare ould twister ? " The only other remark I
overheard was after we had narrowly missed being mined at a
cross-roads. Private Flaherty calmly said : " They do say the
War is over." The inhabitants of Arc-Ainières turned out to
welcome us, carrying fruit and plates of bread and butter for the
men. We fell out on a ridge just east of the village and piled arms.

An enemy shell burst some 300 yards away—*the last shot the
Battalion saw fired in anger in the war.*

One of our aeroplanes was flying ahead of us, and was being
" archied " occasionally by the pom-poms, but we couldn't see
the shells bursting. The 7th Dragoon Guards of the 7th Cavalry
Brigade rode past. They were a fine-looking regiment, all well
mounted on black horses, as pre-War, which gave them the nickname of " The Black Horse." The 7th D.G.s were famed for their
exploit in the War, when charging with the 20th Deccan Horse
at Delville Wood on the Somme, on the 14th July, 1916, when
they belonged to the Secunderabad Brigade.

We advanced, and got to St. Sauveur without incident. We
were all tired, having covered over 15 kilometres, partly by road
and partly across country. C Company was allotted a farm to

billet in for the night. I received a chit from the Adjutant, stating the hostilities would cease from 11.00 hours on the morrow, the 11th November. We were approximately ten miles due south of the famous battlefield of Oudenarde.[1]

11th November.

Company paraded at 7.30 a.m., and marched to the Battalion rendezvous. At 8 a.m. the Battalion marched off from St. Sauveur. Wodecq was given as our destination. Our Divisional Commander wanted us to cover as much ground as possible during the morning. The Brigadier rode past us, accompanied by his staff. He told Farrell (acting C.O.) that he was riding on to make good the bridge-head over the Dendre at Lessines before 11 a.m., in case the Huns violated the terms of the Armistice and fighting did not cease. (This he did at 10.50 a.m., with " A " Squadron of the 7th D.G.s.)[2] The enemy put up a " scrap " but were all either killed or captured. To make matters worse for them, a party of British prisoners of war, who were working at Lessines, turned on their recent captors, and gave them hell ! We had only a few casualties. At about 10 a.m. we passed through the 2nd Hampshires, and became advanced guard to the Brigade. It was a glorious morning. The route lay over broken country ; sometimes by road, more often by rough tracks through thickly wooded and hilly terrain. The men were in their usual good spirits. Many discussed the situation, some arguing that the Boches were bluffing. But optimism and pessimism centred more on the question whether or no a sequence of four rumless days would be broken. We could not realise that the War was coming to an end.

THE ARMISTICE

Every now and then officers and signallers would furtively glance at their watches. At last the hands pointed to the hour, and I called out to the Company the words : " Eleven o'clock ! "

Thus, the most dramatic moment passed, as we marched on in silence.

[1] We were less than 8 miles north of the battlefield of Fontenoy where the Irish Brigade in the service of France under Marshal de Saxe so distinguished itself against the Duke of Cumberland's forces. Detachments from these Irish regiments later fought at Culloden where my ancestor, the Chevalier de Johnstone, was serving as A.D.C. to Prince Charles Edward, and who has left an account of the campaign under the title of *Memoirs of the Rebellion, 1745-46*.

[2] The value of cavalry was well demonstrated in this advance to secure the Dendre bridgehead at Lessines against time. As all the bridges over the Scheldt had been demolished by the enemy in his retirement, a mechanized force, had it been available would not have been able to function.

Then some of the men began to speak of India, and of the prospects of being sent there with the 1st Battalion now that the War was over. Quite a number spoke about their dead comrades, and I overhead : " If only Colonel Murphy could be with the old Battalion now ! "

Shortly afterwards a thin rain began to fall, and we tramped into our billets at Wodecq, tired but contented, for we all felt as if a great weight had been lifted off our shoulders. The Company was billeted in a convent ; the rest of the Battalion throughout the village. The nuns gave us an enthusiastic reception, and forthwith started to put up beds in the large schoolroom for the men. To give it its " pukka " name, the " Pensionnat de la Divine Providence " had been a girls' school pre-War. I had a fine room with a parquet floor. The nuns fed us for the first 24 hours after we arrived, as our rations were held up owing to the difficulties of the transport with the demolished bridges. The nuns brought us round early morning coffee and bread.

Whenever the Battalion came in contact with the nuns of Flanders it received most hospitable treatment. At many places, notably at Ypres and Poperinghe, they went out of their way to be kind to us. No doubt this was partly due to the fact that we were Irish, and the majority R.C.s. The Ypres nuns[1] had originally all been Irish, and had rendered great assistance just two centuries earlier to another Irish regiment—Clare's— fighting in the French service, after the Battle of Ramillies, 1706. (See p. 79.) Food was very scarce in this district. I think what pleased the nuns most was seeing our sentries pacing up and down in front of the main gate. They told me that ever since '14 they had watched a Boche, complete in *pickelhaube*, doing likewise ! We remained three days in the convent, having short cleaning parades and rifle inspections only. The Company just mustered 100 strong.

14th November.

In the evening we paraded and moved with the Battalion into Lessines. All cross-roads were mined, and we had to make several detours. The men had behaved splendidly at the convent, and we all bade tender farewells to the charming old ladies who had been so hospitable.

---

[1] The convent of the Irish Nuns of Ypres was founded by Queen Mary of Modena, James II's wife, for Irish women exiled after the capitulation of Limerick. The original Mother Superior was a Clare, sister to Lord Clare, the Colonel of Clare's Regiment in the service of France.

15th to 17th November.

The Battalion received a draft of several senior N.C.O.s, including Sergt. Kells. 2nd Lieut. Staines went down the line with dysentery. The *entende cordiale* pervaded everywhere in Lessines. The town seemed to have suffered severely from Hun oppression, and most of the " municipal counsellors " had only just been released from Germany, where they had been slaving in mines, etc.

Owing to the terms of the Armistice, we had to remain at Lessines, and give the Huns so many days' grace to retire before us. The whole Division was concentrated in or about Lessines, and on the 17th we watched troops of all our Army pouring through. I particularly noticed the 17th Lancers, a magnificent-looking regiment still wearing their steel helmets, and carrying their lances, less pennons ; the 18th Hussars, Machine Gun Corps Cavalry, R.F.A., Pontoon Companies, and Signal Corps. We received information about the grant of the 1914–15 Star, a medal to which I would be entitled.

18th November.

Battalion marched off from Lessines at 9 a.m. It was a bitterly cold, frosty morning. Thousands of mounted troops and batteries of artillery, British and Canadian, preceded us. R.E. officers were busily employed ahead, de-detonating mines at all cross-roads. On this day the Allies started their march to the Rhine. The British Army of Occupation was composed of a Cavalry Division, 9th and 29th Infantry Divisions, and a Canadian Division. Belonging to the 29th, the Battalion was to have the honour of marching as victors into German territory. This honour was shared by but one other Irish battalion, the famous " Blue Caps," or 1st Battalion Royal Dublin Fusiliers of the 86th Brigade. Thus, we commenced our march of 204 miles to Germany, and the Battalion stepped out in true Leinster fashion this crispy morning over the cobbles, led by the pipe band playing lustily.

19th to 20th November.

Billeted in Enghien, a fairish-sized town. Here we met batches of our recently released prisoners of war. They were in a deplorable condition from lack of food. We got orders to " dump " our iron rations for their use. The men were comfortably accommodated in a large school, and in the mornings we marched off to our company parade grounds allotted to us near a small park, and went through the usual drill and P.T. exercises. In the evenings the Battalion pipe band paraded in the town square, and played "Retreat," in the midst of an interested throng of inhabitants. Just four miles south of this straggling town, lay the battlefield of Steinkerque,[1] where the British Army under William of Orange had met with a reverse from the French under Luxembourg in 1692.[2]

21st November.

Companies rendezvoused in the Square, and the Battalion halted for some minutes while men were picked out of the four companies to make a contingent to represent the Regiment at Brussels on the morrow, when the King of the Belgians was to enter his capital officially. Val Farrell was detailed to take command of this contingent (1 platoon per company), and 2nd Lieuts. Mallins and Moran, along with myself, were also detailed to go with it. This selected contingent marched in rear of the Battalion.

Nearing Hal the Battalion branched off to the right for their billets at Brain-le-Château, leaving us to march on to Hal in the failing light on this typical winter evening. At Hal we fell out, and piled arms to await motor lorries which were to convey us to Brussels. We were joined by detachments of the 2nd Hampshire and 4th Worcestershire Regiments. Brigadier-General Freyberg, V.C., then appeared in a taxi, and said he would bring an officer from each regiment to find billets for the contingents.

I was detailed for this duty, and set off with the Brigadier in our ramshackle motor, which I thought would fall to pieces over the rough *pavé*. Going through the heart of the Belgian capital reminded me of London with all the lights shining through the foggy atmosphere. We drew up in the Ganshoren vicinity, north-west of Brussels, where the Brigadier talked to some officials and the *gendarmerie*. We took over our billets and allotted them to the various detachments, and then awaited their arrival. At about 10 p.m., they came in motor lorries. Food was scarce, and we were all hungry. I slept in the château (a fine moated one with good stabling) on an old iron bedstead. Brigade H.Q.s were also accommodated in this building, which had been left in a filthy condition by the Germans.

22nd November—Friday.

Got up at dawn, very stiff ! We all had a very meagre breakfast in a small house where Farrell was billeted.

[1] In our surprise night attack which preceded this battle, the officers of the French regiment were asleep, and dressing hurriedly had not time to adjust their stocks correctly, which they threw over their shoulders. The ladies of the French Court copied this method of wearing a scarf, which they alluded to as a *Steinkerque*.

[2] Maréchal de Luxembourg received the soubriquet of *Tapissier de Notre Dame* for having decorated the cathedral with so many colours captured in battle from the Dutch and the Germans.

Paraded at 7.30, a cold, chilly morning. We marched off to the main road past another château, which was said to be undermined by the Germans, and had been left unoccupied. All the Allied Armies were represented in this triumphal march, and the British had a Battalion formed of contingents from the 29th and 9th Divisions. English, Irish, Scottish, and Welsh troops were all included in this composite battalion, which was headed by the pipers of the Seaforth Highlanders. The 1st Dublins and ourselves were the Irish representatives. A Battery of R.F.A. looked very smart, head ropes " blancoed," all saddlery and bits and chains all burnished. As we marched on, the crowds lining the sides of the roads became denser. Tier upon tier of forms and seats had been erected ; every window, balcony, roof, lamp-post, and kiosk was packed along the whole route. At all street corners the various official organisations, under large banners, were formed up. The city was a mass of decorations and flags ; all the houses were covered in electric light bulbs for illuminations at night. It was said that half a million had been spent on these decorations, and that the inhabitants had been assisted in installing the electrical illuminations by the Boches ! Some of the spectators paid equivalent to £10 for seats along the route.

On the march the King and Queen of the Belgians overtook us in a motor on their way to the saluting base. Swinging on to a great wide thoroughfare, we split up into two parties and marched eight deep down this broad *chaussée*.

PRINCE ALBERT

The Belgian Royal Family accompanied by Prince Albert[1] and the Belgian General Leman, the heroic defender of Liége, were all mounted and drawn up on our left outside the gates of the Royal Palace. We gave " Eyes left " and " Eyes front " and marched on.

It was now midday ; we had been marching all morning without proper halts ; to ease matters the order " Change arms " had been given every ten minutes. I noticed that King Albert was wearing his steel shrapnel helmet ; he was a particularly distinguished-looking figure.

Behind us marched the Belgian Army, with a bugle band. At 1 p.m., we drew up in the large square of the main infantry barracks, piled arms, took off equipment, and fell out to await our two cookers, which had gone astray in the city. A guard was mounted on the main entrance, and all troops of the 29th Division were C.B.

[1] Later Duke of York and now His Majesty King George VI.

We were all dreadfully hungry after our poor breakfast at 06.00 hours, according to the 1918 B.E. Force method of describing the time. In turn officers were allowed out into the city to get food. We were charged exorbitant prices for food and cigarettes. I had to pay 10 francs for a few slices of horseflesh in one of the principal restaurants.

Numerous effigies of the Kaiser were hanging from the lampposts throughout the town. Brussels is a fine city, and the Grand Place is one of the finest I have ever seen, surrounded by large handsome buildings. I was very taken with an equestrian statue to the late King Leopold of the Belgians outside the Royal Palace, but the snaffle bridle looked most incongruous with the rest of the military saddlery.

It always surprised one that the Belgians put up such a great fight in the first weeks of the War, harassing the Germans with their sniping and *franc-tireur* warfare. Their holding of the enemy hordes before Liége made a power of difference to the situation. At 6 p.m., the lost cookers turned up, and the men got their first meal since breakfast.

At 8 p.m. lorries arrived to convey us back to our regiments, and we left Brussels magnificently illuminated, and in a mad state of jubilation. After a freezingly cold drive, we pulled up at Brain-le-Château, where the Battalion was billeted. There was a curious description of the triumphal march next day in the Brussels papers to the effect that the American and French contingents had acknowledged the greetings of the people, but that the British khaki-clad warriors, with set faces, looked neither to the left or right."

Doubtless, the War had destroyed many of the trammels of military discipline, and the sight of a contingent from a division of British troops marching to attention, completely baffled the Belgian journalists !

23rd November. Saturday.

Paraded early and left Brain-le-Château at 8 a.m. The Battalion was advance guard to the Division, C Company being in front. It was a fine morning, and we were looking forward to marching over the famous battlefield of Waterloo, which lay in our route.

Before we came to the Lion monument, a deafening cheer burst from the Company—one of the houses on the left-hand side of the road was a public house with the name O'Brien in large letters over the door, and this homely inscription was joyously recognised by the Leinsters. Leaving the Lion (where we had a ten-minutes' halt) on our right, we marched over the cross-roads close to La Haie St. Farm, and struck off across the famous battlefield.

It was the kind of country one imagined as the typical battle-
ground of a century ago, with its great rolling plains. On we
marched over this partly cultivated terrain, our route leading
us across what in 1815 was probably " No-Man's-Land."

We were all frightfully interested as we marched, picking up
the famous landmarks with the aid of our maps. We then took
the famous sunken road which runs from west to east to Ohain.
It was here that the French cavalry met with such unexpected
disaster when charging the British left flank. One recalled the
striking picture by Meissonnier, depicting those heavily armed
cuirassiers with their metal casques, breastplates, and long horse-
hair plumes, plunging headlong into this unseen, but natural
trap.

Strange to say, only one infantry regiment represented Ireland
in that great battle. Although the Royal Irish Fusiliers and the
Connaught Rangers fought in all the Peninsula battles, they were
not present for the Hundred Days' Campaign. The Royal
Inniskilling Fusiliers,[1] the 27th Foot, is the sole Irish infantry
regiment bearing the proud battle honour " Waterloo " on its
colours.

We covered 21 kilometres during this day over very undulating
ground, but our interest in this historic and picturesque country
took our minds off the stiff march. Pushing out outposts, we
billeted in the small but pretty village of Ohain, which lay in a
deep depression south-south-east of the Forest of Soignes. Some
days previously, one of our cavalry regiments had crossed over
the famous battlefield, but the honour of being the first British
infantry regiment to march across the fields of Waterloo since the
18th June, 1815, fell to the 2nd Battalion The Leinster Regiment.

24th November.   Sunday.

Remained at Ohain. R.C. church parade. Rations arrived
complete with a rum issue.

---

[1] The 1st " Skins " were one of the battalions which formed part of the Irish
Brigade and which fought so courageously at Pieter's Hill, Colenso.
This regiment happened to be stationed at Enniskillen in 1899 when they
received orders for the Cape. An officer who was serving with the battalion at
the time told me the following story : As Enniskillen was their home town the
regiment got a tremendous send-off. The town turned out *en masse* and at the
station before entraining the battalion was formed up to receive an address of
good wishes from the townspeople. Three cheers were called for the regiment
and in reply the C.O. called for three cheers for the citizens of Enniskillen.
After the cheering had subsided a voice from the ranks called out, " Boys, three
cheers for Kruger ! " Very annoyed, his Company Commander strode up to the
man and demanded an explanation, to get the reply : " Sure, sir, if it wasn't for
Kruger we wouldn't be going to the war at all."

25th November.

Paraded at 9 a.m. Heard that 2nd Lieut. Hickie (deceased) and 2nd Lieut. FitzSimon had been awarded the M.C. Climbing the high ground going eastwards, the famous Lion monument on its pyramid-shaped plinth, or the " Butte du Lion, Waterloo," was still visible when we looked back.

Reached Ottignies by 3 p.m. in a shower of rain. The Battalion pipe band played splendidly on the march. Good billets.

26th November.

Company training and an inspection by the C.O. In the afternoon the Battalion football team played the 2nd Hampshires in a hollow near the railway. The inhabitants, though friendly to us, did not show the same consideration towards some of their own people, especially those who had been friendly with the enemy during their occupation. It was the time for revenge, and those who had fraternised with the Hun had their houses smashed up. I saw all kinds of furniture being thrown out of the windows of two houses going through the town. In the majority of cases, the objects of hate were the women of easy virtue who were known to have " liaised " with the enemy. All these had their hair closely cropped in order to brand them before the world. I saw one of the unfortunate victims being chased by some of the inhabitants across a field in the pouring rain.

27th November.

Paraded at 9 a.m., in pouring rain, for an unknown destination. On the march our billeting area was given as Walhain St. Paul. At 5 p.m. we got to this town, having covered more than 14 miles over bad roads, running through very broken and wooded terrain. However, it turned out that there was not sufficient accommodation for the Brigade, and we had to trek on for another three miles to a village called Sart lez Walhain. The billets were poor, and we were short of food.

28th November.

Left Sart and marched to Hanret—a long march just under 20 kilometres. Here we were billeted just six miles as the crow flies due south of the famous battlefield of Ramillies.

29th November.

Left Hanret and marched to Moha, the famous fortress of Namur lying to our south. The march was over 20 kilometres long, but fortunately over a first-class road, although owing to the hilly nature of the country we were very fatigued when we arrived in our billeting area, Moha, at dusk. Men accommodated in barns.

30th November.

Paraded at 8.30 a.m. Very cold morning. There had been a thick frost in the night, and the roads had a glassy surface.

On approaching the eastern frontier of Belgium, the scenery changed, flat and rather dull country giving place to deep river beds with precipitous sides, and swift-flowing water. The country was thickly wooded with pine and fir forests. The change, though delightful, made marching more difficult, owing to the many hills and valleys.

We crossed the Meuse at Huy.[1] Huy is a fine old town lying in a hollow, with a network of narrow cobbled streets. This city came into great prominence in Marlborough's campaigns. Our transports had considerable difficulty in negotiating the steep gradients of the road leaving Huy. We had a ten-minutes' halt in the town.

We got into billets at Ouffet, a small town which lay nestling in a hollow. A large rocky promontory rising up behind it reminded me of the Rock of Cashel in Tipperary. Our billets were good, and the inhabitants very friendly. "Madame" in my billet gave me a glass of cognac on arrival. The 1st Battalion K.O.S.B. of the 87th Brigade were also billeted in this town.

1st December.

Leaving Ouffet at 8.30 a.m., by a steep straggling road, we struck out for Awan, a small village due south of Aywaille on the River l'Ameleve. I was in charge of the Battalion stragglers party, and marched in rear with part of the transport—Maltese cart and officers' mess cart. Behind marched the 4th Worcesters.

A lovely morning. The march brought us through thickly wooded terrain. Coming to the River l'Ourthe we branched off

---

[1] It was at Huy that an incident, which was somewhat reminiscent of the transference of General Monck's Regiment of Coldstream from the Parliamentary Army to serve King Charles II at the Restoration, occurred.

Owing to excessive casualties in the First Battle of Ypres the remnants of the 2nd Battalion Connaught Rangers were absorbed by their 1st Battalion. After the Armistice it was decided to re-raise the 2nd Battalion by the conversion of their 5th Service Battalion which had fought gallantly at Gallipoli.

The transformation took place on the parade in the above historical town in February, 1919. The commands were given " 5th Battalion Connaught Rangers, Ground Arms ! "—" 2nd Battalion Connaught Rangers, Take up Arms ! "

That great Irish soldier, Patrick Sarsfield, the defender of Limerick in the Jacobite War, died of the wounds which he received in the Battle of Landen, 1693, at Huy. A descendant, Major W. S. Sarsfield, 2nd Connaught Rangers, died of wounds received on the Aisne in September, 1914, and until their disbandment in 1922, his son, Lieut. Patrick Sarsfield, was serving in the regiment.

to our left, and marched northwards along the left bank of the river.

The scenery was most picturesque. At times we were marching round the mountain-sides, and below us rushed the river in a great ravine. Cutters were working in the forests, felling the pines, which they then floated down-stream to some saw-mills. Everything seemed very peaceful ; the only reminders of the terrible conflict which had waged for the past 4¼ years being the enemy billeting notice-boards, which were nailed up beside the doors of all the houses along the main road and in the villages, stating the accommodation within, in the German vernacular (viz.) :

8 MENSCHEN (8 men)

5 PFERDEN (5 horses).

This alone shows the thorough organisation of the Q.M. branch of the German Army.

All along this march since the Armistice we noted that there was a great scarcity of live-stock, especially cattle on the land. This was due to the fact that the enemy had plundered them during his occupation, and in many cases had driven them before him on his retreat.

Passing Comblain au Pont, we crossed the rushing mountain torrent, and marched parallel on the south side of the Ameleve. Having had a half-hour's halt for lunch, we got to our billets in Awan as it was growing dusk. We were all tired, and some of the men, especially my small band of stragglers, suffered severely owing to bad boots. The Brigadier halted by the bridge at Aywaille to watch the regiment marching through.

2nd and 3rd December.

Complete company billeted in a very comfortable farm, where we got beer, butter, eggs, and bread. Some of the men played football. Shelly and I walked into Aywaille, and had a look round this quaint and picturesque town. The reason for this halt was that we had got too far ahead of our supplies ; owing to the numerous demolished bridge-heads, railway bridges, and crossroads, the lines of communication were not yet completely restored.

4th December.

Left Awan for La Reid, which we reached in pouring rain. We were allotted filthy billets, along a straggling road.

A supply of boots came up for the Battalion by lorry, but they turned out to be boots, high, mounted branches, for the use of, 200 pairs ! I suggested cutting the tops off, but the Quartermaster would not hear of it. They were returned to Brigade H.Q. Officers and men of the Battalion very " hostile " towards the Quartermaster Stores branch of the Army.

GERMANY

5th December.

Paraded at 8.30 and marched off from the miserable and squalid village of La Reid. A winding road brought us to the picturesque town of Spa, in a shower of rain. The place was crammed with Allied Commissioners and German representatives of the Peace Delegations, each with their string of retainers in various coloured uniforms. We were all interested at the sight of an armed enemy sentry on duty over the enemy Headquarters. We had a ten minutes' halt in the town, and a group of German soldiers sauntered over to try and fraternise with the men. The ribbon of the Mons star, which some of the men were wearing, seemed to interest them greatly. Spa was usually the residence of the Kaiser, when the German War Lord ventured so near the Western Front to review his troops.

Two friends of mine, a Highlander who had been at the machine-gun school at Le Touquet with me, and a Lancashire Fusilier whom I had met at Proven in October, seeing the Leinsters going through their billeting area, came along and " ran me to earth."

Leaving Spa, we marched due east, and proceeded to climb a stiff hill between two and three miles long. Derelict motors were ditched here and there along the roadside. We were all quite thrilled at the prospect of getting into Germany, and as we topped the rise we strained our eyes looking at a chain of hills in the distance, which were in German territory. Here we had a short halt for lunch. Descending into a small valley, we reached a hamlet called Francorchamps, all decorated with the Allies' flags. We swung over a level crossing, and a kilometre to the south-east crossed a little stream, on the far side of which was a signpost (iron) bearing the words " Belges Halte."

And so the 2nd Leinsters passed from Belgium into Germany at exactly 1.48 p.m., the pipers playing " Let Erin remember the days of old." Climbing a steep hill which curved round to the right, we in front had a fine view of the rest of the Battalion, with the pack-horses and stretcher bearers in the train of each company crossing the frontier.

The country was solemn, glum, and uninviting. We passed many isolated farmhouses, but the inhabitants lay " doggo," and did not, like the Belgians, come out to watch us march through, though no doubt there were many eyes glued to peep-holes ! All there was to be seen was refuse and dirt where the enemy had camped, and dead horses which had been attacked by the natives for the value of their meat.

Descending a steep winding road which ran through a thick pine forest, we reached Malmédy. Here we spent our first night in German territory, and in a restaurant the officers of the Battalion assembled and drank lager beer.

The Kaiser was reputed to have stayed on several occasions in this hotel, and there were several life-size oil paintings of him " adorning " the walls. The shock-headed Boche proprietor made himself very affable.

6th December.

Left Malmédy for Weywertz. Several of the men were given cigars and cigarettes by the inhabitants on leaving. Arrived in Weywertz at midday. It was a fairly short march, but the " going " had been heavy, the roads had a terribly bad surface, and were all cut up by countless deep ruts caused by the retiring enemy transports. Came across many " dumps " left by the Huns. Several fields just off the road were littered with colossal stacks of their coal-scuttle-shaped shrapnel helmets and gas masks. Here and there were abandoned motor cars and lorries pulled into the ditch. We noticed that all the tyres and leather upholstery had been hacked to pieces ! Lying beside an evacuated aerodrome was the skeleton of a burnt-out aeroplane. The hangars had all been dismantled.

This march brought us through one of the enemy's pre-war manœuvre grounds. It was studded with " crows'-nests," such as one sees in some racing centres to enable owners and trainers to watch trials. From these vantage-points we were told the Kaiser watched his troops on field days, galloping from one to the other as various stages of the " battle " progressed. Parts of this training area were intersected with networks of trenches for the instruction of Landsturm armies on the Western Front in trench warfare. All devices necessary for teaching position warfare were there ; bombing trenches with shell craters, and stretches of wire entanglements of all descriptions. There were also numerous hutments. It was the famous Elsenborn camp where many Divisions of the German Army concentrated for the invasion of Belgium in July, 1914.

After we had crossed the German frontier we noticed numbers of recently disbanded men from the Boche army in every town, and outside their houses which lined our route. These ex-soldiers continued to wear their field-grey uniform, but with civilian hats.

Some of them at first objected to salute, or raise their hats. Leinster law was drastic ; the offender would be hauled into the ranks and made march to the evening destination of the Battalion. A truculent Hun, wedged in between two tug-of-war Leinsters, had not what was exactly a " soft passage."

The Germans all expressed their astonishment at our horses, which, despite the conditions and march, were in fine condition. The enemy had suffered from the inefficiency of their horse transport in their 1918 offensives, largely due to lack of feeding.[1]

We were surprised to see oxen dragging the farm carts.

On this day we passed a large building, at the entrance of which were a number of flaxen-haired women, all carrying babies. It was one of the German " stud farms," which was instituted and maintained by the State.

7th December.

Left Weywertz for Vlatten in heavy rain. We passed through more of the enemy's manœuvre area. I was detailed to march the stragglers of the Battalion to our next destination. These men were not really stragglers, as they could not keep up, owing to their rotten boots. Some of them were actually marching on the hard roads without any soles to their boots ! I had about twenty-five men, including Pte. Mansfield, an old tough of A Company. No maps were available for this march ; we were given rough sketches of the areas, and instructed to fill in the roads. We got to Vlatten after the very devil of a trek. I managed to get all the men carried on a spare lorry, and joined up with the Battalion. We marched along the banks of the River Roer.

8th December.

I looted a very fine Boche map of Belgium which I still possess, but Montjoie was the most easterly point shown on it. Marched 15 kilometres to Konzen. Rations delayed, and my tobacco supply ran out.

9th to 12th December.

Left Konzen and marched to Frechen on the outskirts of Cologne. Here the 88th Brigade concentrated and prepared for the entry into Cologne, and the crossing of the Rhine. The Company had good billets. Mine was in a large detached house, and was very comfortable. The owner had lost his son, killed in one of the last battles. Naturally, my " host " and his family were very bitter about my being under their roof, but were not openly hostile.

[1] *General Ludendorff, in his memoirs, states that they had to mix sawdust in the horses' feeds towards the end, to make up for the deficiency of bran and oats !*

I took advantage of the four days' halt to have my boots repaired by a local cobbler.

The Adjutant informed me that my name had been submitted for the instructors' course at Berkhamsted.

CROSSING THE RHINE

13th December.

Battalion paraded at 8.30 a.m., in a downpour of rain, for the march across the Rhine at Cologne. The men were conspicuously well turned out ; new serge, new boots, shining buttons, and the web equipment had all been pipe-clayed with ordinary khaki-coloured earth found behind the billets. Before marching off, the order to put on ground sheets was given. A special limbered G.S. waggon followed the Battalion, as we were going to discard these ground sheets in the suburbs of the city.

The rain had almost ceased as we got to the outskirts of Cologne, having had a wet and uninteresting march along flat roads running through root fields. Here we halted ; ground sheets were dumped and bayonets fixed.

At first there were few enemy spectators to be seen, but as we marched on through some of the shopping centres, which reminded me of London, the Germans turned out to see us. At every street corner were numbers of the inhabitants, with their many flaxen-haired children, awaiting us. Here and there, mingled in the background, were demobilised soldiers in uniform, who took stock of us from under the brims of various kinds of civilian head-dress.

Three attempts were made to break through the ranks of the Battalion. The first was by a tram-driver just on the outskirts. Two of the men were sent to " beat him up." They pulled him down off his platform and inflicted necessary summary punishment ! A disbanded soldier attempted to pass between the interval of my platoon and the one in front. Another ex-soldier tried the same stunt in front of the signalling officer, and he, too, was left lying in the gutter.

We swung round to the right, passing the famous Cathedral, the tramp of the marching men re-echoing in the cobbled square. The pipers began to play. General Plumer, attended by General Jacob, II Corps, stood on the right-hand side of the entrance to the Hohenzollern Bridge under a large Union Jack, just ahead of us. Opposite to the famous II Army Commander, on the left-hand side of the bridge, was a colossal equestrian statue of the Kaiser. Some days previously it had been bespattered with mud by the revolutionary troops! Platoon commanders gave " Eyes right," and " Eyes front," as we marched over this great iron structure to the skirl of the pipers, at exactly one o'clock. In the distance we could see the battalions which were in front, winding off to the right and left to their billeting areas, playing their regimental tunes.

The British army to cross the Rhine was composed of the 29th (Regular), the 9th (Scottish New Army), and the 1st Canadian Divisions. The three divisions crossed over different bridges simultaneously, the place of honour going to the Regulars.

By 3 p.m., altogether 32,000 British soldiers were billeted in Cologne. The enemy Press reports next day alone testified to our splendid appearance, remarking on the physique and turn-out of the " khaki-clad 29th Division." They refused to believe that it was composed of troops who had been engaged in the recent fighting, and said it had been obviously nursed and formed recently in England especially for this event! They also remarked that the British battalions crossed over to well-known English marching airs (the 86th Brigade, consisting of three Fusilier Regiments, all played " The British Grenadiers "), but they omitted to mention that the 2nd Leinster Regiment were played over to " Paddy McGinty's Goat!

No wonder we impressed them! Their own " conquering heroes " returned on transport waggons, without equipment; or on the roof of a train (unless swept off by a tunnel, as many of them were), or on looted French bicycles. All the triumphal arches erected by the Cologne citizens in honour of their returning troops had been removed before our entry.

Our company billets were all quite convenient to each other in Mülheim. C Company was allotted a school building, and as we marched up to it we found swarms of women and children awaiting us, with typical German curiosity. We were closely followed by our company cookers. We mounted a guard at the entrance, and in an incredibly short space of time the men had got settled down. They were allowed out in pairs, and it was inter-esting to see them taking their web equipment to pieces to get at their belts and side-arms preparatory to " walking out " in Cologne. Officers messed, as usual, by companies. C Company " struck oil " in the way of a good billet in a residential part of the town. The house where we were billeted was divided into flats. Two of the officers slept in the flat below mine, where our mess was. Orders were issued to the effect that officers were not to billet alone, and that our batmen were to be within earshot. This was owing to the fact that some Belgian soldiers had been murdered up north. However, we had no trouble whatever, and we all found the Germans only too eager to fraternise. Cologne presented an extraordinary appearance at night.

At about 6 p.m. we went out to sample the beer in one of the numerous restaurants, wearing our revolvers. As we walked along the well-lit streets we passed some of the men of the 88th Brigade walking arm-in-arm with German wenches ! In this " pub " were numerous small marble-topped tables, round which were seated typical Germans with shaven heads and double necks, sipping Munich beer out of long glasses or tankards, and puffing away at long-stemmed pipes.

As we entered, silence fell on the whole place. Beer was ordered, which was served by a barman wearing a " field grey " jacket and the ribbon of the Iron Cross. As we drank our beer, the German occupants looked sullenly towards us.

Our life in Cologne was not too bad. After the first day the inhabitants realised that the British Tommy was a cheery individual, without a care in the world, but that they could not take any liberties. The Germans, as a disciplined people, were quick to appreciate this, and gave up the idea of trying to find out how far it was expedient to go, with the Irish in particular. Everything was orderly, due to the work of our Military Police, in co-operation with the German force, and the splendid behaviour of the men of the 29th Division. Perhaps the numerous notice-boards and placards bearing the word " Verboten " had a restraining influence ! The streets were always crowded, but there was very little motor traffic, as we had forbidden all motor-cars inside the town or across the Rhine bridges. The people interested us as much as we interested them. What struck us most was their methodical way of carrying on amidst their hardships (shortage of food, coal, etc.). What they seemingly could not get over regarding our men was that they were always, as they said, " cleaning up." The old Frau in our billet told us that the hardware stores close by had been completely bought out of brushes for boots and buttons by the men in the Battalion.

There was great reluctance on the part of our " landlords " to give us baths, owing to shortage of coal ; when we groused they blamed our Allies, the Belgians, who, as they said, had stopped the coal supply for Cologne coming up the Rhine from the Belgian area of occupation.

14th December.

Kit and rifle inspections only. Supervised a rum issue to the Company in the evening. Shelly and I were asked to go round and have a chat to a London woman, who had married a German pre-war. Her husband was a recently disbanded flying corps officer. They went out of their way to be nice. The flying man told us about some interesting experiences he had had observing over the Russian trenches. He said the Russian anti-aircraft guns at the commencement of the War were much more accurate than either ours or the French. I was surprised at this, as "Archie" work is supposed to be the most intricate branch in gunnery. We drank some Grand Marnier with them before leaving. They told us of the effects which our bombing planes had had on Cologne in the War. I remember the wife asked pathetically about the plays in the London theatres.

15th December.

At 9 a.m., in a misty morning we paraded and marched to Altenburg. It rained heavily towards the end of our march, and we had a stiff climb up a cork-screw road to our billets. Here the people were friendly enough, bar a son, a pukka Prussian wearing the ribbon of the Iron Cross on his coat lapel. Large crowds, mingled with ex-soldiers, watched us leaving Mülheim.

16th December.

Marched off in pouring rain for the 88th Brigade outpost area. A terribly wet march along muddy roads. At 2 p.m., we relieved the 18th Hussars near Donn. This regiment had only been able to stay out in the outpost line for 24 hours, as their forage had run out. I noticed a certain number of lame horses in one squadron.

TWO VICTORIA CROSSES

17th December.

C Company Headquarters were in one of the few decent houses in the area ; it belonged to a gamekeeper who was in charge of some thickly wooded preserves close by. The Company was distributed as follows : 2 platoons in the piquet line with head-quarters, and 2 platoons in support accommodated in some houses opposite Company Headquarters at the cross-roads. The platoons in the piquet line of the neutral zone were billeted in very dirty isolated farms. Their duties were to halt and turn back all vehicles coming towards them, and keep back German patrols, etc. These piquet platoons had a very miserable time in this bleak and sodden countryside.

It was bitterly cold and rained continually. Accompanied by my batman, I tramped over in a downpour of rain, and liaised with the regiment on our right, the 1st Lancashire Fusiliers. They were no better off than we were regarding billets, and seemed to have even a more depressing locality to piquet. We received official news of the award of two Victoria Crosses to the Battalion. The recipients were No. 4119 Sergt. J. O'Neill, M.M., and No. 18321 Pte. Martin Moffat.[1] Both won their V.C. on the same day, the 14th October, at Ledgehem near Courtrai, on which occasion 11 field guns, 60 machine-guns, and 240 prisoners, were captured by the Battalion.

18th to 20th December.

Two officers joined the Company, one of whom was Lieut. Schoales, who had been promoted on the field with the 2nd Battalion in 1916 and an army championship boxer. I visited the piquets.

21st December.

I was highly delighted at getting orders to proceed to " U.K." on the morrow, and attend the instructors' course at Berkhamsted,[2] and so to get away from this most depressing locality. There seemed to be no further interest in belonging to the Army of Occupation once Cologne was left, and we all talked about leave, and a number of the men about demobilisation.

A short service scheme was started for the men, whereby those serving for the duration of war were allowed to sign on for service in the Regular Army. A number accepted this offer, and more would have done so, had it not been for the new Education Scheme, which fell on us like a black cloud just before Christmas. Men were to be taught how to read, write, and do arithmetic ; the more advanced were to learn languages, and to read Shakespeare ! Some of them who wanted to go to India with the 1st Battalion, flocked to a Hindustani class got up by McNamara, but the enthusiasm soon waned.

I found the time in Germany flat and monotonous. When the novelty had worn off it became wearisome, and the inevitable reaction after the War made itself felt. I spent a lot of time

---

[1] This soldier, who hailed from Sligo, later received his V.C. under unique circumstances. At an open-air investiture held in the quadrangle of Buckingham Palace, the following three names were called out : Admiral of the Fleet Sir David Beatty, Order of Merit, Field-Marshal Sir Douglas Haig, Order of Merit, Private MOFFAT, 2nd Leinster Regiment, Victoria Cross.

When they descended from the dais, Martin Moffat, who was somewhat abashed with the ceremony, was reported to have said that what with following Sir Douglas Haig and shaking hands with the King he was " all of a fluster."

[2] By a happy coincidence I was destined to find Alyn Palin on this course, on the termination of which I was recommended as an instructor at Sandhurst. Colonel H. S. Poyntz, D.S.O., of the 2nd Bedfordshire Regiment, was C.O.

walking with the gamekeeper's dog, an intelligent and well-trained kind of pointer with a docked tail! As for the composition of the Battalion, apart from the transport and the senior N.C.O.s the bulk of the personnel was from the Special Reserve. Racially, the Battalion was still overwhelmingly Irish. I do know that the percentage of Englishmen serving with it was not more than 8 per cent. I record this especially, as I have heard it stated that at the end of the War the Irish Regiments were Irish only in name.

On the morrow I was to leave the Neutral Zone for the U.K. From Lille to Cologne and our outposts I had marched every step of the way, and for most of the journey I was accompanied by Sergt. Warton, M.M. Side by side we trekked the 220 miles, talking away and smoking our pipes. I couldn't have had a better marching companion. He was always in good spirits. Well over 48 in 1914, he left his prospering business, joined the Leinsters, and had won the Military Medal for gallantry in action.

Summing up the march to the Rhine, with the exception of the march across the field of Waterloo and the entry into Cologne it was most uninteresting and monotonous. We never got time to appreciate the lovely scenery as we got into East Belgium. It was always like Rudyard Kipling's " Infantry Columns " :

" Boots—boots—boots—boots—movin' up and down again ! "

22nd December.

Tramped down to Orderly Room in the rain to get my railway warrant. Here I found my servant with my valise awaiting me. I got into the Battalion mess cart, driven by Pte. O'Brien, and we rattled off down a hill along through dismal-looking country, over uneven roads. At Wermelskirchen I got into a train for Cologne. At the East Station I got out and struck up with some 29th Division officers, going on leave. A German ex-soldier pushed our valises across the Rhine bridge on a cart to the West Station. A Boche official asked me to pay toll going over the Hohenzollern Bridge, but I naturally refused. Men of the recently-arrived Guards Division were on sentry-go on the Bridge entrances. Crossing the square opposite the Cathedral, a German ex-soldier came up to me, and in English asked me to buy his war medals, which he produced, in a case. They were the Iron Cross, an Austrian decoration, and a medal for some pre-war Colony " scrap." I did not buy them, as I was terribly short of cash, and after paying for my lunch I had only some 10 francs left. I had sent my " Advance Field Pay Book " some days previously to the Adjutant, but it had not returned from the

Field Cashier when I left. For one mark I purchased a small nickel match-box cover, with a machine-gun (German) emblazoned on it, and the words " Andenken an den Weltkrieg " (Souvenir of the World War) on the reverse side, which was sold to me by an old frau, who remarked as she pointed to the machine-gun : " That held you up for over four years ! "

I entrained at night in a fast and comfortable German train. However, we weren't to be comfortable for long, as on the frontier just west of Aix-la-Chapelle our train stopped. Much to our chagrin we were transferred into horse-boxes of a " Froggie " train marked : " 40 hommes, 8 chevaux." This was a come-down. However, we were all for Blighty, so swearing like troopers, we transferred into the waggons in pouring rain. Amongst those proceeding on leave was Brig.-General Freyberg, V.C.

23rd December.

Passing Liége in the night, we went through Namur, with its formidable-looking fortress, in the early hours. Here I noticed any amount of German rolling-stock, dumps of guns of all calibres, and aeroplanes, all having been handed over according to the terms of the Armistice.

We breakfasted in Mons railway station. Waited in Mons for two hours, and I went into the famous town. The train went very gingerly over the newly-laid rails at Valenciennes. It was raining hard, and the war-scarred town, with its shattered railway station decorated with shrapnel-peppered advertisements, looked most depressing. The train jolted terribly going over this country, which was all pitted with shell craters. We had no food all day, and we all lay on our backs, heads on valises, cursing and kicking our heels on the manure-dried floor. We all wondered if we'd get home for Christmas.

24th December. Xmas Eve.

Woke up to find ourselves in a shell-ravaged region at dawn. It turned out to be Arras. Here we were issued with food—bread and butter and tea from a ration waggon, which had crept up mysteriously in the night. Just as well, as our last meal had been eaten just 24 hours previously. Men very hostile, and threatening to slay the driver—a cheery old tough ! Got into Boulogne at 6.30 p.m. after the worst train journey I have ever had—48 hours on two meagre meals.

Marched a party of bobbery leave men to a soldiers' hostel for the night. Poor devils had missed being home for Christmas ! Slept at the Officers' Club.

25th December. Xmas Day.

Lunched with a Munster Fusilier at the Officers' Club, and at 3 p.m. I embarked, having conducted my draft through the town to the wharf.

The boat glided slowly down stream past the russet-sailed fishing smacks and the buildings which overlook the harbour, and out into the Channel. I was detailed to inspect the men in their life-belts, which they had donned with much " grousing." Though the submarine menace was over, yet there was always the chance of bumping into a drifting mine. I came across a man who had belonged to my platoon at Ypres in 1915—Pte. Eldridge —now a Sapper ; much water and blood had flowed under the bridge since those far away days in " Fifteen," and together we wondered how many men of the old platoon could answer the Roll Call this Christmas Day.

As we talked the giant cliffs of Dover loomed out in their whiteness against the evening sky.

APPENDICES

SECRET

GENERAL PLAN FOR ENTERPRISE TO BE CARRIED OUT BY TWO COMPANIES OF THE 2ND BATTALION THE LEINSTER REGIMENT ON TRIANGLE CRATER

1. GENERAL IDEA. The raid will be carried out by two separate parties (X and Y) furnished from two different companies.

Party X will operate from the direction of Sap H against the western face of the Salient.

Party Y from the abandoned trench M.5.1 against the eastern face of the Salient.

2. ASSEMBLY. The preliminary assembly for the raid must be very carefully and slowly carried out, and will commence early in the afternoon. Party X (two platoons) will assemble outside our own wire in front of Sap H, passing through our parapet and wire man by man and crawling into line outside our wire. Party Y (two platoons) will assemble in or near the old front-line trench (M.5.1) joining TRIANGLE CRATER and RUSSIAN SAP.

Both parties will be deployed at about 4 yards' interval at their approximate assembly places before Zero hour.

At the same hour two supporting parties, each one platoon strong (X's and Y's), will be in position, X's in Sap J.1 and J.2 and extended along the lip (northern) of TRIANGLE CRATER, and Y's in the old advanced line in front of RUSSIAN SAP (M.5.c.44.83). Each of these platoons will have two Lewis guns.

The fourth platoon of each raiding company will be in reserve in our main front line.

3. DEMONSTRATION. During the preliminary assembly a demonstration with Artillery and Trench Mortar bombardment will be carried out on another portion of the Brigade front. This will distract the attention of the enemy O.P.s.

4. ASSAULT. The assault of the two parties will commence at Zero hour, probably about 4 p.m. Both parties will then rise to their feet and make for their objective in the enemy's line at top speed. Party X will move in two waves at 20 yards' interval. Y will move in one wave. The O.C. raid will be on the right of the party.

5. OBJECTIVES. The first objective of Party X is the front line from M.5.c.10.85 to M.5.c.15.95, including believed emplacement at the former point. Immediately the trench is reached a block and post

will be established at H.5.c.10.85 and a patrol will move down the trench leading to CRATER SAP to gain touch with Party Y.

The first objective of Party Y is the front-line trench from M.5.c.20.98 to M.5.c.32.79, including the sap-head at CRATER, and at M.5.c.30.85. A block and post will be established about M.5.c.32.78 and a communicating post at the enemy's sap on the southern side of CRATER. Touch will be obtained with Party Y at the TRIANGLE apex. The headquarters of the O.C. raid will be established at the tip of enemy's sap-head on southern lip of TRIANGLE CRATER.

After the first objective has been gained and consolidated an advance from both flanks will be ordered by O.C. raid along first support trench forming the CRATER retrenchment which is the second objective. Probable mine-shafts and dug-outs will be bombed and the trench-mortar MOORHEN destroyed. Touch with our own line must be kept throughout across the crater and all subsequent movement between the occupied line and our own line during daylight must be across or round the crater.

6. ACTION OF ARTILLERY AND TRENCH MORTARS. The action required from Artillery and Trench Mortars during the occupation of the enemy's trenches will be normally under three headings :

    (1) A smoke barrage to cut off the invaded area from view of the DOUBLE CRASSIER and direction of HILL 70. This barrage, weather permitting, will commence at Zero hour and will be kept up till dusk.

    (2) The engagement by Howitzers and Heavies of probable O.P.s and known M.G. and T.M. emplacements. This bombardment will commence at Zero hour and will continue at a slow rate till dusk.

    (3) An intense bombardment by concentrated Artillery and Trench Mortars on back lines, trench junctions, and on both flanks of raided area to cover the withdrawal of the two companies. This bombardment will commence on a signal of one or more golden-rain rockets sent up from TRIANGLE CRATER or when called for by telephone (probably required about Zero 45).

From Zero hour onwards Field Guns and Trench Mortars will be laid on suitable targets in rear of area to be raided, and will be prepared to deliver short, heavy bombardments on the right or left rear of raided area, on receipt of Code word by telephone.

SUPPORT A (for the right rear) or SUPPORT B (for the left rear). These bombardments will only be asked for if or when they are necessary to assist the raiders or repel local counter-attack. They must not in any case be allowed to interfere with the final intense bombardment.

N.B.—If difficulty is experienced in assembling outside our own wire unobserved it may be necessary to call for a smoke barrage *before Zero hour.*

7. WITHDRAWAL. The withdrawal will take place about three-quarters of an hour after Zero and will be ordered by O.C. raid, who

will inform Directing Officer across the Crater as soon as he is satisfied
that the withdrawal has commenced. The Directing Officer will then
send the Signal from his position in J.1 Sap by rocket or by telephone.
A large bonfire will then be lighted near TRAVERS KEEP to indicate
direction for withdrawal and the intense bombardment will begin.

(Sd.) A. D. MURPHY,

2.1.17.   *Lieut.-Colonel, Commanding 2nd Leinster Regiment.*

APPENDIX A

1. *Composition of parties.*

(a) Raiding Party X .	.	.	2 platoons D Company (40 men)
(b) ,, ,, Y .	.	.	2 platoons A ,, (40 men)
(c) Support Party X's	.	.	1 platoon D ,, (20 men)
(d) ,, ,, Y's	.	.	1 platoon A ,, (20 men)
(e) Reserves .	.	.	2 platoons D and A Companies (40 men)
(f) Patrols .	.	.	I.O. and 16 scouts

Parties X and Y will be under the direct command of Capt. F. C.
HITCHCOCK who will be the Officer in charge of the Raid. Each platoon
of X and Y will be under the command of an Officer. Capt. N. ALGEO
will command the Reserves.

APPENDIX B

Communications.

Battalion Headquarters.	The present right Company Head-quarters in CORDIALE AVENUE.
Advanced Battalion Headquarters.	The deep dug-out in rear of Sap J.1 and J.2 about M.5.a.20.08.
Directing Officer.	In Sap J.1.
Observation Post.	Advanced Post on NORTHERN CRASSIER.

Battalion Headquarters to be connected with advanced

Battalion Headquarters ⎫
Artillery Group   ⎪
Stokes Gun Headquarters ⎬by telephone.
Vickers Gun Headquarters ⎪
Observation Post   ⎭

Advanced Battalion Headquarters to be connected with Battalion
Headquarters by telephone.

(Sd.) A. D. MURPHY,

2.1.17.   *Lieut.-Colonel, Commanding 2nd Leinster Regiment.*

INTELLIGENCE SUMMARY

73rd Infantry Brigade. From 12 noon 30/11/16 to 12 noon 1/12/16.

OPERATIONS

3. *Artillery.* 3.45 p.m. 2 7·7 cm. on QUEEN STREET.

Bombing. 7.30 a.m. 5 heavy minenwerfer behind HARTS CRATER at about M.6.a.7½.2.

11.30 a.m. A few T.M. bombs near MIDDLE ALLEY.

Our STOKES fired 265 rounds, a few aerial darts and rifle grenades were fired in retaliation at M.6.c.2.9 and M.6.c.3.7½.

8.30 a.m. 12 rifle grenades at about M.6.a.9½.4½.

Machine-guns. NIL, except for one firing on the right battalion front between 9 a.m. and 10.30 a.m.

4. *Sniping.* Our snipers claim a hit on the SOUTHERN CRASSIER.

5. *Patrols.* 5.30 p.m. An officer's patrol left RUSSIAN SAP, and proceeded by our old front line towards M.5.c.7.5. The patrol halted about 20 yards from the enemy's wire, and the officer went on to the wire. A double telephone wire was discovered, running from the enemy trench to our old front line, where it was earthed ; the patrol unearthed the wire and marked its position. The enemy wire is in good condition, about 2′ 6″ high and 20′ deep. No sounds were heard from the enemy trenches. The patrol returned at 7.20 p.m.

12.30–2 a.m. An officers' patrol was out between RUSSIAN and BARRICADE SAPS. A white tape was found, running from a point 30 yards to the right of BARRICADE SAP in our old front line to a recent gap in the enemy's wire. This tape was left for further investigation, but a reel at the enemy end was, in the absence of a knife, bitten off and brought in. 3 bags of white chalk were also found ; it is thought that they may have been intended to mark the route of a raiding party. This patrol reports the enemy wire weak in places and very low : all gaps have been filled in with loose wire.

12.45 p.m. A patrol left M.5.d.2.9 and proceeded along the road to M.5.d.2.5 in order to examine the enemy wire : on the road this is in good condition, and very thick on the left of the road : on the right it is not very strong.

A dead man of the 26th I.R. (7th Division) was found at M.5.d.1.7 ; he had been dead for a long time : no papers were found on him. A revolver (Mk. IV WEBLEY Patent 1916, with broad arrow on side, No. 283722), rusty but in good working order, was found about 20 yards from the dead German.

The 7th Division (IV Corps) relieved the 53rd Reserve Division (XXVII Reserve Corps) about 6th October—*vide* First Army Intelligence Summary No. 636, 8/9th October.

The 165th Regiment (7th Division, IV Corps) was formerly in the line between LOOS and the DOUBLE CRASSIER where it was identified by contact in the first half of October. They left about 8 days ago, 15/11/16, being relieved by a division from the SOMME, number of which prisoner could not say, *vide* " Examination of deserter of 165th Regiment, 7th Division, IV Corps, who came over from LITTLE WILLIE, G.4.b, on morning of 23rd November, '16." (Supplement to First Army Intelligence Summary, No. 682.)

The 165th Infantry Regiment, together with the rest of the 7th Division, was relieved in its former sector on the southern portion of the Loos salient at the end of October, by troops from the SOMME— apparently PRUSSIANS. *Vide* " Further information from the above deserter." (Supplement to First Army Intelligence Summary, No. 685, 26th November, 1916.)

INTELLIGENCE

1. (*b*) " OWL " and " HAWK "[1] fired at 11.30 a.m.
Thick fog made observation impossible.

Correction. Summary of 28/29th November. 2nd Canadian Division Summary of Intelligence. " Suspected T.M. at M.4.b.9½.1½ " should read " M.4.*d*.9½.1½."

Addendum. 40th Divisional Artillery Report, 27/28th November. To " Company Headquarters " add reference " M.6.c.04.28."

To-morrow, 2nd December :

SUN.	Rises 7.35 a.m.	MOON.	Rises 12.17 p.m.
	Sets 3.42 p.m.		Sets 11.54. pm.

PART II

INFORMATION FROM OTHER SOURCES

24*th Division Observers.*

12.15 p.m. M.5.c.50.65. Smoke issuing from this point.

1.5 p.m. M.5.d.39.34. A few of the stakes, reported to have been at this point on 26th instant, have been removed.

1.45 p.m. M.5.d.56.38. Our artillery obtained a few well-directed hits here.

12.45 p.m. Smoke observed issuing from trench for over 15 minutes at M.5.c.74.29.

1.30 p.m. Enemy has dumped a quantity of timber and corrugated iron in an opening in parapet at M.6.c.23.48.

2.40 p.m. There is a large amount of new earth, placed on parapet of enemy's sap, at M.3.c.40.56.

3.15 p.m. Our T.M.s considerably damaged the enemy's wire and trench in vicinity of M.5.c.90.23.

40*th Divisional Artillery Report.* 29/30*th November.*

A number of 77 mm. and 4·2" were fired on our trenches north of the TRIANGLE between 9 and 10.25 a.m.—short bursts of fire following the sending up of VÉRY lights.

---

[1] " Owl " and " Hawk " were our names for certain enemy trench mortars.

The VÉRY lights sent up from PUITS 11 were immediately followed by about 12 77's on trenches opposite TRIANGLE. Another VÉRY light sent up at 9.5 a.m. was followed by about a dozen VÉRY lights from different parts of the TRIANGLE and then by salvos of 77's and 4·2's between DOUBLE CRASSIER and QUEEN STREET. It is possible that this firing of lights in co-operation with artillery may be practice for a pending night operation. All the lights were white. The explosion of the Bangalore torpedo by our infantry drew a considerable aerial dart and trench-mortar retaliation from the enemy, lasting for half an hour. At the request of our Infantry B/188 fired salvos in connection with the firing of this torpedo, and in retaliation against the resulting hostile trench-mortar fire.

17th Infantry Brigade Summary of Intelligence. 28/29th November.
4. *Movement.* Much movement noticed at M.6.d.4½.9½.

H.Q. 73rd I.B.   (Sd.) N. EGERTON YOUNG,
1.12.1916.   *Lieut. Intelligence Officer, 73rd I.B.*

INTELLIGENCE SUMMARY

73rd Infantry Brigade. From 12 noon 1/12/16 to 12 noon 2/12/16.

OPERATIONS

3. *Artillery.* 12 noon–2 p.m. 5 7·7 cm. shrapnel at RUSSIAN SAP.
9.10 a.m. 2 7·7 cm. near LOOS CHURCH.
9.15 a.m. 5 7·7 cm. at about M.5.b.9.5.
Bombing. 12–2 p.m. 2 minenwerfer near CARFAX ROAD.
3–4.15 p.m. 12 heavy minenwerfer and about 50 aerial darts and rifle grenades behind HARTS and HARRISON'S CRATERS; but artillery retaliated very effectively.
7.15 p.m. 6 aerial darts on BOYAU 32.
2.45 a.m. Some retaliation with aerial darts on REGENT STREET behind HARRISON'S CRATER, caused by our STOKES Mortar fire.
7.30 a.m. 4 aerial darts at M.6.c.8.9½.
8.30 a.m. 1 aerial dart at M.6.c.1.7.
Our STOKES Mortars fired 564 rounds; this total includes 131 rounds omitted from yesterday's report.
Machine-guns. Quiet.
4. *Sniping.* Our snipers claim a hit at M.4.c.9.3½.
5. *Patrols.* 1.15 a.m. An officers' patrol left Sap G to reconnoitre the enemy sap opposite; on reaching the enemy wire they heard a working party about half-way down the sap; a sentry near the head of the sap was heard coughing. On working to the right, the patrol located a wiring party, approximately at the place where the BANGALORE torpedo was exploded; this party was dispersed by LEWIS-gun fire on the return of our patrol at 3 a.m.

An officers' patrol watched the white tape found yesterday in "No-Man's-Land" but no movement of the enemy was observed.

A patrol from M.6.a.9.2 reports that no gap can be found in the enemy's wire to the left of HARTS CRATER : the enemy was bombing his wire. A wiring party was heard at M.6.d.1.9½.

12 midnight. An officers' patrol left our trench at M.5.d.2.9 and reached the enemy's wire at M.5.d.2.5. The enemy has a post on the road, from which the voices of at least 3 men were heard, and smoke was seen rising.

The following further information has been received about the daylight patrol reported in yesterday's summary :

This patrol was able to move under cover of the mist to within 15 yards of the enemy's wire ; at this point the wire is very close to the trenches and a bomb can be thrown into the enemy's trenches with ease ; the enemy were heard coughing and walking on footboards at about M.5.d.3.4. The body reported before had no identity disc ; in addition a helmet was found with the number 72 on the cover. Another body in a bad state lay under the wire close to the helmet. The patrol brought in on its return two coils of German wire-netting strips, as if used for crossing wire ; the netting is lined with tarred felt.

The following report was delayed, and has just been received :

On the night of 26th November, a patrol of 3 men left our lines and proceeded to the mound on the right of HARTS CRATER (at M.6.c.70.82), where they found 5 or 6 bodies ; no clothing was found and it was at first thought that they were our own troops, as they were lying on our side of the mound. Further investigation discovered a leg with a jack-boot on the foot, which was German. The bodies were all lying within about a 6-yards' radius and some were partially covered with earth. A partly dug hole appeared as if at some time an effort had been made to bury one or more, but as far as could be discovered, this was made some time ago. The bodies also appear to have been there some time. There was a hard frost at the time the patrol was out. There is a large hollow on the top of this mound, with a ruined dug-out inside the far lip.

INTELLIGENCE

1. (b) " OLIVE " and " HELGA " reported firing.

The T.M. firing aerial darts at 2.45 a.m. had a premature and did not fire again.

The reference of the new T.M. reported on 29/30th November is M.5.c.08.38, and not as stated ; this fires a heavy shell in rear of QUEEN STREET. Only 8 rounds have been fired. The flash and smoke were plainly seen.

3.45 p.m. " OWL " fired 2 rounds on CRASSIER SAP and " PHEASANT," two near QUEEN STREET.

3. *M.G. Emplacements.* M.G. firing from M.6.d.2.9. This may be an alternative emplacement for the gun from M.6.d.1.9 (reported 23/11/16, M.G. in action 31/10/16).

4. *Movement.* 4.20 p.m. Transport heard going up and down BETHUNE–LENS ROAD behind HARRISON'S CRATER ?

9.15 a.m. Movement seen behind canvas at M.6.d.1½.9.

9.45 a.m. Movement seen in trench at M.11.b.5.8.

5. *Trenches and Works.* 11.15 a.m. Work in progress in sap at M.5d.63.

11.45 a.m. 2 men driving stakes at M.5.c.7.5½ ; they were fired on. New " gooseberry " wire at M.5.d.7½.3½.

9.30–10.30 a.m. Earth thrown on to parapet and a large mallet in use at M.5.d.6.3.

M.5.c.1½.7. The parapet has been cut away and a sheet of iron put up with a board running down the centre.

6. *Identifications.* The man killed yesterday on the SOUTHERN CRASSIER was wearing a soft cap with a white band, and (7. *General*) was carrying a plank towards the enemy advanced post ; at the first shot he ducked and shook his fist ; at the second he fell and lost his cap.

9.30 a.m. What was thought to be a periscope appeared on the top of RUDOLF'S RISE ; it was fired at and knocked down.

2.30 p.m. Three train whistles were heard from the direction of CITE ST. PIERRE.

Smoke was seen at M.4.d.9.5½ and M.10.a.6½.8½.

To-morrow, 3rd December :

SUN.	Rises 7.37 a.m.	MOON.	Rises 12.33 p.m.
	Sets 3.41 p.m.		Sets 12.34 a.m.

PART II

INFORMATION FROM OTHER SOURCES

24th Division Observers.

11.15 a.m. Two German soldiers, wearing greatcoats, were observed moving between the 2nd and 3rd house in CITE ST. PIERRE, probably on railway at M.12.a.10.85.

40th Divisional Artillery Report. 30/11/16–1/12/16.

2 p.m. M.5.c.77.00. Movement seen and fired on. 1 round.

2–2.30 p.m. M.5.c.18.52. Sand-bag erection. 15 rounds.

2.50–3 p.m. M.12.a.12.85. Suspected O.P. 8 rounds.

4–4.20 p.m. M.12.a.10.89. Suspected O.P. in house. 17 rounds.

H.Q. 73rd I.B.   (Sd.) N. EGERTON YOUNG,

2.12.1916.   *Lieut. Intelligence Officer, 73rd I.B.*

INTELLIGENCE SUMMARY

73rd Infantry Brigade. From 12 noon 2/12/16 to 12 noon 3/12/16.

OPERATIONS

3. *Artillery.* NIL.

Bombing. 3.30–4 p.m. 12 aerial darts at about M.5.d.9.7.

12 midnight. 20 aerial darts and L.T.M. on REGENT STREET at about M.5.b.5.1½.

1 a.m. 20 heavy bombs on CORDIALE AVENUE.

2.30–4.30 a.m. 6 heavy minnenwerfer at M.6.a.7.3, doing some damage to trench. 30–40 aerial darts at same place.

8 a.m. 8 rifle grenades at about M.6.b.3.6.

9.15 a.m. 3 rifle grenades at about M.6.c.2.7.

10–10.15 a.m. 3 heavy minnenwerfer at about M.6.c.2.7½.

4 aerial darts at M.6.c.2.7.

4 ,, ,, ,, M.6.a.8.0.

3–4 p.m. 17 ,, ,, behind HARTS CRATER.

1–4 p.m. 22 ,, ,, between QUARRY and LOOS CRASSIER.

Our 2″ Mortars fired on the TRIANGLE ; STOKES fired 454 rounds. During the night the enemy bombed his wire from saps opposite Sap G and Sap H.

Machine-guns. Enemy M.G.s quiet, except one opposite the QUARRY between 6.30 and 7 p.m.

Between the night of 26th November and the night of 1st December, our Vickers Guns fired 25,000 rounds on the LENS–BETHUNE Road, and 21,000 rounds on the dump at M.11.b.9.8½ and C.T.s in M.5.c. During the mist of 1/12/16 three Vickers Guns retaliated throughout the morning for an enemy M.G. firing on the LOOS–MAROC Road.

4. *Sniping.* Our snipers claim a hit at M.4.d.½.2.

5. *Patrols, Enemy.* About 12 midnight a small enemy patrol (about 3 men) was observed from DEAD MAN'S SAP on the right of HARRISON'S CRATER, and dispersed by rifle fire.

Right Battalion. A patrol left RUSSIAN SAP about 8.15 p.m. and followed the enemy wire to M.5.d.2.4 ; up to this point the wire was good. Here the patrol listened for about 15 minutes ; much talking was heard, and work was in progress, the rattling of tools being heard ; at this point there is a well-beaten path very close to the enemy's wire, probably used by patrols. From this point to M.5.d.4¾.3½ the wire is not very good, and is much scattered by our T.M. fire. Two men of the patrol crawled over and looked into a trench which appeared to be disused ; many German grenades are lying about in it. The patrol returned along the middle of " No-Man's-Land," and came in by RUSSIAN SAP at 10.30 p.m. No enemy patrols were seen.

The same patrol was out again, and reconnoitred the ground between M.5.c.7.6 and M.5.d.2.5, returning the second time at 11.30 p.m.

A patrol of 1 officer and 2 N.C.O.s left RUSSIAN SAP and went south, till they reached a shell-hole about 20 yards from the enemy's wire ; here the officer ordered the 2 N.C.O.s to wait while he went on to examine the wire, intending to rejoin them and proceed south-east. After about 20 minutes, a light went up and the two N.C.O.s saw the officer at the enemy wire ; later, when another light went up, and they could not see him, they decided to go up to the wire and follow it along. Soon after this they heard a call, and 4 or 5 revolver shots, followed by 3 rifle shots ; as nothing more could be seen or heard, they returned and reported to the Company Commander. A strong fighting patrol was sent out under an officer, which thoroughly searched the whole of " No-Man's-Land " from RUSSIAN SAP to well beyond BARRICADE SAP. They were challenged by a German sentry at about M.5.d.2.5 and saw 2 men, who ran away, near the enemy wire. It is certain that this officer's body is not in " No-Man's-Land," and there can be no doubt that, whether killed or wounded, he is in the hands of the enemy.

Left Battalion. 11.15 p.m. An officers' patrol reports that the gaps in the enemy's wire at M.5.d.7.6 and M.5.d.9.6 have not been repaired.

11.25 p.m. An officers' patrol went out between HARTS CRATER and MANNINGS MOUND ; of the many shell-holes in this area, the majority are very deep and contain wire at the bottom. Our own wire in this part is quite good as an obstacle. No sign of the enemy was observed, but a whistle blast was heard in the enemy's trench when the patrol went out.

Emission Bombing. Occasional T.M. bombs on CARFAX Road between 12 noon and 3 p.m.

INTELLIGENCE

1. (*b*) A heavy T.M. firing on our right battalion was on a true bearing of 230° from M.5.d.4$\frac{1}{2}$.9 ; it fires at 3-minute intervals (probably SWAN, but this bearing also passes through FALCON and ELIZA).

4. *Movement.* 9.45 a.m. 2 men on parapet at M.5.d.2.5.

11.10 a.m. 1 man at M.5.d.7$\frac{1}{2}$.4.

5. *Trenches and Works.* 9.45 a.m. 3 men seen at M.10.a.6$\frac{1}{2}$.9 were bringing up sandbags from a sap ; their clothes were covered with chalk. They were fired on.

7. *General.* 8.15 a.m. Smoke seen on SOUTHERN CRASSIER about 10 yards behind enemy's advanced post.

The right Battalion reports that the enemy's attitude is more quiet ; fewer lights sent up, and an absence of sounds of work.

To-morrow, 4th December :

SUN.	Rises 7.38 a.m.	MOON.	Rises 12.49 p.m.
Sets	3.41 p.m.	Sets	1.53 a.m.

PART II

24th Division Observers.

8.10 a.m. Sheets of corrugated iron have been placed over enemy trench at M.11.a.80.80.

9.30 a.m. Enemy heavy T.M. sent 6 shells from M.11.a.75.80 (probably the emplacement shown on aeroplane photographs at M.11.a.72,82 by I Corps) into our lines at M.5.a. Our T.M.s retaliated on his lines in M.5.c damaging trench and wire.

10.45 a.m. Our artillery shelled enemy's lines in M.5.d damaging trench, and timber was observed to be hurled into the air.

11.30 a.m. Our artillery again shelled enemy front line, greatly damaging wire in places at M.5.c.

H.Q. 73rd I.B.   (Sd.) N. Egerton Young,
3.12.1936.   *Lieut. Intelligence Officer, 73rd I.B.*

DETAIL OF OPERATIONS TO BE CARRIED OUT BY THE 2ND BATTALION THE LEINSTER REGIMENT ON OCTOBER 5TH, 1916

1. Preliminary Dispositions. Each of the two raiding parties will be drawn up in single file just in front of the covering party from A.1, and will remain there until reports of the reconnoitring party are received. The forward movement will then be ordered by the Directing Officer.

Party B will lead, and Party D will follow at 2 minutes' interval.

2. Action of Party B. Party B will proceed as quietly as possible towards the German trench in the order shown below, making for Lonely Sap. On reaching the German wire they will (if unobserved) lie down and wait until Party D reaches their objective ; Party B will then pass through the wire and enter the German main trench either by Lonely Sap or over the parapet, at the junction of Lonely Sap with the main trench (whichever is easiest). Two scouts will be left at outer end of Lonely Sap lying outside to watch the left flank and to keep touch between the raiders and the reconnoitring party (who after their reconnaissance will be lying down between Lonely and Crater Saps about 10 yards outside the German wire). The previously detailed post of one Corporal and four men will be left at Point D—the two riflemen lying outside on the parapet and the bombers inside the trench, all facing north. The remainder of party will move southwards along the main trench until they reach Point C (about 40 yards).

Any Germans found must be accounted for silently or taken prisoner. Any useful trophies or identifications will be collected.

If no hostile party is encountered the patrol will halt at Point C and block the main trench beyond this point. They will await the arrival of Party D at this point. If fighting is in progress round the crater, a portion of Party B may move to the right to help Party D, but a post MUST be left at Point C.

3. ACTION OF PARTY D. Party D will move across "No-Man's-Land" in the order shown below at 2 minutes' interval behind Party B. They will make for the CRATER SAP which they will enter at Point A or B (whichever is easiest). If there is an enemy post at B endeavour must be made to surround it and cut it off from the south as silently as possible. When the post is accounted for, or if no enemy are met, Party D will advance to Point C, leaving the previously detailed post of a corporal and four men to watch Points B and B.1 and the trenches running south from them. At Point C the party will join hands with Party B. If the latter have not arrived they will block the main trench running southwards from Point C, and await arrival of Party B.

PARTY D WILL NOT UNDER ANY CIRCUMSTANCES ADVANCE BEYOND POINT C.

N.B.—At the first sounds of fighting or bombing the Directing Officer at A.1 will telephone the code word to O.C., T.M. Batteries and the T.M. Demonstration on mock point will begin.

PRELIMINARY FORMATIONS

		PARTY B.			PARTY D.
		2 scouts.			2 scouts.
		1 officer.			1 officer.
		1 rifleman.	POST		1 rifleman.
PATROL.	{	1 bomber.	AT	{	1 bomber.
		1 N.C.O.	C.		1 N.C.O.
		1 rifleman.			1 rifleman.
		1 bomber.			1 bomber.
		1 rifleman.			1 rifleman.
		1 bomber.			
		1 rifleman.	POST		1 N.C.O.
		1 bomber.	AT B		1 rifleman.
D POST.	{	1 N.C.O.	AND	{	1 bomber.
		1 bomber.	B.1.		1 rifleman.
		1 rifleman.			1 bomber.

4. ACTION OF BOTH PARTIES AT POINT OF JUNCTION AND AFTERWARDS. As each party approaches Point C the leading man will give one blast on acme siren to signify the approach of friendly party. This signal will be answered by the other party if they are already at Point C. A similar signal will be made by either party when waiting at Point C on hearing the approach of another party and will be similarly answered.

At Point C both parties will compare notes and if no enemy have been encountered or captured it will be for the senior officer to decide whether a withdrawal is advisable or whether it is feasible to remain in the trench occupied in the hopes of surprising some of the enemy as they arrive. In the latter event, the posts at Points B, C, and D will be reinforced and a patrol will move constantly between Points B and D. If enemy are encountered at any of the points during this new phase they will be captured as silently as possible and the commander of the post will signal his success by sounding two blasts on his acme siren. Help will then be sent from the patrol and the whole party will get ready to withdraw.

5. WITHDRAWAL. In all eventualities withdrawal will take place in the following manner :

The order will be given by the senior officer and will first be communicated to the patrol and to the post at Point C. The patrol and post at Point C will then move back along the trench past Point B and back to our line along the lip of LOVE CRATER. The post at Point B will follow at a short interval after the patrol and Post C has passed through them.

The senior officer will remain at Point A and will check the patrol and Posts B and C as they pass him. He will then sound three blasts on acme siren as a signal to Post D to withdraw. As an additional precaution he will send the two scouts at Post A to warn the reconnoitring party who in their turn will warn the two scouts at Point E who will warn the post at D if they have not already passed through. In any case the reconnoitring party must remain out until they are certain that all parties have withdrawn. If there are any casualties they must assist to get them in, and if necessary send back to the supporting party for assistance and direct them to the right spot.

All ranks as soon as they reach our own line will make their way at once to the head of UHLAN ALLEY where they are to report personally to the Directing Officer.

As soon as the Directing Officer has satisfied himself either by personal observation or by other means that the withdrawal is in progress he will telephone the code word to the supporting artillery who will commence their bombardment of the enemy's support lines and communication trenches. The covering party and supporting party will remain out during the bombardment and will seize any opportunity of inflicting loss on any of the enemy who may show themselves.

(Sd.) A. D. MURPHY,

4.10.16. *Lieut.-Colonel, Commanding 2nd Battalion the Leinster Regiment.*

INDEX

349

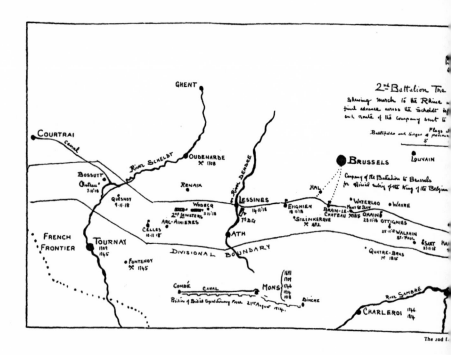

The map shows the march of the 2nd Battalion The [Regiment] and various locations including GHENT, COURTRAI, BRUSSELS, LOUVAIN, OUDENARDE (1708), RENAIX, BOSSUTT Chateau (7.11.18), QUESNOY (9.11.18), WODECQ, 2nd LEINSTERS (11.11.18), ARC-AINIERES, CELLES (10.11.18), LESSINES (14.11.18), 7th D.G., ATH, ENGHIEN (13.11.18), HAL, WATERLOO, WAVRE, BRAIN-LE-HUNT LE DUC, CHATEAU JOLIE ORAINE, STEINKERQUE (1692), OTTIGNIES (23.11.18), WALFAIN ST. PAUL (23.11.18), SUST HA, FRENCH FRONTIER, TOURNAI (1709, 1745), FONTENOY (1745), DIVISIONAL BOUNDARY, QUATRE-BRAS (1815), CONDE CANAL, MONS (1691, 1709, 1746, 1792, 1818), BINCHE, RIVER SAMBRE, CHARLEROI (1746, 1794).

2nd Battalion The [Regiment]

Shewing march to the Rhine and final advance across the Scheldt and route of the company sent to [Brussels]

Battlefields and Sieges of previous [...] Flags of [...]

Company of the Battalion to Brussels for official entry of the King of the Belgians

Position of British Expeditionary Force 21st August 1914.

The 2nd [Battalion ...]

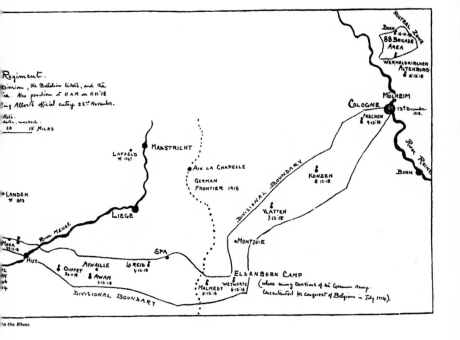

Regiment.

Division, the Battalion billets, and the
.... Also position at 11 A.M on 11·11·'18
King Albert's official entry. 22nd November.

..... deaths marked .
10   15 MILES

NEUTRAL ZONE

DORN 6·12·18·18
BB BRIGADE AREA

WERMELSKIRCHEN
ALTENBURG
6·12·18

MÜLHEIM
COLOGNE   13th December 1918.
FRECHEN
9·12·18

River RHINE

BONN

LAFFELD
× 1141
MAASTRICHT

AIX LA CHAPELLE
GERMAN FRONTIER 1918

KONZEN
6·12·18

DIVISIONAL BOUNDARY

VLATTEN
7·12·18

LANDEN
× 1693

LIEGE

River MEUSE

MORA
31·11·18

HUY

OUFFET   AYWAILLE   Lo REID
30·11·18   6·12·18
AWAN
1·12·18

SPA

MONTJOIE

ELSENBORN CAMP
(where many Divisions of the German Army
concentrated for conquest of Belgium in July 1914).

MALMEDY   WETWERTZ
5·12·18   6·12·18

DIVISIONAL BOUNDARY

to the Rhine.